CW01090811

Languedoc Roussillon

for John.

In recollection of a great evening

The Wines and Winemakers

Paul Strang

19·02·19

Jasper Strang

Published by Jeanne and Paul Strang Partnership

JPS

The author and photographer would like to express their gratitude
to Jessica Heslop for her invaluable work in copy-editing the text,
to Fiona Holman and Mike Parsons for devising and producing the
maps, Nathan Burton for layout advice and to the many hundreds of
vignerons who have been so generous with their time and their wines
to enable this book to happen.

Finally to Jeanne Strang and Caroline Heslop for constant support,
help and encouragement.

Languedoc Roussillon

The Wines and Winemakers

Paul Strang

Photographs by Jason Shenai

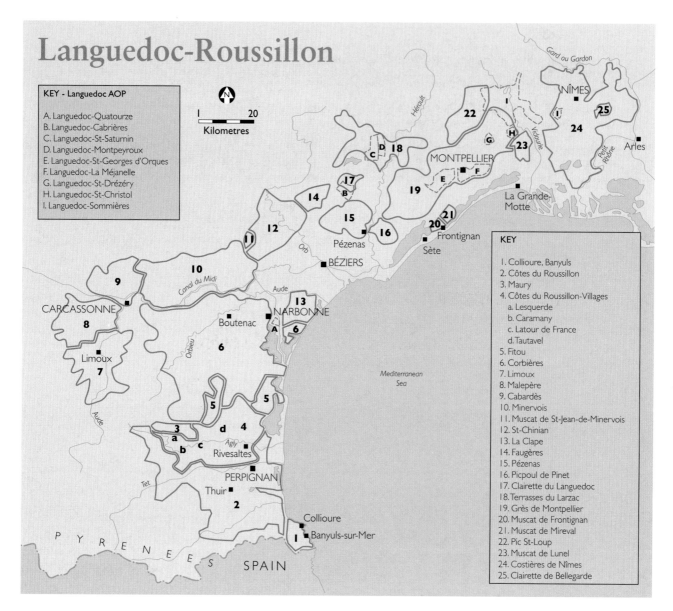

Languedoc-Roussillon

KEY - Languedoc AOP

A. Languedoc-Quatourze
B. Languedoc-Cabrières
C. Languedoc-St-Saturnin
D. Languedoc-Montpeyroux
E. Languedoc-St-Georges d'Orques
F. Languedoc-La Méjanelle
G. Languedoc-St-Drézéry
H. Languedoc-St-Christol
I. Languedoc-Sommières

KEY

1. Collioure, Banyuls
2. Côtes du Roussillon
3. Maury
4. Côtes du Roussillon-Villages
   a. Lesquerde
   b. Caramany
   c. Latour de France
   d. Tautavel
5. Fitou
6. Corbières
7. Limoux
8. Malepère
9. Cabardès
10. Minervois
11. Muscat de St-Jean-de-Minervois
12. St-Chinian
13. La Clape
14. Faugères
15. Pézenas
16. Picpoul de Pinet
17. Clairette du Languedoc
18. Terrasses du Larzac
19. Grès de Montpellier
20. Muscat de Frontignan
21. Muscat de Mireval
22. Pic St-Loup
23. Muscat de Lunel
24. Costières de Nîmes
25. Clairette de Bellegarde

This edition first published in 2017 by Jeanne and Paul Strang Partnership, 34 Hamilton Terrace, London NW8 9UG, United Kingdom.
paulstrangwine@gmail.com
Original edition first published 2002 by Mitchell Beazley

A CIP catalogue record for this book is available from the British Library.
ISBN 978-1-5262-0708-1
Brand and product names are trademarks or registered trademarks of their respective owners.

Printed in Great Britain by Halstan & Co. Ltd.

CONTENTS

INTRODUCTION

Languedoc-Roussillon encompasses the largest vineyard in the world, its production exceeding that of Australia or Bordeaux. Until the last quarter of the 20th century, little save very poor wine was made here and, since the appearance of the first edition of this book, the leap forward in quality and variety has been unbelievable. How such a change? Why were things so bad in the old days? And how does one explain the revolution? The *terroirs* and the climate are constant – more or less: only the intervention of man has been responsible for such swings in quality.

Marseille was founded by the Greeks and was a busy wine port six centuries BC. But the Greeks did little to explore or develop the rest of the southern coastline. The Romans were bolder: their lines of communication were shorter, they had stronger armies, a more sophisticated administration, and they were not frightened of the local inhabitants, who at once showed an insatiable thirst for wine. Their drunkenness became proverbial. The Romans were quick to plant vines in their new colonies and to profit from the market which they had unwittingly uncovered. Loyal military and administrative service was rewarded by the grant of lands for the purpose.

Expansion west of the river Rhône resulted in a colony which became known as the province of Narbonne (Narbonnensis). It extended up both banks of the Rhône as far as Vienne, westwards as far as modern Montauban, and south to the Pyrenees.

It thus included the whole of what we now know as Languedoc-Roussillon, as well as the Côtes du Rhône and parts of the South-West. Avoiding the insuperable barrier presented by the Massif Central, where only 'barbarians' lived, viticulture spread westwards to the valley of the Garonne river, which gave access to the Atlantic and what is today Bordeaux.

The Roman empire declined and fell, but despite successive invasions by vandals, and later

Harvesting cinsault

by the Saracens, the vineyards survived and even thrived. Wine was no longer just a crop to be traded like olives or cereals: the vine itself was regarded as having an intrinsic value quite apart from the religious associations within the rites of the fast-expanding Christian Church. It was an important badge of culture, one of the obvious expressions of the quality of life. It was a sign to the outside world that the Church was looking after the interests of the citizens on a secular as well as a spiritual level.

Wine was also an important source of Church revenue. Its vineyards expanded to supply outlying parishes and smaller churches with wine for sacramental purposes. The Church carried out many of the functions of today's catering industry, receiving pilgrims en route to holy places, or merely giving travellers refreshment

and rest. Wine was core to such activities. Vineyards sprang up around the monasteries and abbey churches. Valmagne (Montpellier/Pézenas), Fontfroide (Corbières), Caunes (Minervois), Saint-Gilles (Nîmes) and Saint-Hilaire (Limoux) became, among others, centres of what to this day remain productive wine regions.

REVOLT

The religious struggles which engulfed Languedoc from the Middle Ages onwards slowed its development, leaving scars which still have not healed. The Cathar movement was inspired largely by resentment at the corruption and luxurious decadence of the Catholic Church. The Cathar heresy, which struck at the heart of Catholic doctrine in fundamental respects, spread like wildfire among the people of Languedoc. They saw in it not only a way of purifying the Church, but of standing against the combined power of the foreign French king who was bent on securing the total subjugation of Languedoc to the French crown; and of the Pope in Rome, equally determined to exterminate heresy. After many years of resistance and persecution, the last of the Cathars, confined to almost impregnable fortresses in the mountains of the south, were gradually eliminated by torture or massacre in one of the most shameful episodes in Christian history, the horrors of which still resonate 800 years later.

The Cathar story is a living part of Languedoc tradition, like the Protestant influence around Nîmes, and in the Cévennes the later Protestant heresy was countered just as determinedly and with only marginally less cruelty. The people of the Midi, though conservative in character, are dissident politically. Languedoc is reluctant to promote or accept change, but votes solidly against the Parisian political establishment to this day.

ECONOMIC CONFINEMENT

Vineyards in the rest of France gradually consolidated their position and their hold on markets, particularly overseas. Languedoc had only two routes by which to compete: the historical corridors established by the Romans, unattractive because of the exaction of greedy tolls which made the wines uncompetitive; or a sea voyage round the south of Spain, which was expensive and liable to ruin the wines, except those fortified with alcohol.

The rise of France as a world power in the 17th century should have brought with it corresponding economic expansion, but the stranglehold of the centralised power in Versailles and the cost of ruinous territorial wars sucked the economic blood from the provinces, and Languedoc suffered with the rest. Taxation was administered by tax-farmers who were not slow to cream off the receipts from their efforts, today evidenced by the many fine châteaux and vineyards which they have left behind them, for example in the vicinity of Montpellier.

Until the building of the Canal du Midi, little of the wine produced in the south was exported either to the rest of France or abroad, and virtually none at all from Roussillon, which until the middle of the 17th century was part of Spain and not France. It might be thought that the opening of the canal would have brought an immediate boost in trade, but in fact what was really needed was the ability to compete on equal terms with the rest of the French vineyards. This could not happen until the abolition in 1776 of the tolls and privileges enjoyed by Bordeaux. Even so, the 18th century did see the development of an important trade in brandies which were distilled from the local wines and shipped down the canal. Brandy would travel well and did not mind how long it was in transit.

BOOM....

The brandy trade and the free use of the port of Bordeaux resulted in a frenzy of vine-planting after the Revolution. Vines, until then grown mainly on the best higher terrains, spread downward to the plains. Gradually wine became the principal regional crop. Growers were encouraged by the drop in the price of cereals to plant more and more vineyards, mostly consisting of high-yielding grape varieties such as aramon and clairette. The boom both in spirits and wine was fuelled by the rise of the new industrial proletariat generated by the Industrial Revolution. Gradually the larger landowners were able to concentrate on vines as a monoculture, and at last the Canal du Midi came into its own. This extraordinary feat of civil engineering was the brainchild of Paul Riquet, who was born in Béziers in 1604. His vision was to create a link between the Atlantic and the Mediterranean so that boats did not have to go around the Straits of Gibraltar. The concept coincided with the unquenchable appetite of the Crown for prestige and the ambition of its clever finance minister Colbert to develop France into a merchant-nation. The idea was not new, but earlier schemes had foundered on the problem of feeding a canal with water in such a way that it would fall towards Toulouse in the west and the Mediterranean in the east. Riquet's solution was to locate the high point of the canal, as it crossed the watershed between the two seas, at a spot where it could be fed by the waters coming off the Black Mountain. The project received the royal go-ahead in 1666, and the canal took 12,000 labourers and 12 years to build. The lack of a port on the Mediterranean to serve as the eastern terminus was solved by the creation from scratch of what is today the town of Sète. The canal, with its 99 locks and the 45,000 trees planted specially along its banks, was opened in 1681, but Riquet had died just six months earlier.

The first 80 years of the 19th century were a golden age for Languedoc, made even more golden by the coming of the railways. In this heyday, Languedoc had very nearly 300,000 hectares under vine, yielding often more than 100 hectolitres of wine to the hectare in the plain. In Roussillon, the yields were lower because of the more difficult nature of the terrain. In Hérault, the area under vine doubled between 1850 and 1870.

BUST....

Then the phylloxera struck. Many smaller growers could not afford the only effective antidote to this voracious aphid and the disease it spread: the grafting of vines on to immune American rootstocks, which of course had to be purchased and planted. But the demand for cheap wine did not abate, and the Government even promoted the creation of supplementary vineyards over the sea in Algeria, from which the shortfall required to satisfy the market was imported to stretch the supply. Sète became a net importer of wine, not an exporter. Fraud was rife too: wines were produced artificially in the north of France by adding raisins or sugar to sour, inferior juice. Eaux-de-vie made cheaply from sugar-beet, maize and potatoes flooded the market. This led to demonstrations in the streets of the big towns as early as 1893. The larger growers were less affected, their newly replanted vines starting to yield huge quantities of inferior wine to sell to the cheap markets in the north. By the turn of the century over-production had become a real danger. Prices between 1890 and 1901 had fallen by three quarters. Wages to vineyard workers were slashed and not restored when a brief respite in the market occurred at the turn of the century. In 1903/4 the workers went on strike, having successfully unionised themselves. With the next downturn in the market, the big bosses and the workers became united and there were riots in 1907. Government troops were sent to keep order, but sympathy for the plight of the vineyard workers was such that many troops mutinied in the streets of Béziers, and their general refused to discipline them.

This episode is little publicised today, but in 1907 it had profound consequences, boosting the embryonic cooperative movement in Languedoc. The first legislation was introduced at national level to prevent fraud, and to protect the distilleries of the South. New measures encouraged the replanting of land with better quality grapes, the reduction of the total area under vine and the introduction of mechanisation. Thus, the seeds for the later renaissance were sown rather earlier than generally supposed, but the people of the South are slow to respond to change, and the effects were felt only very gradually.

Bélesta, Roussillon

The switch from quantity to quality production was not encouraged by the continuing rise in French wine-consumption, which by 1926 had reached 136 litres per year per person, women and children included. So, for the greater part of the 20th century it was business as usual. People made as much wine as they could, and to make it saleable, they beefed it up with stronger, dark-coloured wine from Algeria and Morocco. The blends were bottled and marketed throughout France at knock-down prices. Nearly as much money could be had back on the bottle as the cost of the wine inside. The quantity sold made up for the lack of quality, at least temporarily.

REBIRTH

It is surprising that the growers had not learned the lessons of history. Over-production eventually led to the same poor returns as had been suffered in the 1900s. It was influences from outside the region which were to ensure a recovery in Languedoc fortunes.

The market for wine was gradually changing. The post-war era saw the first lasting economic revival in France for nearly a century. Consumers started to look for better quality wine, while others started to switch to beer. Today, half the French nation does not drink wine at all – a far cry from 1926.

Algerian independence in the 1960s led to a ban by the new Muslim regime there on the export of wine to France, so the blenders and dealers in the south of mainland France found they had nothing with which to cover up the weaknesses of their own product. Although the making of wine in Algeria was not illegal, many of the French growers there felt constrained by the explosive political situation to repatriate themselves to France, bringing back with them techniques which they had developed in Africa. A spirit of innovation was about, and a new generation of growers began to emerge alongside the established bulk-producers and traders, and they saw that the future lay in a search for better quality. At the same time, there was the problem of what to do with the ever-increasing 'wine-lake' caused by over-production in Italy as well as France. Growers were offered grants to dig up inferior rootstocks and either to replant with quality grapes or diversify into other crops. In total about half of all vines disappeared, and this is a process which continues to this day, though you would hardly guess as much from seeing the apparently interminable landscape of vines which still greets visitors to the region. Statutes of Appellation d'Origine Contrôlée (AOC) were decreed throughout the region, setting out the terms on which wines could enjoy protection and thus a better chance of a market, in exchange for compliance with certain requirements as to terroir, grape variety and limitation on the scale of production. There had been no such controls in the bad old days.

The sons and daughters of vignerons who had once been *coopérateurs* took themselves off to college and studied winemaking techniques. These days it is rare for a young vigneron to take over from his or her parents, or to acquire a vineyard of his or her own, without technical qualification. The new generation has set new standards, as well as teaching its forebears new tricks. More and more have left the *coopératives*, and every year sees fresh names enter the list of independent growers, even as the total area under vine in Languedoc is diminishing. The ranks of modern producers have been further swollen by the arrival of enthusiasts from overseas, some already experienced in wine-production, others beginners in search of a change in lifestyle.

THE PRESENT STRUCTURE OF THE WINE TRADE

Before the First World War, the vineyards had belonged largely to the big landed estates, whose owners would have a manager and workers regularly employed in the vineyards and cellars. There were some lesser proprietors who operated similarly but on a smaller scale. The mass of people engaged in the industry were paid workers.

The picture has changed fundamentally. There are still a few large estates, but they are far less important than they used to be. Many of them belong to the *coopératives* who still dominate the bulk of production. Some *coopératives* work to a much higher standard than others, and some of them are listed in this book alongside the independent growers. It is true to say, however, that in general, it is the independents who are making the more characterful wines.

The second half of the last century saw also the growth of a number of important *négociants*. These dealers/wholesalers may work in different ways. The traditional dealer will buy in wine which has been made by growers who are not members of a *coopérative*, but do not have ageing or bottling facilities of their own. They may even buy in wine from each other or from *coopératives*. They then blend their wines and either sell them on to other traders, or make them up into blends themselves. Some *négociants* have several regular suppliers, perhaps of varietal wines such as viognier or chardonnay, which they either bottle as they are, or blend with the wines of other growers of the same grape varieties to achieve the best mix they can. Others may have their own domaines, or at least work with independent growers who may or may not have their own *chais*, but who do not mind sacrificing a certain amount of their own independence in order to achieve the market which the *négociant* is able to provide. It is in this category that one finds some of the best *négociants*, such as Boisset (formerly Skalli), Jeanjean (now called Advini), Castel, Gérard Bertrand, Foncalieu, Val d'Orbieu, Bésinet, Paul Mas et al. Among the *coopératives*, standards vary enormously. The best are very good indeed, insisting, often by rewarding higher standards with higher prices to their best growers, on best practice within the vineyards to ensure that the grapes which have to be processed are of top quality.

It has, however, also to be said that all too many have poor standards, and in the depressed market for bulk wines seen in recent years, grower-members have had to be satisfied with as little as 40 cents a litre for their crop. It is not surprising that younger growers are deserting the poorer *coopératives* in droves, tempted to emulate the top independents, some of whom can market their wines at 100 times that price. Others are simply turning to other ways of making a living.

APPELLATIONS, IGPs AND VINS DE FRANCE

In an effort to delineate those wine-growing areas in Languedoc with the longest history and reputation for quality, the wine authorities in Paris drew up a map of wine-producing regions which would be entitled to the status of *Appellation d'Origine Contrôlée* (nowadays rebranded as *Appellation d'Origine Protégée*, or simply *AOP*). Partly with the object of compelling an increase in quality, the appellation rules defined, amongst other things, what varieties of grapes could be grown and the maximum amount of wine which could be made, expressed in hectolitres per hectare (hl/ha). This created a problem for growers, particularly those belonging to *coopératives* who had traditionally relied on vast yields in order to make a living. The more you produced, the more you got paid.

Parallel with this, many growers also saw the possibility of making wines from grape varieties other than those prescribed by the rules. Alongside the AOP system, there quickly grew up a parallel culture of what were then called vins de pays (now called wines entitled to an *Indication Géographique Protégée* or IGP for short). These could be sold either by reference to virtually the whole of the South (Pays d'Oc), the region of production (e.g. Hérault, Aude), or a more localised grouping together of a number of neighbouring communes (e.g. Côte Vermeille). The rules for IGP offer much more freedom, especially since they authorise much higher yields and the production of varietal wines (wines from a single grape variety) such as chardonnay, merlot etc., seen as one way of competing with the wines from the new World.

AOP wines, in theory at least, have to be a blend of two, sometimes three specified grape varieties. Some growers went even further; so as to escape any kind of control, they forfeited the benefits of the *appellation* system by making their wines simply as *Vins de Table*, nowadays called *Vins de France*. This hierarchisation of production, once validly seen as a protection to growers against fraud, is now seen as over-complicated and often meaningless. What becomes increasingly more and more important is the name of the grower on the label of the bottle, as is the case in other quality wine-growing areas of France. In an area as large as the Minervois for example, there are many producers – both good and bad – and the AOP system does not enable you to tell one from another. However, it is also true that the definition of different areas can give an indication of the terroir and style of the wine, if not its quality. So, it is useful to have at the back of one's head (even if not at the front) some knowledge of the system. Full details are to be found in their own section of this book.

It is no wonder that many people feel that the new hierarchy is even more complex than the old one, and what is really needed is a complete re-think of the whole system. In an area where any change, as well as lack of change is likely to cause riots, this may be wishful thinking. The need for more effective marketing often takes second place to individual pride and sense of place.

TERROIR

This one word carries, for the French, a wealth of associations, which makes it almost untranslatable into any other language, summed up in a feeling that a wine has come from one particular place, just as every artist has a unique style which determines the character of his or her work. It is a combination of the kind of soil and subsoil to be found in the vineyard, the way the ground faces, how it is drained, the gradient on which the grapes grow, the micro-climate which it enjoys – all these factors influencing the choice of grape varieties which will succeed there, and the way they are grown and pruned. Thus, there is no single 'terroir' common to any region in the South. But there are certain factors that give the area a sense of unity.

The first is geographical. The whole area is sandwiched almost without break between the mountains and the sea. Behind the entire coastline, from the Camargue to the Spanish frontier, the vineyards start almost at the water's edge and gradually climb into the mountains, until either the geology or the altitude make viticulture impossible.

Climate is another unifying element. The popular picture of hot, uninterrupted sunshine throughout the year sometimes seems to be true. Certainly, the summers are torrid and the total rainfall figures are low everywhere in the region. Winters can be mild but frosts are not unknown, and the occasional downpour can be ferocious.

The autumns in particular can be stormy and turbulent. The stony beds of the rivers can be turned instantly into raging torrents, and flooding is frequent. The growers in Corbières and the Minervois will long remember the terrible floods of 1999. Generally speaking, however, the reality lives up to the idyll, and there are few bad vintages. Some are just better than others.

The grape varieties also lend a kind of unity to the whole of Languedoc-Roussillon and give the key to the general style of the wines. Red AOP wines derive from syrah, grenache, mourvèdre, carignan and cinsault.

Some older kinds are sometimes permitted, but less often seen in practice. White wines represent a rather smaller proportion of the total production, but the whole list of permitted AOP varieties is longer than the list of the reds, with more variation from one district to another.

The most striking feature of the climate is the nearly incessant wind. Near Nîmes, the mistral blows from the north, dry and cold. Further west, the wind from the Cévennes is called the tramontane and is again a drying wind. Towards the Minervois, the wind often blows from the northwest and is called the cers, and in Corbières and Roussillon, the *tramontane* blows with renewed vigour. These winds are good for the grapes because they dry off any moisture quickly, and so reduce the number of chemical treatments which a grower needs to apply to

Tower near Octon

BEST VINEYARD PRACTICE

Over the last decade and more, a movement towards organic and even biodynamic production has gathered pace to an extraordinary extent – sometimes officially certified, sometimes not – but always in recognition of the virtues it entails. The so-called *culture raisonnée* is a sort of halfway house to strict bio principles, recognising the superiority of natural fertilisers and composts to chemical ones, and of natural ways in keeping down undesirable insects to the use of chemical insecticides. It has the advantage of leaving the door open to growers who feel they need recourse to old bad practices if otherwise irretrievable disaster overcomes their vines.

But full organic certification is more and more the norm, especially for younger, smaller producers who are more infused with the idealism of beginners than older and more cynical hands. Organic viticulture is also easier to practice in smaller than larger estates, and in a climate which is generally more reliable than that further north. But whatever the motivation, the tendency is to work the soil by hand rather than machine, thereby properly aerating the upper part of the root system while avoiding the main and deeper roots of the plants.

Growers today have learnt the lesson that good wine can only come from small crops of grapes. The smaller the yield, the higher the concentration within the fruit. They will therefore prune their vines hard, whether grown in *gobelet* form as is usually the case with carignan, cinsault and grenache, or on wire, which is the norm for syrah and mourvèdre. Just before the grapes start to turn colour, today's grower may carry out what he calls a *vendange verte*, by removing and sacrificing all but a few bunches of the best grapes on the plant.

He will also remove some of the leaves around the remaining bunches, while carefully nurturing

prevent disease. The wind from the sea brings moisture. It can shroud the plain with mist on summer mornings, yielding as much water as a good shower. This is called '*le marin*' and it brings rain particularly in spring and autumn.

For the IGPs made outside AOP rules, the permitted red grapes include merlot and the two cabernets, pinot noir being planted occasionally in the cooler areas. The AOP varieties are also permitted, as are cot and portan. For rosés, cinsault is a mainstay everywhere. White counterparts include chardonnay and sauvignon of course, but also the increasingly popular viognier, chenin, mauzac, colombard, sémillon, and all the permitted AOP white grapes.

the foliage of the upper part of the vegetation – the 'motor' of the vine – which ensures a proper feeding of the roots for the following season. It is easy to imagine how much persuasion was required to impose these techniques on growers who were traditionally remunerated only by the quantity of grapes produced. The less convinced *coopératives* who still encourage bulk rather than quality should understand why they are having difficulty in marketing their product. Harvesting is increasingly done by hand. Smaller growers can sometimes twist the arms of their friends and relations to pick with them, sometimes they take on students and holidaymakers on an ad hoc basis. Larger growers have teams which they hire, sometimes through Spanish agents who specialise in this eclectic form of fixing. Grapes tend to be brought in from the vineyard in small *cagettes* rather than large containers – a practice which reduces the pressure from the weight of the grapes and ensures that the fruit reaches its destination in perfect condition. Speed is also essential to avoid oxidisation of the grape juice on the way. Harvesting is often done by night, or at least as early in the morning as possible, before the heat of the sun increases the risk of oxidisation. Fussy growers will discard inferior fruit even before it has a chance to get into the baskets, and the grapes will be examined on a specially manned table at the entrance to the chais where unripe or rotten grapes are eliminated.

Macération carbonique, still controversial with some growers, is not just a method of making fruity and quick-maturing wines. It has become a sophisticated way of extracting flavours which balance the characteristics of other grapes in a blend, while at the same time making a wine which is capable of ageing. It involves hand-harvesting to avoid the grapes being bruised by machines, because the grapes must go, without their skins being broken, straight into the tanks where they are covered with a layer of carbonic gas. Fermentation is by explosion from within.

This technique accentuates fruit flavours, especially in the carignan grape, and is sometimes applied to syrah and even grenache. Some growers believe that it destroys the feeling of *terroir*, and prefer the traditional method of vinification.

Macération pelliculaire, as applied to white wines, consists of allowing the grapes to rest with their skins in the *cuve* before fermentation begins. This is carried out under refrigeration and is calculated to develop maximum freshness of the fruit. Other wines are fermented in barrel, much in the New World style, and some are allowed a malolactic fermentation to develop richness and complexity, though sometimes at the expense of freshness and fruit.

Temperature control has always been one of the bugbears of winemakers in the south. Inside the *chais* elaborate systems, some computer-controlled, have been evolved to maintain temperatures at a constant and desired level, ensuring a disciplined and regular vinification. Sometimes this includes the introduction of gentle refrigeration in the case of white and pink wines. Vinification tanks nowadays tend to be made either of stainless steel or concrete lined with epoxy resin. Some growers are loath to part with their old concrete tanks, which are enjoying a comeback: concrete as a storage medium is less liable to temperature fluctuation than steel. There is also a fashion for egg-shaped amphora-like jars, said to produce natural homogenisation of the wine and so avoiding too much pumping over. Corresponding improvements have been made in the conditions in which wines are matured and then stored, often, where geological conditions permit, by the construction of underground cellars, the best of them air-conditioned.

Château de Nouvelles, Fitou

OAK

Languedoc-Roussillon has embraced the general fashion of raising at least part of its production in new oak barrels. This is thought to correspond with public demand, as created by the media and pundits. Professional judges tend to promote oaked above non-oaked wines automatically, and so the oaked ones get the medals. The French particularly swear by medals, and so it is conventionally believed that there is an inherent merit in oaking wine. Research also shows that younger people and newcomers to wine generally prefer the oaked style. Largely it is a question of taste whether one prefers some or more oak to no oak, but most growers use new oak only for a small percentage of their

total production because it increases substantially the cost of their wines. £500 or more for a 225-litre standard-sized barrique has to be passed on to the consumer, as does the additional cost of labour in overseeing the ageing of wine in these generally smaller containers. Sometimes growers oak their wine because they feel they have to. All the same, there seems to be a reaction against the over-use of wood which was common in the 1990s. Many growers will tell you that they seek to avoid the taste of wood in the wine, but value oak for the extra complexity and richness it adds. Certainly, it is now common for brand-new wood to be used mainly for white wines, before being passed on to the reds in its second and subsequent seasons, by which time the oaky flavours will have been partly exhausted.

THE WINES AND THE MARKET

The emergence of truly fine wines from this region in the closing years of the last century is indisputable. The problem for the consumer is to sort out the good from the bad.

Anglophones, accustomed to the marketing styles of the New World, are especially attracted to *vins de cépage*, wines made from a single grape variety. The name chardonnay or cabernet on a bottle will help sell the wine, whether it comes from Australia or Languedoc. But so many excellent wines from the South are sold under the AOP designation, which by law are supposed to be blends, and it is here that the new generation of independent producers often excel. The tension inherent in these distinctions runs parallel with the debate about globalisation and *terroir*, between those who promote the standardisation of wine from one region or country to another, and those who believe that wine is not a product like Coca-Cola, and that its excitement lies in its sense of origin – its unpredictability from one vintage to another, and even from one bottle to the next. Why should all bottles of wine marked 'merlot' taste the same? In truth, these distinctions are unreal. There are only two kinds of wine: good and bad. Even so, this book concentrates on the creativity of the individual grower, whether of AOP wines or others, held preferable to the undoubted skill of the industrial blender or chemist. A real winemaker will inevitably be a person who regards his métier as a way of life rather than the production of just another crop. Good wine is a product of passion, not the test tube.

'Value for money' has become a catchphrase which has sadly come to concentrate more on the money than the value. More often than not, 'cheapest is best.' A Languedoc merlot priced at £X may be better or worse than a Chilean merlot priced at £Y. The cheaper may or may not be better, but the average shopper will more likely choose it than not. At the same time, many growers in Languedoc-Roussillon are getting too greedy too soon, profiting from media attention, the medals they have won, or the buzz which those who have a talent for marketing can create with their personalities. But their wine can at the same time be very good. So, the question of 'value for money' must be addressed from the point of view of quality, just as much as price. In this book, an assessment is made of the quality of each vigneron, and the prices charged for his range of wines are also given. It is for the reader, occasionally with a little help from the commentary, to solve his or her own 'value for money' equation when he or she tastes the wines.

THE PRINCIPAL GRAPE VARIETIES

Many of the traditional Languedoc-Roussillon grapes survive only as a reminder of the region's inglorious past, and they are today overshadowed by modern rivals. While some excellent producers still cling on to the older grapes, these have largely been replaced by imports from Spain and the Rhône valley. There follows a list, not exhaustive, of the varieties likely to be found in practice today.

RED VARIETIES

Syrah
is the noble grape from which Hermitage and Côte Rôtie are made. The New World calls it shiraz. It has always been present in the Midi, but until recently, comparatively little has actually been grown. Now it is suddenly fashionable. It is one of the two so-called '*cépages améliorateurs*', considered by the authorities as a corrective to the more traditional carignan and cinsault. Its complex tannins give concentration

Carignan

and structure, deep colour, sometimes a roasted, smoky character, spice and some finesse. When mature, it can suggest game and mushrooms, even burnt rubber or tar. Usually grown on wire with hard pruning, its leaves have five lobes with deep sinuses. The berries are small. It grows less well in excessive heat and can therefore suffer in drought conditions from what is called 'hydric stress'.

Grenache
is the workhorse grape of the south, absent from few vineyards. It is a relative newcomer from Spain, planted after the phylloxera plague. It gives good fruit and alcohol, though it is short on acidity and it can oxidise fast. It can lack colour and tannins too, but is invaluable for blending. It is the backbone of red *vins doux naturels* in particular, and prefers gravelly conditions to limestone. Prone to disease, it is often given a mild pre-winter pruning, the main pruning being deferred until spring when the growing cycle can be delayed beyond the time when disease is a danger. Grenache is usually grown *en gobelet*. Its leaves are curly and the lobes pronounced, the grape-clusters large.

Lledoner pelut
is a close relative of grenache, and is to be found where grenache is absent. The two do duty for each other, though lledoner is not often found today.

Mourvèdre
(also known as Mataro, particularly in Roussillon)is Catalan by birth, but has become the mainstay of the red wines of Bandol in Provence, where it thrives on the moisture from the sea. It contributes pepper and spice flavours to its deeply coloured, structured juice, which has good acidity. Mostly found as a supporting grape, it is not easy to grow and takes time to come to maturity, just as its wine needs ageing. It thrives only in some terrains, needing moisture as well as heat, so is particularly suited to maritime con-

ditions. It is the second *cépage améliorateur*. Its leaves are round and with noticeable teeth, and it is usually grown tall to give maximum foliage to the upper parts of the vine. The grape clusters are quite large.

Carignan
is another post-phylloxera Spanish import, suited to poor soils such as schist, and resistant to the strong winds of the south. Dark and alcoholically generous, but tannic and sometimes lacking in fruit and softness, it is often vinified by *macération carbonique*, which maximises its fruit flavours. It is usually blended, though some growers make a varietal wine from it. The leaves are rather large and curly and the plant is usually grown *en gobelet*. It was once scorned by the authorities who have spent much energy and money persuading growers to dig it up, but it is having something of a renaissance, and could even be called fashionable. It requires hard pruning and drastic action to reduce yields, but many growers will challenge the orthodox view that carignan is only good when produced from old vines, and some are even planting it anew.

Cinsault
is officially frowned on too, although it has the longest history of all in the Languedoc. It will give fruity, pleasant, soft wines if yields are kept low and the soil is poor enough. Lighter in colour than any other of the main grapes, it is much valued for making pink wines and for moderating the power of grenache. It is thought sometimes to have poor ageing potential. The plants are not vigorous and often seem to droop. The leaves are sharply indented and the berries very large.

Other native grapes of Languedoc include **Oeillade** (a first cousin of cinsault), **Ribeyrenc** (also known as **Aspiran**), **Piquepoul Noir**, **Marselan** (a modern cross between grenache and cabernet), **Portan** (grenache crossed with portugais bleu) and **Mourrastel**.

Merlot, Pinot Noir, Petit Verdot and the two Cabernets are at the base of many of the IGPs to be found throughout the region, either as varietals or blended with each other and sometimes with the main Languedoc AOP varieties.

WHITE VARIETIES

Traditionally, the wines of the region were sweet, but in modern times producers have adopted new techniques, particularly in the *chais*, to make dry-style whites, often with varieties imported from other regions.

Muscat
appears in two forms in the South – 'Alexandria', almost entirely limited to the *vins doux* of Rivesaltes – and 'Petits Grains', found in all the *vins doux naturels* of Languedoc-Roussillon. There is a fashion for dry Muscat too. It is one of the few wines to taste of grapes. Its leaves have sharp teeth. 'Petits Grains' has small clusters and grows well on chalky soil and, much beloved by birds, bees and wasps, it ripens early. It is generally considered finer than 'Alexandria', which has large bunches and does better on gravelly or acid ground, maturing later.

Mac(c)abeu (or Mac(c)abeo)
is another Catalan grape still important in Spanish sparkling wines. It is not often found further east than Minervois. The plant is vigorous and easily snapped by strong winds. It makes a surprisingly pale wine, with pronounced floral character when unblended, but sometimes it lacks acidity. It is choosy about soils, not liking those that are either too dry or too damp. The leaves have long, pointed lobes and the bunches and the berries are big.

Roussanne
comes from the Rhône valley, but has settled down well in the Languedoc. It likes poor stony soils with good exposure to the sun. The wines are fine and complex with flavours of honey, flowers and apricot. Good acidity and strength ensure that they keep well. The plant is easily recognised by its leaves, which have pronounced, almost circular lobes, separated from each other by deep sinuses. Clusters and berries are rather small.

Marsanne
does not quite enjoy the same status as roussanne, with which it is often blended, but the wines can be good, with some acidity and an attractive bouquet. The plant is vigorous and fertile, and needs sharp pruning to limit yield. The leaves are very rough and have practically no teeth, while the lobes have very shallow sinuses. The clusters are large, but the berries, which turn deep golden or even reddish when ripe, are small.

Vermentino (also called **Rolle**)
probably comes from Corsica, where it is much in use. It is resistant to drought and likes poor soils. The juice is pale, sometimes lacking in acidity, but can make well-balanced wines, said to have hawthorn and pear aromas. The leaves have deep sinuses and sharp teeth, and hard pruning is needed to control the yield. The bunches and the berries are rather large.

Grenache Blanc
is the white cousin of grenache noir, to which it is very similar except in colour, though it has an earlier cycle. It is well-adapted to drought and wind, but likes magnesium in the soil. The grapes can give either dry or sweet juice, soft and full, sometimes high in acidity and alcohol. It is the backbone of the whites of the Midi. Its other cousin, Grenache Gris, is less often found, but in good hands it can be excellent.

Viognier
is a variety only recently permitted in AOP wines. Currently all the rage in Languedoc, just as chardonnay was a few years ago, it needs

high density of planting and careful pruning. It is also sensitive to wind. It buds early so is vulnerable to spring frosts. The wines are aromatic and complex, with notes of peach, apricots and tropical fruits. The grapes are naturally high in sugar and so need careful vinification to avoid vulgarity and coarseness, especially since they are lacking in acidity. The clusters and grapes are both small, and the leaves are roughish and curly at the margin.

Bourboulenc (also called **Malvoisie** or **Tourbat**) is a rustic variety that ripens late and needs warmth. Delicate rather than powerful, the wines are fine, aromatic and high in alcohol. It is a particular feature of the wines of La Clape, which accounts for 70% of its production. The plants tend to droop so need careful pruning and tying-in. The leaves have three lobes and are rough in texture. The clusters are large and sensitive to mildew.

Clairette

was once the principal white grape of the Midi, but its presence has been cut by almost ninety per cent during the last half-century. It is at its best in the two small AOP regions bearing its name. It likes dry, shallow, chalky ground. The wines are alcoholic and though sometimes hard, they can lack acidity. Apple aromas are common. The grapes, olive-shaped when mature, can make wines both dry and sweet, which need early drinking.

Piquepoul Blanc

is the sole constituent of the popular wines called Picpoul de Pinet, dry, fresh and fruity, often and mistakenly regarded as the Midi's answer to Muscadet. Grown close to the sea in sandy or chalky ground, the grapes make a wine which is perfect with the oysters and mussels of Bouzigues and Sète. The leaves of the plant have five or seven distinct lobes with teeth, and the grape clusters are large. The grape is also used as a supporting variety.

Terret

is today found chiefly in mid-Languedoc, and makes crisp, dry wine which can transcend the ordinary in the hands of a good grower. It is mildly cultish. The grapes are medium-sized and elliptical, the bunches large, compact, late-ripening and prone to mildew.

Chasan

is a modern, early-maturing cross between chardonnay and listan (the latter being better known as palomino, the sherry grape). It is well adapted to cooler soil, its acidity dropping fast as the grapes come to maturity. It oxidises fairly quickly but is valuable for its aromatic qualities. It is recognisable in the vineyard by its clearly lobed leaves with deep sinuses and very long teeth. The clusters are very large.

Carignan Blanc

is another cult grape, in clever hands making delicious minerally fresh wine. Best grown on very poor, dry and windswept soil, it can be found either blended or sometimes as a *vin de cépage*.

Mauzac

can be recognised instantly by the downy-white underside of its leaves, and its wine by the aromas of apples and pears. Acidity weakens as the grapes mature, so it is beefed up in some versions of the wines from Limoux by blending with chenin and chardonnay. The leaves are round and rather rough in texture. Mauzac likes chalk.

Chardonnay

is not yet admitted as an authorised variety in AOP wines of the region other than Limoux, but its immense popularity explains the considerable production of IGPs which are made with it, either on its own or with other grapes. Grown in cooler and higher areas, it can be fine. Otherwise it tends to be fat and rather blowsy in this climate.

Chenin
appears in some blends, increasingly so, and very occasionally as a *vin de cépage*, as does

Sauvignon,
which in this warmer climate tends sometimes to lose some of its zing.

AOPS AND IPGS

APPELLATIONS D'ORIGINE PROTÉGÉES (AOP)

and

INDICATIONS GÉOGRAPHIQUES PROTÉGÉES (IGP)

For explanation of these terms see introduction page 15

ROUSSILLON
See also APPELLATION LANGUEDOC below

AOP VINS SECS (i.e. unfortified) for all three colours unless otherwise specified; blend of at least two grape varieties required except for Muscats.

Collioure	reds and rosés;	grenache,syrah, carignan and mourvèdre.
	whites;	grenache blanc and gris.
Côtes du Roussillon	reds and rosés;	carignan, grenache, syrah, mourvèdre, lledoner pelut.
	whites;	grenache blanc, maccabeu, roussanne, marsanne, vermentino and bourboulenc.

Côtes du Roussillon Villages (reds only); grapes as above with four communes able to add their own names:
> Caramany
> Latour de France
> Lesquerde
> Tautavel

Côtes du Roussillon Les Aspres (reds only); from 37 communes in southern hills.Blend of at least three grape varieties required, oak- ageing compulsory.

Maury sec (red only) from four communes; Maury, Tautavel, Saint Paul and Rasiguères Minimum of 60% grenache.

IGPs in all three colours

IGP d'Oc;   non-AOP varieties include merlot and cabernet
                                           sauvignon in the reds and rosés, chardonnay in whites.

IGP de la Côte Vermeille;   sauvignon blanc and viognier in the whites.

AOP VINS DOUX NATURELS

Rivesaltes;   grenache for 'grenat red',
                                           grenache blanc and gris, the two muscats,
                                           maccabeu and bourboulenc for *'ambrés'*, all
                                           allowed in the *'tuilés'*.

Maury;   same as Rivesaltes for the whites, grenache, carignan
                                           and syrah for reds.

Banyuls;   grenache noir and gris (reds),
                                           blanc and gris (whites).

Banyuls Grand Cru ('tuilé' style only);   minimum 75% grenache.

Muscat de Rivesaltes (white only);   muscats 'alexandria' and 'petits grains'.

LANGUEDOC; blend of at least two grape varieties required unless otherwise specified

APPELLATION 'LANGUEDOC' which covers specified vineyards throughout the whole of
Languedoc Roussillon.

reds and rosés;   mainly grenache, syrah, mourvèdre, carignan and
                  cinsault

whites;   mainly grenache blanc, clairette, bourboulenc, viognier,
                  piquepoul, marsanne, roussanne, vermentino and ugni
                  blanc.
                  The following 'crus' are entitled to add their names to
                  'Languedoc,' while in some cases waiting to join the
                  list of inner AOPs below;

                  Montpeyroux (reds only);

                  Grès de Montpellier (reds only) including:

                  St Georges d'Orques and La Méjanelle.

INNER AOPs listed alphabetically

Cabardès (reds and rosés only);   syrah, grenache, cabernet sauvignon and merlot. Secondary grapes; cot, fer servadou and cinsault must not exceed in total 20% of blend.

Clairette du Languedoc (white only);   exclusively from clairette grapes grown in communes in and around Adissan.

Corbières;   all three colours;   The largest AOP area in Languedoc. Corbières-Boutenac; a sub-appellation of Corbières, covering 10 communes from Lézignan southwards towards Thézan. Syrah must not exceed 30% in the grower's vineyard. Carignan must be hand-picked and taken in whole bunches to the chais.

Faugères;   the usual quintet of grapes for red and pink wines, grown on schist. Roussanne, grenache blanc, marsanne and vermentino for the whites.

Fitou;   reds only;   Carignan and grenache mainly (often 40% each) with syrah and mourvèdre in support.

Limoux;   Reds from merlot (min. 50%), cot, syrah, Grenache (minimum 30%), carignan (max 10%).
whites;   'Blanquette' from mauzac (min. 90%) 'Crémant' from chardonnay (min. 40%), chenin (min.20%) with mauzac and pinot accessories

'   'Limoux Blanc' (not sparkling), mauzac (min 15%), chardonnay and chenin. Oak ageing compulsory. 'Blanquette Méthode Ancestral' 100% mauzac

La Clape;   carignan and cinsault cannot exceed 70% in the reds. Bourboulenc and/or grenache blanc must constitute at least 60% in the whites. Viognier maximum 10%.

Malepère;   no AOP whites, but some overlap with Limoux.
reds;   merlot (min. 50%), cabernet franc, cabernet sauvignon, cot (min. 20%), grenache and cinsault.
rosés;   cabernet franc (min 50%), merlot (min.20%), cabernet sauvignon, cinsault, cot, and grenache.

Minervois;	all three colours:	
	reds;	syrah, mourvèdre (min. 20%), grenache and/or lledoner pelut (minimum 60%), carignan, cinsault, also terret noir, aspiran and piquepoul as accessories.
	rosés;	pressed direct from the above.
	whites;	marsanne, roussanne, maccabeu, bourboulenc, clairette, grenache,, vermentino and muscat à petits grains.

Minervois-la-Livinière;   a sub-appellation of Minervois.

         reds only;   from six communes around the village of La Livinière; syrah, grenache and mourvèdre which must account for 60% (syrah or mourvèdre being a min. of 40%). Accessory grapes; carignan, cinsault, terret, piquepoul and aspiran.

Muscat de St Jean de Minervois

         whites only;   100% muscat petits grains (*vin doux naturel*)

Muscats de Frontignan, Lunel, Mireval;

         whites only;   yields must not exceed 28 hl/ha, exclusively muscat petits grains. Sugar at maturity minimum 252 gr/l. Final alcohol between 15 and 18%.

Pézenas;   reds only;   Syrah, grenache and mourvèdre, with carignan and cinsault as ancillary

Saint Chinian;   with two inner appellations Roquebrun and Berlou.

         all three colours;   usual quintet of grapes (inc. lledoner pelut) for reds and rosés.
Grenache blanc, marsanne, roussanne and vermentino for whites.

Pic Saint Loup;   1,000 hectares in 17 communes. Reds and rosés only. Minimum 90% syrah/grenache/mourvèdre

Terrasses du Larzac.   reds only;   Max. yield 45 hl/ha.
Grenache, mourvèdre, syrah and carignan must together represent 75% of the blend, and no one of them can exceed 75%.

LANGUEDOC IGPs

La Bénovie	Bérange
Bessa	Cassan
Caux	Cessenon

Cévennes   La Cite de Carcassonne
Collines de la Moure   Coteau du Libron
Coteaux de Béssilles   Coteaux de Cèze
Coteaux d'Enserune   Coteaux de Fontcaude
Coteaux de la Cabrerisse   Coteaux de Laurens
Coteaux de Miramont   Coteaux de Murviel
Coteaux de Narbonne   Coteaux de Peyriac
Coteaux du Salagou   Côtes de Lastours
Côtes de Pérignan   Côtes de Prouille
Côtes de Thau   Côtes de Thongue
Côtes du Brian   Côtes du Céressou
Côtes du Vidourle   Gorges de l'Hérault
Hauterive   La Haute Vallée de l'Aude
La Haute Vallée de l'Orb   Hauts-de-Badens
Mont-Baudile   Monts de la Grage
Pays du Torgan   Val de Cesse
Val de Dagne   Val de Montferrand
La Vicomté d'Aumelas

GARD AOPs

Costières de Nîmes; all three colours; mostly reds and some rosés from syrah, mourvèdre and grenache (minimum 25%) and some carignan and cinsault (max. for each 40%)
Sprinkling of whites from bourboulenc, clairette, grenache blanc, maccabeo, vermentinno, roussanne and ugni blanc.

Clairette de Bellegarde; whites only; a tiny appellation with only 40 hectares planted; exclusively clairette.

Sommières; all three colours; also entitled to use the Languedoc name. Same grape varieties.

GARD IGPS

Coteaux -Faviens   Duché d'Uzès
Petite Crau   Pont du Gard
Sables du Golfe du Lion   La Vaunage
La Vistrenque

TO HELP READ THIS BOOK

First, every entry in this book is a snapshot in time. Producers frequently change their email addresses and contact details.

Secondly, they change the range of wines they offer. Sometimes these are of style, but more often they are new names for earlier products. Wines supplied to supermarkets and the larger retailers may be given different names (or no name at all other than the domaine), and may be blended to the specification of the customer.

Thirdly, an appointment is always the best guarantee that you will get to meet the grower and taste the wines. If the text gives no information as to visits, always make an appointment. Few vignerons spemd their day in the tasting-room hoping that someone might call. Sunday visits are not encouraged. Mobile phone numbers are the best means of contact..

Fourthly, a visitor is not under any obligation to buy. But the grower will have taken time to receive you and it is a normal courtesy to purchase at least some wine.

Producers are listed by region, not always the recognised *appellations*. The section devoted to each region is prefaced by a brief, not necessarily technical, description of the area in question, followed by a list of growers, not in any order of merit but so as to make vineyard visits as convenient as possible and with the minimum of travel between one grower and another. Each chapter has its own map, and the citation of every grower includes a reference to his approximate position on that map. If you have access to the internet, you will hopefully be guided to any grower you select.

Organic (biological) growers are indicated by a large red **B**, biodynamic ones by a further large **D**. They are officially certified except where stated.

A star system indicates the general quality of wines produced at each estate, not necessarily every individual wine coming from there :

*	- above average standard
* *	- greater excellence
* * *	- some of the best wines of Languedoc-Roussillon
* * * *	- world-class.

Stars represent basically the author's own judgment, sometimes augmented and/or modified by the opinions of experienced tasters, sommeliers, cavistes , journalists and fellow wine-writers. The aim is to give as objective a judgment as possible, and also to ensure that good wines at all price-levels are fairly represented.

Prices are graded as follows, each wine being shown in the text by the appropriate grade :-

A ; up to 8€
B; between 8€ and 13€
C; between 13€ and 20€
D; above 20€.

These estimates are based on growers' ex-cellar lists, which can change (upwards usually). They include tax. Sometimes wines are available only by the case, while some growers offer a discount for quantity. Wines purchased away from the grower's premises may cost more.

Finally, this is not an encyclopaedic guide. About a quarter only of all the growers in the region are represented, so many excellent ones are not listed. Sincere apologies to them and to critical readers.

ROUSSILLON

South of the Corbières, where the ruined châteaux of Quéribus and Peyrepertuse dominate the plains to the south, the valleys below give way to the foothills of the Pyrenees, and you are suddenly in Roussillon. Today it is rather prosaically called 'Pyrenées-Orientales', but until 1659 it was part of Spain. The ruined castles bear witness not so much to the persecution of the Cathars, but to the wars between France and Spain. Roussillon is, although now French, essentially and almost entirely Catalan in its culture, language, gastronomy and in the physiognomy of its people. The wines are correspondingly more southern in style, something of a cross between Châteauneuf-du-Pape and the wines of Spain made just the other side of the Pyrenean chain.

Several threads run through the history of these wines during the second part of the 20th Century. The greater profitability of fruit farming saw the conversion of many of the lower-lying vineyards into orchards, causing winemaking to retreat into the higher, more arid interior, which is more conducive to the production of quality wines. The relative fall in public demand for the sweet *vins doux naturels*, which for many years had been the mainstay of the vineyards, is another feature. Also, the better education of the winemakers' families at agricultural college has led to a desire to make their own wines instead of selling off the family grapes to the *négociants* or *coopératives*. This is resulting in a corresponding change in the role of the *coopératives* themselves, which nevertheless today still account for 70% of the production of all Roussillon wine – a statistic which compares with the number (about 600 and growing) of independent producers in the region. Of these, many are newcomers to the area, not always welcomed by the locals. The latter often find themselves having to accept a pittance for their crop, while invaders from all over the world are making wine which sells for a high price because of their greater skills and ability to adapt to changing tastes in the market place.

One factor remains constant: winemaking here is split between the growing production of dry table wines on the one hand and the shrinking making of *vins doux naturels* on the other. Roussillon nevertheless accounts for the production of over 90% of the French wines made in this latter style.

VINS DOUX NATURELS ('VDNs')

The region is the biggest producer of wines fortified by the addition of alcohol (*'mutage'*). The process was invented in the middle ages to enable wines to travel long distances. Many had to be exported round the straits of Gibraltar before the building of the canal du Midi, and were

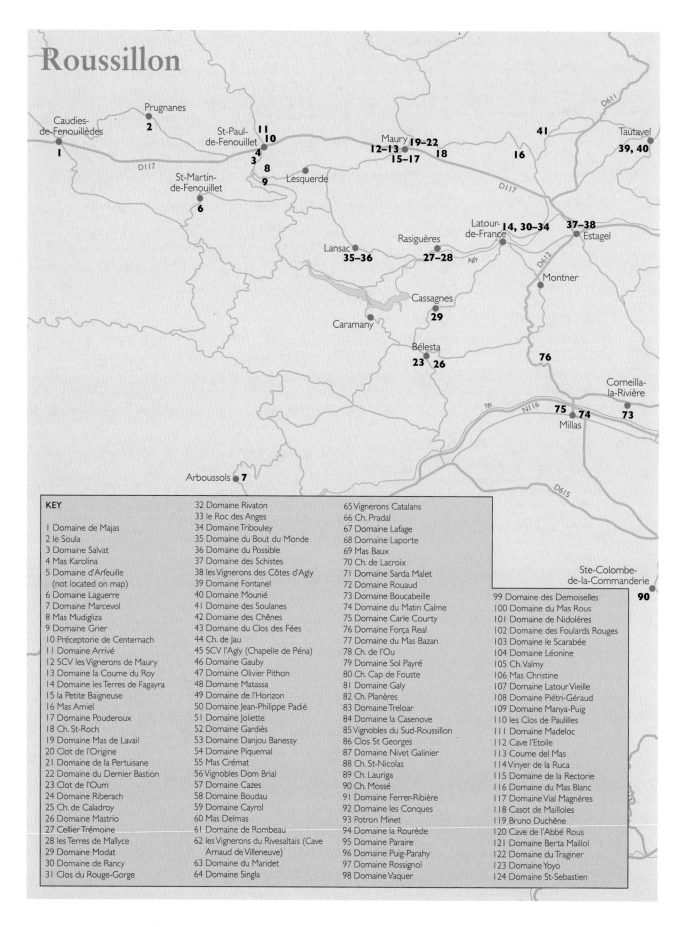

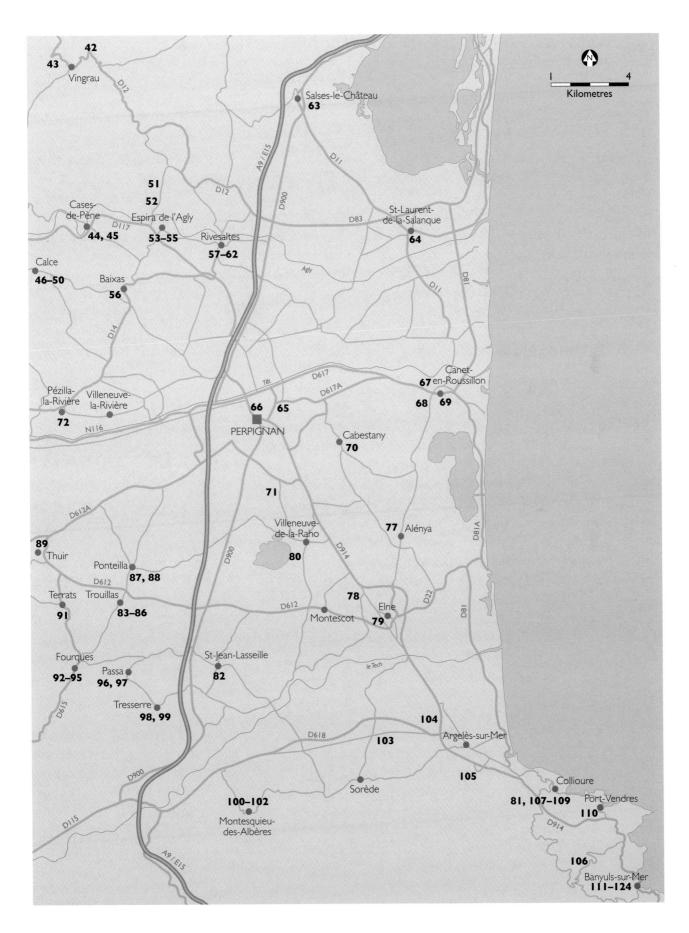

42
43
Vingrau
D12
Salses-le-Château
63
A9 / E15
D11
D900
D12
51
52
Cases-de-Pène
Espira de l'Agly
D117
44, 45
53–55
Rivesaltes
57–62
St-Laurent-de-la-Salanque
D83
64
Agly
D11
D81
Calce
46–50
Baixas
56
D14
Pézilla-la-Rivière
Villeneuve-la-Rivière
72
N116
Têt
D617
Canet-en-Roussillon
67
D617A
68 69
66 65
PERPIGNAN
Cabestany
70
71
D612A
Villeneuve-de-la-Raho
77 Alénya
89 Thuir
D900
80
D914
Ponteilla
87, 88
D612
Terrats
Trouillas
91
83–86
D81A
78
Elne
Montescot
79
D612
D22
Fourques
St-Jean-Lasseille
92–95
Passa
96, 97
82
le Tech
Tresserre
98, 99
D615
104
Argelès-sur-Mer
D618
103
D900
105
Sorède
Collioure
81, 107–109
Port-Vendres
110
D115
100–102
Montesquieu-des-Albères
D914
106
A9 / E15
Banyuls-sur-Mer
111–124

Kilometres
1 4

spoiled in the process. In the Roussillon and some adjoining areas to the north, VDNs may be either aged by oxidisation and matured in open containers, or given brief conventional vinification either in wood or vat before being bottled soon after the vintage. In the case of red VDNs, this latter process is called 'Vintage' or 'Rimage'. These are the different and confusing styles of VDNs:

Muscat de Rivesaltes: Made from either or both of the muscat varieties: Muscat Petits Grains (often favoured) and Muscat d'Alexandrie. Found all over the district but not in Banyuls.

Rivesaltes: May be red, white or, rarely, rosé. If white, the muscat content is limited to 20% to give differentiation from the *Muscat de Rivesaltes*, the remaining authorized grapes being grenache blanc or gris, maccabeu and vermentino. In the case of red *Rivesaltes*, the grenache grape must make up 50% of the traditional-style wine and 75% of the vintage style. Sometimes the reds are described as *'Grenat'*. Other authorised grapes are syrah, cinsault and carignan, though these are comparatively rarely used for VDNs.

'Ambré' is a term used to describe white VDN if aged by the oxidisation method for at least two years.
'Tuilé' denotes a red VDN which has been aged for two years in the oxidisation style or for one year in the vintage style.
'Hors d'Age' denotes at least five years' ageing.
The suffix *'Rancio'* may be used where the wines have acquired a distinctly Madeira-like style through long ageing.
'Maury' is a distinct appellation for red and white VDNs, and more recently dry table wines from grenache.

Meanwhile the making of dry wines has become increasingly important, especially dry white muscat for early drinking. A range of reds is a natural development of the interest in the wines of Languedoc to the north and a falling off in the demand for the *vins doux naturels*. There are two principal AOPs:

Côtes de Roussillon: applicable generally in specified areas throughout the region to wines of all three colours

Côtes de Roussillon Villages: limited to red wines.

All AOPs must be a blend. Wines from the communes of Caramany, Lesquerde, Latour-de-France and Tautavel may also add their names to their labels on account of their special *terroirs*. *'Les Aspres'* is an additional description for wines from certain specially delimited parcels in the south of the area, and for which oak-ageing is compulsory.

The grapes permitted are the same as in Languedoc (including the rather rare lledoner pelut), although the use of carignan is restricted. Syrah and/or mourvèdre are obligatory. These restrictions account for the rise in production of IGPs that give much greater freedom to the growers, many of whom are producing from grapes not permitted in the AOPs, or from varietals or blends which do not meet the percentage requirements of the AOPs. 'Côtes Catalanes' is the most commonly found of these denominations, which also include 'Côte Vermeille' and 'Pays d'Oc'.

Dry white wines are less common than the reds, but may be made from a variety of grapes including grenache blanc and gris, maccabeu. malvoisie, vermentino, marsanne and roussanne, as well as the two muscats.

Finally, there are separate AOPs for Collioure (dry wines of all three colours) and Banyuls (limited to *vins doux naturels*). See below.

LES FENOUILLÈDES

At the western end of the valley of the Agly in the north-west corner of Roussillon, this arid, schistous region has suddenly become home to a number of very interesting and successful growers, often preferring to make their wines as IGPs rather than labour under the restraints of the *appellation* rules. They used to have their own IGP, but are angry that it has been subsumed into Côtes Catalanes. Their resentment is in part due to the fact that the small frontier area of Fenouillèdes was always pure French rather than Catalan.

Entries in this section run broadly from west to east, and not in any order of merit. Because of its altitude, the grapes here ripen up to a month later than those in the hot valleys further east, and tend to have lower alcohol potential and the ability to produce wines of greater finesse and lightness. Sometimes the minerality can be overdone, and acidity can mask the fruit.

BD ****LE SOULA
Mark Walford and Gérard Gauby
66220 Prugnanes
Tel 04 68 35 69 31
info@le-soula.com www.le-soula.com

MAP 2
Telephone for appointment.

At between 1,000 and nearly 2,000 feet above the sea, these must be some of the highest vineyards in the South. On a soil mostly of decomposed granite, otherwise of schist, the 24 hectares of vines are dotted over several communes and are divided roughly equally between white and red grapes. The wines are made in the former *coopérative* building at Prugnanes, acquired by the growers and now completely modernised. From low yields of 14-18 hl/ha, there are just two *grand vins* wines. The white (C) is mainly a blend of maccabeu, sauvignon and grenache blanc, but with other grapes added such as viognier, chardonnay and malvoisie (the latter adding good acidity but not much else). For the red (C), the mix is more conventional; roughly 40% each carignan and syrah, the rest grenache. In addition there are two second wines, a red and white called 'Trigone' (B) made from the younger wines of the *domaine*. The character of the whites derives from the unusual *terroir* of the vineyards; they are unusually fresh for Roussillon wines, flinty and minerally with powerful fruit. The reds, again because of the altitude of the vineyards, are fine and elegant, pure, fresh and fruity, characteristics which are developing more and more as the vintages go by. These are undoubtedly some of the finest wines of the Roussillon. The latest creation is an 'orange' wine which may be a blend of more than one vintage, made from vermentino and maccabeu and grown at 400 metres above the sea. It has orange and dried flowers on the nose and is clean and well-built on the palate (D). Gérald Standley was in charge here for six years until 2014 and imprinted his own style on the policy of the domaine's owners with huge success. The wines get better every year. Challenged to explain why he had not gone for official bio certification, he replied that he could not be bothered because of all the paperwork, snooping and 'silly questions' involved. Now the future is in the hands of Philippe Salvat, president of the local Fenouillèdes growers.

November in the Fenouillèdes

**DOMAINE D'ARFEUILLE

Dominique and Stéphane d'Arfeuille
1 Rue Mongiran 33750 Nérigean
Tel   04 57 24 46 73
contact@domainedarfeuille.com
www.domainedarfeuille.com

Phone ahead for directions. Owner based in Bordeaux

Although M. d'Arfeuille does not allow his Bordeaux experience to influence his activities in Roussillon, he manages to retain a few vines in Bordeaux from which he produces a dry white blend of sauvignon, sémillon and muscadelle, perhaps a digression from his now very serious work in Roussillon. He has nearly eight hectares of vines, some of them venerable, grown on austere schist. Nothing remarkable about the *encépagement*: carignan and grenache both grown *en gobelet*, the syrah on wire. There is too a centenarian plantation of maccabeu which goes to make a varietal IGP. It is floral and honeyed and remains dry, but the *élevage sur lies* gives a certain richness to the wine (A/B). Of the reds, the Roussillon Villages (B) is deep garnet coloured, but remains bright and transparent, often with cherry and spices on its bouquet and a good balance overall. 'Les Gabax' (C), 50/50 syrah and grenache has darker fruits, but the same lively appearance and persistent aromas. The top red 'Vieilles Vignes' (B/C) is pure grenache and therefore IGP, a fine example of unblended grenache which is something unusual.

B ***DOMAINE LAGUERRE Eric Laguerre

12 rue de la Mairie,   St. Martin-de-Fenouillet
Tel   04 68 59 26 92
Mobile   06 15 35 78 92
domaine.laguerre@free.fr   www.domainelaguerre.com

MAP 6
Best to phone ahead; Eric has plenty of irons in the fire round here.

Eric Laguerre is one of the pioneers of the Fenouillèdes, having discovered the potential of making wines with a fine minerality as compared with the rather fatter style of wines (in particular the whites) which so often come from Roussillon. For many years he was manager of the local *coopérative,* then associated with Le Soula (q.v.) .He has today been joined by others, or perhaps it is his interest in other *domaines* of the region, but he seems to have moved sideways in recent years. Nevertheless, his whites, 'Cistus', and reds, 'Eos', as well his newer wines such as 'Eclipse' still show very good style and explain why it was that he fell in love (one of the first to do so perhaps) with this extraordinarily wild and inhospitable region. His wines remain undeniably attractive and very good value, mostly (B) tending to (C). Compared with many, they appear to have put on weight recently (the influence of oak-fermentation and ageing?), or is it that the other growers round here have lightened their style?

**DOMAINE GRIER

La Famille Grier (manager Raphaël Graugnard)
18 Avenue Jean Moulin, 66220 Saint-Paul de Fenouillet
Tel   04 68 73 34 39
GPS: 42.81 11 21 N,   2.507942 E
contact@domainegrier.com   www.domainegrier.com

MAP 9
Visits by appointment.

Proprietors of the Villiera vineyard at Stellenbosch in South Africa, the family longed for a domaine in the south of France, a dream ultimately realised with the help of Jean-Louis Denois of Limoux fame. Specialists in sparkling wine, they naturally have put their passion into practice in the Roussillon with a fizz (B) mostly from maccabeu, but they also make a full range of wines from other grapes: syrah, grenache, mourvèdre and carignan for the reds and some viognier too. The 22 hectares are mostly on schist a few kilometres above Saint Paul, while the state-of-the-art *cave* is in the middle of the village. The still white is all early-picked maccabeu, a small part of which is barrel-fermented, but the wine is bottled early to preserve freshness. The rosé is two parts grenache one part carignan, vinified separately. The reds include 'Galamus' (B) from roughly equal quantities of syrah, carignan and grenache, transferred to wood for the malolactic fermentation and aged there for a few months. There is a tank-raised grenache varietal (B), a syrah/carignan/grenache blend called 'Odyssea' (B/C), where the barrel-ageing is restrained in order to balance the fruit. 'Crusade' (C) is the 'top' wine, from old vines and given generous oak-ageing. Very skillful winemaking here.

OTHER GOOD GROWERS IN THE FENOUILLÈDES

B ** DOMAINE DE MAJAS

Agnès and Alain Carrère
21 Rue de la Bartasse, 66220 Caudiès-de-Fenouillèdes
Tel   04 68 59 94 41
Mobiles (Agnès) 06 13 32 03 27 and (Alain) 06 21 61 38 74
GPS 42 48 49 96N 02 22 36 67 E
domainedemajas@wanadoo.fr www.domainedemajas.com
MAP 1
Rendezvous recommended.

**DOMAINE SALVAT Jean-Philippe Salvat

8 Avenue Jean Moulin, 66220 St Paul de Fenouillet
Also at Rue de l'Horte 66610 Villeneuve de la Rivière
Tel (St Paul) 04 68 59 29 00 (Villeneuve) 06 03 32 42 59
salvat.jp@wanadoo.fr   www.domainesalvat.com
MAP 3
Cellars open: St Paul 9.00. Sat and Sun, 10.00-12.00 and 14.00-18.00. At Villeneuve Tue, Wed, Fri and Sat at 15.00-18.00.

⁎⁎MAS KAROLINA Caroline Bonville
29 Boulevard de l'Agly, 66220 Saint-Paul-de-Fenouillet
Tel 06 20 78 05 77
mas.karolina@wanadoo.fr   www.mas-karolina.com
MAP 4
Cellars open Monday to Saturday 10.00-13.00 and 15.00-19.00.

B ⁎⁎DOMAINE MARCEVOL
Pascal Verhaeghe   Manager Guy Predal
66320 Arboussols
(business address 164 Avenue General de Gaulle 66320 Vinça)
Tel 04 68 05 74 34
jean.predal@sfr.fr
MAP 7
Telephone ahead for visits.
Pascal Verhaeghe is better known as partner and animator of
Château le Cèdre in Cahors.

⁎⁎MAS MUDIGLIZA
Dimitri Glipa and Muriel Samson
20 Rue de Lesquerde, 66220 Saint Paul-de-Fenouillet
Tel 04 68 35 01 99
Mobiles 06 79 82 03 46 / 06 08 15 66 83
masmudigliza@neuf.fr   www.masmudigliza.fr
MAP 8
Appointment advised.

Drying *rafle*

MAURY

A few kilometres east of St.-Paul-de-Fenouillet, and in the lee of the ruined Château of Quéribus, is the small town of Maury which, until 20 years ago, was known only for its famous wine estate Mas Amiel. Today there is a born-again *coopérative* and a dozen or so other good growers, specialising in the production of *vins doux naturels*. They also produce a range of dry table wines rather in the style of the Fenouillèdes, but from a slightly less forbidding *terroir* (still mainly black schist) and a less extreme climate. The grenache grape dominates both the sweet and dry wine production.

B ⁎⁎⁎PRÉCEPTORIE DE CENTERNACH
Joseph Parcé
La Préceptorie, ZAC le Réal, Rue de la Fou
66220 Saint Paul de Fenouillet
Tel 94 68 59 26 74

Mobile   06 72 23 08 58
lapreceptorie@gmail.com   www.la-preceptorie.com

MAP 10
Tastings by appointment only.

Though owned by the Parcé family of Banyuls fame, this is no mere colonial outpost of the Domaine de la Rectorie (q.v.), but a free-standing enterprise, begun in 2000 when Vincent Legrand, Marc Parcé's son-in-law, took along to the Maury *coopérative* some red Grenache grapes. This was an experiment in making a dry red wine, with a view to bringing about AOC recognition of what had theretofore been an area uniquely devoted to VDNs. Though geographically based in the Fenouillèdes, this is an essentially Maury operation. 'Coume Marie' is the name given to one white wine and one red (both B). The white, from grenache gris (a Parcé favourite), grenache blanc, maccabeu and white carignan is fermented in old 400-litre barrels and aged in them for six to eight months. The red from grenache and carignan is aged in old standard size barriques for 12 to 15 months. These wines have freshness, fruit and great charm, and show well the so-called 'minerality' of this *terroir*. 'Terres Nouvelles' (C) is the name given to another pair of wines: the white all from grenache gris, this time fermented as well as aged in old barrels; the red fermented in small containers and once again aged in old wood. Don't overlook a vin de plaisir called 'Copain comme cochon' (B), pure grenache and designed for early and copious drinking and to accompany charcuteries or plain meat dishes. There are three Maurys (B/C), a red from grenache made and aged in cuve, a white aged in barrel for a year, and a more upmarket solera

In the Agly Valley

style red (C/D) which has fruits such as cassis, raspberry and blackberry as well as sweet spice. High-class winemaking throughout.

*SCV LES VIGNERONS DE MAURY
Mme Ute Hauke,
14 Avenue Jean-Jaurès 66460 Maury
Tel 04 68 59 00 95
contact@vigneronsdemaury.com
www.vigneronsdemaury.com

MAP 12
Cellars open Monday to Friday and Saturday morning at usual hours.

Founded in 1910, this *Cave* expanded rapidly at the turn of the century (there are now about 250 members, though many have tiny holdings) to reflect the growing demand for dry table wines and the corresponding dip in the market for VDNs. The long history of the *Cave* is further illustrated by the age of the vines, which cover 1,100 hectares, most of which are between 50 and 100 years old. The range of dry wines (all A) includes 'Nature de Schiste' a delicate dry white from grenache gris; 'Terra Novo', a barrel-fermented white from grenache blanc; and a 'Maury Sec', a red blend

of grenache and carignan made under their new appellation. The VDNs include 'Maury Blanc' (A), bottled early with a character of pears and flowers; 'Maury Ambré' (B), raised in old foudres or demi-muids in the traditional manner, eventually yielding preserved fruits such as orange and honey; and an aperitif-style red grenache called 'Pollen' (A), early bottled for easy drinking.

B ***DOMAINE LES TERRES DE FAGAYRA
Marjorie et Stéphane Gallet, 1 Rue de Montner, Montner
Tel 04 68 29 16 62
rocdesanges@wanadoo.fr www.terresdefagayra.com

MAP 14
Phone ahead.

Marjorie and Stéphane, already so well known for their wines at Le Roc des Anges at Montner (q.v.), have now acquired five hectares of vines at nearby Maury, on a mixture of pure schist and limestone. The vines are huddled under the mountains on the north side of the valley, enjoying more rainfall than some. The bedrock is fractured, which allows quick drainage and encourages the vines to burrow deep into the sub-soil. Cultivation has been organic here since

2009. Stéphane's earlier years as manager at Mas Amiel have given this couple the necessary know-how to equal and even overtake his former tutors. The white Maurys (both D), are not only from grenache blanc and gris but one ('Op. Nord') has also a little white carignan, the other ('Falgayra Blanc') a little maccabeu. Fresh and tingling, the contrast of sweetness and acidity is intensely satisfying. The red (D) is 90% grenache from slightly differing terroirs, one with some limestone mixed within the schist, the other on pure black schist. Sometimes a little carignan ensures a lighter feel to the wine. These wines are not cheap, but as examples of VDNs, hard to beat.

***MAS AMIEL

Olivier Decelle, Manager Nicolas Raffy
66460 Maury
Tel 04 68 29 01 02
www.masamiel.fr

MAP 16
Tours Monday to Saturday 9.00 to 18.00.

Once the only estate in Maury of which anyone had ever heard, its colourful history is almost as well-known as its wines: how a former owner had won it off the Bishop of Perpignan in a game of cards, and how another had been first disappointed by the failure of the King of Portugal to fulfill a promised visit, and later was ruined by the collapse of the wine market in the South in 1907. Today the property belongs to a former frozen food entrepreneur, 'the man who came in from the cold', who has had to face the problem of how to make viable an estate of 155 hectares famous for a style of wine no longer commercially possible in such bulk. Today much of the old style production of Maury and its reserve of stocks is still available. Decelle continues to make Maury in all its styles, but much of the vineyard has now been turned over to the making of dry table wines, while there are also new plantings of syrah and mourvèdre. It is something of an irony that the pure Maury flame has been largely passed to smaller growers who don't have so many hectares to turn to account. Nevertheless, Mas Amiel is still hugely worth the visit, if only to see the old glass *bonbonnes* with their cassoulet-tin lids, in which the wines are allowed to oxidise out in the open sunlight, and to taste what is still a fine range of Maury wines (B upwards to D according to age). The '10 ans d'age' is transferred from the demi-johns to 130 hectolitre casks and aged there for nine years more, the '15 ans d'age' is similarly made but given more time in cask, and the 1980 even longer, and so on back over the years. The modern style of traditional vinification (no *bonbonnes*) seems to be taking over because the taste these days is for a more port-style of wine rather than the old-fashioned flavours. There is also a white Maury from grenache gris and a range of Muscats de Rivesaltes. The Roussillon table wines are largely raised in new oak and will not disappoint.

**CHÂTEAU SAINT-ROCH

Proprietors Domaine Lafage
Mas Miraflors Route Canet 66000 Perpignan
Domaine at 66460 Maury
Tel 04 68 80 35 82
contact@domaine-lafage.com   www.domaine-lafage.com

MAP 18
Cellars open Monday to Friday 9.00-12.00 and 14.00-18.00

This 40-hectare property, which once enjoyed one of the highest reputations in Maury, was acquired in 2007 by the ambitious and go-ahead Domaine Lafage between Perpignan and the sea (q.v.). No doubt, economies of scale have enabled Lafage to reduce the previously high prices asked for the wines here, but only those fortunate enough to have known the property during the time of the Bourmazeau are in a position to say whether quality has been maintained. Certainly, the wines available today are good, for example the 'Petit Blanc' (A), sauvignon-based, and the more ambitious 'Cuvée Centenaire Blanc'(B) (see the Lafage entry), a blend of grenache blanc and roussanne that hits the spot nicely, as does the syrah-grenache rosé (A/B). The top red under the château name (D) is from Maury-grown grenache and is excellent. The 'Vieilles Vignes rouge' (A/B) and the red Maury VDN (C) are carried over from the old régime, albeit at reduced price.

**DOMAINE MAS DE LAVAIL

Nicolas and Jean Batlle
Route d'Estagel, 66460 Maury
Caveau at 18 rue Henri Barbusse, Maury
Tel 04 68 59 15 22
Mobile 06 20 71 38 57
info@masdelavail.com   www.masdelavail.com

MAP 19
Rendezvous required.

This is a large estate (80 hectares), run by father and son, at the eastern end of the *appellation*. For the Maury wines the grapes come from the schist, in the lee of the Château de Quéribus, while for the dry wines the more chalky-clay parcels round the *mas* itself are more propitious. There are too some vines up at Saint Paul, and grapes for the white Maury come from as far away as Tautavel. The dry wines include IGPs (C): a white from the two grenaches, hand-picked and aged in barrel, with hints of dates and figs; and a red from old grenache, again raised in wood, soft and rather plummy. The Côtes de Roussillon Villages red, 'Tradition' (A), has rather less character, but another red, 'La Désirade' (B), has a bit more syrah which is given new wood. The two Maurys (B) can best be described as mainstream, but an IGP (A) based on old carignan, though severe on the nose, has been found full of lovely black fruit on the palate.

BD ** CLOT DE L'ORIGINE Marc Barriot
66460 Maury
Tel 04 68 53 10 38
Mobile 06 75 03 71 71
www.vin-de-l-origine.com

MAP 20
Telephone ahead.

A small *domaine* of just over five hectares spread over several communes, but all run on biodynamic principles since 2004. Work in the vineyards is entirely manual, and Marc uses a mule for much of it. Only indigenous yeasts are used and no sulphur is added until the final stages of bottling, and then only in minimal quantities. Praise has been lavished on his dry Muscat, with more structure and less of the perfume-shop than many wines of this style; and on two reds, one an IGP (C/D) from 50% grenache, carignan and syrah, fermented together in old wood, the other an AOP(C/D) with rather more carignan, some of which is made by *macération carbonique*, notable for elegance and soft fruit rather than power. There is too a Roussillon Villages Latour de France 'Soif de plaisir' (B/C) which has just the extra class together with the buzz words, 'minerality', 'spice' and 'dark fruits', which the village name implies,. Perhaps because of their neo-'natural' character, the wines are controversial and attract polarized views… .maybe not a bad thing in itself?

OTHER GOOD GROWERS AT MAURY

** DOMAINE ARRIVÉ Marie-Pierre and Arnaud Arrivé
39 Rue de la Fou, 66220 Saint-Paul-de-Fenouillet
Mobiles 06 70 79 90 86 / 06 84 17 61 10
domainearrive@hotmail.fr www.domainearrive.fr
MAP 11
Promising growers, and to be followed.

** DOMAINE LA COUME DU ROY
Agnès and Jean-François de Volontat Bachelet
7 Avenue Jean-Jaurès / 13 route de Cucugnan   66460 Maury
Tel 04 68 59 67 58
Mobile 06 86 49 39 52
contact@lacoumeduroy.com www.lacoumeduroy.com
MAP 13
Telephone for an appointment.

B ** LA PETITE BAIGNEUSE Philippe et Céline Wies
4 Route de Lesquerde 66460 Maury
Tel 04 68 73 83 25
philippe.wiess@orange.fr

MAP 15
Phone ahead.

B ** DOMAINE POUDEROUX
Cathérine and Robert Pouderoux
2 Rue Emile Zola, 66460 Maury
Tel 04 68 57 22 02
domainepouderoux@sfr.fr www.domainepouderoux.fr
MAP 17
Appointment recommended.

/* DOMAINE DE LA PERTUISANE
Richard and Sarah Case
18 Rue Antoine Fauché 66460 Maury
Tel 04 68 59 26 31
Mobile 06 71 45 15 70
domaine@pertuisane.com www.pertuisane.com
MAP 21
Rendezvous advised.
A hard-to-rate *domaine*. It depends whether you like new world-style wines, powerful, alcoholic, oaky and dense, or whether you think this *terroir* better suited to something else.

** DOMAINE DU DERNIER BASTION
Jean-Louis Lafage
29 Avenue Jean-Jaurès 66460 Maury
Tel 04 68 38 97 68
Mobile 06 73 03 24 71
dernierbastion@orange.fr www.dernierbastion.com
MAP 22
Appointment suggested. A traditional, even old-fashioned *domaine*, but none the worse for that.

THE FOUR VILLAGES AND THE AGLY VALLEY

This section covers the vineyards between Maury and the Agly Valley as far as Rivesaltes. Travelling eastwards, the landscape gradually becomes less wild, though the effects of the extreme climate and the north-westerly *tramontane* wind are everywhere manifest. Although the postal addresses below mention the two villages of Latour de France and Tautavel, the other two villages entitled to put their names on the wine labels (Caramany and Lesquerde) are sometimes disguised by the postcodes of adjoining communes. Within this section are some of the best dry table wines of the whole of Roussillon.

The team, Domaine Mastrio

B ***CLOT DE L'OUM Eric and Lèla Monné

66720 Bélesta
Tel   04 68 57 82 32
Mobile 06 60 57 69 62
emonne@web.de   www.clotdeloum.com

MAP 23
Visits by appointment.

The seemingly strange name translates as 'Hill of the Elm'. Eric trained at Clos des Fées, whose wines were at first a model, but as he developed his own organic practices, he arrived at a point where his and Hervé Bizeul's styles could not be more different. At first he sent his grapes to the co-op, and it was only in 2001 that he made his own first vintage. He has 18 hectares of grapes, spread over countless parcels on the hillsides of Bélesta and Maury, at an altitude of 400 to 600 metres. The soil is granite and this, together with the high altitude, has drawn comparisons with Chablis in the case of his white wine 'Cine Panettone' (C/D), appropriately steely from a mix of grenache blanc and gris, maccabeu and muscat. The reds are said to recall those of the northern Rhone, but with more flint and minerality. They start with 'Compagnie des Papillons' (C), a blend of carignan and old grenache, with just a touch of the obligatory syrah. This,

like all the other wines here, has plenty of fruit but is not an oaky monster, and the low alcohol levels are a feature of the production. 'Le Clot' (C), mostly from younger syrah vines is aged in *foudres*, and does not require as much time as its elder brother 'Numéro Un' (D). 'Saint Bart Vieilles Vignes' (C) is dark, chunky and powerful, and needs time.

***DOMAINE MASTRIO

Michael and Caty Paetzold
Lieu-dit Lous Sarradets, Route de Caladroy, 66270 Bélesta
Tel 05 57 83 85 90
Caty.dhoine@domaine-mastrio.com
www.domaine-mastrio.com

MAP 26
Visit by appointment.

Starting in 2006, and operating at the beginning with a kind of mobile winery (now replaced by a more permanent conventional chais reminiscent of the old Eurostar terminal at Waterloo), these growers are heading for the top of the Roussillon tree. Caty was a nurse and therefore of a disposition to be a part of the local community. Michael is Belgian and a former businessman. Together they have about 20 hectares of tiny-yielding vines, some of them going back over 100 years. They have a winemaker called Didier working with them. They are keen on experimenting with the introduction of dried *rafle* from various vine varieties into their wines, apparently without making them over-stalky. There seems to be just one white here, 'Pain d'Oiseau' (C/D) from very old carignan blanc and raised like all their wines in vat (they don't do oak barrels). It has plenty of fruit and *gras* without heaviness, and the unique flavour of this rare grape. Their rosé ('Libertine' B) is red carignan-based and quite a hefty food-demanding pink. Of three reds, two are AOP Roussillon Villages: 'Dynamique' (B), more than half syrah, the rest carignan, heart-warming, spicy and garriguey; and 'Généreux' (C), which has some grenache too. Perhaps the best wine is a pure carignan IGP called 'Élégant' (D), once again from veteran wines, and with the warm roundness which seems to be the hallmark of this *domaine*. Hugely promising.

B***DOMAINE MODAT
Henri and Philippe Modat
Les Plas' 66720 Cassagnes
Tel   04 68 54 39 14
Mobile   06 72 26 50 66

MAP   29
Tastings by appointment (mobile).

Laurent Abet, working here since November 2008, has encouraged and supervised the transition of this 19-hectare estate to bio status. The brand new *chais* is also built to bio specification. The Modats' ambition is reflected in these new developments – it is a domaine that should improve further and go far. They make two white wines, both quite rich and powerful: 'De ci et de là' (B), a blend of all their white grapes; and 'Les Lucioles' (C), which includes a little young viognier which they have planted, some customers having spotted similarity in the terroir here to that of Condrieu. These wines are partly raised in tank and partly in wood, as are their reds. 'Comme Avant' (B) is a typical syrah/grenache/carignan blend. 'Sans Plus Attendre' (B) has the grenache is raised in tank, the carignan and syrah in wood. 'Le Plus Joli' (D) is from syrah with a 1/3rd dose of carignan. These reds proudly carry the Caramany name. The rosé (B) should not be passed over; indeed, they aim to make it a rich, quite powerful food wine.

****DOMAINE DE RANCY
Brigitte and Jean-Hubert Verdaguer
Place du 8 mai 1945 66720 Latour-de-France
Tel   04 68 29 03 47
Mobile   06 87 11 15 18
info@domaine-rancy.com   www.domaine-rancy.com

MAP 30
Appointment strongly recommended.

You will be hard put to find better exponents of the art of Rivesaltes *ambré* VDN, the cellars here being packed with legendary vintages going back 50 and more years. The Verdaguers have 17 hectares of vines in all, of which 11 (dotted about all over the region) are devoted to their beloved maccabeu, and their cellars are full of barrels of varying sizes, from old *foudres* to kiddies' miniatures, packed with their golden treasure. Vinification, nowadays carried out by their daughter Delphine, seems simple; six months in concrete before being transferred to wood where the wines will remain until they are required for bottling and sale. Start with their young *ambré*, perhaps a mere four years in barrel, the style and colour of a montilla, and a fitting partner for the local anchovies. Another 10 years in barrel and the wines will taste quite different, of figs perhaps, and if you go back say 40 years, the wine will have lightened in weight but will have acquired added complexity and length. You may be lucky enough to taste their 1959, matured all these years in old wood until it has acquired the colour of old Madeira. Prices for these wines range from B to D++ with advancing age. The Verdaguers have relatively recently (this century) started making dry red table wines (B) and these are hardly less remarkable than their VDNs, made from various blends of grenache, carignan and mourvèdre with lovely dark fruits, with some rusticity but also good grip, real tannins but elegant all the same.

BD***CLOS DU ROUGE-GORGE Cyril Fhal
6 Place Marcel Vie 66720 Latour-de-France
Tél   04 68 29 16 37
Mobile 06 31 65 25 89
cyrilfhal@gmail.com

MAP 31
Appointment is essential, if you are able to make contact (difficult).

The lack of a website is not surprising considering the almost reclusive character of this highly respected winemaker. With only five hectares of mostly north-facing vines he has made huge waves since his arrival from the Loire in 2002. Eschewing syrah and mourvèdre, which he regards as not indigenous and making for fat plummy wines, his vineyard consists of carignan and grenache, with a little cinsault for the reds, and maccabeu and grenache blanc for the whites. A boutique vineyard indeed, where nothing will cost you less than C, but where the quality makes the price seem cheap, M. Fhal aims for finesse, what the French call precision and delicacy, his wines being compared by some with fine burgundy. His 'Blanc' (C) is made in a mix of 500-litre casks and other old *barriques*, without *bâtonnage*, fining or filtering and with minimum sulphuring. It will keep from five to ten years, developing herb, citrus and smokey tones. Of the reds, the wine from 'Jeunes vignes' (C) is fruity and light, giving immediate pleasure but with some complexity too. It is mostly grenache, given a taste of wood in its early life and then transferred to stainless steel to complete its *élevage*. The Old Vine wine (D), largely carignan but with some grenache, is the 'top' wine here, unless you include a rarity

Marjorie Gallet, Le Roc des Anges, p.48

called 'Ubac' which does not seem to be marketed along with the rest of the range.

BD **DOMAINE RIVATON** Frédéric Rivaton
26 Boulevard Carnot / 9 rue Gabriel Péri 66720 Latour-de-France
Tel 04 68 51 76 08
Mobile 06 24 92 49 63
rivaton66@orange.fr and/ or frederic.rivaton@sfr.fr
www.rivaton.vinsnaturels.fr

MAP 32
Rendezvous necessary.

Rivaton is a self-styled producer of 'natural' wine from his 12 hectares of old vines growing on schist and gneiss. Working of the soil replaces weed-killers, and there are no sprays other than the usual *bouillie bordelaise* and sulphur against the oidium. Gravity is exploited both for the vinification and the racking of the wines. Rivaton's first vintage was in 2009 and no doubt he will develop a range of wines beyond those he started with: a 'Cuvée Blanc' (B) vinified and aged in barrel and made from 50% maccabeu, 30% carignan blanc, and the remainder from various grapes including grenache gris; a rosé called 'Poil dans la main' (B) from a mix of grenache gris and syrah; and two reds, a pure carignan vin de France, vinified by *macération carbonique* (C), and an AOP 'Gribouille' (C/D) made from 70% carignan and 15% each syrah and grenache, the whole vinified and aged in a large new *foudre* of 20 hectolitres (the equivalent of 8 normal barrels). There is also a Rivesalte Grenat (D) in 50-cl. bottles, promised to last until 2040. Expensive, but then the yields are only 10 hl/ha and every attention is given to detail both in the vineyard and the chais.

BD **** LE ROC DES ANGES

Marjorie and Stéphane Gallet
1 Route de Montner 66720 Latour de France
Tel   04 68 29 16 62
rocdesanges@wanadoo.fr   www.rocdesanges.com

MAP 33
Appointment required.

After a stage with Gauby, Marjorie, who comes from the Rhône valley, set up in her twenties at Montner with 10 hectares of very old vines, and since then the vineyard has grown to 30 hectares. Her husband, Stéphane, a native of Normandy, started with Cuilleron in Condrieu, before moving south to take over as régisseur at Mas Amiel (q.v), a post which he held until 2007 when he left to join Marjorie at home. Together they have established a reputation among the finest growers in the Midi, proving that wine can be elegant and fresh, even in a hot climate. Their use of barrels is well-disciplined, most coming from Burgundy and between three to five years old, just a few smaller ones bought from coopers in whom they have confidence. Extractions and alcohol levels are unusually low. Of their three whites, 'Llum' (a re-naming of the former 'Vieilles Vignes') is mostly grenache gris with some maccabeu and shows off the classic house style very well, the acidity and minerality well marked (C); 'Iglesia Vella' (D) so named because it comes from vines near to the site of the old local church is also from grenache gris, this time 80 years old; while 'L'Oca', all maccabeu will also shock you by its D+ price until you savour its wonderful quality. More modest are 'Imalaya' (C), all carignan gris, 'Chamane' (C), a dry muscat, and a rosé, neither quite white nor pink, and containing many local, some rare, grape varieties, which is aged a while in five-year-old barrels, and has been noted as being grapefruity, mineral and even salty. The reds start with 'Segna de Cor' a blend of the youngest grapes on the *domaine* (C); then come 'Reliefs', a carignan/grenache blend with a touch of syrah; '1903' (D) and 'Les Trabasserres', which are both pure carignan, planted in that year on *terroir* perfectly suited to it, and which must be kept a while before opening. Great stuff despite the cost.

B *** DOMAINE DES SCHISTES

Jacques and Mickaël Sire
I Rue Jean Lurçat 66310 Estagel
Tel 04 68 29 11 25
Mobile   06 89 29 38 43
sire-schistes@wanadoo.fr   www.domaine-des-schistes.com

MAP 37
Appointment required.

Combining the vineyards of their parents and grand parents, the Sires today have 55 hectares of vines straddling the communes of Estagel, Maury and Tautavel, planted mostly on the slopes of the Agly valley, *en gobelet* and thus mostly requiring hand harvesting. Three easy-drinking IGPs (allA) start their good-value range; a white from maccabeu, picked early to ensure freshness and to avoid excessive alcohol levels; a rosé with syrah, mourvèdre and a little maccabeu to back up the prevailing grenache, bottled in the spring after the vintage for summer drinking; and the red, half marselan, half syrah from their lowest ground where mechanical harvesting is possible. All three are raised in steel. There are two white AOPs, 'Le bosc blanc' (A), based on grenache gris and 'Les Terrasses Blanches' (C), 70% grenache blanc, the first raised in steel, the other transferred to wood after its first fermentation and left there till bottling the following spring. 'Terrasses Rouges' (C) is a blend from their Tautavel vines, the syrah made in new barrels, the grenache in old and the carignan in steel. 'Tradition' (B), also from Tautavel and quick to mature, is raised in concrete and without racking, so as to ensure freshness of the fruit. 'Les Bruyères' (A) is another early-ready wine from syrah, lledoner pelut (standing in for its cousin grenache) and carignan. The top red is 'La Coumeille' (D), mostly from old low-yielding syrah and aged in barrels of one or two previous wines. Bottling is deferred for two years. The VDNs include a Muscat de Rivesaltes (B), 80% alexandria, raised in steel; the 'Solera' (C), aged in barrels without topping up; and a Maury called 'La Cérisaie' (B/C), all grenache and usually bottled one year after the vintage. Lovers of the *rancio* style can enjoy their version (C) from grenache blanc and maccabeu, again without ullage and made as in Jerez on the solera system (three levels).

*** DOMAINE DES CHÊNES Alain Razungles

7 rue Maréchal Joffre 66600 Vingrau
Tel 04 68 29 40 21
domainedeschenes@wanadoo.fr   www.domainedeschenes.fr

MAP 42
Phone ahead.

Razungles is a professor of oenology at Montpellier University, so there's nothing much you can teach him about wine making. His 35 hectares of vines, facing south out of an amphitheatre of rock which is itself the southern boundary of the Corbières, are at varying altitudes, the highest (about 1,200 feet) being particularly suitable for the white grapes. Wines from these include 'Les Olivettes' (A), half muscat and sold as IGP, crisply mineral with resulting good acidity to balance some richness on the palate; 'Les Magdaléniens' (B/C), an oaked white from grenache blanc and roussanne, aromatic and white burgundy-ish; and 'Les Sorbiers' (A/B), another wine given some months in oak, which has some *gras* but manages to keep its acidity. The fruity rosé called 'Festa Major' (A) is not to be spurned by those in a hurry to get to the reds; the top-selling 'Grand'Mères' (A/B) is mostly carignan and grenache, and sometimes quite tapenade-ish and with rich tannins; and there are two Tautavel AOPs, 'le Mascarou' (B) with spicy soft red fruits and, perhaps better (added mourvèdre), 'La Carissa' (C), richer and holding its alcohol well. Just as good as the reds are the sweet wines; a Muscat de Rivesaltes (B), with strong flavours of the grape variety, fully sweet but with the right mineral balance; a pair of Rivesaltes; a well-balanced *ambré* (B) and a powerful *tuilé* (B). If there's any left, don't miss the bone-dry *rancio* style wine called 'L'Oublié' (C), well-named because it emerged in a barrel of maccabeu which had long been abandoned and left by accident to oxidise on its own. All the wines here, including the whites, seem to age well.

****DOMAINE DU CLOS DES FÉES

Claudine and Hervé Bizeul
69 rue Maréchal Joffre 66600 Vingrau
Tel 04 68 29 40 00
contact@closdesfees.com www.closdesfees.com

MAP 43
Prior appointment strongly recommended.

Former sommelier, restaurateur and journalist, Hervé Bizeul took his courage in both hands in 1997 to become a wine maker without any experience whatsoever. Starting with the simplest of equipment and premises, but with the help of good friends like Gérard Gauby, he has become one of Roussillon's cult growers. Being considered one of the top two or three in the region, he has been able to pitch his prices accordingly. All the wines are D here, often D++, except a grenache blanc-based 'Vieilles vignes' (C), a wine at once pale and delicate, fat and mediterranean and aged for 18-40 months before bottling; and a red four-way blend 'Les Sorcières', the grenache and cariginan coming from old plants, the syrah and mourvèdre from young ones. In the financial stratosphere, try the pretentiously-named 'Un faune avec son fifre sous les oliviers sauvages', an unusual blend of cabernet franc and merlot, picked ultra-late and vinified in steel, then raised in a succession of new wood, old wood and finally *cuve*. The top 'Clos des Fées' and 'Petit Sibérie', produced after the manner of the *vins de garage* in Bordeaux and at prices to match, are hardly for everyday drinking, but perhaps to be tried at least once in a lifetime, especially if you are a lover of rich, powerful, concentrated, dark and sculpted wines. To surprise us all, Hervé pulls out of the hat 'Modeste', a very light and elegant Grenache, a delicious quaffer (B).

BD ****DOMAINE GAUBY

Gérard and Lionel Gauby
le Faradjal 3 route Estagel 66600 Calce
Tel 04 68 64 35 19
domaine.gauby@wanadoo.fr www.domainegauby.fr

MAP 46
Prior appointment strongly recommended

Without doubt one of the star winemakers of France, Gauby is the man who put Roussillon wines on the map. In the middle of a region miraculously preserved from ecological vandalism, Gauby has 45 hectares of vines surrounded by another 40 of wild plants, shrubs, forest and scrub, which give his wines part of their inimitable character. Compost and fertilisers are all made odiferously on the premises and no chemicals are allowed anywhere near, either in the vineyard or in the *chais*. The vines are worked by horse and not tractor. The wines are neither filtered nor fined, and there are no enzymes added, no chaptalisation nor acidification. Gauby began towards the end of the last century, and as time has gone by, his style has purified itself (Gauby is a Burgundy-lover). Today the emphasis is on elegance and finesse, and perfect control of *élevage* rather than up-front assault, and the importance of oak-ageing has been modified towards a style where the fruit and the *terroir* are allowed maximum expression. He has moved to the opposite end of winemaking from, say Hervé Bizeul, his one-time protégé, as it is possible to go. There are three whites; 'Les Calcinaires Blanc' (C), a blend of 50% muscat, 30% chardonnay and 20% maccabeu, given an *élevage* in cuve of eight months; 'Vieilles Vignes blanc' (C) from maccabeu, carignan and the two paler grenaches, all the vines for this wine being up to 100 years old; and 'Coume Gineste' (C/D) from the two grenaches, aged in a mix of new and one-year-used *barriques*. The whites are partnered by three reds; 'Les Calcinaires Rouges' (C), from younger vines, particularly the syrah which Gauby himself planted when he began; 'Vieilles Vignes rouge' (C/D), where the carignan is 125 years old and is blended with grenache, syrah and mourvèdre; and 'Muntada' (D++), the ultimate red Roussillon, reverting to the traditional foundations of carignan and grenache, with just a touch of the other grape varieties, and aged in a mix of *foudres* and barrels for two years. And don't forget his Rivesaltes (C) from grenache noir, which dispenses with a second fermentation and is aged 18 months in barrel.

BD ***DOMAINE OLIVIER PITHON

Olivier Pithon
19 route d'Estagel 66600 Calce
Tel 04 68 38 50 21
GPS 42 45 18 712N 2 44 49 718 E
olivierpithon@live.fr www.domaineolivierpithon.com

MAP 47
Visits by appointment in summer during normal business hours.

What is it about Calce which has attracted so many talented winemakers? Perhaps a guaranteed freedom from chemical sprayers and spreaders? Perhaps the proximity of the great Gauby, a friend of this grower's brother? Perhaps the *terroir*? At all costs, Pithon arrived here from his native Anjou in 2001 and has established himself as a top winemaker. This is another property where you will need good credit facilities. Low yields and biodynamic production on only 15 hectares raise production costs uncomfortably. The 'Cuvée Laïs' IGP blanc (C), named after a cow of theirs, is fermented and

Tom Lubbe, Domaine Matassa

modesty in alcohol and elegance, but at prices which aspire to match Gauby. You will be lucky to find any wine here less than C/D, unless it is the red 'Cuvée L'Estanya', mostly from very old carignan with just 20% mourvèdre, or 'Romanissa Cazot', a highly original light red, 70% grenache gris and the rest carignan, a lovely bright carmine colour. The prices for the others are explained by the tiny yields, and because biodynamic principles are here carried out to their extremes. Lubbe is helped by the fact that the vineyards are entirely surrounded by *garrigue* and woods, so that he is protected from 'infection'. Try the red 'Cuvée Romanissa', mostly lledoner pelut. The wines need opening ahead of time to cast off any signs of reduction, which sometimes occurs with 'natural' wines. 90% of Lubbe's wines are exported to a wide range of countries.

raised in various kinds of wood, but does not have to be aged if the thirst takes you (maccabeu, grenache blanc and gris). 'La D 18' (D) (named after the one road which runs through Calce) is another white from the two grenaches given 12 to 16 months in barrel. Relax now, because there are two affordable, easy-drinking wines, a white and red called 'Mon P'tit Pithon' (A/B), which have all the hallmarks of the grander *cuvées* – freshness and roundness. The red 'Laïs' (C) is a blend of all four of the regular grapes, aged in concrete to retain sappiness and zip. 'Le Pilou' (D) is a pure carignan, the vines grown on chalk and the wine raised in *demi-muids* for 18 months or so. Back to the stratosphere for 'Le clot' (D++), produced from grenache and only bottled as a limited edition in magnums. Hence the price. The name of their sweet grenache noir 'Le vitriol' (C) is not a joke, but chosen presumably because there are some people who don't get on with this kind of thing. See if you do.

BD ***DOMAINE MATASSA
Tom and Nathalie Lubbe
10 route d'Estagel 66600 Calce
Tel 04 68 64 10 13 / 09 62 50 17 99
matassa@orange.fr   www.matassawine.com

MAP 48
Prior appointment strongly advised. April to October best. Lubbe spends a lot of time on the road.

A 'natural' winemaker, Tom Lubbe spent four vintages on a *stage* with Gérald Gauby before settling down in Gauby's village, and marrying his sister Nathalie. He then set about acquiring a patchwork of vines in and around the village of Calce. Today he has about 13 hectares of vines and two of olives. The style of the *domaine* is quite austere; the whites are viscous but minerally to the point of being aggressive, wonderfully long and fruity all the same. 'Cuvée Marguérite' is a blend of the two muscats with touches of viognier and maccabeu, and the 'Matassa blanc' is from centenarian grenache gris with some maccabeu added. They are a far cry from the more normal fat and heavy wines that come from so many lower-flying domaines. The reds are marked by a

B ***DOMAINE DE L'HORIZON
Thomas Teibert
4 rue des Pyrénées 66600 Calce
Tel 04 68 28 49 98
Mobile 06 23 82 24 59
info@domaine-horizon.com   www.domaine-horizon.com

MAP 49
Appointment needed.

Teibert has had extensive experience in all aspects of the wine business, particularly as a representative for the Austrian barrel-maker Stockinger, for whom he was an agent in the Roussillon. This was how he met Gauby and Lubbe and bought two and a half hectares of vines in Calce. Today he has just about 15 hectares, all grown *en gobelet*, and from which yields are as low as 12 hl/ha. He explains that the soil contains a deal of ferrous oxide which gives the wines a freshness and mineral quality. The wines are expensive (nothing less than D) but top quality. The grapes are destalked but not crushed and given as little punishment in the cellar as possible. Ageing is, of course, in Stockinger barrels, large ones, and *foudres*. There are two whites: 'Esprit' from 2/3rds maccabeu and 1/3rd muscat; and 'Domaine', in which the maccabeu is supported by the two paler grenaches. The rosé is all grenache and the single red, 'Esprit', a syrah/carignan blend. The wines are presented in Burgundy bottles.

***DOMAINE JEAN-PHILIPPE-PADIÉ
Jean-Philippe Padié
11 rue des Pyrénées 66600 Calce
Tel 04 68 64 29 85
Mobile 06 99 53 07 66
contact@domainepadie.com   www.domainepadie.com

MAP 50
Prior appointment by mobile recommended.
Jean-Philippe arrived here from the South-West, and over the space of 10 years, two of which were spent working with Gauby (q.v.), has acquired from local *coopérateurs* a

Jean Gardiès, Domaine Gardiès

like number of hectares split among thirty or so different parcels, home mostly to carignan and grenache, as well as some grenache gris (which Jean-Philippe marginally prefers to grenache blanc). The latter does however form the bulk of his first white, 'Fleur des Cailloux' (C), aptly named, with 30% of the gris and 20% maccabeu, and raised partly in steel and partly in 300-litre barrels for eight months. 'Milousie' (D) is a straight blend of the two paler grenaches and entirely aged in old *demi-muids* of 600 litres for a year. The whites here, as everywhere in Calce, are outstanding, rivalling the reds for quality. Jean-Philippe's first red, 'Petit Taureau' (B), is aged wholly in concrete and is half carignan, otherwise syrah with just a little grenache and mourvèdre. It can be drunk young if desired, but will also keep a few years. 'Ciel Liquide' (C/D), notable for its fruit, is aged in various kinds of barrels and has a little more grenache, while 'Calice' (A/B) is pure carignan raised in steel, well-balanced and full. The wines here are very much after the Gauby style, finely elegant with good acidity and an attractive astringency which calls for bottle-ageing.

B ＊＊＊＊DOMAINE GARDIÈS Jean Gardiès
Chemin de Montpins 66600 Espira d'Agly
Tel   04 68 64 61 16
Mobile 06 08 53 07 50
GPS 42 80 447N 2.8267 E
domgardies@wanadoo.fr   www.domaine-gardies.fr

MAP 52
The domaine, outside the village on the way to Vingrau, is open Mon. to Fri. 9.00 – 17.00 for tasting of four to six wines at 10€ per person, refundable on purchase of six or more bottles. Prior appointment requested.

From his 45 hectares spread over varying terroirs at Espira and Vingrau (schist, argilo-calcaire, marnes) Gardiès makes a range of widely differing wines. These include some relatively uncomplicated IGPs (B) from his 'Mas Les Cabes', a property which he bought in 1999 just down the road towards Espira, a white muscat sec, and a simple, clean, fruity and easy red. There is also a pink, oaked wine (B) which will (unusually) keep a few years, and a blended red called 'Les Millères' (B/C), only half of which is given any oak. Prices start to rise with the white 'Les Glaciaires' (C) from the home-*domaine*, a blend where 40% roussanne and the two paler grenaches are vinified together and a little maccabeu is added before the wine is matured in old barrels for eight months. 'Le Clos de Vignes blanc' (D), almost all grenache blanc and gris is given 12 months in *demi-muids*. A red is made under the same name (C/D) and is a grenache/ carignan blend with just a touch of mourvèdre and held in barrels and *demi-muids* for 12 months. The top wines of the house are 'Les Falaises' (D), mostly syrah and grenache in equal quantities, which will keep 10 years or more after its 20 months in *barriques*, and 'La Torre' (D), a largely mour- vèdre wine which spends two years in *demi-muids*, as does a pure mourvèdre called 'Mataro' (D). Grannies and babies might be safer with the fresh 'Flor Blanc' (B), a Muscat de Rivesaltes which has just eight months on its lees and is for drinking young, and a glorious *ambré* (D), nutty, sweet but not cloying and marvellous with just about any cheese.

***DOMAINE DANJOU BANESSY

Benoît and Sebastian Banessy
1b Rue Thiers 66600 Espira d'Agly
Tel 04 68 64 1,8 04
bendanjou@hotmail.fr www.domainedanjou-banessy.com

MAP 53
Domaine open Mon. to Sat. during usual hours.

Organic, even biodynamic, but working without official certification, this *domaine* of just about 20 hectares con- centrated in former times on the production of VDNs, but Benoît has switched largely towards the production of dry table wines, like many others in the region. If you ask how long the family have been making wine here, the answer will be '*depuis toujours*'. The present regime being relatively new and still finding their feet, the range of wines on offer will change no doubt (they could do with some entry-level wines), but those likely to prove constant are: two dry whites based on combinations of the two grenaches and maccabeu. 'Coste' (C) and Estaca' (D); and more unusually, a pure carignan gris, 'Vieilles vignes' (C), with a bakery nose and a long, quite salty and thirst-provoking finish. Barrels here are used purely as containers and not to give any added flavour to the wines. The reds include 'Roboul' (C), with dark fruits and sometimes a rather austere finish; 'Truffière' (C) from carignan and grenache and given a long *éle- vage*; 'Estaca' (D), a pure grenache by *macération carbon- ique*; and a very original and unusual pure cinsault called 'Espurna' (D). Then comes a range of VDNs (D) from vintages going way back and in the *rancio* style, some decadently sweet but with redeeming acidity to lighten the wine magically, and others quite differently dry.

OTHER GOOD GROWERS IN THE AGLY VALLEY

**DOMAINE RIBERACH Jean-Michel Mailloles
2c Route de Caladroy 66720 Bélesta
Tel 04 68 50 56 56
Mobile 06 21 42 08 13
GPS 42.71 N 2.60 E
cave@riberach.com   www.riberach.com
MAP 24
Shop open during usual business hours.
The production here is one of the mainstays of an ambitious de luxe hotel complex recently opened in this 'lost' little town, and of which Mailloles is one of the partners.

*CHÂTEAU DE CALADROY Mme Valérie Maurin
66720 Bélesta
Tel 04 68 57 10 25
chateau.caladroy@wanadoo.fr   www.caladroy.com
MAP 25
Cellar open all year from Monday to Friday 10.00-18.00, 19.00 in summer. Saturday and Sunday in summer only 10.00-18.00
This is a handsome medieval *château*, a real one right in the middle of its vineyard, and its former chapel has been converted into a cellar for visitors. The less expensive wines here are excellent value for money.

*CELLIER TREMOINE
5 Avenue de Caramagny 66270 Rasiguères
Tel 04 68 29 11 82
Mobile 06 20 82 83 08
contact@tremoine.com   www.tremoine.com
MAP 27
Open 8.00-12.00 and 14.00-18.00 from Monday to Saturday. Closed Sundays and public holidays.
'Cuvée Moura Lympany' is named after the famous pianist who had vines in the village and used to hold a music festival every year in the Coop's chais.

B *LES TERRES DE MALLYCE
Corinne and Yvon Soto
21 bis Rue des Vignes, 66720 Rasiguères
Tel 04 68 73 86 37
Mobile 06 81 70 12 34
yvon.soto@yahoo.fr   www.lesterresdemallyce.com
MAP 28
Appointments necessary for visits every day between 10.00-12.00 and 15.00-19.00. Formerly members of the Cellier Trémoine at Rasiguères (q.v.), they set up on their own in 2007 and immediately began conversion to organic methods. To be encouraged.

B **DOMAINE TRIBOULEY Jean-Louis Tribouley
9 Place Maréchal Vié, 66720 Latour-de-France
Tel 04 68 29 03 86
Mobile 06 83 50 89 62
jean-louis.tribouley@orange.fr
MAP 34

Visits every day by rendezvous. One of many of Gauby's pupils/ disciples, Jean-Louis farms biodynamically on his 14 hectares of widely spread vineyard.

B **DOMAINE DU BOUT DU MONDE
Edouard Laffitte
13 Avenue des Platanes 66720 Lansac
Tel 06 77 50 94 22
edouard.laffitte@laposte.net
www.domaineleboutdumonde.sitew.com
MAP 35
Appointment required.

B **DOMAINE DU POSSIBLE Löic Roure
13 Avenue des Platanes 66720 Lansac
Tel 04 68 92 52 78
MAP 36
Appoinment advisable.
Roure bought the disused *Coopérative* in the village of Lansac in 2003, and has been converting the upper storey into a flat to live in ever since. The space in the cave he shares with Edouard Laffitte (see above).

**LES VIGNERONS DES CÔTES D'AGLY
Avenue Louis Vigo, 66310 Estagel
Tel 04 68 29 00 45
commercial@agly.fr www.agly.fr
MAP 38
Open during usual business hours.
While many of the smaller *coopératives* have closed or merged into bigger units, the Caves des Côtes d'Agly (an amalgam of many of these) seem to go from strength to strength.

**DOMAINE FONTANEL
Pierre and Marie-Claude Fontaneil (sic)
25 Avenue Jean-Jaurès, 66720 Tautavel
Tel 04 68 29 04 71 or 04 68 29 45 21
domainefontanel@hotmail.com   www.domainefontanel.com
MAP 39
Visits at Tautavel (Pierre) April to October from 10.00 to 19.00 and all year round at Caveau d'Estagel, 37-39 Avenue du Docteur Torreilles (Marie-Claude) 66310 Estagel

**DOMAINE MOUNIÉ Claude and Hélène Rigaill
Avenue Jean Badia, 66720 Tautavel
Tel   04 68 29 12 31
domainemounie@free.fr
MAP 40
Appointment advisable. Check for possible change of ownership.

B **DOMAINE DES SOULANES
Cathy and Daniel Laffite
Mas de las Frédas 66720 Tautavel
Tel 04 68 29 12 84
Mobile 06 12 33 63 14

daniel.laffite@nordnet.fr   www.domaine-soulanes.com
MAP 41
Rendezvous strongly recommended.

*CHÂTEAU DE JAU La famille Dauré
66600 Cases-de-Pène
Tel 04 68 38 90 10 (restaurant 04 68 38 91 38)
contact@chateau-de-jau.com   www.chateaudejau.com
MAP 44
Visit during normal business hours.
The Dauré family have been here since 1974, in which time they have not only restored the château, but installed a restaurant and art gallery too.

*SCV L'AGLY (CHAPELLE DE PÉNA)
2 Boulevard Maréchal Joffr, 66600 Cases de Pène
Tel 04 68 38 93 30
contact@chateaudepena.com   www.chateaudepena.com
MAP 45
Open during normal business hours Monday to Saturday and Sunday mornings in July and August.
55 members of this *coopérative* share 400 hectares, making a range of wines of which half are IGPs from the Côtes Catalanes and the other half split AOP reds and VDNs

B *DOMAINE JOLIETTE Philippe Mercier
route de Vingrau, Montpins, 66600 Espira d'Agly
Tel 04 68 64 50 60
mercier.joliette@wanadoo.fr   www.joliette-mercier.com
MAP 51
Rendezvous recommended.
Value here for all purses in an area not renowned for its bargains.

**DOMAINE PIQUEMAL Famille Piquemal
Lieu dit Della Lo Rec, RD 771 66600 Espira de l'Agly
Tel 04 68 64 09 14
contact@domaine-piquemal.com www.domaine-piquemal.com
MAP 54
Phone for appointment.
A big range of wines, some of which have found their way to the tables of the Elysée, the Matignon and the Paris Mairie. But the reputation of the *domaine* rests more famously on its dry Muscat (A).

**MAS CRÉMAT Catherine, Christine and Julien Jeannin
66600 Espira d'Agly
Tel 04 68 38 92 06
mascremat@mascremat.com   www.mascremat.com
MAP 55
Open weekdays (avoid lunchtime). Rendezvous required at weekends.
Whether it is the black schist or the hot climate which gives its name to the domaine, 'burnt' is an apt epithet, 'crémat' meaning just that in Catalan.

**VIGNOBLES DOM BRIAL

66390 Baixas
Tel 04 68 64 22 37
contact@dom-brial.com   www.dom-brial.com
MAP 56
Open for visits Monday to Saturday at usual hours (not lunchtime). One of the more important *coopératives* in the northern part of Roussillon, created in 1923, and enlarged through the absorption of smaller *caves*. Everything here is value for money and there is something for all tastes and purses, including a range of old vintages (C).

RIVESALTES

This is the heart of the production of Vins Doux Naturels, and also the birthplace of Muscat de Noël, Roussillon's white vin nouveau for drinking within months of its vinification. With the overall decline in taste for sweeter fortified wines, the production of dry table wines is increasing, although the growers here are persisting in their love for the fortified styles.

BD ***DOMAINE CAZES

Director Lionel Lavail, winemaker Emmanuel Cazes
4 rue Francisco Ferrer, BP 61, 66600 Rivesaltes
Tel   04 68 64 08 26
Mobile 06 84 62 05 31
GPS 42 77 01 921 N 2 8773664 N
info@cazes.com   www.cazes-rivesaltes.com

MAP 57
Open Monday to Saturday during usual hours, also Sundays between June and September.

220 hectares (including the estate of Marshal Joffre, whose name is perpetuated on the labels here), 15 or so IGPs, three AOP table wines, a stock of one million bottles. All this and its association with the big négociant Jeanjean (Advini) does not sound much like an artisanal production. Nor is it. Nevertheless, this is a benchmark estate for the production of the whole range of Roussillon wines, and biodynamic to boot. All the usual Roussillon grapes are represented, as well (for the IGPs) as some tannat, petit manseng and colombard. Broadly speaking there are three ranges of wine: 'Les Vins Plaisir' (mostly A) in all three colours, and made for immediate consumption; 'Les Vins prestige', in a bigger, fleshier style, the reds showing typically forest-floor and spice character (of which particularly note the oaky 'Credo' (C) a cabernet/merlot IGP blend); and 'Les Vins d'Exception', consisting of older vintages, particularly the 'Cuvée Aimé Cazes' (D++), named after Emmanuel Cazes' grand-

Olives and vines, near Estagel

father. Then there is the run of VDNs, perhaps the stars of the house (mainly B/C) but at all prices up to and including the wonderful but expensive Rivesaltes *ambré* (D++). In the lower ranges the wines are good value, but rather dear otherwise. This establishment also boasts a fine restaurant, serving mostly organically produced food.

***DOMAINE BOUDAU

Véronique and Pierre Boudau
6 rue Marceau, 66600 Rivesaltes
Tel   04 68 64 45 37
info@domaineboudau.fr   www.domaineboudau.fr
MAP 58
Open Monday to Saturday usual hours. Closed Sunday.

This vineyard was created in the 1920s by Hippolyte Boudau, and is today owned and run by his great grandchildren, who took over the reins in 1993. The domaine consists nowadays of 119 hectares, partly at the entrance to the Agly valley, and partly on the flatter ground near Baixas. The present owners have gradually increased the importance of dry table wines (with the plantation of grenache produced by *selection massale* in Châteauneuf-du-Pape). They also continue to produce some VDNs of excellent quality, for example their 'Rivesaltes grenat' (B), redolent of cherries. The Boudaus recommend strong soft cheese such as Munster to go with it. The dry whites include, of course, a very dry muscat (A) and a maccabeu 'Le Petit Closi' – a name shared with their much-praised rosé (A). There is also a fruity red meant for early drinking (A). The AOP reds start with a spicy 'Le Clos' (A). There are four Roussillon Villages wines, 'Tradition'(A), 'Henri Boudau' (B), 'Padri' (C) and 'Patrimoine' (C), the last three given varying degrees of oak-ageing and Patrimoine needing some time in bottle. As well as the grenat, there is a good Muscat de Rivesaltes (B). Excellent value for money at this property.

B **DOMAINE CAYROL** Danièle Cayrol
15 Rue du 4 septembre, 66600 Rivesaltes
Mobile 06 86 53 82 71
dancay@hotmail.fr
MAP 59
Appointment suggested.
The cellars are in Rivesaltes town, but the vines are away towards Espira. A quietly admired domaine, converted to organic production from 2011.

OTHER GOOD GROWERS IN RIVSALTES

*MAS DELMAS** André and Mercédès Delmas
29 Avenue du Stade, 66600 Rivesaltes
Tel 04 68 51 88 10
info@masdelmas.com   www.masdelmas.com
MAP 60
Phone ahead.
This is a worthy, finely intentioned *domaine* on the lower slopes of the Corbières mountains, on a terrain swept by winds from whichever direction they come.

B *DOMAINE DE ROMBEAU**
Pierre-Henri de la Fabrègue
2 Avenue de la Salanque, 66600 Rivesaltes
Tel 04 68 64 35 35
Mobile 06 88 88 79 78
domainederombeau@wanadoo.fr www.domaine-de-rombeau.com
MAP 61
Open every day from 08.00 to midnight. Best before midday or evening meals.
Here you will find a comfortable hotel and a fancy restaurant, as well as a wine estate, the latter with fifty hectares. Here was born the style, 'Muscat de Noël'.

*LES VIGNERONS DU RIVESALTAIS (CAVE ARNAUD DE VILLENEUVE)**
Rue de la Roussillonaise, 66600 Rivesaltes
Tel 04 68 64 06 63
econtact@caveseady.com   www.arnauddevilleneuve.com
MAP 62
Open every day (including holidays) during normal hours.
Arnaud de Villeneuve, the man who invented the technique of making VDNs, has given his name to this *Cave Coopérative* (a Rivesaltes/Salses merger) which can give an instant overview of the wines of the region, both dry and sweet, and at prices affordable to all.

*DOMAINE DU MARIDET**
Jean François Tisseyre and Hélène Constantin
Chemin de Boto Nord, 66600 Salses-le Château
Tel 04 68 51 73 24

Mobile 06 15 25 25 42
domaine.maridet@gmail.com
MAP 63
Phone ahead.

B **DOMAINE SINGLA** Laurent de Besombes Singla
52 Boulevard Arago, 66250 Saint-Laurent-de la Salanque
Mobile 09 67 30 77 90 ;
laurent@domainesingla.com   www.domainesingla.com
MAP 64
Appointment recommended.
The Singla family is of Huguenot origin and came south from the Cévennes at the time of the persecution in the 1760s, settling in Roussillon where they began trading in wine between Spain and Africa.

PERPIGNAN AND THE VALLEY OF THE TÊT

The river Têt rises just below Mont Canigou and flows eastwards through a relatively fertile valley until it reaches Perpignan and thence flows into the sea at Canet Plage. The previous section having dealt with the wines of Rivesaltes, it is logical to start the exploration of this valley on the coast and work inland.

*VIGNERONS CATALANS**
directeur Daniel Dumanois
1870 Avenue Julien Panchot, 66000 Perpignan
Tel 04 68 85 04 51
contact@vigneronscatalans.com   www.vigneronscatalans.com
MAP 65
Open usual hours.

This is Roussillon's largest *coopérative*, responsible in one way or another, whether as winemaker, *négociant* or distributor, for over half of all the wines made in the Pyrénées-Orientales, and for the efforts of over 2,000 growers. It has links to other *coopératives* throughout the region. Space prevents a detailed account of their entire repertoire which runs from simple IGPs for quick and easy drinking (the Fruité Catalan brand A) to AOP wines from the four prestige villages. The best advice is to go along and put yourselves in the hands of their sales team. You won't be ruined either. It's all Price A.

Cave at Domaine Mastrio

**DOMAINE LAFAGE

Jean-Marc Lafage and Eliane Salinas-Lafage,
Mas Miraflors, Route de Canet, 66100 Perpignan
Tel 04 68 80 35 82
Mobile 06 19 15 75 81
contact@domaine-lafage.com   www.domaine-lafage.com

MAP 67
Cellars closed Sunday and Monday. Open Tuesday to Saturday during usual hours, not lunchtime.

Jean-Marc has travelled the world, working with Gallo in California before going to Australia, South Africa , Chile and more, while Eliane is a trained oenologist. They now have 138 hectares under vine, mostly around the home-*domaine* at Perpignan, but there are vines too near Fourques further south in the Aspres. Most of the grapes for Jean-Marc's AOP reds come from the latter, and also some chardonnay which goes into a barrel-fermented IGP (A/B). He also has vines at Maury, where he himself comes from; "C'est dans le sang," he says. Hence his '*grenat*' (B) and the Muscat *ambré* (C). There are also IGP varietals from muscat (dry, pale but fragrant) and grenache 'Cuvée Nicolas' (both B). The AOPs start with a white 'Cuvée Centenaire' (A/B) from roussanne and grenache blanc, peachy and surprisingly intense.

The rosé (A) is deeply coloured, but not as heavy as it looks. Then there are the reds: 'Le Vignon' and 'Cuvée Léa' (B/C) from syrah, grenache and carignan, hailing from the southern vineyards; and the 'Cuvée Authentique' (B) from nearer home, rich and chocolatey. Under the Rivesaltes banner, there is a muscat called 'Grain des Vignes' and a *tuilé* style called 'Rimage' (both B).

B ***DOMAINE SARDA MALET

Suzy et Jérôme Malet
Mas Saint-Michel, Chemin de Sainte-Barbe, 66600 Perpignan
Tel   04 68 56 72 38
info@sarda-malet.com   www.sarda-malet.com
MAP 71
Appointment requested. Monday to Friday during usual hours.

Although effectively organic for many generations, this 50-hectare domaine has only recently sought official certification. The vineyard and *chais* were brought up to date some years ago by Jérôme's father Max, and today Jérôme and his mother (a former law professor) have taken the improvements one stage further and are making benchmark Roussillon wines. Don't be put off by the fact that their catalogue begins with a series of Vins de France. For example, white 'L'Insouciant Blanc' (C) is a blend from grenache blanc and gris, their vines going back to 1958, allowed a malolactic fermentation and then matured on lees in barrel without any racking. The red version (B/C) is from grenache which yields a bare 15 hl/ha, and is fermented slowly. The name of another red 'L'Intransigent' (C) is suggested by the character of the mourvèdre grape, tannic and restrained during youth and needing time to develop. 'Fandango' (B/C) is pure syrah, this time smooth and silky and to be enjoyed rather than analysed. The AOPs are, paradoxically, much more orthodox: the white (C), made from grenache blanc, gris and some malvoisie, is partly fermented and raised in barrel, partly in cuve; the rosé (B) is from syrah and mourvèdre; while the red (B/C) from grenache, syrah and mourvèdre is, like the white, partly oak-aged, lively, fruity and long. 'La Réserve' (B) is another red and is given added oomph by the reincorporation of the *vin de presse* and the lees during the spring following the vinification. It is then aged for the most part in barrels renewed on a three-year cycle, with just a part kept in tank to preserve the balance of fruit. Finally the VDNs are represented by a Muscat de Rivesaltes (B), vinified as dry as the law allows; an excellent *ambré* (D) left to oxidize in cuve for many years; and 'La Carbasse' (C), a sweet grenache, vinified in barrel for 10 days before the addition of the alcohol. Fermentation is resumed and lasts a further six weeks, then the barrels are sealed and left for 18 months.

B **DOMAINE DU MATIN CALME

Anthony Guix and Véronique Souloy
5 Rue Rouget de L'Isle, 66170 Millas
Tel   04 68 51 73 08
Mobile   06 63 13 58 82
a_guixfr@yahoo.com

MAP 74
Rendezvous required.

This tiny five-hectare *domaine* makes wines as 'naturally' as nature will permit. Organic in the vineyard, no unnatural yeasts, no sulphur (except sometimes a tiny point of it when bottling), otherwise additive-free in the cellar, no fining or filtration. The quality shows in the almost burgundian style of the wines: two whites from grenache blanc called 'Chamboultou' and 'Green H' which are not cheap (Both D). Less expensive is 'Ose' (C), a blend of virtually all of the roussillon white *cépages*. The reds have attracted rather more attention. 'Sans Temps' (C) is all carignan and a splendid example of what this grape can do in sensitive hands. 'Mano Mano' (B) is mostly grenache with less than a third carignan, a tank-raised vin de soif made by *macération carbonique*. 'Bonica Marieta' (B/C) translates as "pretty ladybird," so we are told, and is a development of Mano, the carignan being just that bit older. 'Sans Temps' (C) is another carignan wine: this time the grapes are over 100 years old. This couple are among the more interesting of the cult natural winemakers.

**DOMAINE FORÇA REAL

Jean-Paul and Cyril Henriquès
Mas de La Garrigue, 66170 Millas
Tel 04 68 57 37 08
info@forcareal.com   www.forcareal.com

MAP 76
Phone ahead

Cyril is now in charge of the *domaine* created by his father. They have 10 hectares of olives as well as 38 of vines, and the property (whose name translates to 'Château Royal') has magnificent views over the Roussillon plain, which alone make the visit worthwhile, almost as much as the reasonable prices charged here for very good wine. Neither whites nor rosés are currently on offer, but there are three fine AOP reds. The entry-level 'Mas de la Garrigue' is from a conventional blend of syrah, grenache and carignan, and has good fruit on the nose, with blackberries and cassis on the palate. It is raised in tank (A). 'Domaine Força Real' (B) omits the carignan, and is noted for its red fruit, especially cherries and its spicy palate. No wood here either. The top wine is 'Les Hauts de Força Réal' (C/D), almost all syrah and aged in barrel for two years. The oak is gently evident on the nose where it sweetens ripe fruit, and the palate is rich and complex. The range is completed by a honeyed Muscat de Rivesaltes (A), with its hints of honey, lime and citrus fruits and an *ambré hors d'age* (A) aged for at least eight years in *foudres*. Both are excellent value.

OTHER GOOD GROWERS AROUND PERPIGNAN

**CHÂTEAU PRADAL   André-Coll Escluse

58 rue Pépinière Robin, 66000 Perpignan
Tel   04 68 85 04 73
Mobile   06 11 13 61 57
chateaupradal@orange.fr
MAP 66
Appointment strongly advisable.
The suburbs of Perpignan now surround this 20-hectare vineyard, which has been in the same family for five generations, back to a time when the vines were surrounded by windmills. Today André is the only grower to make wine in the precincts of the city, so that the *caveau* is easily reached from railway station, airport and autoroute alike.

*DOMAINE LAPORTE   Patricia Laporte

Château Roussillon, route de Canet, 66000 Perpignan
Tel 04 68 50 06 53
domaine-laporte@wanadoo.fr   www.laporte-vins-roussillon.com
MAP 68
Visits during normal business hours.
This is a frankly 'commercial' property, where the wines (mostly A) are all well made, even if they lack a *terroir* voice.

B * * MAS BAUX Serge and Marie-Pierre Baux
Voie des Côteaux, 66140 Canet-en-Roussillon
Tel 04 68 80 25 04
contact@mas-baux.com www.mas-baux.com
MAP 69
Prior rendezvous recommended. Monday to Friday. Quickly the wines have made a name for themselves. They are not expensive... yet.

* * CHÂTEAU DE LACROIX Yanne Tanguy,
Chemin des Mas del Chots, 66330 Cabestany
Tel 04 68 50 48 39
Mobile 06 16 40 62 99
chateau-de-lacroix@wanadoo.fr www.chateau-de-lacroix.fr
Appointment preferred.
This is an ambitious go-ahead property, whose wines should be enjoyed before the prices rise.
MAP 70

B * * DOMAINE ROUAUD Jérôme and Sophie Rouaud
66370 Pézilla-la-Rivière
Tel 04 68 92 46 59
Mobile 06 33 96 81 57
rouaud.vigneron.66@orange.fr www.domaine-rouaud.com
MAP 72
Cellars open Monday to Friday 17.00-19.00, Saturdays 10.00-12.30 and 14.30-18.30. Otherwise by appointment.
This is a relatively recent vineyard (2003), organic from the word go and Ecocert certified 2009.

B * * DOMAINE BOUCABEILLE
Jean Boucabeille
66550 Corneilla-la-Rivière
Tel 04 68 34 75 71
domaine@boucabeille.com www.boucabeille.com
MAP 73
Appointment required. Again a good value vineyard especially with the dry table wines.

B * * DOMAINE CARLE COURTY
Frédéric et Véronique Carle
6 Route de Corneilla, 66170 Millas
Tel 04 68 57 21 79
Mobile 06 62 78 05 63 or 06 23 91 14 38
domaine.carlecourty@orange.fr www.domaine.carlecourty.com
MAP 75
Best by appointment.
Essentially a (B) property and so welcome.

TOWARDS THE PYRENEES: LES ASPRES

B * * CHÂTEAU DE L'OU
Philippe et Séverine Bourrier
Route de Villeneuve, 66200 Montesco
Tel 04 68 54 68 67
Mobile 06 82 19 82 87
www.chateau-de-lou.fr

MAP 78
In theory open all year from 16.00 to 18.00, but better to phone ahead.

'Ou' means 'egg', the domaine named after an egg-shaped water resource formerly used by the animals as a drinking supply. This ambitious and quite pricey 48-hectare domaine, whose history goes back to the Knights Templar, has been bio since 1998. It is spread over three distinct terroirs: the alluvial terraces of a dried-up river at Montescot, near the sea, brown schist at St Paul de Fenouillet, and black leafy schist higher up at Caudiès, the western limit (so far) of viticulture in the Roussillon. From Montescot comes the range (all B) called simply after the château: a white blend of grenache blanc and roussanne with citrus and white fruit flavours; a rosé which can accompany food throughout a meal; and a syrah/grenache red, fruity, complex and very moreish. A more ambitious low-yielding syrah (D) is called 'Infiniment de l'Ou', powerful, fermented and aged in barrel. The château name is also borne by a Muscat de Rivesaltes (B) and Rivesaltes Grenat (D), the latter made in tiny quantities. From St Paul comes a pure garriguey syrah called 'Secret Des Schists' (D). At Caudiés another pure syrah (the emblem grape of the property), peppery, cedarish and even with liquorice hints called 'Velours Noirs' shows the virtues of high altitude and cool nights. Here they also make a pure barrel-fermented chardonnay (C), which manages to retain a spiky elegance. You can also buy a version (D++), which has been literally submerged for seven months in the waters of the Étang de Leucate.

* * * DOMAINE TRELOAR
Jonathan Hesford and Rachel Treloar
16 Traverse de Thuir, 66300 Trouillas
Tel 04 68 95 02 29
GPS 42.6113, 2.8065
info@domainetreloar.com www.domainetreloar.com
MAP 83
Open for visits every day except Sunday from 16.00-18.00. Tuesday and Thursday 9.00-12.00 and 14.00-18.30, also Saturday mornings. Otherwise by rendezvous.

Jonathan had been an IT consultant in New York at the time of 9/11. The trauma of this, which coincided with his being made redundant, brought about a damascene conversion

58   Languedoc Roussillon

Jonathan Hesford, Domaine Treloar

which took him to New Zealand to learn the art of wine-making. He and his partner Rachel arrived in Roussillon only in 2006. They have 10 hectares spread over three different *terroirs*. All their grapes are hand-picked because, they say, harvesting machines break up the grapes which oxidise fast in the local heat, and also they are able to use only the best grapes whereas machines put in the lot (including snails). They also find that less sulphur is required to protect hand-picked fruit. IGPs include 'One Block Muscat' (A), not over-perfumed and good with oriental food; 'La Terre Promise' (B) from grenache gris, maccabeu and carignan blanc, raised in barrel for 12 months; and a rosé from syrah (A), light in alcohol at 11.7% alc. Their AOPs include 'Le Ciel Vide'(A), 50% carignan, rich, smokey and leathery, then other reds (B) which include 'One block Grenache', given 12 months in oak; 'Three Peaks' (syrah, grenache and mourvèdre); and a syrah-based 'Secret', rich and spicy. The two top reds are Motus (C), (80% mourvèdre) for long keeping with lovely bite and from American oak, and 'Tahi' (D), superbly spicy. Very fine wines here.

BD ✻✻✻ DOMAINE NIVET GALINIER
David Nivet
Lou Jassal, route du Soler, 66300 Ponteilla
Tel 04 68 56 51 20
Mobile   06 27 25 44 23 / 08 99 10 34 69
GPS 42.631136-2.810897
nivet-galinier@orange.fr   www.nivet-glinnier.over-blog.com

MAP 84
Visits by appointment every day from 11.00-14.00 and 17.00-19.00.

Nivet mistrusts the word 'vigneron', which he says is a term invented to misdescribe the basically peasant-style of the métier. He, his wife and son do all the work themselves, and this includes keeping chickens and bees and growing fruit on the higher ground in the hills. You would be wrong to expect from this a rustic, simple establishment, because the premises are spick and span, incorporating a very pretty chapel. From only seven hectares of vines, all of which yield tiny amounts of juice (between eight and 15 hectolitres per hectare), one can hardly expect bargain prices at this fully bio-dynamic domaine. Such methods of production can often, as here, produce highly individual, quirky wines, which some so-called experts call 'wild'. Nevertheless they last well, as demonstrated by their pure maccabeu (B), slightly

David Nivet, Domaine Nivet Galinier, p.59

oxidized in style, which manages to be dry and rich at the same time, and which retains its nervous character even after some years in bottle. The reds have plenty of carignan in them, for example 'Les Aspres' (C), which combines some rusticity with power and even elegance. VDNs include a *tuilé* (D) and an all-grenache Rivesaltes (D). The wines seem to get better every year, hence the third hopeful star.

B ***DOMAINE LA CASENOVE
Etienne Montès
66300 Trouillas
Tel   04 68 21 66 33
chateau.la.casenove@wanadoo.fr
www.rhone.vignobles.free.fr/pagesqb/montes.htm

MAP 88
Visits by appointment.
The rules for Les Aspres limit the amount of carignan which may be used in an AOP blend. But carignan is Montès' favourite and most-grown grape on his 65 hectares, so many of his wines are sold as IGPs. The house style here has become more Rhone-ish, due to the influence of Jean-Luc Colombo, who has been advising Montès now for over a decade. The wines usually show a substantial reliance on new wood, sometimes at the expense of finesse, but the wines remain top quality examples of the *sudiste* Roussillon school. They all keep well, including the white blend (B) from grenache blanc and roussanne, fresh, and well balanced. The easier reds include 'MasiaM', a peppery, fruity carignan/grenache blend, and 'La Garrigue', the latter from carignan and syrah and aged in tank to accentuate the red fruits and spice (both B). 'La Colomina' (B/C) is spared new wood too, but raised three years in cuve, by which time the tannins have softened the power of the wine. The more ambitious reds include 'Torrespeyres' (C), a dense, powerful wine from carignan raised in tank and from syrah, given two years in Bordeaux barrels. 'Cuvée Commandant Jaubert' (D) is named after a predecessor who served under Napoleon III. It is all syrah, its sweet vanillin oaky flavours deriving from its two years in barrel. Of the VDNs, the Ambré is an outstanding example (D).

**CHÂTEAU MOSSÉ Joëlle and Jacques Mossé
66300 Sainte-Colombe-de-la-Commanderie
Tel 04 68 53 08 89
chateau.mosse@worldonline.fr
www.chateaumosse.chez-alice.fr

MAP 90
Appointment advised.

Jacques' first love is his vines; *"plus que moi"* jokes Joëlle. He has 50 hectares of them, and it is Joëlle's job to market them, something she does well since they are to be found in Hong Kong and China these days. The range covers just about every style, most of the reds being syrah-based, except that is 'Le Carignan' (B), from vines no less than 120 years old, and which are treated to 12 months in four-year-old barrels. The result is complexity and sweetness without the taste of floorboards. There are whites from 100% Muscat d'Alexandrie (A). 'Bianca' (B) is a viognier/grenache blanc blend given a touch of wood, and there is a very rose-coloured rosé (A), mostly syrah with strong hints of redcurrants. The syrah wines start with 'La Belle Jardinière' (A/B), which comes in large part from young vines, and 'Tradition' (B) which has but 12 days' maceration and is fruity, though with some moderate tannins. The syrah for 'La Coume d'Abeille' is grown on unusually pale schist and the wine is raised half in tank and half in barrel for 12 months. 'Le Temporis' (B/C), 'Les Reines' (C) and 'Les Aspres' (C) are variations on the same theme, though the latter has less syrah and more carignan. The so-called top wine 'Le Blues' (D) spends two years in new barrels and is half syrah and half carignan with just a touch of grenache. It is a *vin de garde*, time being needed to absorb all the oaky influences. The range of VDNs generally on the market is quite standard, but there are also some fabulous old vintages going back nearly a century which will set your bank manager reeling.

BD ***DOMAINE FERRER-RIBIÈRE

Denis Ferrer and Bruno Ribière
20 rue du Colombier, 63300 Terrats
Tel   04 68 53 24 45
GPS   42°36' 25" N - 02°46' 13" E
domferrerribiere@orange.fr   www.vinferrerribiere.com

MAP 91
Phone ahead.

Denis was already a member of the local *coopérative* when in 1993 he met Bruno, a retired *fonctionnaire* looking for an open-air life. Starting with barely four hectares of unfashionable vines, their enterprise has grown (with some commercial assistance from outside) to 44. Their original philosophy remains intact: to make wine as naturally as possible from those grape varieties most suited to their varied *terroirs*, wines they themselves could be proud of, even if the market looked somewhat askance at their efforts. All but their flagship wines are extremely keenly priced. From the long list one might pick from their 'Empreinte du Temps' range (all varietals and B), the grenache gris white, an ideal partner for the local anchovies, or its red counterpart, which can also be chilled to go with fish. There is the pure carignan, partly given four months in old barrels and redolent of blackberries and deep spice; its mourvèdre cousin, from low-yielding vines and with an attractive violet-tinted colour,

uninfluenced by oak; or even 'Syrahnosaurus Rex', finished in tank after its six months in wood. There are entry-level wines (A) from Muscat d'Alexandrie, a mostly syrah rosé, deep pink, as well as blended AOP reds (B). Top of the range are 'Cana' (C), from old low-yielding vines, "bottled on the falling moon and with the wind in the north-west;" and 'Sélénae' (D) from the oldest vines of all and given the luxury of three years in old barrels. The Muscat de Rivesaltes (B) is fine, but less interesting than the curious 'Cuvée Sans Interdit' (C) from overripe shrivelled grapes, but vinified like a dry wine and cellared on the solera principle, then finished in the open air. Or there is 'Perle d'Octobre' (D) only eight hl/ha, from a blend of grenache blanc and gris, over-ripened on straw and matured for four years to develop the authentic *rancio* style.

B **DOMAINE LES CONQUES

François Douville
5 place de la Mairie, 66300 Fourques
Tel   04 68 52 82 56
Mobile ; 06 81 51 36 99
francois.douville@wanadoo.fr   www.lesconques.fr

MAP 92
Telephone ahead of visits.

This is a barely 10-year-old *domaine* which Douville took over when he came south from his native Loire and converted the existing vines at this property to organic production in 2008. There are only 10 hectares, the white grapes including maccabeu and grenache blanc with some grenache gris and carignan blanc in support. The reds are dominated by carignan, supplemented by some grenache and new plantings of syrah. The white wine is called 'Bohème' (A) and is raised partly in wood for a few months, which gives it concentration and texture, while the red 'Vitis' (B) has typical spice from syrah and good structure from the grenache included in the blend. There is also a rosé called 'Nonette' available only in bag-in-box, from grenache gris and a little syrah. Nodding to the local tradition, Douville also makes a Rivesaltes *ambré* (C), given three years to oxidise in barrel without the addition of suphur. Douville is a winemaker of promise.

B ***POTRON MINET Jean Sébastien Gioan

40 Avenue du Vallespir, 66300 Fourques
Mobile 06 14 19 83 69
domainepotronminet@free.fr

MAP 93
Appointment necessary.
"Potron-Minet" is old French for "break of day" or, alternatively, "little cat" (take your pick). Jean-Sébastien is the second of a clutch of natural winemakers centred on this village. A youth spent biking messages round Paris elided into a passion for 'natural' wines, which in turn led Sébastien to abandon Paris and work with Tuzelat in the Loire and

Jean Sébastien Gioan, Potron Minet, p.61

then Nicq at Foulards Rouges (q.v.). Jean-Sebastien finds himself after five years of being on his own with just over 12 hectares in the lee of Mont Canigou. The soil is a mix of clay and *galets roulés* on a bed of schist. 'Pari Trouillas Blanc', white, pink and red are all (B), 'Roulé Boulé (B) is mostly syrah with some grenache, 'L'Amandier' is pure Grenache (C), and 'Quérida' (C) (a four-way blend, of which the syrah is aged in barrel) is cherry-coloured with good body. Good value here, and a welcome change from the heftier style traditional to the region.

***DOMAINE PUIG-PARAHY Georges Puig
LeFort St Pierre, 16 rue du Presbytère, 66300 Passa
Tel   06 14 55 71 71
www.puig-parahy.fr
MAP 96
Best to phone ahead.

George's grandfather played rugby for France and, to prove it, there is a photo of him being presented to King George V on the rugby field. Does this explain why Georges is called Georges? The family has been making wine in the region since before the phylloxera. Georges feels the weight of tradition, but has been finding the task of exploiting his initial 140 hectares impossible in today's conditions, so the vineyard has been shrinking. He has been careful to preserve the oldest vines, planted immediately after the phylloxera. He also has in his 13th Century *cave* an amazing collection of old vins doux naturels, made and kept for the celebration

of new members of the family as they came along. The modern range, which is of almost incomparable value for money, starts with a pale but quite powerful Muscat Sec (A), followed by 'Les Miserys' (A/B) from the two pale grenaches, part oak-aged. Then there is a strawberry-coloured Rosé (A). The reds include 'Le Fort Saint Pierre' (A), a blend of all four Roussillon grapes together yielding only 23 hl/ha; a pure syrah (A), aged in tank after a maceration of four weeks, and 'Georges' (A/B), half carignan and the rest mostly grenache, slow to mature, clean with grippy tannins and good length, a wine eulogised by Robert Parker, despite its lack of oak ageing. The Muscat de Rivesaltes (A/B) is a blend from both varieties of muscat, aged six months in tank before bottling.

***DOMAINE VAQUER Mme Frédérique Vaquer
2 Rue des Ecoles, 66300 Tresserre
Tel   04 68 38 89 53
domainevaquer@gmail.com   www.domaine-vaquer.com

MAP 98
Rendezvous recommended.

Madame is a Burgundian by birth, taking over this long-established domaine from her husband Bernard who died in 2001. Bernard's father was the first to christen the local wines 'Les Aspres', long before the present AOP was introduced. He was also one of the first to commercialise his own bottlings in the Roussillon. 'Aspres' means arid in Catalan, and the terroir has plenty of the *galets roulés* which characterise the wines of Châteauneuf-du-Pape. This 15-hectare *domaine* however strives after elegance, while expressing fully the character of its *terroir*. Over-ripeness of grapes and over-extraction are avoided. So is new wood, though there are some older barrels which are brought into play in suitable vintages. A visit may offer some remarkable old vintages to taste, but the commercial list is based on a grenache called 'Est-ce Spécial?' (B). There is a pure carignan (B/C), which is perhaps the most interesting and characteristic wine here; a pure Grenache (B), an 'Aspres' blend of carignan and Grenache (B); and a madeira-like Rivesaltes *Hors d'Age* matured on the solera principle as used for making sherry.

**DOMAINE DE NIDOLÈRES
Pierre and Martine Escudie
66300 Tresserre
Tel   04 68 83 15 14
pierre@domainedenidoleres.com
www.domainedenidoleres.com

MAP 101
Visits possible every day.

This 50-hectare *domaine* is at the limits of Les Aspres, overlooking the river Tech, with a soil which has plenty of sand and pebbles suiting especially the mourvèdre grape. While

Georges Puig, Domaine Puig-Parahay

Pierre makes the wine, Martine, an excellent cook runs a restaurant with an inviting air, and there are rooms and gîtes too. None of the dry table wines is raised in barrel. The old *foudres* have been replaced by stainless steel and the winemaking is done in concrete. The result is good value for such exciting quality. Start with varietals from muscat and Grenache, or a rosé 'D'Un Soir', largely syrah and Grenache (all A). There are five AOPs: the entry-level wine (A) being a blend of equal quantities of syrah, mourvèdre and grenache; 'L'Angelette' (B) with 60% carignan (all 90-year-old vines), revealing red berries and spice; 'La Justine' (B/C) featuring 60% grenache, again from old vines; 'La Pierroune' (B) from 80% syrah, dark ruby in colour and with hints of liquorice and spice; and 'La Raphaelle' (B/C) from 80% mourvèdre, suggesting blackcurrants, cherries and chocolate, a wine which needs a little ageing. Then there is the range of sweet wines; unfortified late harvested IGPs, one from grenache blanc and the other from grenache noir (both B/C), as well as the more conventional Muscat de Rivesaltes (B), held in vat for a year before bottling, a Rivesaltes *ambré* from Grenache blanc, and a Rivesaltes grenat (both B).

**DOMAINE DES FOULARDS ROUGES

Jean-François Nicq
10 Chemin du roi, 66740 Montesquiou des Albères
Mobile 06 75 73 48 65
lesfoulardsrouges@orange.fr

MAP 102
Appointment suggested.

Nicq came to the area in 2002 and bought just seven hectares of vines, from which he produces 'natural' wines of a style wholly atypical of Roussillon as a whole; wines which are fine, elegant and not at all beefy or soupy. They are fairly light in alcohol too. They are not cheap and the names of the various *cuvées* seem to come and go with alarming rapidity. Whatever you find is likely to be very interesting, and names which have cropped up over the years are 'Zéro de Conduite Blanc' (C/D) for a dry unmuted muscat of extraordinary purity; another white called 'Soif du Mal' (C) from grenache blanc; grenache-based wines called 'Glaneurs'; the pure syrah 'Fond de l'Air Rouge' (C); or a varietal cinsault, 'Cuvée d'Octobre (C). There may be bottle variation, but that's a chance you take with really 'natural' wines.

Pierre Escudie, Domaine de Nidolères, p.62

B **DOMAINE LE SCARABÉE Isabelle Frère,
Moli d'en Cassanyes, 66690 Sorède
(the cave is at nearby St. André)
Tel   06 14 73 34 80
isabellefrere@hotmail.fr

MAP 103
Phone before visiting.

It is hard to imagine a larger contrast with the makers of big, extracted wines such as Bizeul than this wacky ex-teacher from Perpignan who has set up with nine hectares of vines, many of them rescued from virtual exhaustion and converted to organic production. She inherited them from her uncle who, she said, made disgusting wine, and with whom she fought for many years to make wine her way. Isabelle is not interested in *appellations*, nor much in technical blah-blah, merely in making wines which are light, un-tannic, fruity and easy to drink – such as her white 'Pied d'Nez' from a mix mainly of maccabeu and grenache gris. Like her rosé 'P'tit Scarabée' this is finished off in old wood (both B). She gives that name also to a pure syrah (B), which she describes as "easy and subtle". Syrah also features with grenache in her 'Volubile' (B), while grenache is at the base of 'Sur un nuage' (B). Her carignan stars in 'Murmure' (C). She describes her wines as "*vins de dentelle*" (lace), and they are sold as non-vintage Vins de France to give her maximum freedom in their making. She makes new *cuvée*s with abandon, so be prepared for name changes and different blends. But they're all going to be good and good value too.

B **DOMAINE LÉONINE Stéphane Morin
Mas Lamon, Route ND, 66700 Argelès-sur-Mer
Tel   04 68 81 81 83
domaineleonine@live.fr

MAP 104
Rendezvous recommended.

Stéphane took over this *domaine*, which now extends to 13

hectares, in 2005, and has since made a name for himself in the world of natural wines. Experts use the word 'wild' to describe a wine which they can't make fit any of their conventional vocabulary, and in this sense Stéphane's wines are indeed a bit wild. The aim is to concentrate on fruit, lightness and minerality, and hence a predilection for *macération carbonique*. Examples include 'Fond de tiroir' with its gentle hint of torrefaction, and 'Que Pasa' (both B). 'Bottle Neck' (B/C) is a syrah/grenache blend, while 'Carbone' (C) is a celebration of grenache in all three colours. Stéphane's handling of wood is exemplary.

****MAS CRISTINE Philippe Gard and Andy Cook
c/o Coume del Mas, Les Cosprons, 66650 Banyuls-sur-Mer.
Mobile   06 11 84 16 97
info@tramontanewines.com   www.tramontanewines.com

MAP 106
Visits afternoons only by appointment.

There is no cellar at Mas Cristine, the vines being leased to Gard and Cook in partnership under the name 'Tramontane Wines'. Visits are through Gard's flagship winery at Cosprons (see above and also under Banyuls). The vines in the past were used mainly to make Muscat de Rivesaltes, and this style continues at the Mas (B), sweet but with good acidity to balance. Other whites may include a cocktail blend of all the local varieties, with a similar rich mineral balance, but of course this time dry (B), or perhaps a varietal roussanne or grenache gris under the name 'Consolation' (both B/C). The main red is mainly grenache and syrah (B), but there is also a curious all-mourvèdre wine called 'Dog Strangler' (D) from tiny yields, seriously ripe and complex. The fourth star is awarded in certain expectation that these wines will go to the top, if they have not already done so.

OTHER GOOD GROWERS IN LES ASPRES

B *DOMAINE DU MAS BAZAN Myriam Garnier
Route de Saleilles, 66200 Alénya
Tel   04 68 22 98 26
Mobile   06 83 51 51 13
contact@masbazan.fr   www.masbazan.com
MAP 77
Visits without appointment from June to September inclusive. Otherwise phone ahead.
Well-known as a handsome place to stay close to the heart of Perpignan and the sea.

**DOMAINE SOL PAYRÉ
Pascale and Jean-Claude Sol
Route de Saint Martin, 66200 Elne
Tel   04 68 22 17 97

Isabelle Frère, Domaine Le Scarabée

domaine@sol-payre.com   www.sol-payre.com
MAP 79
Tasting cellar at Caveau Ville Haute d'Elne (tel 04 68 37 22 48), best to phone ahead. Or visit their shop at St Cyprien Plage, Carrefour Maillol, 27 Avenue François Desnoyer, 66750 St Syprien Plage
(tel 04 68 37 22 48).

*CHÂTEAU CAP DE FOUSTE
Caisses Centrales et Régionales de Groupama
66180 Villeneuve-de-la-Raho
Tel 04 68 55 91 04
capdefouste@free.fr www.chateau-cap-de-fouste.com
MAP 80
Visits every day (usual hours) except Sundays and public holidays.

*DOMAINE GALY Christian Galy
33 avenue Jean-Jaurès, Bages 66670 , also 11 Aristide Maillol, Avenue de la Gare, 66190 Collioure
Tel at Bages 04 68 66 71 59   at Collioure 04 68 88 54 46
Mobile 06 07 29 79 70   at Collioure 06 18 20 11 37
lamaison.galy@orange.fr www.maisongaly-collioure.com
MAP 81

Shop open at Collioure every day except Sundays. At Bages by appointment.

*CHÂTEAU PLANÈRES
Vignobles Jaubert et Noury
66300 Saint Jean Lasseille
Tel 04 68 21 74 50
gilles.jaubert@orange.fr   www.chateauplaneres.com
MAP 82
Visits Monday to Friday at usual hours, also by appointment in summer on Saturdays.

*VIGNOBLES DU SUD-ROUSSILLON
1, Ave du mas Déu, 66300 Trouillas,
Tel 04 68 53 47 08
GPS 42°36'57" N - 02°48'38" E
info@vignobles-sud-roussillon   www.vignobles-sud-roussillon
MAP 85
Opening hours at Trouillas Monday to Saturday 9.00-12.00, and 14.30 to 18.30.
Also at cellars at Bages (04 68 21 60 30 phone ahead), and Saint-Jean Lasseille (mornings only Tuesday to Saturday inclusive, and Monday 0afternoons).
This is a merger of the *caves* at Trouillas, Bages and St Jean Lasseille. A haven for the thirsty and thrifty, and in an amazing building.

**CLOS SAINT GEORGES Dominique and Claude Ortal
66300 Trouillas
Tel 04 68 21 61 46
clortal@wanadoo.fr www.clos-saint-georges.fr
MAP 86
Cellars open during usual business hours Monday to Friday. This estate has recently expanded from 70 to 120 hectares, partly by acquiring vines from neighbouring estates such as Château Canterrane, whose well-known name it rebrands as a *marque*.

**CHÂTEAU SAINT-NICOLAS Pierre Schneider
Route de Canohès, 66300 Ponteilla
Tel 04 68 53 47 61
contact@chateausaintnicolas.com
www.chateausaintnicolas.com
MAP 88
Visits weekdays at usual hours.
Schneider has been in charge of these 66 hectares since 2007, and has developed this historic building into a pleasant place to stay and visit.

*CHÂTEAU LAURIGA René and Jacqueline Clar
Traverse de Pontheilla, 66300 Thuir
Tel 04 68 53 26 73
info@lauriga.com   www.lauriga.com

MAP 89
Phone ahead.
There are good-value, typical wines to be bought at this 60-hectare vineyard between Perpignan and Thuir.

B **DOMAINE LA ROURÈDE
Jean-Luc and Josiane Pujol
66300 Fourques
Tel 04 68 38 84 44
vins.pujol@wanadoo.fr   www.larourede.fr
MAP 94
Open Monday to Friday 9.00-12.00 and 15.00-18.00.

B *DOMAINE PARAIRE Jean-Michel Paraire
28 Avenue du Vallespir, 66300 Fourques
Tel 04 68 38 84 86
Mobile 06 10 51 02 01
paraire.jean-michel@orange.fr
MAP 95
Cellars at Vignerons de Constance, 1 rue des Tastevins, Fourques, open every day except Sunday.

B **DOMAINE ROSSIGNOL
Pascal and Fabienne Rossignol
Route de Villemolaque, 66300 Passa
Tel 04 68 38 83 17
GPS 42.58 268 N 2.815858E
domaine.rossignol@free.fr   www.domainerossignol.fr
MAP 97
Visits during usual hours, weekdays and Saturday mornings. Excellent value here.

B **DOMAINE DES DEMOISELLES
Isabelle Raoux and Didier Van Ooteghem
Mas Mulès, 66300 Tresserre
Tel 04 68 38 87 10
Mobile 06 83 04 34 62
domaine.des.demoiselles@wanadoo.fr
domaine-des-demoiselles.com
MAP 99
Visits Monday to Saturday, 9.30-12.00 and 15.00-19.00 except Monday from September to June. Sundays by appointment.

**DOMAINE DU MAS ROUS José Pujol
66740 Montesquieu-des-Albères
Tel 04 68 89 64 91
masrous@mas-rous.com   www.mas-rous.com
MAP 100
Cellar open daily except Sundays and public holidays. 9.30-12.00 and 14.00-18.00.
This is a good value domaine, knocking on 40 hectares of vines, where you can find a big range of IGPs and AOPs.

*CHÂTEAU VALMY
Martine and Bernard Carbonnell
Chemin de Valmy, 66700 Argelès-sur-Mer
Tel 04 68 81 25 70
contact@chateau-valmy.com   www.chateau-valmy.com
MAP 105
Cellar open Monday to Friday during usual hours. Also Saturdays from mid-April to mid-October. Closed Sundays. Perched high on a hill above Argelès, this extraordinary folie of a castle is unmissable. You can stay here too; exquisitely comfortable though it's not cheap.

COLLIOURE AND BANYULS

Driving south along the flat coast road south of Perpignan towards Spain, you are suddenly in mountains, as the Pyrenean chain literally tumbles into the sea away to your left. On the hillsides, mostly dark schist, are terraces, 6,000 kilometres of them built with walls called locally '*feixes*' to prevent the erosion of soil down the steep slopes. These in turn are interlaced with mini canals ('*peus de gall*'), built to drain the hillsides after storms and also to help prevent erosion. Such terrain makes any kind of mechanisation impossible. Yields are low and the wines are consequently less cheap than those grown in more conventional areas.

Collioure and Banyuls are two well-known coastal resorts, the former especially owing its fame to the painters of the first half of the twentieth century who made it their home. Nowadays the economy is divided between tourism and wine. The still dry table wines of all three colours from both towns are called Collioure, sturdy, concentrated and quite powerful, while the name Banyuls is reserved for *vins doux naturels*. Because of the frequency of storms around vintage time, some growers pick earlier than the rules allow, and market the resulting wines as IGPs, here usually called 'Côtes de Vermeille'.

Storm drain near Collioure

Banyuls has different rules from those applying to other VDNs. It is found in both the oxidised style and the '*vintage*' style (here called '*rimage*'). There is also a Banyuls Grand Cru with a higher grenache content and a requirement for long *élevage* in wood. Sometimes it is aged in the solera manner, like sherry, stored in three layers of barrels from which wine is drawn off as required from the lower barrels and replaced by wine from the barrels higher up. There is a small quantity of white Banyuls which may be dry or sweet, and an even rarer pink version.

***DOMAINE LA TOUR VIEILLE

Vincent Cantié and Christine Campadieu
12 route de Madeloc, 66190 Collioure
Tel 04 68 82 44 82
www.latourvieille.com

MAP 107
Appointment advisable.

This 12-hectare domaine represents a merger of the family vineyards of the two proprietors. In 2000 they built a brand new *chais* in the heart of their vines above crowded Collioure. Their quaffing red is called 'Sur la route' (A) and is an IGP from mourvèdre and (mostly) grenache, lighter and less structured than their AOP Collioures. These begin with a big white, 'Les Canadells' (B/C), a five-way blend from grenache blanc and gris, roussanne, maccabeu and vermentino, partly raised in barrel, robust, not scared of being partnered with strong cheese, for example. The pink is called 'Rosé des Roches' (B), a plump mix of syrah and grenache for early drinking. The reds (all aged without the benefit of barrels) start with 'La Pinède' (B/C), a quarter carignan the rest grenache, which can be drunk lightly chilled and is good with fish. 'Puig Oriol' (B/C) is half syrah, half grenache. Open ahead of drinking. The top red is 'Puig Ambeille' (C) from roughly equal proportions of mourvèdre, carignan and grenache, given long maceration and aged 18 months before bottling. The VDNs include a sweet white Banyuls (B), *muté sur grains* like all the VDNs here, and aged partly in old barrels; a *rimage* (B) which has some carignan in it, macerated for three months before the addition of alcohol, and then quickly bottled; another *rimage* (C), which is aged in old *foudres* for three years (without oxidisation) before bottling, and a 'Réserva' (C) which is in fact a *tuilé*, aged in open glass *bonbonnes* for a year before being transferred to *foudres*. Unusual specialities include a white 'vin de Méditation' (D++), in a *rancio*-aged solera style; 'Mémoire' (C) a sweet white wine without added alcohol but left to mature in old barrels for four years; and finally 'Cap de Creus' (D), another *rancio* style wine like an old sherry.

***DOMAINE PIÉTRI-GÉRAUD

Laetitia Piétri-Géraud with her mother Maguy
22 rue Pasteur, 66190 Collioure
Tel 04 68 82 07 42
domaine.pietri-geraud@wanadoo.fr
www.domaine-pietri-geraud.com

MAP 108
Cellar open every day during summer between 10.00-13.00 and 15.30-20.00. Otherwise Tuesday to Saturday 10.00-12.30 and 15.00-18.30, but best to phone in advance. Open on public holidays and on Sundays during school holidays.

You are in a pedestrianised street in the crowded town centre, but trolleys are available if you have parked outside. Laetitia belongs to Vinifilles (q.v.). She has 26 hectares, 16 of which are on the schist above the town, the remainder on chalky clay in the village of Ortaffa, near Elne. Some may prefer to concentrate on the excellent Banyuls, but there are white and red Collioures. The white 'L'Écume' (C) is from barrel-fermented grenache gris and vermentino, the red 'Sine Nomine' (B) has typical Collioure power. 'Le Moulin de Cortine' (C) has a good dose of mourvèdre, while 'Trousse Chemise' is aged for two years in barrel (C/D). The rosé is more modest (A/B), with strawberry/raspberry character. Grenache blanc is the base of their white Banyuls (C), raised in new wood. The reds comprise 'Cuvée de Soleil' (D), aged in the open in glass *bonbonnes*; the traditional 'Cuvée Joseph Géraud' (C) with seven years in old *foudres*; while the *rimage* 'Mademoiselle O' (C) is a fine example of the style. Enjoy too the Muscat de Noël (B) from grapes grown near Elne. The wines are not cheap here, but win medals and high accolades from the press and are widely exported.

***DOMAINE MADELOC Pierre Gaillard

1 bis Avenue du Général de Gaulle, 66650 Banyuls-sur-Mer
Tel 04 68 88 38 29
domaine-madeloc@wanadoo.fr
www.domainespierregaillard.com

MAP 111
Advance appointment strongly recommended.

This modernising grower has vines in the Loire, famously in the Côte Rôtie, as well as these 29 hectares in Collioure-Banyuls. Grenache blanc and vermentino, grown on slopes plunging into the sea, make up a barrel-fermented white called 'Tremadoc' (B/C), deprived of malolactic fermentation to ensure freshness. Grenache gris replaces the blanc in 'Penya' (B/C), but the style is similar. There is a rosé, saigné from syrah, grenache and mourvèdre and called 'Foranell' (B), which is an overture to three red Collioures: 'Serral' (B/C), mostly grenache, made in tank and one third barrel-aged; 'Magenca' (C), with 20% each of syrah and mourvèdre and aged for 18 months in oak, one third of it new; and 'Crestlall' (C), a syrah-mourvèdre blend, whose ageing is wholly in new barrels. The 'mutés' Banyuls start with a white 'Asphodèles' (B/C), all grenache gris, fermented in tank but oak-aged for 12 months. Then there are three reds: the all-grenache 'Cirera' (C) in *rimage* style, 'Robert Pagès' (B/C) (named after the former owner here), left to oxidise in *foudres* and old *bonbonnes* out in the sun; and 'Soléra' (D), toffee-nosed and whose name says it all. A curiosity is a mix of Maury and Banyuls styles called 'Terre-Mer' (C), made in association with Stéphane and Marjorie Gallet (Le Roc des Anges q.v.), pure grenache, aged in closed barrel, to produce a wine of distinct cherry and dark fruit character.

****CAVE L'ÉTOILE

26 Avenue du Puig del Mas, 66650 Banyuls
Tel 04 68 88 00 10
info@cave-letoile.com   www.banyuls-etoile.com

MAP 112
Visits all year round (check around harvest-time), also at their stands at the port and opposite the Sol Hôtel (both April-October only).

This is more a club than a *coopérative*, founded in 1921 by a family of enthusiasts, many of whose old *foudres* are still in place in the cave. The members have a mere 150 hectares between them. The wines include Collioure in three colours (all B) under the brand 'Les Toiles Fauves', the white from the two pale grenaches, the pink and red being syrah/grenache blends. There are also reds from older vines; 'Clos du Fourat'(C) and 'Rouge Montagne'(B/C). But it is the astonishing range of Banyuls which has made the fame of this group. The younger and fruitier styles include a white (C) which can either be drunk young or older when it develops a dried-fruit character; a good-value *rimage* called 'Rim's' (B) bottled young for its fruit; and two more serious Rimages (C) with residual sugar of 100 grs./litre, which also age well. There is a range called 'Grand Cru' the '2000' (C) being rather more affordable than the 'Réservée' (D+) or the 'Doux Paillé' (D+), both exposed to the sun in *bonbonnes* for one or two years before being aged in wood for at least 10 years. The more traditional style, aged for varying lengths of time in old *foudres*, comes in five different qualities: an inexpensive 'Doré' (B); a Tuilé (C); a Rancio (D); 'Extra Vieux'(D) (and aged in *demi-muids* and *foudres*); and 'Select Vieux', which undergoes ageing in wood for at least 15 years and is bottled only just before sale. Fabulous wines, and the visit is just as memorable.

Philippe Gard, Coume del Mas, p.72

Terraces above Banyuls

Bonbonnes

****COUME DEL MAS

Philippe Gard (with Andy Cook)
3 rue Alphonse Daudet, 66650 Banyuls-sur-Mer
Tel 04 68 88 37 03
Mobile 06 86 81 71 32
info@coumedelmas.com   www.coumedelmas.com
MAP 113
Note; the cave is NOT at the business address but on the rue de la Madeloc, Cosprons (see Mas Cristine above).
Visits p.m. by appointment.

Though there are but 12 hectares of vines, this estate has rapidly become one of the stars of the Midi. Philippe, a native of Aveyron, where he still helps former school friend Laurent Mousset with his red wine called 'La Pauca', started in Roussillon in 2000 with some really old vines, but has since planted some more which are not yet on stream. While not officially certified organic, Philippe tries to make his wines as naturally as possible. The top-of-the-appellation Collioures include the white 'Folio' (C), mostly grenache gris, barrel-fermented and aged on its lees for six months, rich and intense, and a pink made only in abundant years and called 'Farniente' (B/C), of which a small part is barrel-fermented (only wild yeasts at this property) There are three reds: 'Schistes' (C) from 100% old-vine grenache, matured in tank for about nine months before bottling; 'Quadratur' (C/D), a blend this time from old-vine fruit aged in barrel for a year, bottled unfiltered; and 'Abysses' (C/D), made only in tiny quantities, a syrah/grenache blend aged in barrel (some new wood) for over a year, a big, bold colourful affair. There are also fine Banyuls: a white (C) aged in wood for six months; 'Galateo' (C/D), all grenache, matured in cask for at least six months; and finally the knock-out 'Quintessence' (D), not made every year, and bottled after 12 months in cask.

NOTE: Philippe and Andy (a Scot with a New Zealand wine degree) also have other ranges of wines from this property and from Mas Cristine (q.v.), sold under the quasi-brands 'Tramontane', and 'Consolation' (both C). The curiously named Collioure red, 'the Dog Strangler' is (D). These last wines are just as impressive as the wines detailed above, perhaps a little lighter in style.

**VINYER DE LA RUCA Manuel di Vecchi Staraz

Rue de L'Artisanat, 666580 Banyuls-sur-Mer
Mobile 06 65 15 78 38
info@vinyerdelaruca.com   www.vinyerdelaruca.com

MAP 114
Appointment essential to avoid disappointment.

No Collioure here, just Banyuls, and only 1,000 40-centilitre bottles a year from fifty-year-old Grenache, which yield a bare 300 kilos of fruit per hectare. A doctrinally purist *boutique de garage* at that. Hand-blown bottles and an artist-designed label are preceded by all-manual work in the vineyard, no mechanisation at all, and, of course, no chemicals, fertilisers or weed-killers. Natural yeasts only, hand-harvesting and a minimum of sulphur (if any). No filtration or fining. With only two hectares, Italian agronomist Manuel di Vecchi Staraz has to charge D+++ in order to keep alive, but there will always be a market for this kind of perfection whatever the price. The single Banyuls from here yields crisp fruit, hints of chocolate and orange peel. Fresh but full-bodied and deliciously chewy. Huge concentration, a meal on its own.

****DOMAINE DE LA RECTORIE

Marc Parcé and Vincent Legrand
28/65 Avenue du Puig del Mas, 66650 Banyuls
Tel   04 68 48 31 24
Mobile 06 82 67 04 10
la-rectorie@orange.fr   www.la-rectorie.com

MAP 115
Appointments advisable for visits every day except Sunday from 10.00-12.00 and 16.00 to 19.00.

Coming from an old Banyuls family, Marc Parcé and his family, whose grapes had been sent in their absence for many years to one of the local *coopératives*, returned to Banyuls in 1976 to resume control of the vineyards. He began making his own wine in 1984. Today there are 30 hectares spread over as many different parcels, most of the production being of Collioure table wines, Banyuls accounting for only 15%. Traditionally there were grenache noir, blanc and gris, together with carignan. Since the recognition of Collioure as a separate *appellation*, there have been more recent plantings of syrah, mourvèdre and more grenache. This is one of the star properties in the deep south. Parcé was one of the first to recognise the merit of grenache gris, which still forms the basis (90%) of his white Collioure, 'Argile' (C), fermented in barrel and bottled the following April. The Collioure rosé (B) is fermented the same way from grenache, carignan and syrah. 'Montagne' (B/C) is the name currently given to the red, aged in a mix of *foudres* and *barriques* for 18 months. In addition to grenache and carignan, it also contains mourvèdre and a little counoise (rare in Roussillon but found in Châteauneuf-du-Pape). The three Banyuls comprise 'Mise Précoce' (B), bottled after seven months in tank and no wood, and 'Léon Parcé' (C), in which the fruit is more

Caves, Banyuls Reno

developed and there is more backbone after 18 months in wood. 'L'Oubliée' (D++) is a solera-style, old-fashioned Banyuls from grenache gris of great delicacy. For the visitor, the problem here is that the names of the wines seem to change with alarming rapidity, but the house styles are fairly represented by the above citations.

****DOMAINE DU MAS BLANC SCEA

Docteur Parcé et fils (Jean Michel Parcé),
9 Avenue Général de Gaulle, 66650 Banyuls-sur-Mer
Tel 04 68 88 32 12
www.domaine-du-mas-blanc.com

MAP 116
Rendevous best.

Unlike his namesakes at the Domaine de la Rectorie (q.v.), Jean Michel Parcé represents the Banyuls establishment. He is the only member of the family to have devoted his life to wine, rather than medicine. The wines from this estate are often regarded as the benchmark in fine wines from the area. From his 21 hectares, Jean Michel makes roughly equal quantities of Collioure table wine and Banyuls, and there is a multiplicity of different *cuvées* of each. Traditionally the alcohol added to the VDNs is white armagnac, the family having been great hunters in that region. None of the wines is exactly cheap, but among the red table wines one might pick out 'La Llose' (B) for earlier drinking, or the red Collioure 'Les Junquets' (D), mostly syrah with a small amount of marsanne and roussanne. It has a cassis character. 'Cuvée du Docteur Parcé' (C), an everyday Banyuls, is suitable either as apéritif or dessert, while 'Dry' (D) with hints of madeira, is not as sweet as the name suggests, because the *mutage* is introduced late in the fermentation so as to keep the sugar levels low. There is too a *rimage* 'La Coume' (D) and an 'Hors d'Age Vieilli en Sostrera' (D+), powerful, complex, with hints of fig, walnuts and quince. Note also a pair of rare speciality vinegars.

***DOMAINE VIAL MAGNÈRES

Bernard Sapéras
Clos St. André, 14 rue Edouard Herriot,
66650 Banyuls-sur-Mer
Tel 04 68 88 31 04
info@vialmagneres.com   www.vialmagneres.fr

MAP 117
Phone ahead

A small (10 hectares) but highly regarded estate, its vines spread on the hillsides close to the sea shore on decomposing schist. Nearly all the grapes are grenache (all three varieties), with just a little syrah and carignan, and a tiny parcel of mourvèdre. The vines average 40/50 years old, all grown *en*

At Les Clos de Paulilles

gobelet. There are Collioures in all three colours. 'Le Petit Couscouril' (B) is a white from the two pale grenaches, raised in tank and allowed a malolcatic fermentation. The red is called 'Les Espérades' (B/C), with just a little carignan to blend with the grenache. Its short *cuvaisons* and a short stay in old barrels give the wine finesse and there is plenty of fruit. The Banyuls start with a 'Blanc Rivage' (C), part of which is set aside for oxidising in the solera style (C); a straightforward '4 ans' (B), and a 'Tradition' (B/C), which is given three or four years in big old foudres. 'Gaby Vial' (C) is similar to the Tradition but is given seven years. It is a non-vintage wine because it is usually a blend of two or more years, as is the 'Grand Cru André Magnières', made from the oldest vines here. Finally, the star of the show is 'Al Trigou' (D+), one of the finest of all Banyuls *rancios*, which is matured for 20 years and more in demi-muids and is priced accordingly. A by-the-fireside wine.

BD ★★★★ CASOT DE MAILLOLES Jordi Pérez
17 Avenue du Puig del Mas, 66650 Banyuls
Tel   04 68 88 59 37   No computer!

MAP 118
Phone for appointment

M. Pérez has taken full control of one of the great (and most eccentric) domaines in the South: tiny too, just five hectares farmed to the strictest natural standards. If 'natural' wine needs a definition, start here, one of the first vineyards in the region to espouse 'natural' philosophy; no filtering, no fining, no sulphur, vineyards worked by pick-axe (*xadic*), and every bunch of grapes sorted by the growers. Tiny yields. All this means that the wines (only 5,000 bottles a year are made) have to be expensive, but everyone should try them, even if just once. They taste like no one else's, and one bottle may not taste like the next. Why should it? Your adventure may start with a couple of whites, 'Tira Blanc' (C) perhaps, or Blanc du Casot (D+), mainly from grenache blanc and gris. The rosé is called 'Canta Manana' (C), and there may be three reds ('maybe' because the names as well as the styles seem to change unexpectedly). 'Poudre d'Escampette'(B/C) has a lot of mourvèdre, 'Soula' (D+) is all grenache, or there is the spicy 'Visinum' (D). His wines should qualify for AOP Collioure, but he has been refused his *agrément* twice because his wines are not typical. You can say that again. Fabulous. The wines have as much character as their maker. The range of wines may change with their new maker

OTHER GOOD GROWERS IN COLLIOURE AND BANYULS

**LES CLOS DE PAULILLES
Domaine Cazes (Advini, Jeanjean)
Baie de Paulilles, 66660 Port-Vendres
Tel 04 68 81 49 79
contact@clos-de-paulilles.com
www.cazes-rivesaltes.com/en/Les-Clos-de-Paulilles
MAP 110
Appointment best. Wine-shop open every day from 9.30–19.30. Restaurant open from May to October every day for lunch and dinner.
As well as being one of the most beguiling of all seaside restaurants in this part of France (though rather more expensive than it used to be), this is a wine estate of 65 hectares, recently acquired by the Domaine Cazes of Rivesaltes fame (q.v.)

**DOMAINE MANYA-PUIG Cathy and Guy Puig
7 Avenue de la République and 6 rue Berthelot 66190 Collioure
Tel 04 68 98 02 59
domaine.manya-puig@orange.fr
www.domaine-manya-puig.com
MAP 109
Group visits by arrangement, including a tasting of local produce. Appointment also recommended for personal visits. They have a stand at Collioure market on Wednesdays and Sundays.

BD **BRUNO DUCHÊNE
3 Rue Jean Bourrat or 3 Rue Voltaire , 66650 Banyuls-sur-Mer
Tel 04 34 10 12 02 or 04 68 55 94 22
MAP 119
Appointment advised. This domaine must be one of the smallest in Banyuls. Just four hectares.

**CAVE DE L'ABBÉ ROUS
56 Avenue du Général de Gaulle, 66650 Banyuls-sur-Mer
Tel 04 68 88 72 72
contact@banyuls.com   www.abberous.com
MAP 120
Sales are through the trade only.

**DOMAINE BERTA MAILLOL
Jean-Louis and Michel Maillol
Mas Paroutet, Route des Mas, 66650 Banyuls-sur-Mer
Customer Service; Impasse Foment de la Sardana
Domaine, Route des Mas (4k. outside town)
Tel 03 85 20 36 54 (*caveau*)   Tel 04 68 88 00 54 (*domaine*)
domaine@bertamaillol.com   www.bertamaillol.com
MAP 121
If you find noone at the *caveau* in town, phone the *domaine* before visiting.

BD **DOMAINE DU TRAGINER
Jean-François Deu
56 Avenue du Puig del Mas 66650 Banyuls-sur-Mer
Tel 04 68 88 15 11
Mobile 06 79 17 19 31
jfdeu@hotmail.com www.traginer.fr
MAP 122
The 'shop' is open from April to October 10.00-12.00 and 16.00-19.00. Otherwise by appointment. To see Deu (pronounced 'Déou) himself, phone him on his mobile in advance.

BD **DOMAINE YOYO Laurence Manya Krief
14 Impasse Aristide Maillol BP 37,   66650 Banyuls-sur-Mer
Mobile 06 12 19 05 79
yoyomk@aol.com www.vinyoyonature.fr
MAP 123
Visits by appointment. Another exciting boutique 'natural' winery, this has to be one of the smallest. Only three hectares!

**DOMAINE SAINT SEBASTIEN
manager Jacques Piriou, sales Romuauld Peronne
10 Avenue de Fontaulé, 66650 Banyuls-sur-Mer
Tel 04 68 88 30 14
contact@domaine-st-sebastien.com
www.domaine-st-sebastien.com
MAP 124
Cellar open usual business hours on weekdays. There is an adjoining restaurant. Good marketing here, but the wines are not cheap and the accueuil could be warmer.

FITOU AND CORBIÈRES

FITOU

This is the oldest *appellation contrôlée* in the Midi, going back to 1948. Growers in Corbières rejected overtures to join in the application for *appellation*, some believing that it would only involve them in extra taxation!

The name Fitou may be used only for red wines, other wines in the area being designated Corbières (esp. white and rosé), Muscat de Rivesaltes or other *Vin Doux Naturels* as appropriate. The reds can be fairly powerful and sometimes rustic in an agreeable sense.

There are two distinct sub-regions of Fitou. There is the '*Montagnée*' area in the mountains which are a southern extension of Corbières. Here the soil is largely schist and wonderfully suited to carignan, which is the dominant grape. There is also the '*Maritime*', centred on the village of Fitou itself and close to the sea, where the soil is mostly chalky clay. The *coopératives* at Cascastel and La Palme are in no way to be considered as different in class from even the best of the independents, while at Tuchan the hitherto excellent *coopérative* is looking for a new direction.

For the most part the carignan grape (often regarded as the basic grape of Fitou) is supplemented by grenache noir, which balances with its soft plummy fruit the bite and astringency of the carignan. Some-times the grenache is grown alongside or as a substitute for its cousin lledoner pelut, a grape not often seen these days. In their wisdom, the French wine authorities have made it compulsory for growers to have a proportion of syrah and/or mourvèdre in their vineyards, perhaps because they have mistakenly

Ruins near Tuchan

despised carignan in the past. Syrah appears more in the '*Montagnée*' region and mourvèdre on the coast. The mourvèdre grape thrives on the moisture coming off the sea and is a compulsory ingredient down there in the AOP wines. Some growers prefer to stick with the traditional grenache/ carignan formula whenever they can, although others welcome the 'class' which syrah can bring. Generally speaking, the '*Montagnée*' region produces wines which are more powerful; the land is mostly schist and the climate is drier. By the sea, the soil is more chalky clay, deriving from the old sea bed, and the wines tend to be more supple and delicate. Annual production amounts to about 13 million bottles, of which the various *coopératives* are responsible for a good 80 percent.

FITOU 'MONTAGNÉE'

The suggested visits go from north to south. Many growers overlap with Corbières to the north (particularly for their whites because there is no AOP for Fitou white) and Rivesaltes to the south. Old records from Cascastel show that in 1907, the vineyards there were planted with 80% carignan and 20% Grenache, and that there were 50,000 hectolitres (nearly 7 million bottles) of wine produced from 450 hectares, which suggests an average yield of 110 hectolitres to the hectare! Nowadays, many growers manage a maximum of 18. Carignan remains however the essential ingredient.

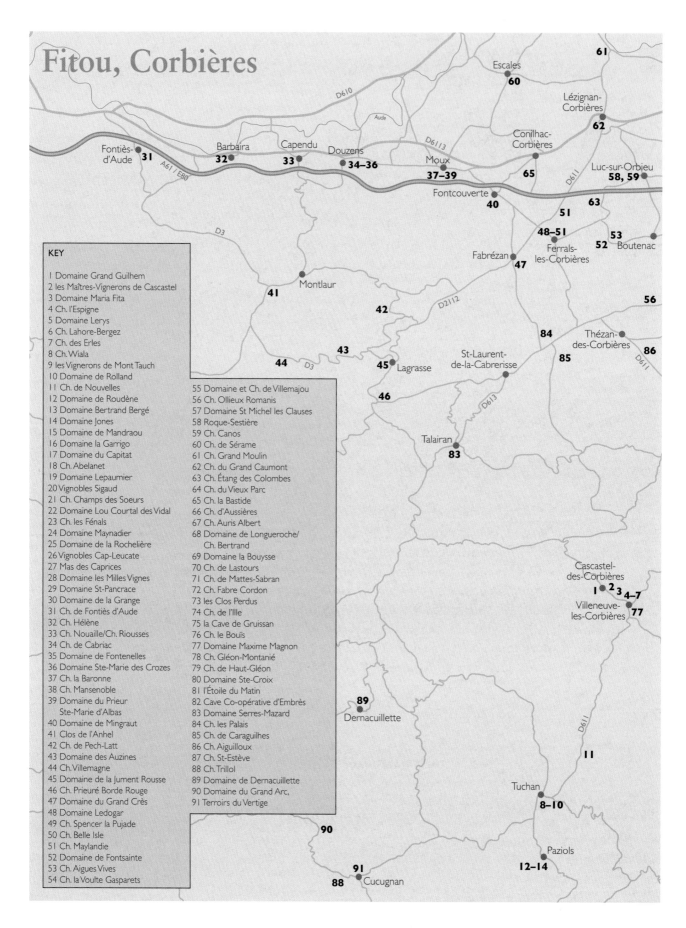

Fitou, Corbières

KEY

1 Domaine Grand Guilhem
2 les Maîtres-Vignerons de Cascastel
3 Domaine Maria Fita
4 Ch. l'Espigne
5 Domaine Lerys
6 Ch. Lahore-Bergez
7 Ch. des Erles
8 Ch. Wiala
9 les Vignerons de Mont Tauch
10 Domaine de Rolland
11 Ch. de Nouvelles
12 Domaine de Roudène
13 Domaine Bertrand Bergé
14 Domaine Jones
15 Domaine de Mandraou
16 Domaine la Garrigo
17 Domaine du Capitat
18 Ch. Abelanet
19 Domaine Lepaumier
20 Vignobles Sigaud
21 Ch. Champs des Soeurs
22 Domaine Lou Courtal des Vidal
23 Ch. les Fénals
24 Domaine Maynadier
25 Domaine de la Rochelière
26 Vignobles Cap-Leucate
27 Mas des Caprices
28 Domaine les Milles Vignes
29 Domaine St-Pancrace
30 Domaine de la Grange
31 Ch. de Fontiès d'Aude
32 Ch. Hélène
33 Ch. Nouaille/Ch. Riousses
34 Ch. de Cabriac
35 Domaine de Fontenelles
36 Domaine Ste-Marie des Crozes
37 Ch. la Baronne
38 Ch. Mansenoble
39 Domaine du Prieur
    Ste-Marie d'Albas
40 Domaine de Mingraut
41 Clos de l'Anhel
42 Ch. de Pech-Latt
43 Domaine des Auzines
44 Ch. Villemagne
45 Domaine de la Jument Rousse
46 Ch. Prieuré Borde Rouge
47 Domaine du Grand Crès
48 Domaine Ledogar
49 Ch. Spencer la Pujade
50 Ch. Belle Isle
51 Ch. Maylandie
52 Domaine de Fontsainte
53 Ch. Aigues Vives
54 Ch. la Voulte Gasparets

55 Domaine et Ch. de Villemajou
56 Ch. Ollieux Romanis
57 Domaine St Michel les Clauses
58 Roque-Sestière
59 Ch. Canos
60 Ch. de Sérame
61 Ch. Grand Moulin
62 Ch. du Grand Caumont
63 Ch. Étang des Colombes
64 Ch. du Vieux Parc
65 Ch. la Bastide
66 Ch. d'Aussières
67 Ch. Auris Albert
68 Domaine de Longueroche/
    Ch. Bertrand
69 Domaine la Bouysse
70 Ch. de Lastours
71 Ch. de Mattes-Sabran
72 Ch. Fabre Cordon
73 les Clos Perdus
74 Ch. de l'Ille
75 la Cave de Gruissan
76 Ch. le Bouïs
77 Domaine Maxime Magnon
78 Ch. Gléon-Montanié
79 Ch. de Haut-Gléon
80 Domaine Ste-Croix
81 l'Étoile du Matin
82 Cave Co-opérative d'Embrès
83 Domaine Serres-Mazard
84 Ch. les Palais
85 Ch. de Caraguilhes
86 Ch. Aiguilloux
87 Ch. St-Estève
88 Ch. Trillol
89 Domaine de Dernacuillette
90 Domaine du Grand Arc,
91 Terroirs du Vertige

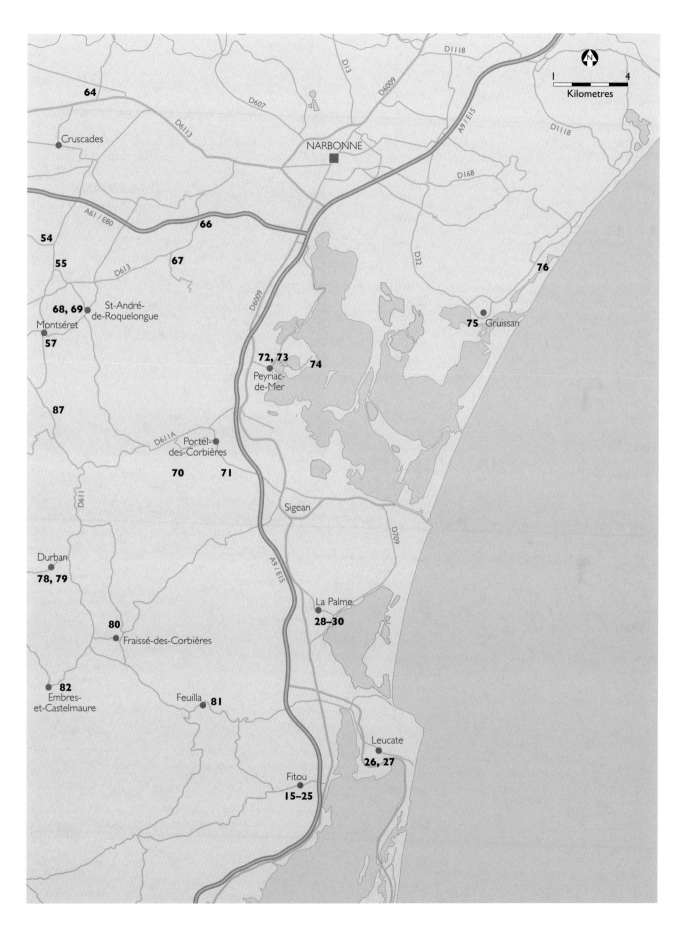

64

Cruscades

D1118

D13

D607

D6009

A9/E15

D1118

NARBONNE

A61/E80

66

D6113

D168

54

55

D613

67

D32

76

68, 69
St-André-
de-Roquelongue

Montséret

75 Gruissan

57

72, 73

74

Peyriac-
de-Mer

87

D611A

Portel-
des-Corbières

70

71

D6009

D611

Sigean

A9/E15

D709

Durban

78, 79

La Palme

28–30

80

Fraissé-des-Corbières

82

Embres-
et-Castelmaure

Feuilla

81

Leucate

26, 27

Fitou

15–25

B ***DOMAINE GRAND GUILHEM

Sévérine and Gilles Contrepois
1 Chemin du Col de la Serre,11360 Cascastel-des-Corbières
Tel   04 68 45 86 67
gguilhem@aol.com   www.grandguilhem.com

MAP 1
Visits during normal hours, but appointment required for anyone seeking lessons in winemaking and/or evening musical entertainment by the winemakers. There is also good accommodation in *gîtes* and *chambres d'hôte* for up to 32 people.

Nearly 13 hectares of vines are grown by this former IT expert and his Parisian wife on high-altitude schist. Maccabeu (80%) dominates the unoaked white Corbières (B) and the yields are as low as 19 hl/ha. It is pale gold in the glass, floral on the nose, and lively and aromatic on the palate. The rosé (B) derives from grenache and syrah and is given nine hours on the skins. In the glass it is a deep pink, aromatic and rich with red fruits on the nose; a wine equally good as an apéritif and with light food. Of the two Fitou reds, the 'Domaine' wine (B) is half carignan from very old low-yielding vines, the rest mainly grenache with a little syrah (to acknowledge the diktats from Paris) which is not allowed to over-ripen "and thus cause banality". Generally speaking this wine is not aged in oak, but sometimes a special parcel of old carignan, planted in 1892, is made by *macération carbonique* in barrel as the main ingredient in 'Angels' (D) – a wine where elegance and finesse are surprisingly reminiscent of wines made well to the north of Languedoc.

Gilles Contrepois, Domaine Grand Guilhem

***DOMAINE MARIA FITA

Jean-Michel Schmitt
12 Avenue du Pont-Neuf, 11360 Villeneuve-les-Corbières
Tel   04 68 45 81 21
vins@mariafita.com   www.mariafita.com

MAP 3
Appointment required.

Schmitt prides himself on not being interested in making standardised wines for the wider market, but wines which are 'different' and intensely personal, whatever colour, and in whatever style. With only about 10 hectares on wild and barren schist and limestone between Villeneuve and Cascastel, he concentrates on getting the best out of his terroir without imposing himself on the fruits of it. Schmitt relies mainly on grenache and carignan with a little syrah and mourvèdre. The range of wines (B/C) will vary from year to year, so the past is not necessarily a guide to the future, except to underline the importance of the originality and freshness of attitude on the part of this vigneron. Sometimes the wines are aged only in tank, sometimes partly in wood, as in warmer vintages such as 2007. Sometimes the grenache will be blended with a minimum of syrah, or they may make a less serious IGP from younger vines. They make an IGP white too sometimes, for example from maccabeu

and grenache (both white and *gris)*, quite rich and strong on the palate but with good balance. Altogether very high quality and way out of the ordinary.

***CHÂTEAU DE NOUVELLES

Jean and Jean-Rémy Durat-Fort
Nouvelles, 11350 Tuchan
Tel   04 68 45 40 03
Mobile   06 75 13 72 77
durat-fort@terre-net.fr   www.chateaudenouvelles-fitou.com

MAP 11
Cellars open (except Sundays and public holidays) 8.00-11.00 and 14.00-17.00.

One of the longest established as well as one of the best Fitou estates. It owes its name to a distinguished previous owner, an Avignon pope called Novelli. There are still a medieval tour and a chapel to prove it. 76 hectares of vines are divided between red Fitou and Rivesaltes (q.v. in Roussillon chapter). The Fitou wines come half from carignan, the rest mostly from grenache, with just a little syrah and mourvèdre. Many of the wines are aged in old *foudres*, varying in volume from 12 to 200 hectolitres, with regular topping up. 'Cuvée Augusta' (B) is aged in *cuve*. Their *entrée de gamme*, aged for one year partly in old wood and partly in tank, is from the same grapes and far from being a quaffer, rather Rhonish in style. Opening ahead of drinking is recommended as with the other reds. 'Vieilles Vignes' (B) spends 18 months in tank before bottling. 'Cuvée Gabrielle' (C) is 60% 70-year-old carignan from just one parcel of vines on schist and has a different *élevage*, half in fine-grained French oak for 18 months, the other half in steel or concrete, and the wine is bottled one month after the *assemblage*. Good value here for the quality. The VDNs, which make up about a third of the production are good too. They are stored in immense old *foudres* and bottled as required, gradually gaining in oxidisation. This family has three permanent staff, all from Portugal, and for the harvest and other busy times they summon their families to help with the work on this large estate.

**DOMAINE DE ROUDÈNE

Bernadette, Jean-Pierre and Sylvain Faixo
5 Espace des Écoles, 11350 Paziols
Tel 04 68 45 43 47
Mobile 06 75 06 68 13
GPS lat. 42° 51' 33" - long. 2° 43' 9"
domainederoudene@orange.fr   www.domainederoudene.fr

MAP 12
Visits during normal hours but prior appointment may be wise.

The family Faixo, beginning in 1975 with only seven hectares, have expanded the vineyards to 28 by digging up scrubland and snapping up other parcels which have come on the market. As well as a Rivesalte *ambré*, good enough though tending to be on the light side (B), and a red Corbières, apparently only available in Belgium, the red Fitou wines are the main business of this estate. 'Selection' (A/B), based on carignan which, depending on the vintage, is sometimes vinified by *macération carbonique*, sometimes not. It may be followed by 'Jean de Pila' (also A/B), their best-selling wine, where the carignan is complemented by 30% Grenache and 20% syrah. The oaked *Tête de Cuvée* 'Fitou Fût de Chêne' (B) makes up the range available at the *domaine*, although another red, 'Les Pys' is marketed (exclusively?) through the *négoçiant* Advini /Jeanjean; a wine which adds mourvèdre and cinsault to the blend. These wines have the ruggedness of the inland Fitou style, but soften and mature well with a few years behind them. A quality Fitou property.

B ***DOMAINE BERTRAND BERGÉ

Jérôme Bertrand
Avenue du Roussillon, 11350 Paziols
Tel 04 68 45 41 73
Mobile   06 80 02 30 13
GPS 42 85834 N 2.72184 E
bertrand-berge@wanadoo.fr   www.bertrand-berge.com
MAP 13
The cellars are open daily except Sunday, but lunch times should be avoided as a matter of courtesy. By arrangement there are guided tours of the vineyards in a 4x4.

This justly admired *domaine*, with its headquarters in the main street of Paziols, has been independent on and off since 1911, but has seen a rapid climb to fame under Jérôme Bertrand's direction. He has been able to convert the *chais* and the *cave* into a magnificent state-of-the-art establishment, well-stocked with the barrels which he was not able to house or use before. However, little has changed in the 33-hectare vineyard where the average age of the vines is 60 years. Some are given over to Muscat de Rivesaltes, but it is the reds which generally attract the attention (and the medals) here. For example, 'Origines' (A/B), carignan and grenache from the relatively younger vines (a mere 20 years) is ripe, flowery, smoky, jammy and intensely fruity, and all without benefit of oak. 'Ancestrale' (C) adds syrah to the blend and the wine spends some time in wood, all of which make together for a more complex and deeper kind of wine. 'Mégalithes' (B) is almost pure carignan from low-yielding and very old vines indeed. It is raised in *cuve* for 18 months and neither filtered nor fined, deep ruby in the glass, round on the palate with notes of the *garrigue* and the minerality you would associate with the carignan grape. A recently developed wine is a carignan/mourvèdre/grenache blend called 'La Boulière' (C), for which the wines come from high ground vines on a *terroir* of *galets roulés*. In some years, a super-cuvée (D) called 'Fitou Jean Sirven' is made to show off the contrast between spicy wood and rich ripe fruit. There is also a "simple, naughty range" called 'Le Méconnu' (all A), varietals from merlot, syrah and muscat, without oak ageing and not to be taken too seriously. As well as a range of Rivesaltes (B/C), there is an ultra-sweet Muscat (D), made as a 'vendanges tardives' style of wine. An outstanding estate.

***DOMAINE JONES   Katie Jones

15 chemin des Rebouls, 11350 Paziols
Mobile   06 86 67 94 68
hello@domainejones.com   www.domainejones.fr

MAP 14
Visits by appointment.

Katie Jones used to be the Export Manager and Sales Director for the once powerful Fitou *coopérative* Mont Tauch (q.v.), and has now set up on her own as a grower. She admits that it took a great deal of courage to "forsake a well-paid job selling wine in order to take up the pruning shears and the sheer hard work of making it." Starting with only a tiny vineyard in Maury she has today two and a half hectares of vines there, and 12 in Tuchan. From the former she makes white and red *Vins de France* (both B); the white from grenache gris and the red nearly all from grenache noir. For such southerly located wines, these are surprisingly sprightly in style, the white being fresh and vital, the red with good fruit and quite sunshiny, and her use of oak is wonderfully gentle. Katie, already a multiple medal-winner, gets better as she goes along – her experience in the region

Katie Jones, Domaine Jones

Tél   04 68 45 91 74
info@cascastel.com   www.cascastel.com
MAP 2
Visits weekdays during usual hours, not lunch time, also Saturday in July and August. Otherwise closed Saturdays and Sundays.

**CHÂTEAU L'ESPIGNE Jean-Philippe Cassagnol
21 Rue des Moulins, 11360 Villeneuve-les-Corbières
Tel 04 68 41 92 46
Mobile 06 81 17 64 88
contact@chateaulespigne   www.chateaulespigne.com .
MAP 4
Appointment recommended.

*DOMAINE LERYS Maguy and Alban Izard
1 Rue du pech de Grill, 11360 Villeneuve-les-Corbières
Tel 04 68 45 95 47
domlerys@gmail.com   www.domainelerys.com
MAP 5
Phone ahead.

*CHÂTEAU LAHORE-BERGEZ
Dominique Bergez
11 Rue Pech de Grill
11360 Villeneuve-les-Corbières
Tel 04 68 45 82 27
lahore-bergez@wanadoo.fr
MAP 6
Better to phone ahead.

**CHÂTEAU DES ERLES François Lurton
11360 Villeneuve-les-Corbières Business ; Domaine de Poumeyrade, 33870 Vayres Tel 04 68 45 82 27
francislurton@francoislurton.com   francislurton.com
MAP 7
For visits, telephone Mme Croft for information.

*CHÂTEAU WIALA
Alain Voorons and Wiebke Seubert
3 rue de la Glacière, 11350 Tuchan
Tel 04 68 45 49 49 Mobile 06 86 43 21 81
contact@cheateau-wiala.com   www.chateau-wiala.com
MAP 8
Appointment recommended.

tells. Her AOP Fitou (C), of which her first vintage was the 2010, is a blend of carignan, grenache and syrah, and again is not a heavyweight but rather distinguished and quite elegant. The syrah shows through with spicy flavours, and perhaps liquorice and/or anise according to the vintage. At Maury, she also makes a Muscat, deliciously fresh but off-dry and a perfect aperitif. Her aim is to make a wide range of small quantities of perfectly crafted wines. For example, her range of what she calls her 'Perles' includes a varietal from carignan gris (B/C), and others from maccabeu, black carignan and syrah (the latter being D+). She is deliberately positioning herself at the top of the Fitou market she knows so well after her long experience at Mont Tauch. Local spiteful vandalism in her early days suggests some resentment at her success.

OTHER GOOD GROWERS AT FITOU 'MONTAGNÉE'

**LES MAÎTRE-VIGNERONS DE CASCASTEL Pascal Toussenot and Louis Arnaud
Grand Rue, 11360 Cascastel-des-Corbières

? LES VIGNERONS DE MONT TAUCH
director Hubert Busquet
11350 Tuchan
Tel 04 68 45 44 73 or 04 68 45 41 08
Fax 04 68 45 45 29
caveau@mont-auch.com   www.mont-tauch.com
MAP 9
Open usual business hours.

It seems that it is all change at this once respected *coopérative*, which has now altered its strategy, no longer rewarding its members at a premium for better quality, with a resulting falling of standards. Apparently no wine for export is bottled here nowadays, being sold off *en négoce* to Les Grands Chais, the giant French *négociants*. Recent changes suggest a return to quality.

B *DOMAINE DE ROLLAND
Louis et Sabine Colomer
Impasse Saint-Roch, 11350 Tuchan
Tel 04 68 45 42 07
Mobile 06 07 02 66 01
contact@domainederolland.com
www.domaine-de-rolland.com
MAP 10
Visits Monday to Friday 10.00-12.30 and 15.30-19.30, but make an appointment if you want to tour the property.

FITOU MARITIME

At Fitou the *maritime* half is quite separate and differs widely from the '*montagnée*' sector. Here the mourvèdre grape adds a tannic and aromatic structure which helps the wines to age. The wines are nevertheless by no means heavy.

***DOMAINE LES MILLE VIGNES
Valérie Guérin
24 Avenue San Brancat, 11480 La Palme
Tel 04 68 48 57 14
les.millevignes@free.fr   www.lesmillevignes.fr

MAP 28
Appointment strongly recommended.

This 12-hectare *domaine* clearly positions itself (by price if nothing else) among the top wines of this *appellation*, but one expects to pay for such care and control in the vineyard and the *chais*. Yields are low (between nine and 25 hl/ha), the vines are fertilised organically, pruning is short and of course there are *vendanges vertes*. Macerations (in small *cuves)* are long, but the time spent in wood is short. The accent here is on soft tannins, lowish acidity and a politeness not characteristic of most of the wines of this region. All the Fitou (there are Rivesaltes and Muscats too) rely heavily on mourvèdre, often a feature of these seaside vineyards. They are all (D), aimed successfully at some of the top restaurants in France. Try 'Cadette', with a promised life of 15 years

and calling for red meat or game to accompany it. There is 'Atsuko', all from *gobelet*-grown grenache with a yield of barely 10 hl/ha, and 'Vendangeurs de la Violette' (named after the team of pickers), from 90% mourvèdre, garnet in colour with spice and red fruits in abundance on the nose, deep on the palate with soft tannins. Recommended if your credit card is healthy.

OTHER GOOD GROWERS AT FITOU MARITIME

*DOMAINE DE MANDRAOU
Evelyne and Eric Suzanne
20 rue de l'Abreuvoir, 11510 Fitou
Cellars and tasting rooms at 3 rue Gilbert Salamo, Fitou
Tel 04 68 70 65 88 or 05 68 45 63 31
Mobile 07 86 18 89 00 or 06 15 95 63 42
evelyne-suzanne@wanadoo.fr   www.mandraou.com
MAP 15
Appointment recommended.

BD **DOMAINE LA GARRIGO
Valérie and Christian Coteill
10 rue des Condomines, 11510 Fitou
Tel 04 68 45 00 69
Mobile 06 62 78 62 64
christian.coteil@wanadoo.fr
www.11510.fr/domaine-la-garrigo
MAP 16
Appointment requested.

*DOMAINE DU CAPITAT Pierre Abelanet
39 Route Nationale 9, 11510 Fitou
Tel 04 68 45 76 98
pierre.abelanet@wanadoo.fr   www.abelanet-capitat.fr
MAP 17
Phone ahead.

**CHÂTEAU ABELANET
Marie-Françoise and Romain Abelanet
7 Avenue de la Mairie, 11510 Fitou
Tel 04 68 45 76 50
contact@chateau-abelanet.com   www.chateau-abelanet.com
MAP 18
Appointment advisable

*DOMAINE LEPAUMIER
Pierrette and Christophe Lepaumier
2 rue de l'Église (cellar), 15 Av. De la Mairie (sales), 11510 Fitou
Tel 04 68 45 66 95
Mobile 06 12 26 27 71
lepaumier.christophe@hotmail.fr
MAP 19
Visits at usual hours. Groups of up to 30 welcomed.

Venerable old Fitou

??? VIGNOBLES SIGAUD Jean-Marie Sigaud
Clos L'Aventure, Le Courtal de Marty , 11510 Fitou
Tel 05 65 22 41 80
barat.sigaud@wanadoo.fr
MAP 20
Appointment essential. Plan well ahead.
M. Sigaud is president of the Union Interprofessionelle des Vins de Cahors, in which area he has important vineyards. The Languedoc is relatively new ground for him, but in 2010 he established legal protection for the name of his 'Clos l'Aventure' and early reviews of his wines suggest a big potential

** CHÂTEAU CHAMP DES SOEURS
Marie et Laurent Maynadier
19 Avenue Corbières, 11510 Fitou
Tel 04 68 45 66 74
Mobile 06 03 68 26 94
laurent.maynadier@orange.fr www.champdessoeurs.fr
MAP 21
Open every day by appointment.

*DOMAINE LOU COURTAL DES VIDAL
Thierry Vidal
25 rue du Pla, 11510 Fitou
Tel 04 68 27 66 08
Mobile 06 29 67 47 36
m.vidal.thierry@orange.fr www.domaine-vidal.com
MAP 22
Visits every day from 10.00-12.30 and 14.30-20.00.
Admirers of the late actor Jean Marais and his circle will want to come here to relive the days when the stars came to this auberge-winery run by the Vidal family in Fitou. A fun visit.

**CHÂTEAU LES FÉNALS
Marion and Mickael Moyer
11510 Fitou
Tel 04 68 45 71 94
Mobile 06 81 00 94 78
les.fenals@wanadoo.fr www.lesfenals.fr
MAP 23
Usually safe to visit without appointment because there are two *gîtes* attached to the *domaine* and so someone on hand to look after them.

**DOMAINE MAYNADIER
Cécile and Marie-Antoinette Maynadier
45 route D6009, 11510 Fitou
Tel 04 68 45 63 11
Mobile 06 81 35 65 80
cecile@domainemaynadier.com www.domainemaynadier.com
MAP 24
Cellars open in summer season daily 9.00-20.00 non-stop. otherwise 9.00-12.00 and 14.00-18.00 but not Sundays.

**DOMAINE DE LA ROCHELIÈRE
Jean-Marie and Émilie Fabre
17 rue du Vigne. 11540 Fitou
Tel 04 68 45 70 52

Mobile 06 14 69 65 07
GPS 42 53.648 N 2 58.956E
la.rocheliere@orange.fr www.domainedelarocheliere.com
MAP 25
Visits April to October inc. daily 9.00-12.00 and 14.00-19.00.
November to March inc. Mon. to Sat 14.00 to 18.00.

*VIGNOBLES CAP-LEUCATE
contacts Joël Castany and Stéphane Roques
Chais La Prade, 11370 Leucate
Tel 04 68 33 20 41
commercial@cave-leucate.com www.cap-leucate.com
MAP 26
Visits during normal business hours. Not Saturday afternoons, nor Sundays or lunchtimes.
This is a successful *coopérative* covering the maritime half of Fitou, and the result of a number of mergers with other smaller coops. The total production of 54,000 hectolitres a year on average gives some idea of its size and scope. The range of wines (mostly A) is huge, including six whites (some produced as AOP Corbières) including an oaked maccabeu/grenache blanc blend called 'Tresmoulis', four vins rosés, 12 reds, both Corbières and Fitou, especially 'Terre Natale' and 'Cap 42', and nine *Vins doux Naturels*, as well as some sparkling oddities.

B **MAS DES CAPRICES Pierre and Nireille Mann
37 Avenue George Brassens, 11370 Leucate Village
Tel 04 68 40 96 19
Mobile 06 89 15 18 50
masdescaprices@free.fr or pierremann@free.fr
www.mas-des-caprices.com
MAP 27
Visits during summer weekdays (not Monday) 18.00-20.00, Sunday 11.00-13.00.
Spring and autumn; Friday and Saturday evenings 18.00-20.00 and Sunday mornings 11.00-13.00. Winter visits by telephone appointment.

B *DOMAINE SAINT-PANCRACE
Jean-Marie Bourrel
23 rue des Corbières, 11480 La Palme
Tel 04 68 48 62 73 or 04 68 48 50 21
bourrel.jean-marie@wanadoo.fr
MAP 29
Open daily in the mornings and from 17.00-20.00 in the afternoons. Appointments required on Sundays.

B *DOMAINE DE LA GRANGE
Thierry and André Dell'Ova
Les Cabanes de la Palme 11480 La Palme
Tel 04 68 48 17 88
contact@dellova-freres.fr www.dellova-freres.fr
MAP 30
Visits during normal hours.

Coopérative's colours at Castelmaure

CORBIÈRES

Corbières is by far the largest area of AOP wines in Languedoc. It represents nearly half of the total production of Languedoc wine. The red wines dominate, contributing over 90% of all the AOP. The vineyards cover about 13,000 hectares, and produce over 70 million bottles of wine per year. They stretch from close to the Narbonne/Toulouse motorway in the north to the boundaries of Roussillon to the south; from the sea in the east to the high mountains separating the Mediterranean from the valley of the Aude around Limoux. It is hardly surprising that the variation in quality is huge, as is the range of wine styles. 11 geographical divisions have been promulgated, representing the many different

terroirs. One of these, Boutenac, has been promoted to having its own AOP.

The usual quintet of red grapes is to be found in Corbières, although cinsault is allowed only as a supporting variety in the red table wines. Just as surprising is the range of white grapes for the tiny production of white Corbières. Clairette, muscat, piquepoul and terret may appear sometimes in a supporting role. The production of rosé wines is noticeably less important here than in other parts of the Midi.

The official maps show the 11 different *terroirs* in a rather haphazard way, not making life any easier for visitors. In this book the *terroirs* have been retained but renumbered in such a way as to make a tour of the region more practicable. Starting from the outskirts of Carcassonne, the journey takes one east to Narbonne before heading south towards the Rousssillon.

SERVIÈS

*CHÂTEAU DE FONTIES D'AUDE

Mme Bastié Loyer, Lisane et Bertrand Loyer
11800 Fonties d'Aude
Tel   04 68 78 67 14
Mobile   06 17 78 24 40
www.chateau-de-fonties.fr
MAP 3
Phone ahead of visit.

MONTAGNE D'ALARIC

B ***CHÂTEAU LA BARONNE

Paul and Jean Lignères
11700 Fontcourverte
Offices and tastings 21 rue Jean-Jaurès, 11700 Moux
Tel   04 68 43 90 07
Mobile 06 11 56 37 43
info@chateaulabaronne.com   www.chateaulabaronne.com

MAP 37
Phone ahead to determine venue.

The family is often described as being "doctors with wine in their veins." Jean is indeed the village doctor in Moux, and Paul is a local dentist, but the family's ties with winemaking go back to the nineteenth century and beyond. Their parents bought the La Baronne estate in 1957 and since then the family have expanded it, acquiring another *domaine*, Las Vals, in the 1980s, and then the Domaine Plo de Maorou in 2006 in partnership with the Jackson family, this wine going entirely to the USA. Nowadays they work closely with Tuscan wine consultant Stefano Chioccioli on their 90-hectare vineyard. There is nothing extraordinary about the grape varieties they grow except their predilection for carignan, some of which goes back to the 19th Century and which they refuse to submit to *macération carbonique*. They say it strips the grapes of the sense of *terroir*. The large estate produces a big range, from which one might pick out the white 'Las Vals', a pure roussanne (B/C), 'Montagne D'Alaric', a half carignan blend (B/C) and 'Les Chemins' which has a little Grenache (B). Further up the scale, the red 'Las Vals' is virtually a *mono-cépage* from mourvèdre (C),

as is 'Notre Dame' (C) from syrah. 'Alaric' (C) is a blend from carignan, syrah and mourvèdre, while 'Pièce de Roche' (C/D) is pure carignan from the 1892 planting. Ageing here is done in a mixture of tank and *cuves tronçonniques*, the barrels coming from St. Émilion and renewed on a seven-year cycle. Top Corbières.

***CHÂTEAU MANSENOBLE

Alexandre Chekalin and Tatiana Korolchuk
Consultant Guido Jansegers-de-Witte
15 Avenue de Bataille, 11700 Moux
Tel   04 68 43 93 39
chateaumansenoble@gmail.com   www.mansenoble.com

MAP 38
Appointment desirable.

The property has new owners but their predecessor remains closely connected. Guido Jansegers, a former insurance broker by profession, knows all about taking on risks. But alongside that career, he rapidly acquired a reputation as a wine taster. He is known as "The Nose of Belgium" in his native country. At the age of 50 he gave up everything to buy this estate in Corbières, which he saw one morning and signed up for the same day. He at once reduced the vineyard from 38 to 20 hectares, allowing his vendor to keep the rest and claim the reward for ripping up vines. Thus Guido kept only the best parcels in production. His reputation was instant and meteoric, partly because he was able to cash in on his Belgian connections. He was never interested in making white wines, and the red grapes are syrah, grenache and carignan (with just a little mourvèdre) for the AOPs, and merlot and cabernet sauvignon for his IGPs. Of the latter he makes just two (both A/B), adding a little carignan to one of them (Le Cyprès), the other being called 'Le Nez'. Unless the new owners make changes there are currently three AOP wines: 'Montagne d'Alaric' (B), raised in *cuve* where the accent is on grenache and carignan; 'Réserve' (C) using the mourvèdre, partly aged in once-used barrels; and 'Cuvée Marie-Annick' (C) where there is a little more oak ageing, but still only in one-year-old barrels. This wine is made only in the very best years, and is said to last 15 years. A fine Corbières estate.

B ***DOMAINE DE MINGRAUT

Véronique Robin-Cuculière
Sud domaine Maingraut, 11700 Fontcourverte
Tel   04 68 43 40 01 or 06 82 00 50 66
info@domaine-mingraut.fr   www.domaine-mingraut.fr

MAP 40
Visits by appointment.

Although the vines were planted over a hundred years ago, Véronique arrived only in 1997, and without any previous

Chapel in the vines

history or experience in winemaking. Wisely concentrating on a modest vineyard of eight hectares, she has made quite a name for herself and her wines, now having converted to organic methods in the vineyard. She is known for her varietal viognier, with its typical apricot/peach character, combining good acidity with some weight. She also makes an oaked chardonnay which is given six months in barrel. Her AOP reds, from syrah, grenache and carignan, which go under constantly varying names, are big and well-built with plenty of black and red fruits and, with age, hints of undergrowth and even cinnamon. Véronique also makes in small quantities a sweet dessert wine from muscat and viognier (B), otherwise the wines here are all (A), going towards (B). Excellent value.

OTHER GOOD GROWERS

**CHÂTEAU HÉLÈNE

M. Villalonga-Shelly (maître du chais M. Estèbe)
34 route de Narbonne 11800 Barbaira
Tel   04 68 79 00 69
Mobile 06 10 54 59 65
chateauhelene@sfr.fr www.chateauhelene.net
MAP 32
Open Monday to Saturday   8.00-12.00 and 14.00-18.00.

**CHÂTEAU NOUAILLE / CHÂTEAU RIOUSSES   Gilles Nouaille

4 rue Joseph Quaranta 11700 Capendu
Tel   04 68 79 13 85
chateauriousees@wanadoo.fr
MAP 33
Appointment suggested.

*CHÂTEAU DE CABRIAC

Jean and Michèle de Cibeins
11700 Douzens
Tel   04 68 79 19 15
cabriac@wanadoo.fr   www.chateau-de-cabriac.com
MAP 34
Visits best by appointment.

**DOMAINE DE FONTENELLES

Thierry and Nelly Tastu
78 avenue de Corbieres 11700 Douzens
Tel   04 68 79 12 89   Mobile 06 11 02 48 41
info@fontenelles.com   www.fontenelles.com
MAP 35
Visits by appointment.

**DOMAINE SAINTE-MARIE DES CROZES   Dominique and Bernard Alias

11700 Douzens
Tel   04 68 79 09 00
Mobile   06 59 00 67 90
d.alias11@orange.fr   www.saintemariedescrozes.com
MAP 36
Phone for appointment.

**DOMAINE DU PRIEURÉ STE-MARIE D'ALBAS

Laurence and Vincent Licciardi –Pirot
45 Avenue Henri Bataille, 11700 Moux
Tel   04 68 49 61 54
Mobile 06 98 83 47 36
gigalibert@wanadoo.fr   www.saintemariedalbas.com
MAP 39
Appointment advisable.

LAGRASSE

B **CLOS DE L'ANHEL   Sophie Guiraudon

2 rue des Montlauriers, 12200 Montlaur
Tel   04 68 43 18 12
Mobile   06 77 09 65 48
anhel@wanadoo.fr www.anhel.fr.

MAP 41
Appointment required.

Sophie's vineyard may be only 10 hectares in extent, but she believes in biodiversity and has planted a variety of trees all round it to encourage the fauna; she has even imported some bats. She has a lot of old carignan, which forms the backbone of her four red *cuvées* (she makes neither white nor rosé). 'Le Lolo d'Anhel' ('anhel' means 'lamb') is her "*vin des copains*" (A) but all the same it spends one month in wood before being aged in tank. Cuvee 'Les Autres' (A), described as being for "*les autres copains*", is a *Vin de France*, because it is an unblended carignan varietal. 'Les Terrassettes' (B) is one step up and 'Les Dimanches' (C) (70% carignan, 20% raised in old barrels) one step further, for "drinking only on Sundays." Sophie and her colleague Philippe Matthias also manage Pech Latt (described next).

B ** CHÂTEAU DE PECH-LATT   Louis Max,

director Philippe Matthias
11220 Lagrasse
Tel   04 68 58 11 40
Mobile 06 85 40 99 72
GPS   43.09962   2.37 40
chateau.pechlatt@louis-max.fr   www.pechlatt.com

MAP 42
Phone before visit.

This organic estate is managed by Sophie Guiraudon and her partner Philippe Mathias for Burgundy dealer Louis Max, and is best visited in conjunction with a pre-arranged visit to Clos d'Anhel (q.v.) They have their work cut out because there are no fewer than 100 hectares making AOP Corbières. The Burgundy connection means that there is an IGP from pinot noir as well as the AOP, largely as at Clos d'Anhel nearby from carignan. The mainstream 'Tradition' (A) is marketed widely and is notably silky and fruity. It is dark in colour with plenty of red and black fruits, with suggestions of spices and leather. 'Vieilles Vignes' (B) is deeper and richer, but still built on its fruit. 'Tamanova' (C) is the top red, redolent of the barrels used, and needs time. There is also a sweet red wine from grenache noir. These are quirky wines. Some hesitate, others plunge.

B **DOMAINE DES AUZINES
Laurent and Measa Miquel
11220 Lagrasse
Tel   04 30 16 14 66
nessa@laurentmiquel.com   www.lesauzines.com

MAP 43
Appointment advisable.

'Auzine' is the name given to the species of evergreen oak with holly-like leaves found everywhere on the *garrigue* which surrounds this property. Organic since 1998 (the date of its first vintage under previous owners), this 41-hectare vineyard is now in the hands of St. Chinian winemaker and *négociant* Laurent Miquel and his Irish wife Measa. A height of 1,000 metres above sea-level is too much for the mourvèdre grape, but perfect for producing brilliant deep-coloured fresh wines from syrah, grenache and especially some old carignan. There is a barrel-fermented white mostly from grenache gris, popular with those who like their white wines well-oaked (B). But most of the production is of reds, of which 'Fleurs de Garrigues' (B) features the carignan raised in tank, fruity, spicy and with good body. 'Hautes Terres' (B) is from grenache and syrah, usually given 12 months in barrel – firm, deep and with good tannins. A micro-*cuvée* called 'Les Roches' (C) is mostly syrah and quite modern in style, chocolatey and spicy with well-handled wood.

B *** CHÂTEAU PRIEURÉ BORDE ROUGE
Patrick Chénevas-Paule
Route de Saint-Pierre, 11220 Lagrasse
Tel 09 64 13 04 39
Mobile 06 30 33 60 23
contact@borde-rouge.com   www.borde-rouge.com

MAP 46
The property is two miles out of town so an appointment is recommended

This former priory is as old as the Abbey at Lagrasse, and the Benedictine monks who had their home here were quick to understand how good the place might be for growing vines. The Carrères acquired the property in 2005, he a management consultant and she a designer for Dior, so their arrival here must have been quite a culture shock to them and the locals. The Carrères are fully aware of the historical distinction of the property and vow to carry on and improve the tradition. The estate comprises 130 hectares, but only 23 are under vine and all are surrounded by *garrigue*. There is some very old carignan, and forty-year-old grenache too, as well as the more recently planted syrah. A small production of white is made from grenache blanc called 'Carminal Blanc' (B), of which 20% is aged in barrel for eight months. A rosé blended from syrah and grenache is called 'Rubellis' (A), with suggestions of citrus fruits as well as the more regular red summer varieties. A fruity IGP marketed as bag-in-box opens the reds (A), an easy-to-drink wine with some syrah to give it oomph. 'Rubellis Rouge' (A) is made from carignan vinified by *macération carbonique* and conventionally vinified syrah and grenache. The wine is all tank-raised to preserve the fresh fruity character. The red 'Carminal' (B) is a blend of tank-raised grenache, with syrah and carignan raised for a time in wood which is renewed on a four-year cycle – a more serious wine which will keep well. The top red is the highly praised 'Ange' (C) and is made only in small quantities in the best years.

OTHER GOOD GROWERS

*CHÂTEAU VILLEMAGNE
Sophie et Christophe Hebraud, Paulette and Roger Carbonneau
Hameau de Villemagne, 11220 Lagrasse
Tel 04 68 24 06 97 or 04 68 76 29 53
villemagne@chateau-villemagne.fr
http://chateau.villemagne.free.fr
MAP 44
Visits every day from 09.00-20.00.

BD ** DOMAINE DE LA JUMENT ROUSSE
Sandrine Puech
44 Boulevard de la Promenade, 11220 Lagrasse
Tel 04 68 43 13 29
Mobile 06 73 39 62 29
sapuech@wanadoo.fr   www.la-jument-rousse.fr
MAP 45
Open 11-00-12.30 and 17.30-20.30 during school holidays, otherwise by appointment. A property to be followed.

BOUTENAC

Boutenac enjoys its own inner *appellation*

within the Corbières AOP, and the growers are entitled to put the Boutenac name on their labels. The right also extends to parcels of Boutenac vines owned by other Corbières growers who may have their base of operations outside the Boutenac limits. The wines are notable for their good balance, and the carignan grape is especially successful here. It must be hand-picked and taken to the *chais* in whole bunches. The syrah grape is limited to 30% of a grower's vineyard.

***DOMAINE DU GRAND CRÈS

Pascaline and Hervé Leferrer
26 rue Sainte Elizabeth, 11200 Fabrézan
Mobile 09 61 48 72 67
grand.cres@wanadoo.fr   www.domainedugrandcres.fr

MAP 47
You can take pot luck, but appointment is wiser.

Hervé was once manager at the Domaine Romanée-Conti. Much as he would have liked to have just a small corner in Burgundy, the price of vineyards there is exorbitant, and Corbières offered a much less risky bet for someone starting up on his own. This *domaine*, on 19 hectares of some of the most ungrateful land in Corbières, produces wines of elegance and, not surprisingly, Burgundian finesse. Not too proud to offer BIBs, their bottled whites include an AOP blend of roussanne and viognier (A), as well as an IGP medium sweet muscat (not fortified B). A very dark rosé called 'Le Claret' is bled from cabernet sauvignon, which goes on to make an IGP red (both A). The AOP rosé (A) is more traditional, reminiscent of nectarines, say the makers. The other reds all have more or less oak ageing, the 'Cuvée Classique' (A) least so. The 'Cuvée Majeure' (B) (12 months in barrel) is nearly all syrah and has plenty of power, while 'Cressala' (C) is made only in limited quantities. For those seeking refinement, not blockbusters, these wines are wonderful value for money.

BD **DOMAINE LEDOGAR

Xavier et Mathieu Lédogar
Place de la République, 11200 Ferrals-lès-Corbières
Tel   04 68 43 67 60
Mobile (Xavier) 08 61 06 14 51   (Mathieu) 06 07 06 73 00
xavier.ledogar@orange.fr   www.domaineledogar.fr

MAP 48
Appointment recommended.

The grandfather of these two brothers was already growing grapes in Ferrals in the 1920s. The family sent their grapes to the *coopérative*, but in 1997 Xavier bought an old *chais*, and the first wine of the *domaine* was made in the following year. Mathieu joined him in 2000. Of the 22 hectares under vine, 80% are devoted to AOP Corbières from the typical Languedoc grape varieties, while the rest, under the watchful care of Xavier's forebears, are planted with cabernet sauvignon and marselan, and produce IGPs. These may be phased out in the future when old André is no longer with us to tend them. True to biodynamic principles, some of the ground is worked with horse; there are no chemicals used either in the vineyards nor the *chais* other than a minimum of sulphur, and there are no added yeasts. The wines range from an AOC blended white and a rosé (both A) through a range of reds (mostly B). The oddities here are two pure carignans, both (C): one from the black carignan grape, the other from the rarer white which can be specially recommended. These are natural wines in the best sense of the word, wines which speak their *terroir* with authenticity.

***DOMAINE DE FONTSAINTE

Bruno Laboucarié
16 Route de Ferrals, 11200 Boutenac
Tel   04 68 27 07 63
earl.laboucarie@aliceadsl.fr   www.fontsainte.com

MAP 52
Visits every day except Sunday, 10.00-12.00 and 14.00-18.00.

Bruno's father re-established the vineyards at Fontsainte ('Holy spring') in 1971 and passed on the management to his son in 1995. The *domaine* has always enjoyed one of the highest reputations in the *appellation*, having pioneered the use of carbonic maceration while retaining harvesting by hand. Today, rather mirroring La Voulte-Gasparret in their *encépagement*, they are growing 50% carignan, 30% grenache and the rest mourvèdre and syrah. Bruno's father established the success of his all-carignan 'La Demoiselle' (B), in which the natural fruit is nicely balanced by the austerity of the grape, while being enhanced by gentle oak ageing. The pink 'Gris de Gris' (A) (70% pink and black grenache) is a wine in which many people find a pronounced strawberry character. The 'Domaine Rouge' is also (A). Bruno's contribution has been the new top wine 'Centurion' (B/C), for which the grapes come from selected micro-parcels. The wine is skillfully raised in barrels which give it a beautiful smoothness.

***CHÂTEAU LA VOULTE GASPARETS

Patrick et Laurent Reverdy
11200 Boutenac,
Tel   04 68 27 07 86
chateaulavoulte@wanadoo.fr www.lavoultegasparets. com

MAP 54
Appointment strongly recommended.

The Reverdy family and their many forebears, represented today by Patrick and his son Laurent, have been making wine here for six generations, and their wines give you the

Geoffrey Marchand, L'Étoile du Matin, p.101

feeling that they have settled into a confident mastery of their profession. The 55 hectares of vines are all old, some as many as 115 years of age. The accent is on carignan and grenache, the traditional Corbières varieties, although some of the newcomers, mourvèdre and syrah, are also in evidence. The red wines are those which make this property famous, but don't spurn the rosé (A), saigné from grenache and mourvèdre with a little carignan and syrah, vinified in tank. The white is from vermentino and grenache blanc, with just a little maccabeu, and not shown any wood either. The two reds are permanently established, both made from 50% carignan, and a quarter each of grenache and mourvèdre, though the Cuvée Réservée (B) has a little syrah too. The difference is that the 'Romain Pauc' (C) is given 12 months in barrel, but only 20% of the oak is new, the remainder being two to three years old. These wines can be found frequently in the best wine shops and restaurants of the region and represent good value for their undoubted class.

***DOMAINE ET CHÂTEAU DE VILLEMAJOU Gérard Bertrand
11200 Villemajou
Mobile   06 84 38 26 29
www.gerard-bertrand.com

MAP   55
Appointment recommended.

Ex-rugby champion Gérard Bertrand returns to his family home and native roots to make one of the best known Corbiéres wines from the inner Boutenac region which overlaps into Fontfroide. The estate is notable for its very old carignan, often vinified by *macération carbonique*. The range includes white and rosé wines, as well as reds (nothing less than C). Syrah is added to the carignan to make the top wine 'La Forge' (D), aromatic and round with soft tannins. Bertand almost succeeds in claiming the Boutenac crown.

***CH. OLLIEUX ROMANIS
Jacqueline and Pierre Bories
Route D 613, 11200 Monséret.
Tel 04 68 43 35 20
GPS   43.12177785N 2.78890457 E
ibaccou@chateaulesollieux.com

MAP 56
Visits every day 10.00-18.00.   Conducted tours with tastings of 7 wines available at 15€.

This is today a reunion of the two *domaines* Ollieux and Romanis, historically one but down the years separated. The combined estate (today 150 hectares following the 75 hectares of Ollieux bought in 2006) has rapidly jumped to the top of this appellation. Many organic practices are followed, without the owners yet signing the pledge. The

Pierre Bories, Ch. Ollieux Romanis

grapes are 80% hand-harvested. Jacqueline (Pierre's mother) has all but retired, though she still works front-of-house. It was she who pioneered the production of oak-aged white wines in Corbières, even if they are tending these days to moderate the use of wood. Pierre is almost devout in his worship of the traditional carignan and alicante varieties, from which he produces varietals of each (B). Here you will find a combination of the best of tradition with up-to-date practice. Pierre has recently planted new carignan, and his eyes on the future as well as the past tell him that the best way of managing this large enterprise is to have a team of wine graduates and *stageaires* to ensure that development is perpetually renewed. As often there are two whites, the first straightforward (A) with a flowery, exotic fruit, the second (B) given its malo in barrel and aged there, a bigger, more powerful wine. There are IGPs (A) from sauvignon and a blend which includes some merlot. A delicious rosé (also A) based on grenache gris and cinsault leads to the AOP reds, beginning with 'Alice' (A), carignan-based and to be enjoyed on its fruit and appreciated on the character of the grape variety. 'Classique' (A-, just) , is more complex than most entry-level wines, with good fruits such as blackcurrant and raspberry. Then there is a 'Prestige' (B), raised in mostly old barrels, leading to 'Atal sia' (C) meaning in modern French "so be it", a highly admired tank-raised blend made before it is assembled and raised in *cuve* for a year and a further nine months in bottle. Another top wine, 'Cuvée Or' (C) is still carignan-dominated and vinified by *macération carbonique* before being given 12 months in new barrels.

OTHER GOOD GROWERS

**CHÂTEAU SPENCER LA PUJADE
Sébastien Bonneaud
Rue de l'Église, 11200 Ferrals-les-Corbières
Tel 09 50 26 31 33
Mobile 06 09 04 39 34
GPS 43 08865002N 24387E
contact@chateauspencer-lapujade.fr
www.chateauspencerlapujade.fr
MAP 49
Appointment recommended.

*CHÂTEAU BELLE ISLE
SCEA Belle Isle, Manager Michel Peresse
Chemin Paul Pugnaud, rue de l'Église, 11200 Ferrals-les-Corbières
Tél 04 68 27 90 46 or 08 99 02 96 42
Mobile 06 81 00 06 07
peresse.michel@orange.fr www.chateaudebelleisle.com
MAP 50
Phone ahead, or try pot luck during normal hours Monday to Saturday.

*CHÂTEAU MAYLANDIE
Delphine Maymil, Eric Virion, Anne-Marie and Jean Maymil
18 Avenue de Lézignan, 11200 Ferrals les Corbières
Tel 04 68 43 66 50
Mobile 06 61 93 01 33
contact@maylandie.fr www.maylandie.fr
MAP 51
Visits 09.00-12.30 and 15.00-19.00, Appointment recommended.

**CHÂTEAU AIGUES VIVES Gérard Bertrand
11200 Boutenac
Tel 04 68 45 27 03 or 04 68 27 48 88
vins@gerard-bertrand.com www.gerard-bertrand.com
MAP 53
Prior appointment recommended.

**DOMAINE ST. MICHEL LES CLAUSES
Michel Raynaud
6 chemin de la Source, 11200 Montseret
Tél 04 68 43 36 62
info@dom-st-michel.com www.dom-st-michel.com
MAP 57
Visits Monday to Saturday, usual hours.

**ROQUE-SESTIÈRE Thierry Fontenille
8 rue des Étangs, 11200 Luc-sur-Orbieu
Tel 04 68 27 18 00
Mobile 06 22 24 65 18
roque.sestiere@wanadoo.fr
MAP 58
Cellars open every day from 10.00-18.00 but the growers ask for an appointment 'off-season'.
This much-respected *domaine* is in new ownership since 2014. The emphasis is unusually on the white wines. Formerly they were almost entirely from Maccabeu, but today there is an increasing blending with other varieties.

**CHÂTEAU CANOS Pierre Galinier
Rue des Etangs, 11200 Luc-sur-Orbieu
Tel 04 68 27 10 76 or 04 68 27 00 06
Mobile 04 68 27 61 08
chateau-canos@wanadoo.fr
MAP 59
Appointment essential.

LÉZIGNAN

B **CHÂTEAU DE SÉRAME
Contact M.Vincent Bernard
Chemin de Sérame 11200 Lézignan Corbières
Tel 04 68 27 59 00
Mobile 09 63 60 22 24
contact@cvbg.com www.chateaudeserame.com

MAP 60
Appointment recommended.

Digs suggest that this was truly one of the first Roman vine yards in Languedoc. This is a huge estate extending over 175 hectares and a diversity of *terroirs* (partly in the Minervois), managed and modernised by the Dourthe business from Bordeaux since 2001. The business is too big to be called artisanal, but the wines are impeccably made, though some are not cheap. The AOP reds (B) include 'Les Terrasses', mainly from syrah, grown on north-facing slopes to protect the vines from hydric stress. The wine is aged on its lees in tank for 18 months and suggests a Northern Rhône style. Another syrah-based wine, fruity and spicy, is called 'Le Pégourier' (D) from vines on a *graves* soil lying on a vein of schist. 'L'Icône' (D) is a blend which includes carignan and grenache as well as syrah. 'Réserve du Château' (D), another similar blend, is partly aged in 400-litre oak barrels. The *château* also makes a Minervois under the same name, with a substantial proportion of mourvèdre in the blend. Also notable are two ranges of IGP varietals (A): the first called 'Esprit de Sérame', less ambitious and consisting of wines intended for early drinking, from merlot, cabernet sauvignon and syrah; and a white from viognier. A better quality range of wines from the same grapes (also a chardonnay) goes under the name of 'Réserve' (A/B).

***CHATEAU GRAND MOULIN

Jean-Noël et Frédéric Bousquet
6 maréchal Avenue Galiéni, 11200 Lezignan-Corbières
Tel 04 68 27 40 80
www.chateaugrandmoulin.com

MAP 61
Cellars open Monday to Saturday 9.00 -19.00 and Sunday mornings 10.00-12.00.

M. Bousquet's father was a merchant dealing in pigs, and had a mere three hectares of vines to ensure a supply of wine for his home. Since 1978 the family has built up a substantial holding of 120 hectares, from which his sons make wine very largely for export to the New World and for sale to private customers. They acquired both the present vineyard and their own expertise gradually over the years, starting off as *coopérateurs*. Despite the almost total destruction of the enterprise in the 1999 floods, they have now rebuilt the basis of a flourishing business in some of the best wines of Corbières. Notable among the reds are the 'Vielilles Vignes' and 'Terres Rouge' grown on chalky clay at Lézignan, and a Boutenac red grown on sandstone. Aged partly in new wood and partly in old barrels, the wines will appeal to those who appreciate the added flavours of wood. These are some of the best wines from Corbières, certainly from the point of view of value for money (mostly B), and the reds age well.

**CH. DU GRAND CAUMONT

Mme Laurence Rigal
11200 Lézignan-Corbières
Tel 04 68 27 10 82
fib.rigal@wanadoo.fr   www.grandcaumont.com

MAP 62
Visits Monday to Friday, usual hours.

Mme Rigal's family also founded the famous Rigal brand of Roquefort cheese, while at the same time buying this *domaine* in 1906 and entirely reconstituting the vineyards and *chais*; work which continued throughout the twentieth Century under Mme Laurence's mother. Laurence herself became joint manager of the *domaine* in 2003, having worked for some years in marketing and PR in Paris. The *terroir* of chalky clay and pebbles supports 100 hectares of vines, all 40 years old at least, with some much older carignan too. These form the basis of the red wines (A/B), while there are IGP *vins de cépage* too (A) from merlot and cabernet sauvignon. There is just one white, an AOP (A/B from grenache blanc, sometimes fennelly and floral. The red 'Tradition' (A/B) is 60% carignan, vinified by *macération carbonique*, dark fruits dominating the nose and the palate. It is aged in tank like the 'Cuvée Spéciale' (A/B), in which the carignan is balanced by syrah and grenache to give a character of red fruits and spice. The 'Cuvée Impatience' (B) and the 'Réserve de Laurence' (B) are a pair of wines partially raised in new wood for 10 months or so, and again dominated by carignan and syrah. Another wine of the same type is 'Saint Paul Cuvée Prestige' (B). The only syrah-dominated wine is, curiously, not oaked and specially made for exclusive distribution. The IGP range comprises just one blend, 'Mougin' (A/B), which adds a little cabernet sauvignon to the Languedoc grapes, otherwise it is purely varietal: merlot, cabernet sauvignon or syrah. A good value property.

**CHÂTEAU ÉTANG DES COLOMBES

Christophe Gualco,
11200 Cruscades
Tel   04 68 27 00 03
Mobile   06 18 03 03 43
christophe.gualco@wanadoo.fr
www.etangdescolombes.com

MAP 63
Visits 08.30-12.00 and 14.00 to 18.30, but appointments required at weekends.

This is a well-known and good quality *domaine*, whose wines should appeal to those looking for low alcohol levels. Its 77 hectares are on pebbly, chalky clay. Value for money is exceptional. Outside the AOP, there are varietals (A) from viognier (not too fat, but subtle, flowery and nutty), carignan (with currant flavours) and grenache (also with good fruit). The viognier turns up again in a sweet *passerillé* version (B). The AOP Corbières (none of which show more than 12.5 degrees alcohol, usually less) include a rosé called 'Gris des Colombes' (A), based on syrah, cinsault and grenache. The 'Tradition' range comprises a white (crisp and flowery from grenache blanc, maccabeu and bourboulenc) and a red from all their red grape varieties (both A). A step up to B for the 'Bois des Dames' white (old vine grenache blanc and bourboulenc, fermented and aged in oak) and the red (powerful and vanillin, with spice), also given oak ageing

Jon Bowen, Domaine Sainte-Croix, p.100

for 10 months. A recently introduced 'Bicentenaire' red (A) is from old vines, and is vinified by *macération carbonique* before ageing in wood for six to eight months.

OTHER GOOD LÉZIGNAN GROWERS

**CHÂTEAU DU VIEUX PARC

Louis et Guillaume Panis
11200 Conilhac-Corbières
Tél   04 68 27 47 44
contact@chateau-vieuxparc.fr   www.chateau-vieuxparc.fr
MAP 64
Visits every weekday but by appointment

*CHÂTEAU LA BASTIDE

Anne-Marie and Guilhem Durand
11200 Escales
Tél   04 68 27 08 47
chateaulabastide@wanadoo.fr   www.chateau-la-bastide.fr
MAP 65
Phone for rendezvous

*CHÂTEAU DE MONTRABECH PITT

Marie-Paule and Charly Pitt
10 rue Dantoine,   11000 Carcassonne
Tel   04 68 25 56 18
Mobile   06 11 07 23 38 (Charly) or 06 09 15 83 75 (Marie-Paule)
charly.pitt@wanadoo.fr   www.chateu-montrabech-pitt.com
MAP (not shown)
Ask for instructions where to go when making an appointment (essential)

FONTFROIDE

**CHÂTEAU D'AUSSIERES

Baron Eric de Rothschild
11100 Narbonne
aussieres@lafite.com   www.lafite.com/eng/otherestates

MAP 66
Visits Monday to Friday by appointment only. At least two weeks' notice required.

When famous Bordeaux growers move outside their home base, they tend consciously or not to replicate their own style. Here too: Médoc-orientated Corbières. Never mind. The results are much admired and deservedly successful. There are IGPs (A) from chardonnay (the grapes mostly brought in from outside) and red blends from syrah/mourvèdre and cabernet sauvignon/syrah. The 'entry' wine is called 'Blason d'Aussières' (A) and has all the usual grapes bar cinsault. 20% of the blend is raised in oak, as is the 'Terrasses d'Aussières' (A/B), where the barrel-ageing is a bit longer. 'Ch. D'Aussières' (B/C) is the top wine, made from the best parcels of the vineyard and produced in limited quantity. Nearly half of it is aged in wood for 12 –16 months and widely praised. These modern styled, rather toasted plummy wines are a good choice for those who think they don't like Corbières.

OTHER   GOOD   FONTFROIDE GROWERS

B **CHÂTEAU AURIS ALBERT

Jean-Claude Albert
Route du Massif de Fontfroide, 11100 Narbonne
Mobile   06 04 59 68 44
axeldw@les-bugadelles.com   www.chateau-auris.com
MAP 67
Appointment recommended.

**DOMAINE DE LONGUEROCHE and CHÂTEAU BERTRAND Roger Bertrand
rue de l'Ancienne Poste, 11200 Saint-André de Roquelongue
Tel 04 68 41 48 26
Mobile 06 75 22 85 51
contact@rogerbertrand.fr   www.longueroche.fr
MAP 68
Visit by appointment.

B **DOMAINE LA BOUYSSE
Martine Pagès and Christophe Molinier
30 rue de la Mairie, 11200 St André de Roquelongue
Tel 04 68 45 50 34
Mobile 04 68 45 50 34
domainelabouysse@wanadoo.fr   www.domainelabouysse.com

MAP 69
Caveau open every morning 8.00-12.00, afternoons 16.00-20.00. Appointment advised other than in July and August. Saturdays by appointment. Closed Sundays and public holidays.

SIGEAN

***CHÂTEAU DE LASTOURS Famille Allard
(director Xavier de Rozières)
11490 Portel-des-Corbières
Tél 04 68 48 64 74
contact@chateaudelastours.com   www.chateaudelastours.com

MAP 70
Cellars open during normal hours.

Here there are not only 104 hectares of vines high up in the eastern Corbières mountains and fringed with wind turbines, but a tourist centre offering villa accommodation and a restaurant, as well as long walks and treks through the wild countryside. The height of the vineyards (in places 900 feet above the valley below) ensures cool nights and a huge variation in the dates of maturity of the various parcels of vines. All five Languedoc varieties are represented in different *terroirs* appropriate to each. The equipment and *chais* are ultra high-tech. There are no white wines from this estate but there is a salmon pink rosé (from syrah, cinsault and Grenache (A), made by direct pressing and which boasts white peaches and flowers. The first red is called 'Arnaud de Berre' (A) and is typically fruity and easy to quaff. More ambitious and perhaps the most enjoyable of the wines is 'Simone de Descamps' (B), named after the founder of a previous *régime* which provided employment and training for handicapped people, and who left her personal fortune to that institution. It has a deal of carignan, young carignan at that, which proves that, as long as the yield from this variety is strictly controlled, the vines do not have to be all that old. The Réserve (C) is mostly aged in barrel, but then given a further year in bottle before being marketed.

B ***CHÂTEAU FABRE-CORDON
Monique and Henri Fabre
L'Oustal Nau, 11440 Peyriac-sur-Mer
Tel 04 68 42 00 31
Mobile 06 89 89 96 53
chateaufabrecordon@gmail.com   www.chateaufabrecordon.fr

MAP 72
Rendezvous preferred by growers.

The vineyard, just three kilometres from the sea at Peyriac, covers 15 hectares and has been cultivated organically since 2010. Grenache blanc (A/B) is at the base of their one dry white, sold by *domaine* logo rather than name, and matured in tank rather than wood so as to preserve the character of the fruit. The Rosé, 'Printemps d'Amandine' (A), fresh and quaffable, has all the usual grapes except (curiously) cinsault. The reds start with an IGP varietal from low-yielding cabernet sauvignon, 'Peiriacum Corbierae'(A), grown on sandy soil once covered by the sea. 'Parfum d'été' (A/B), mostly Grenache, is easy drinking and can be bought also in 50-cl. bottles, whereas 'Fragrances Oubliées' (B) derives more complexity and richness from syrah. The oaked 'Fleur de Chêne' (C), which has a little carignan to set off the syrah, is made only in the best years and is given nearly a year in French oak. Its power calls for opening ahead of drinking, preferably overnight. The range is completed by a sweet grenache blanc (C), from grapes shrivelled on the vine and late-picked. Excellent value for wines of this quality.

BD ***LES CLOS PERDUS Paul Old
17 rue du Marché, 11440 Peyriac-sur-Mer
Tel 04 68 48 30 05
Mobile 06 70 08 00 65
info@lesclosperdus.com   www.lesclosperdus.com

also at Botleys Farm, Downton, Salisbury SP5 3NW, UK

MAP 73
Visitors welcomed but long prior notice required.

Seeking to establish themselves in the Langeudoc, this pair of enthusiasts picked up scattered parcels of vines in Corbières and the Agly Valley in Roussillon from local growers who had abandoned them because they did not yield enough, or needed working by hand rather than machine. From the start, they aimed at the top, and have done very well, attracting much attention from the press and experts. Great care is taken over the vinification in small vats with hand-operated equipment, a basket press for example and poles for pumping rather than machines. There are two whites: 'Le Blanc' (B) from maccabeu (mostly), grown in the Agly Valley near Maury, light and fresh; and 'L'Extrème' (C) from the two paler grenaches, barrel-fermented and aged in wood for six months, but without a second fermentation. The Rosé (B/C) is serious, almost a *clairette*, nearly all mourvèdre. The reds range from 'Le Rouge' (B), a mourvèdre from grapes grown on the coastal plain, to 'Cuvée' (C) which varies from year to year but could be carignan-dominated. 'Prioundo' (C) is mostly grenache with a little cinsault and raised in inox, while 'Mire La Mer' (C/D) is from Peyriac, mostly mourvèdre, some of which is barrel-fermented, and sometimes part-oxygenated by *microbullage*. Finally, 'L"Extrème' (D) is a huge affair based on lledoner pelut from the schist at Maury, half the grapes being oak-fermented and barrel-aged for nine months.

CHÂTEAU DE L'ILLE   Régisseur Pol Flandroy
Route Étang, 11440 Peyriac-de-Mer
Tél 04 68 41 05 96
info@chateaudelille.com   www.chateudelille.fr

MAP 74
Appointment recommended.

A maritime vineyard of 65 hectares situated on a remote promontory overlooking the sea between Bages and Sigean. The vines enjoy a very warm Mediterranean ambience, which suits the mourvèdre grape very well. It is a principal ingredient in the top wine here ('Cuvée Louis' B/C), which is partly aged in a mix of French and American wood, renewed on a three-year cycle. 'Andreas' (B) is similarly aged, but has a bigger spread of grape varieties including syrah, grenache and carignan, as well as the mourvèdre, whereas 'Angélique' (B) is raised in tank and is a syrah/grenache blend, excellent value for the quality. 'Cuvée Julia' (A) has no pretensions beyond being a good quaffer and adds carignan to the mix of grapes. An IGP from merlot and marselan (A) completes the range of reds. 'Alexandre' (A) is a syrah based rosé. The white AOP is based on bourboulenc, with vermentino and grenache blanc, while there is also a 100% chardonnay IGP, both (A). A big range of bag-in-box wines should not devalue the image of this good quality, value for money estate.

OTHER GOOD SIGEAN GROWERS

**CHÂTEAU DE MATTES-SABRAN
M. Jean-Luc Brouillat and Mme Brouillat-Arnould
Domaine de Mattes, 11490 Portel-des-Corbieres
Tel   04 68 48 22 77
Mobile 09 77 78 21 35
mattes.sabran@laposte.net   www.mattes-sabran.fr
MAP 71
Prior appointment advisable.

*LA CAVE DE GRUISSAN
1 Boulevard de la Corderie 11430 Gruissan
Tel   04 68 49 01 17
contact@cavedegruissan.com   www.cavedegruissan.com
MAP 75
Visits every day during usual hours, but not Sunday afternoons out of season. September closed mornings. Winter, Monday to Friday 9.00-12.00 and 14.00-18.00. Weekends by appointment.

* CHÂTEAU LE BOUÏS   Frédérique Olivié
Route Bleue, 11430 Gruissan
Tel 04 68 75 25 25
contact@chateaulebouis.com   www.chateaulebouis.fr
MAP 76
Cellars open June-September every day 10.00-13.00 and 15.00-19.30 (but closed Sunday morning). September closed mornings. Winter, Monday to Friday 9.00-12.00 and 14.00-18.00. Weekends by appointment.

DURBAN

BD ***DOMAINE MAXIME MAGNON
Maxime Magnon
11360 Villeneuve-leCorbière
Tél   04 68 45 84 71
Mobile   06 07 55 21 07
maxime.magnon@orange.fr
MAP 77
Appointment essential.

A stable of cult wines, mostly (C), grown from nine parcels spread over 11 hectares on the wild Corbières-Fitou boundary. As he is a disciple of Didier Barral in Faugères, you would rightly expect scrupulously biodynamic sulphur-free principles and an approach to wine completely untrammelled by received wisdom from Languedoc, though much informed by his earlier training in Burgundy. The old-fashioned carignan and cinsault grapes form the backbone of his red production, while the whites are from grenache gris and blanc, maccabeu and terret, all traditional grapes from way back in this desolate region. The white wine is called 'La Bégou' (B/C). Betraying the high altitude at which the grapes are grown, it is wonderfully fresh and floral. The three grape varieties are picked and fermented together in the old-fashioned way. 'La Démarrante' (B), as its name suggests, is the opening red, a carignan and cinsault blend, hugely attractive, which makes you want to pour a second glass before you've finished the first. 'La Rozeta' (C) is carignan-based too, but with some syrah and grenache to give it just a little weight and extra fruit. The top red is 'Campagnes' (C/D), carignan again, with such finesse and delicacy as to make one wonder how such pinot-like wines can be made in this southern outreach of Languedoc. While pundits rave about these wines, others wonder how, with their northern character, they manage to rate so highly with Robert Parker, who must surely (this time at least) be right?

** CHÂTEAU GLÉON-MONTANIÉ
Jean-Pierre and Philippe Montanié
Château de Gléon 11360 Durban
Tel 04 68 48 28 25
info@gleon-montanie.com   www.gleon-montanie.com

MAP 78
For visits you can take pot luck, but it is safer to make an appointment.

Eccentric fermaentation
Domaine Sainte-Croix

This property, which has 50 hectares under vine, has been in the hands of the present family for six generations, since 1861, and they were among the first to bottle their own Corbières at the end of the 19th century. Four hectares are devoted to the bourboulenc grape (a.k.a here as malvoisie), from which they make an aromatic, delicate and quite strong white wine (C). Their rosé (B) is mostly cinsault. There is a red IGP (A), mostly from Malbec, but with some merlot to soften it. For this and their AOP wines, macerations ar-relatively short and, with the exception of their syrah and grenache, the wines are made by *macération carbonique*. As well as these varieties, the red 'Tradition' (B) includes a deal of carignan (which represents over a third of the total plantings). Then there is 'Combes de Berre' (B/C) from 60% syrah. Both these wines are raised in tank, though the malo-lactic fermentation of the latter takes place in wood. 'Cuvée Gaston Bonnes' (C) is also largely syrah, and is discreetly aged in one-year-old barrels for 12 months. The wines here are benchmark quality, traditional Corbières.

**CHÂTEAU DE HAUT-GLEON
11360 Durban
Tel   04 68 48 85 95
contact@hautgleon.com   www. hautgleon.com
MAP   79

In 2012, the Duhamel family sold this rather remote property to Foncalieu, a group mostly of *coopératives*. It was once an ambitious and modern-style estate producing wines rather in the new-world style, and its reputation is still maintained. The new owners are pursuing a policy of developing high-end wine tourism, while continuing the winemaking policies of their predecessors. There are white and red IGPS and an AOP rosé which are all good value (B). The red AOPs from syrah, grenache and carignan range from (B) to (D) as do the whites. The top wines are raised in barrel for 12 months. There are excellent *gîtes* and *chambres d'hôte* for those wishing to stay in the area.

B ***DOMAINE SAINTE-CROIX
Jon and Elizabeth Bowen
7 Avenue des Corbières, 11360 Fraïsse-des-Corbières
Tel 06 85 67 63 88
domaine@sainte-croixvins.com   www.saintecroixvins.com

MAP 80
Appointment strongly recommended.

Here is another *domaine*, just over 13 hectares, seven of which are devoted to carignan, miles from anywhere in the wildest wilds of southern Corbières. This one is the property of two English expatriates who have considerable experience working in wineries all over the place. Their old, almost forgotten grape-varieties say it all: morrastel, alicante and aramon among the red grapes and terret bourret, carignan blanc and blanquette (mauzac) as whites. Many of these are growing among the more familiar varieties, *en foule* as they say. Yields are low, barely 15 hectolitres to the hectare for 'La Serre' (B) from the two grenaches, gris and blanc. There are no additional yeasts and the wine is aged in tank for five months on its lees. The grapes are not de-stemmed, and no wood is used so as not to detract from the lovely fruity bouquet. Also tank-aged is the entry red 'Le Fournas' (A), unfined and only gently filtered. 'Magneric' (B) is largely carignan and raised partly in old barrels to give a slightly more complex wine. 'Carignan' (C) is nearly all from that grape, grown on hundred-year-old vines, and raised in old barrels for two years. 'Célestra' (C) is mostly grenache with some carignan, their top wine, of which three-quarters is raised in barrel for 18 months, and then for another six months in tank before bottling. 'La Part des Anges' (50-cl D) is a sweet Roussillon-styled red (but not as sweet as a Maury) from carignan, late-picked. It starts life in old barrels then grows up in glass *bonbonnes*. "*Surprenant*", say the English makers.

BD **L'ÉTOILE DU MATIN
Geoffrey Marchand
La Planteyre, Route de Treilles, 11510 Feuilla
Tel 04 68 45 01 82
Mobile 06 25 33 47 48
gvin.etoile.du.matin@gmail.com

MAP 81
Visits by appointment.

A relative newcomer to Corbières, Marchand is no stranger to top-class winemaking, having studied in Burgundy, where he learnt his ways from Dominique Dérain at St. Aubin. He then spent two harvests with Hervé Bizeul in the Roussillon. His 17-hectare *domaine* is over 1,000 feet above sea level, yet within minutes of the Mediterranean itself. It has been fully bio since 2006. On various different soils and with no fewer than 32 different parcels, Geoffrey grows the usual Languedoc grapes, but including additionally the unusual lledoner pelut (a relative of the grenache), from which he makes a varietal wine. Some of his vines go back 100 years. Sheep keep the weeds down in winter and provide natural manure, while in spring beehives encourage the pollination of the flowers in the surrounding *garrigue*. Prices are usually (B) throughout the range, though the top wines run into (C). His whites are from grenache blanc and gris, and the rosé from all three grenaches with a touch of cinsault. Among the reds, note in particular his love of carignan ('Védèpe'), the powerful 'Etoile du Matin', and the pure grenache 'Les Agnelles' from grenache grown on schist. When Geoffrey feels strong enough he dispenses with the use of sulphur altogether. A bold, enterprising grower who is going places.

***CAVE COOPERATIVE D'EMBRÈS
Director Bernard Pueyo, President Patrick de Marien
4 route des Canelles, 11360 Embrès-et-Castelmaure
Tel 04 68 45 91 83
vins@castelmaure.com   www.castelmaure.com

MAP 82
Visits during usual business hours (not Sunday or lunchtimes).

This is a small, artisanal and top-of-the-tree *coopérative* at the very southern end of Corbières, remotely sandwiched in the mountains between the two areas of Fitou. There are 60 or so members, but the operation is dominated by roughly a dozen growers who between them own 90% of the vineyards. The whites (B) start with a tank-raised blend from grenache blanc and maccabeu, crisp but with some vivacity, and a barrel-fermented pure white grenache, quite spicy and lively. The rosé is in the 'bonbons anglais' style. It is the reds for which this Cave is famous: the easy to drink, fruity all-grenache *vin de copains* called 'La Buvette' (A); the garriguey, carignan-flavoured 'Castelmaure' (A) with its dark fruit flavours; the well-balanced, good-value and smooth 'Pompadour' (B) from a blend of syrah and carignan made by *macération carbonique* and given six months in old barrels; the modern-style, barrel-raised 'Grande Cuvée' (B/C), sometimes called Marque d'Amour; and finally the famous medal-winning 'No.3' (C/D), a huge wine, powerful but with some elegance, and inspired by the famous winemaker Laurent Tardieu. A visit here is like an expedition to the end of the world, but well worth the journey. Strongly recommended.

SAINT VICTOR

**DOMAINE SERRES-MAZARD

(Cellier Saint Damien)   Jean-Pierre Mazard
11220 Talairan
Tel   04 68 44 02 22
GPS 43.049823 2.663841
mazard.jeanpierre@free.fr   www.serres-mazard.com
MAP 83
Cellars open every day 9.00-17.00.

The tiny village of Talairan (where, according to Mazard, wild boar outnumber the population) hardly needs an *office de tourisme* when it has the Cellier Saint Damien, this *domaine*'s tasting room. It is a veritable village museum and, second only to his wine, Jean-Pierre Mazard's passion is his beloved wild orchids, on which you will be given a long dissertation. No fewer than three white wines will begin the tasting here: 'Origine', a quaffer from grenache blanc, maccabeu and marsanne; 'Cuvée Jules' (B) from the same grapes but raised in a mix of oak and acacia barrels; and a moëlleux called 'Marie Pierre' (B), sold as an IGP because it has the unauthorised clairette, terret and muscat in its make-up. The rosé is called 'Origine' too (A), fresh, fruity and good with salads. There are two more reds (A). The basic 'Domaine Saint Damien' is 60% carignan, and is round and fruity and excellent as an everyday wine. Then there is the red 'Origine' (A/B), which is given six months in barrel. More ambitious is 'Henri Serres' (B), for which the oak-ageing is extended to one year, and 'Cuvée Annie' (C), which is given 18 months. Perhaps the ethos of the *domaine* fits better with the less complicated wines, which are such wonderful value for money, as well as being delicious.

B **CHÂTEAU DE CARAGUILHES

Pierre Gabison
11220 St Laurent de la Cabrerisse
Tel   04 68 27 88 99
chateau@caraguilhes.fr   www.caraguilhes.fr

MAP 85
Take your chance, but appointment recommended.

Lionel Faivre and Pierre Gabison returned from Algeria to create the present-day vineyard in 1958 and immediately converted it to organic production. Gabison bought Faivre out in 1998. An estate of 135 hectares inevitably produces a big range of wines. In addition to a medal-winning rosé, there are three whites from grenache blanc, marsanne and bourboulenc, ranging from a basic 'Domaine de l'Olivette' (A), (with a touch of viognier), an aperitif wine, crisp and dry but with a peachy character. Next, a 'Cuvée Classique' vinified in French oak, and 'Solus', all grenache blanc, raised in barrel (both B). But it is the reds that are best-known and most available. They follow the same name pattern: the 'Olivette' (A) having a deal of merlot being produced

as an IGP; the 'Classique' (B) ("a modern expression of our terroir") having rich notes of black fruits and cherry; a 'Prestige' aged for nine months in oak; and the 'Solus' (a favourite with lovers of the modern style) a more powerful version of the same (both C). 'L'Échappée Bell' (B/C) is the latest *cuvée* from Boutenac terroir, 85% carignan, some old, some newer vines.

**CHÂTEAU AIGUILLOUX

Marthe et François Lemarié
11200 Thézan des Corbières
Tel   04 68 43 32 71
aiguilloux@wanadoo.fr
www.chateau-aiguiloux.com

MAP 86
Visits by appointment.

François is from Normandy, and Marthe was a teacher from the Antilles until they bought this property in 1980. Nowadays, their daughter Anne and her partner Mathieu take a much closer interest in the future of the *domaine*. These 37 hectares are bang in the centre of the Corbières *Appellation*, and they have a variety of soils which is unique, even though the whole vineyard is in one piece. There is also an abundance of small streams ('Aiguilloux'), after which the property is named. The grapes are mostly fermented whole, with only 20% de-stalked. They don't make any white, but the rosé (A) (40% cinsault) is made by direct pressing and is recommended to accompany fish dishes in the Languedoc style. Their first red, 'Tradition' (A), is 50% carignan, raised in inox, the second, 'Trois Seigneurs' (B), has even more carignan but is raised in barrel, and the top wine, still carignan-dominated, 'Cuvée Anne Georges' (C), is for keeping at least five years. This is a long-established and well-regarded Corbières property, which keeps well up to the times, but at the same time is highly respectful of tradition.

OTHER GOOD SAINT VICTOR GROWERS

**CHÂTEAU LES PALAIS

Anne and Xavier de Volontat
11220 St Laurent de la Cabrérisse
Tel   04 68 44 01 63
chateaulespalais@orange.fr   www.chateaulespalais.com
MAP 84
Appointment recommended.

*CHÂTEAU SAINT-ESTEVE

Sylvie, Eric and David Latham
11200 Thézan-des-Corbières
Tel   04 68 43 32 34

contact@chateau-saint-esteve.com
www.chateau-saint-esteve.com
MAP 87
Visits by appointment.

TERMENES

GOOD GROWERS

**CHÂTEAU TRILLOL (formerly domaine du Trillol)
Benjamin Sichel (contact Henry Guiot)
Route de Duilhac, 11350 Cucugnan
Tel 04 68 45 01 13
trillol@orange.fr www.trillol.com
MAP 88
Visits by appointment. Owned by the Sichel family of Bordeaux fame.

B **DOMAINE DE DERNACUILLETE
Guillaume Boussens
15 rue Fleurie, 11330 Dernacueillete
Mobile 06 70 79 38 46
 christelle.dichard@gmail.com
domaine.de.dernacueillette@gmail.com
domainededernacueillete.fr
MAP 89
Appointment requested.
The vineyards are situated in the western lee of Mont Tauch and thus amongst the highest in altitude of all the wines of Corbières, reaching almost to 1,000 metres above the sea. The journey here is long, but the wines are so unusual as to be well worth the trip.

QUERIBUS

There seems to be but one serious independent producer in this remote and wild part of Corbières, but also one very interesting *coopérative*.

** DOMAINE DU GRAND ARC
Bruno and Fabienne Schenk
Le Devez, 11350 Cucugnan
Tel 04 68 45 01 03
domaine.grandarc@gmail.com   www.grand-arc.com

MAP 90
The situation is remote, so it is best to phone ahead.

The Schenks created this *domaine* in 1995. It consists today of 25 hectares of vines planted in the lee of the sinister Château de Peyrepertuse, the Cathar neighbour of the better known Quéribus. Though not officially certified, the growers practice many of the tenets of biodynamism, including hand-picking and the absence of added sulphur to the wines, no extra yeasts or other additives. They currently make just one white, 'Veillée d'Équinoxe', a thirst-quenching blend of roussanne, grenache blanc and maccabeu, and one rosé, 'La Tour Fabienne', mostly syrah and mourvèdre (both A). The bulk of the production is in reds, of which there is a range going from the easy 'Nature d'Orée' (A) to 'Six Terres Sienne Rouge' (D), big and oaked, vanillin, with flowers, herbs and sweet fruits. In between, try 'Réserve Grand Arc' and 'Cuvée des Quarante' (both A), generously endowed with carignan. 'En sol Majeur' (B) is a grenache and syrah blend, while 'Aux Temps d'Histoire' (C) marks a return to carignan. 'La Rose des Jables' is a synthesis of all their red grapes with a careful *élevage* in wood.

**TERROIRS DU VERTIGE
M. Gilles Cutilles (Directeur)
2 Chemin des Vignerons 11220 Talairan
Tél   04 68 44 02 17
 Terroir.vertiges@wanadoo.fr   www.terroirsduvertige.com

MAP 91
Cellars at Talairan and Cucugnan (the latter open only during the season).

There are 124 vignerons who have between them 890 hectares. Note their speciality, the white 'Fraîcheur de Padern', a blend from grenache blanc, marsanne, roussanne, vermentino and maccabeu (A), and wonderful value for a cool, refreshing, summery, light wine of great charm. Because of the high altitude, white wines from the hinterland of Corbières can have more elegance and minerality than many other more famous growers on lower and hotter ground. Do not overlook either their big range of wines in other styles, all good value for money, even if their best rise into the (C) range, but may not be in the same class as their traditional white.

Limoux

As you go south up the Aude river from Carcassonne, you come to the wine-growing area of Limoux, centred on the town of that name. Although in recent years red wines have been making an appearance here, historically the region is famous for its sparkling wines. It is said that the way of making this style of wine originated in the local town of St Hilaire long before Dom Pérignon was born. The local abbots found that their fermentation of white wine stopped when the cold weather arrived, and then restarted in the spring, the resulting ferment causing the bubbles. There was no question of uncorking the bottles or of adding extra yeasts or sugar. The resulting wine is often quite sweet and low in alcohol. Nowadays this simple method is known as *méthode ancestrale*, to distinguish it from the method used in Champagne which has by law to be called misleadingly *méthode traditionelle*. This latter method is also used to make two other kinds of mousseux, a 'Blanquette de Limoux' and a Crémant de Limoux'. In addition to the three sparklers, there is also a still white wine. Pundits have tended to look down on the wines of Limoux, but in recent years the quality has increased dramatically, and the wines can rightfully take their place among the best of sparklers.

The fizzy *méthode ancestrale* has to be made from the mauzac grape, the furry underside of its leaves giving it the name 'Blanquette', a name which is also applied to the more modern method of vinification, but in which case chardonnay and chenin blanc may be used in addition to the mauzac. The crémant must be a blend mainly of the last two grapes, with only a small proportion of mauzac. The characteristic taste of mauzac is apples and pears, particularly prominent in the wines made by the *méthode ancestrale*. The Crémant style produces some very good wines

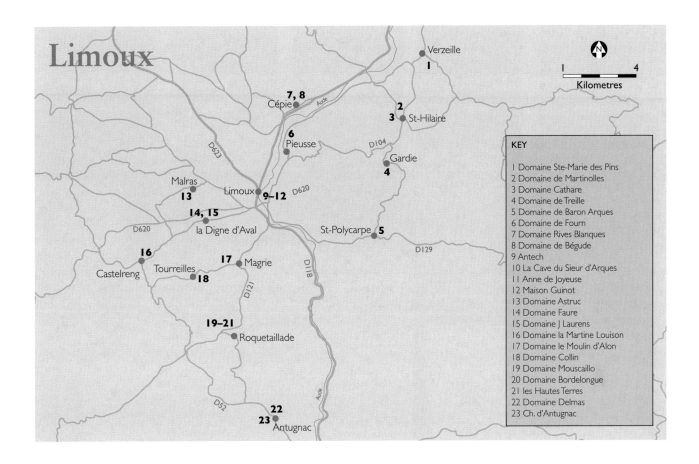

here, but all but the best are rather in the manner of globalised fizz, and do not have the regional taste of the traditional Blanquettes. They came about because of the policy of the winemaking authorities in Paris to reduce the use of local grape varieties in favour of the internationally known ones, just as they tried to reduce the growth of carignan and cinsault in favour of so called '*améliorateurs*'. The red wines may be a blend of several varieties including merlot (which must constitute 60% of any blend), pinot noir (successful on higher ground), syrah, grenache, the cabernets, carignan etc. Some reds (especially the pinot noirs) are marketed as IGPs. Finally, there is the still white Limoux, which may be made only from hand-picked grapes and must be vinified and aged in wood at least until the month of May following the vintage.

**DOMAINE DE MARTINOLLES

Domaines Paul Mas
11250 St. Hilaire
Tel 04 68 69 41 93
info@martinolles.com   www.martinolles.com

MAP 2
Usually open during business hours.

This estate was in the Vergnes family for many years, but in 2011 Isabelle, a charming hostess as well as being an excellent winemaker, sold the 65-hectare property to Paul Mas. The wines continue to be very good, and there is a much extended range available from the new owners: a *méthode ancestrale* (B), particularly elegant and less sweet than some; a fine Blanquette (B); a rather classy Crémant called 'Prima Perla' (C); and IGPs from sauvignon (B) and pinot noir (B). This continues to be one of the best independent estates in Limoux. There's a gîte too if you want to stay in the region.

****DOMAINE DE FOURN**

Robert G.F.A, Jean-Luc and Bernard Robert
11300 Pieusse
Tel   04 68 31 15 03
robert.blanquette@wanadoo.fr   www.robert-blanquette.com

MAP 6

Best to telephone ahead of a visit. Beware of the loud-mouthed donkey.

Pierre Robert started this domaine with a mere one and a half hectares of mauzac. His grandsons now have 38 hectares planted in the white Limoux grapes, and a further six with red grapes. This is one of the most important Limoux estates. There are 20 hectares of mauzac – the only grape allowed in their *méthode ancestrale*, one of the finest and richest of the area, and the base also of their traditional dry Blanquette by the modern method. The chardonnay and chenin are reserved mostly for the Crémant wines, though some chardonnay goes into a varietal IGP (B), raised in tank, and a specialist Crémant (B), which is tinted pink by the addition of a little pinot noir. The *méthode ancestrale* (B) is kept for 15 months in bottle before release and goes well with light desserts. Being low in alcohol it is particularly suitable for younger drinkers, who seem to have a sweeter taste anyway. Of the three dry blanquettes, 'Carte Ivoire' (B) is 90% mauzac, which, being light, makes a fine apéritif. 'Carte Noire' (B), another Blanquette, is recommended as a partner to fish and seafood, while a third Blanquette cuvee, 'Dame Robert' (B), has a shade more chardonnay and chenin to give it length. The 'Crémant Robert' (B) has more mauzac than most others, and is notable for particularly fine bubbles and its apple and hawthorn character. A *demi-sec* Blanquette (B) completes the range, except for the red AOP (B) from 60% merlot, 30% syrah and 10% carignan, fruity and spicy.

*****DOMAINE RIVES BLANQUES**

Jan & Caryl Panman
Le Poudou, 11300 Cépiè
Tel   04 68 31 43 20
GPS 43 11643   2 22585
rives-blanques@wanadoo.fr   www.rives-blanques.com

MAP 7

Prior appointment advised.

These winemakers were much travelled over 12 countries and

four continents before settling in Limoux, where they are in their second decade. Their 30 hectares are all hand-harvested and lie on a plateau 350 metres above sea level. There is a distinct Atlantic feel to the climate here, which perhaps in part explains the Panmans' love of the mauzac grape. More ground though is given over to chardonnay from which they make an unoaked 'Chardonnay du Domaine' and a barrel-fermented 'Cuvée de l'Odyssée', the latter from old uncloned vines. Chenin blanc also appears in two wines; a dry oak-aged 'Dédicace' and a sweet 'Vendange d'Automne' from botrytised grapes. Their *blanquette* is all-mauzac, much medalled and deliciously fresh. Try also their all-Mauzac still Limoux called 'Occitania', particularly delicious and perhaps the only still wine wholly from this grape in the region. Newly planted sauvignon is at the heart of an IGP, barrel-fermented and first marketed in 2009, and there are two Crémants; one wholly from white grapes and the other with just a touch of pinot noir. Prices here are all (B) and very good value for money. No reds – so far.

B **DOMAINE DE BÉGUDE
James and Catherine Kinglake
11300 Cépie
Tel 06 86 05 73 74
Mobile 06 86 05 74 73
james@domainebegude.com   www.domainebegude.com

MAP 8
Tastings by appointment only.

The Kinglakes bought this 29-hectare domaine, which had been farmed organically for some years before, in 2003. They are helped and advised by a team which has had experience all over the world in winemaking. So far they have only white grapes, apart from some pinot noir (17%), mostly chardonnay (55%), sauvignon and chenin, with just a little viognier and gewurztraminer. No mauzac. The vines are all close to the cellar so that oxidisation is minimised between harvesting and winemaking. There are six white wines: an IGP sauvignon (B), citrussy and sharp; a basic IGP chardonnay 'Le Bel Ange' (A/B), unoaked and with a 'splash' of chenin, apples-and-pearsy; and a steel-fermented but oak-aged wine from the same grape called 'Terroir 11300' (B). A wine, 'Exotic' by name and by nature, is from a variety of unusual grapes grown on high ground (B/C). So is 'Surprise du Sud' (B/C) from gewurztraminer, with fragrant aromas of lychees and rose petals. Their still AOC Limoux (B) is all-chardonnay from the best parcels, barrel-fermented and with a bouquet of brioche. The Crémant (B) is again all-chardonnay, their only sparkling white. The grapes from pinot noir go into a rosé (B), the bouquet suggesting strawberries and cherries, and their only red, packed with fruit (B). Fine quality wines with a hint of new world style.

***ANTECH
Georges et Roger Antech, Françoise Antech-Gazeau
11300 Limoux
Tel 04 68 31 15 88
GPS 43 07033 2 22104
courriers@antech-limoux.com   www.antech-limoux.com

MAP 9
Tastings during normal hours. Not Sundays.

A well-known quality Limoux house which makes multi-medalled wines, mostly from their own vines but partly too from carefully selected local growers. Of the four Blanquettes, three are dry and one is half-dry. All are made from 90% mauzac, with just a little chardonnay and chenin. In no perceptible order of quality, there is the 'Tradition', the 'Brut Nature' and the 'Réserve Brut' (all B). The off-dry version is sold as 'Tradition' (B). There are three white Crémants and a rosé (all B), none of which has more than 10% mauzac, the rest of the encépagement being made up of varying proportions of chardonnay (dominant) and chenin. The rosé, called 'Emotion' (B), has a touch of pinot noir. The sparkling wines are notable for their very persistent mousse. Of the still whites (all B), 'Héritage' is from the oldest family vines, 'Eugénie' is named after Eugénie Limouzy, a celebrated ancestor of the Antechs, and 'Grande Cuvée' shows a greater percentage of chenin than the others. The *méthode ancestrale* (A/B) is especially fine, showing a mere seven percent of alcohol and a bouquet of pears and caramelised apples. There is also an IGP chardonnay (A/B) varietal for fish-lovers. Françoise is a member of Vinifilles (q.v.).

***LA CAVE DU SIEUR D'ARQUES
La Grande Cave, Avenue du Mauzac, 11300 Limoux. Also a shop on the Avenue de Carcassonne at Limoux
Tel 04 68 74 63 10
contact@sieurdarques.com   www.sieurdarques.com

MAP 10
Tastings during normal hours.

An excellent and powerful *coopérative*, whose brand name is 'Aimery', and whose members cover 2,800 hectares in Limoux. Quality control is of the strictest. Covering such a wide area and such a diverse range of climates and terroirs, the makers distinguish between four styles: the Mediterranean influence to the east; the more temperate climate to the west due to Atlantic influences ('Terroir Océanique'); a more generalised style round the town of Limoux itself ('Terroir d'Autan'); and a cooler climate to the south due to the nearby presence of the Pyrenees ('Terroir Haute-Vallée'). The first red Limoux is called 'Les Bénédictins' (B) and shows good merlot character. 'Roi de Mari' is rather more interesting. Among the *blanquettes*, 'Diaphane' (B) makes a good start, and there is a big range, but most interest centres on the

'Toques et Clochers' (B) range, presenting still chardonnays from each of the four *terroirs*. You can buy a *coffret* containing one of each, as well as a Crémant (C), which is a blend of all four. There is also a range of still chardonnays from individual producers (C upwards). A cheaper proposition is the pair of wines (red and white) called 'Terroir de Vigne et de Truffe' (A/B). There are often special offers and discounts on quantity purchases. No *méthode ancestrale* unfortunately. The wines from here are available internationally on a wide scale, but are not the cheapest from the region.

**ANNE DE JOYEUSE   Directur Eric Soulard
41 Avenue Charles de Gaulle, 11303 Limoux
Tel   04 68 74 79 40
commercial.france@cave-adj.com

MAP 11
Sales outlets at 34 Promenade de Tivoli in Limoux, at St Hilaire and Montazels. All open Monday to Saturday usual hours.

This *coopérative* is smaller than Sieur D'Arques, but complementary to them because here they make no sparkling wine – only still. As an extension of its 'Protect Planet' policy, it has a range from organic members called 'Camas' (all A) – blends from chardonnay and sauvignon, cabernet and merlot, pinot noir and malbec, as well as a rosé. Apart from these there is a range of oak-aged wines. There are red blends, including 'La Butiniere', 'Coquelicot' and 'Bovin', a pure chardonnay called 'Terroir des Dinosaures', a mono-cépage malbec and finally a light low-alcohol quaffer, 'Social Club'. These are all (A), knocking on (B) in price. Sales are mostly to cavistes, restaurants and wholesalers.

B ***DOMAINE LA MARTINE LOUISON
Monique and Michel Louison
11300 Castelreng
Tel   04 68 31 07 06
Mobile   06 12 24 47 75
louison.lamartine@nordnet.fr
www.louison-domainelamartine.com

MAP 16
Appointment strongly recommended.

Louison, while building his career in Faugères at Les Estanilles, purchased seven and a half hectares of vines in the remote west of Limoux, almost on the frontiers with Ariège. This was virgin territory which he cleared of all plantation and started to plant himself in 1998, following fully organic practice. The vines are in one piece around the domaine; chardonnay and viognier for the white wine, cabernet franc for the rosé and merlot, syrah and cabernet franc (with just a touch of malbec) for the red AOP Limoux. The house style could not be more different from the wines which Louison

made at Faugères. Here, the height of the vineyards (almost 500 metres above sea level) and the much cooler climate provide lighter, more elegant wines, which are all of really fine quality, and remain just within the (B) price category.

***DOMAINE MOUSCAILLO
Marie-Claire and Pierre Fort
6, Rue du Frêne, 11300 Roquetaillade
Tel   04 68 31 38 25
mouscaillo@orange.fr   www.mouscaillo.com

MAP 19
Rendezvous strongly advised.

A tiny five-hectare domaine facing north, 400 metres above sea level, where the owners are able to do all the work themselves. This enables them to pick by hand and to reject on the plant any damaged bunches. Pierre spent ten years at the Château de Tracy at Pouilly-sur-Loire, so he has a natural preference for wines that have a good mineral character. He declines the chance of being officially bio because his approach is more pragmatic, and if it comes to using chemicals to preserve his vines from destruction... Nevertheless, he has many attributes of an organic producer and the wines have many of the characteristics of so-called 'natural' wines. He and Marie Claire make just three (all C): a still white Limoux from chardonnay, barrel-fermented and aged, but managing not to mask the natural flavours of the wine because the majority of the casks are old; a Crémant, for which the grapes are similarly vinified and aged; and a red IGP from pinot noir, made in tank but aged in large demi-muids of 600 litres from two to four years old. This domaine may be small, but it is hard to beat in the region.

** DOMAINE BORDELONGUE (DOMAINE DENOIS)   Jean-Louis Denois
11300 Roquetaillade
Tel   04 68 31 39 12
jldenois@orange.fr   www.jldenois.com

MAP 20
No visits or sales at *domaine*, but wines on sale 7/7 at Vina et Terra, 7 Avenue Lauragais, 11300 Limoux.

Jean-Louis Denois was once the enfant terrible of Limoux, bringing with him from South Africa, where he worked for some while, a breath of freshness. He had the audacity to try experimenting with gewurtztraminer and riesling grapes, to the fury of the Alsace wine people who claimed and failed to gain monopoly over them. Subsequently he explored the Limoux repertoire, including the introduction of pinot noir, before reducing drastically the size of his vineyard high in the hills at Roquetaillade, and then diversifying into buying in grapes from elsewhere, including carignan from further east in Corbières. You may have the opportunity to taste

Marie-Claire Fort, Domaine Mouscaillo

all or any of the fruits of these endeavours. But meanwhile, his chardonnay wines from his own grapes are outstandingly good. There is a 'Tradition Brut Réserve chardonnay' (B), a 'Blanc de Blancs brut' (B/C) and a classy 'Crémant de Limoux' (B/C). Try also his Pinot Noir (B) and his 'Grande Cuvée Rouge' (B) from merlot and the two cabernets.

B ***LES HAUTES TERRES Gilles Azam
11300 Roquetaillade
Tel   04 68 94 16 56
les.hautes.terres@wanadoo.fr

MAP 21
Book an appointment ahead, but Gilles Azam is one of the most elusive growers you will (if you're lucky) meet. The cellars are just close to the château in the village.

Roquetaillade is at the back of beyond with fewer than 100 inhabitants, and everyone seems to be a winemaker. Gilles Azam started in 2000 with just one acre of chenin. Today his vines, not more than eight hectares in total, are grown on a number of different parcels, all 400 metres or more above sea level. Each parcel contributes a distinctive style

to Azam's wines. His range (all B) includes a still white and quite floral Limoux, called 'Louis', 80% chardonnay and 20% chenin, vinified in old barrels for 12 months with regular bâtonnage and topping up. Then there is a 'Crémant' (60% chardonnay, 30% chenin and 10% mauzac) which is given no dosage of sugar after recorking and is as near to a quality champagne as dammit, long on the palate and with a lasting *mousse*. There is also a red Limoux called 'Maxime', a blend of 50% malbec, 20% merlot and 30% cabernet sauvignon, aged 12 months in old oak. Finally there is a varietal chenin IGP, made in rather the same way as his still Limoux. These wines are regarded widely as the best in the region and, despite that, are keenly priced.

B ***DOMAINE DELMAS
Bernard et Marlène Delmas
10 Route Couiza, 11190 Antugnac
Tel   04 68 74 21 02
Mobile 06 78 65 45 36
domainedelmas@orange.fr   www.blanquette-delmas-bio.com

MAP 22
Visits Monday to Friday at usual hours, at weekends by appointment.

Roquetaillade

Production has been organic here since 1986. With a production of 160,000 bottles a year, and with 31 hectares of vines, the Delmas are very important players in Limoux. The vineyards at Antugnac are remotely situated up in the hills in the middle of a very beautiful landscape. Their mainstream Blanquette is a regular prize-winner, rather understated and delicate with gentle and long-lasting bubbles, well balanced and with a long finish. The *méthode ancestrale* is also fresh and fruity, while there are two Crémants, one (Cuvée 'Passion') with some oak-ageing in old wood, the other in tank (Cuvée 'Audace'). The still white Limoux is all-chardonnay. 80% of the production is exported, mostly to Western Europe, Russia, Canada and California. The wines are all (B).

OTHER GOOD GROWERS AT LIMOUX

BD ** DOMAINE SAINTE-MARIE
DES PINS   Marie and Henri Gayzard
11250 Verzeille
Tel   04 68 69 48 24
Mobile 06 34 54 06 01
domainesaintemarie2@wanadoo.fr
www.domaine-sainte-mairie.com
MAP 1
Visits (appointment recommended) every day during April-September, 10.00-12.30 and 14.00-19.00. From October to March, Tuesday to Saturday afternoons 16.00-19.00.

B *** DOMAINE CATHARE   Franck Schisano
Avenue du Béal, 11250 Saint-Hilaire
Tel   04 68 20 08 78
Mobile 06 10 63 41 46
www.cathare.tm.fr

MAP 3
Telephone for appointment.

*DOMAINE DE TREILLE Pascal Eyt

11250 Gardie
Tel   04 68 31 89 54   (régisseur Didier Baldo Tel   04 68 31 23 94)
pascal.eyt-dessus@wanadoo.fr   www.domainedetreille.com
MAP 4
Appointment is safer than pot luck.

*DOMAINE DE BARON'ARQUES

Héritiers de Philippine de Rothschild
11300 Saint-Polycarpe
Tel   04 68 31 96 60
cfoucachon@domainedebaronarques.com
MAP 5
Appointment advisable.
The wines are, as might be expected, good, but the predominance of red grapes, and the total absence of a sparkling wine in any style hardly make this a typical Limoux property.

**MAISON GUINOT   Michel Guinot

Chemin de Ronde, 11300 Limoux
Tel   04 68 31 01 33
guinot@blanquette.fr   www.blanquette.fr
MAP 12
Tastings and visits to cellars Monday to Friday usual business hours and Saturday mornings.

* DOMAINE ASTRUC   Jean Claude Mas

20 Avenue du Chardonnay,11300 Malras
Tel   04 67 90 16 10
MAP 13
Ring during normal hours.

*DOMAINE FAURE   Denis and Manuela Faure

1 Avenue de la Liberté , Cougaing, 11300 La Digne d'Aval
Tel   04 68 31 72 66
vigneron@domainefaure.com   www.domainefaure.com
MAP 14
Rendezvous required, except perhaps during summer. Closed Sundays.

***DOMAINE J. LAURENS   Jacques Calvel

Les Graimenous, 11300 La Digne d'Aval
Tel   04 68 31 54 54
domaine.jlaurens@wanadoo.fr   www.jlaurens.com
MAP 15
This producer is nowhere near a main road, so phone ahead for visits. The complete range of Limoux sparklers includes a notable *méthode ancestrale* wine barely reaching six degrees of alcohol.

B**DOMAINE LE MOULIN D'ALON

Alain Cavaillès
Avenue d'Alon, 11300 Magrie
Tel   04 68 31 11 01
Mobile 06 86 86 20 06
GPS 43 1 34 N   2 11 55 E
cavaille.alain@wanadoo.fr   www.alaincavailles.com
MAP 17
Visits all day every Thursday. Otherwise by appointment.

**DOMAINE COLLIN

Philippe and Marie-Hélène Collin
Route de Magrie, 11300 Toureilles
Tel   04 68 31 35 49
philippe-collin2@wanadoo.fr
MAP 18
Rendezvous advisable.

B**CHATEAU D'ANTUGNAC David Serrodes

11190 Antugnac
Tel   04 68 74 04 81
chateau.antugnac@club-internet.com
MAP 23
Cellars open Monday to Saturday, usual hours.
A strong Burgundian influence here, the property having been acquired by two winemakers from that district in 1997. With over 90 hectares, this is the largest independent producer in the region.

Malepère

Malepère is the name given to a hilly *massif* just north of Limoux and south-west of Carcassonne. Locals claim a long history of winemaking, but it was not until the 1970s that vineyards were replanted and the grant of VDQS status rewarded the efforts put into the improvements. The vines circle the base of the *massif*, starting at the limits of Limoux, going northwest towards the Abbey of Fanjeaux, before switching eastwards again towards Bram and the Canal du Midi.

Because the vines are not grown on the woody *massif* itself, the vineyards seem more extensive than they in fact are. There are fewer than 500 hectares of vineyard all told, three *coopératives* and 18 independent growers, of whom not all bottle their own wines. The rest sell either to one of the *coopératives* or to a *négociant*. The statistics also disguise the large amount of IGPs produced alongside the AOP wines; one of the *coopératives* claims improbably to be the largest in France, and one of the top five in the world.

The Languedoc grapes here are less important than elsewhere, as carignan doesn't seem to ripen in this cooler climate. In addition to cinsault and grenache, there is a fair amount of cot, the two cabernets and a predominance of merlot. Fermentation is traditional, and rarely – if ever – by *macération carbonique*. The tendency is to emulate the wines from the South-West rather than Languedoc, and the region is still searching for a real *typicité*. This is very much a crossover *appellation*. Supple textures are balanced by some power, the aromas of fresh fruits by spices and sometimes a hint of natural (not oak-induced) vanilla.

This sequence of growers starts close to Carcassonne and ends up near Limoux.

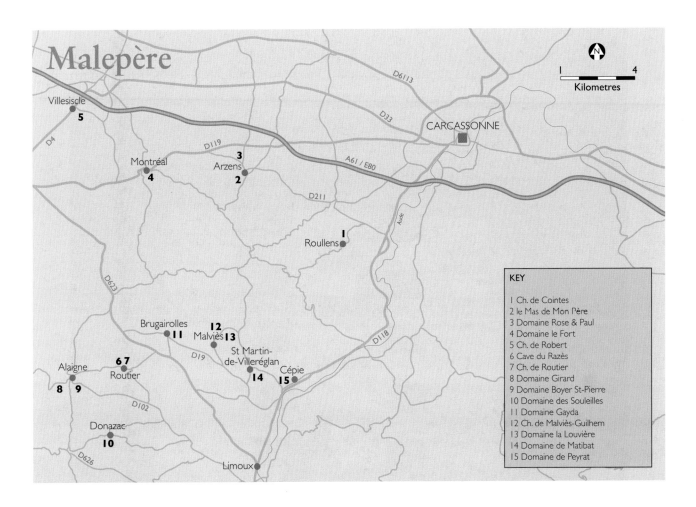

CHÂTEAU DE COINTES   Anne Gorostis

11290 Lavalette   Roullens
Tel   04 68 26 81 05
infos@chateaudecointes.com   www.chateaudecointes.com

MAP 1
The cellars are open every day from 9.00-12.00.
Otherwise appointment is strongly recommended.

One of the best Malepère estates. Nowadays, there are 21 hectares of AOP vines, of which two-thirds have been reconstituted by the present owners to meet the AOP rules. All 12 of the hectares devoted to IGP production have been replanted. The family is Basque, and Anne's grandfather grew despised aramon grapes which he 'cut' with Algerian wine. He was a *négociant*. His son started the replanting and gradual improvement of the estate which Anne and her husband have continued. The IGP wines are sold as Domaine des Consuls – a previous owner was one of Carcassonne's consuls. For the AOP wines, the Bordeaux varieties are complemented by grenache and cinsault (no syrah), but syrah is the feature of their better IGP (B), which is given 14 months *élevage* in oak. More modest merlot and cabernet varietals (A) are good partners with lightly cooked food. The 'Tradition' AOP (A), also available in magnum, comes nearly all from Bordeaux grapes, except for just 10% grenache. This spicy wine is raised in tank. 'Cuvée Croix du Languedoc Marie-Anne' (B) is similarly made but from selected parcels of old vines. The top wine is Croix du Languedoc Cuvée Clémence' (B/C), aged in a mix of old and new barrels. Half of the production is sold to local wine shops, the rest mainly exported to the north of Europe and Asia.

B ***LE MAS DE MON PÈRE

Frédéric Palacios
Chemin le Roudel, 11290 Arzens.

Tel   04 68 76 23 07
Mobile   06 83 48 12 73
lemasdemonpere@yahoo.fr
www.lemasdemonpere.chez-alice.fr

MAP 2
Appointment advisable.

Frédéric describes himself as an artisan-*vigneron* who offers unique wines in limited quantity for a clientele of connoisseurs who do not want a standardised product, but wines which possess a real personality and a strong identity with their maker. This is a boutique vineyard (B) where the grapes are all hand-picked, vinified *cépage* by *cépage* in small steel

Frédéric Palacios, Le Mas de mon Père

tanks, which enables the *chapeau* to be broken up by hand so as to avoid crushing the pips and thereby releasing green tannins. The resulting wines are complex and have a real originality. Frédéric is liable to produce new *cuvées* each year as he gets to know and understand his *terroir*, so the wines currently available may well change. The latest range included: 'Brin de Folie' (A/B), a blend mostly of grenache and cinsault: 'Comme je Suis' (B), all merlot; 'Comme Ça' (B), all carignan and needing time to soften; 'L'Insolite' (C), a pure Malbec; 'Cause Toujours' (C), another grenache/cinsault blend; and 'Quitte ou Double' (C). Frédéric also makes a delicious white from chardonnay and listan (B). For many he is the most interesting of all the Malepère growers.

**DOMAINE GIRARD Philippe Girard
Chemin de la Garriguette, 11240 Alaigne
Tel   04 68 59 05 27
domaine-girard@wanadoo.fr

MAP 8
Appointment recommended.

A top fifth-generation producer in Malepère who makes and bottles a third of the wine himself, the rest being sold *en négoce* or to *cavistes*. His IGPs include two chardonnays – one oaked, the other not – both from grapes grown at relatively high altitude. Good acidity balances the fruit, giving the latter a real sense of minerals. Similarly, his pure pinot noir avoids the kind of plummy excess so common with this grape in the South; with a light cherry and rose bouquet, and red fruits on the palate, it can be drunk chilled. The AOP reds include a blackcurranty-ripe 'Tradition' from merlot and cabernet franc, and the top 'Cuvée Néri' from the same grapes, raised in oak, yielding complex wine which needs keeping. This is the only (B) wine of the property; the rest are all (A) and wonderful value for money.

**DOMAINE GAYDA
Anthony Record, Tim Ford and Marc Kent
Chemin de Moscou, 11300 Brugairolles
Tel   04 68 31 64 14
info@gaydavineyards.com   www.domainegayda.com

MAP 11
Shop open Monday-Friday, 10.00-17.00. Tour of the *cave* by appointment with veronica@domainedugayda.com.

An extraordinary complex, combining winemaking, wine-education and a restaurant, created by this Anglo-South African consortium, not with Malepère particularly in mind, though they have 11 hectares of vines around the *domaine*. They buy in grapes from growers in the Roussillon, la Livinière in the Minervois, and from the Fontfroide area of Corbières. Their marketing takes in the USA and Hong Kong, as well as the UK and Ireland. The result is a range of hugely differing styles and appeal. There are varietal whites, for example from sauvignon, viognier and maccabeu, a pure red syrah, a blend of the two cabernets, and another from grenache/syrah. The wines are technically well-made and good value (virtually all A/B), though any sense of *terroir* is not what you will find. Still, an excellent day out. Avoid Mondays and Tuesdays when the much-praised restaurant is closed, but it is open at lunchtime and evenings on other days.

**CHÂTEAU DE MALVIÈS-GUILHEM
Béatrice Gourdou   Contact M. Bertrand Gourdou
11300 Malviès,
Tel   04 68 31 14 41
Mobile   06 83 88 98 23
contact@chateauguilhem.com   www.chateauguilhem.com

MAP 12
Visits on weekdays from 8.00-12.00 and 14.00-18.00.

This property has been in the Guilhem family for generations, Bertrand having taken over from his mother in 2004. Built on the site of an old Roman settlement (bits and pieces of which turn up in the soil regularly), it has 32 hectares of vines, all (except a little syrah) given over to the Bordeaux grape varieties (including malbec). Bertrand also grows white grapes which do not qualify for AOP, and the wines from them (all A) are thus sold outside the *appellation*. A range of white varietals includes a bone-dry sauvignon, a chardonnay of which 1/3rd is oak-aged, a viognier partly aged in old *foudres*, and a *moëlleux* muscat. A cabernet rosé is pale salmon pink in colour and has a surprisingly fruity power. The red IGPs include a merlot/syrah blend, some of which is given a light touch of wood for four months, and a tank-raised cabernet sauvignon. There are four AOP reds. In ascending order of ambition and price: the 'Tradition' (A), which goes well with charcuterie and lighter meats, is a quaffable merlot-cabernet blend; 'Cuvée Prestige' (B), which is raised in a mix of old and new barrels; the 'Grande Cuvée' (B), from hand-picked grapes grown in the best parcels of merlot and cabernet sauvignon and aged half in new and half in old barrels for a year; finally 'Le Clos du Blason' (C/D), 80% merlot and 20% cabernet sauvignon, given a whole year in new wood. Bertrand has clearly set out to give this already high-quality property a vinous face-lift, but this has not prevented him from perpetuating an extraordinary wine that was his mother's pride: a *vendanges tardives* sauvignon (B), vinified in December and finishing with 100 grams of residual sugar after a year in barrel (the barrel is Bertrand's contribution to this unusual wine).

Cave at Arzens

OTHER GOOD MALEPÈRE GROWERS

**DOMAINE ROSE & PAUL Gilles Foussat
Chemin de la Malepère, 11270 Arzens
Tel   04 68 76 33 96
Mobile   06 03 92 91 11
domaine@rose-paul.fr   www.rose-paul.fr
MAP 3
Visits any day between 17.30-19.00 or by appointment

*DOMAINE LE FORT Stéphanie & Marc Pagès
Domaine Le Fort, 11290 Montréal
Tel   04 68 76 20 11
info@domainelefort.com   www.domainelefort.com
MAP 4
Visits Monday to Saturday (except Wednesday afternoon outside the holiday season). Closed Sundays and *jours fériés*.

*CHÂTEAU DE ROBERT
Lucie and Marie-Hélène Artigouha-Hérail
11150 Villesiscle
Tel   04 68 76 11 86
l.artigouha@wanadoo.fr
MAP 5
Visits in summer every day from 8.00-12.00 and 13.00-20.00. Otherwise 8.00-12.00 and 14.00-18.00.

*CAVE DU RAZÈS
Route Départementale 623, 11240 Routier,
Tél 04 68 69 39 15
caveau@caverazes.com   www.cavedurazes.com
MAP 6
Open mornings and afternoons, Monday to Saturday.
This *Cave Coopérative* is said to be one of the largest in Europe, and so a big player in this compact AOP.

*CHÂTEAU DE ROUTIER   Michèle Lézérat
11240 Routier
Tel   04 68 69 06 13
info@vins-malepere.com
MAP 7
Visits May to September inc., 9.00-20.00. Otherwise 10.00-12.00 and 13.00-20.00.

**DOMAINE BOYER ST PIERRE
Jean Paul Boyer
11240 Alaigne
Tel 04 68 69 01 87
Jpaul.boyer@wanadoo.fr
www.boyer-st-pierre.vins-malepere.com
MAP 9
Appointment advisable. Highly regarded among Malepère estates.

**DOMAINE DES SOULEILLES Sophie Delaude
Pech-Salamou, 11240 Donazac
Tel   04 68 69 53 29
Mobile   06 12 93 69 21
d.souleilles@orange.fr   www.souleilles.com
MAP 10
Visits best by appointment, but pot luck may succeed. Occasional cultural events are accompanied by tastings.

B **DOMAINE LA LOUVIÈRE
Nicolas Grohe/ Thore Könnecke
La Louvière, 11300 Malviès
Tel   04 68 20 71 55
domainelalouviere@wanadoo.fr
www.domaine-la-louviere.com
MAP 13
A shot in the arm here from the arrival of ambitious Australian Jem Harris (ex-Les Fusionels at Faugères q.v.)

*DOMAINE DE MATIBAT
Henri and Jean-Claude Turetti
11300 Saint Martin de Villeréglan
Tel 04 68 31 15 52
domainedematibat@orange.fr   www.domaine-de-matibat.com
MAP 14
Avoiding lunch time, visits possible from Monday to Friday and also Saturday mornings. Honest good-value stuff.

*DOMAINE DE PEYRET (GAEC)
Geneviève and Pierre Andrieu with Thierry Gauché
11300 Cépie
Tel   04 68 31 72 10
domaine.peyret@wanadoo.fr   www.domaine-de-peyret.fr
MAP 15
Visits from 09.00 to 19.00 except Sunday afternoons.
The family is also proud of their Blanquette Ancestrale, authentically 100% mauzac, and attaining only six degrees of alcohol: sweet and recommended on patisseries. There are also the more familiar styles of Blanquette by the same method as champagne, and a Crémant – all exceptional value (B).

CABARDÈS

Like Malepère, this is a crossover vineyard, facing both Languedoc to the east and the Atlantic vineyards to the west. It too is characterised by a mix of Midi grape varieties and those from Bordeaux and Gascony. The latter must represent 40% of a grower's AOP plantation and wines must be a blend of the grapes from both regions.

The vineyards are to the north and north-west of Carcassonne, going up towards the Black Mountain. As well as five *coopératives*, there are 21 independent growers, and 450 hectares are under vine. The annual production is about 20,000 hectolitres. The *Appellation*, one of the more recent in Languedoc (1999), covers red and rosé wines, the latter representing a small but increasingly important proportion. All whites here are made as IGPs. Some growers overlap into the vineyards of Minervois which lie just to the east, and are detailed in that section.

Starting from Carcassonne, the Cabardès growers are described as they go north from the city and then west and south again in a roughly circular sequence.

VIGNOBLES LORGERIL – CHÂTEAU PENNAUTIER Nicolas et Miren de Lorgeril

BP4 11610, Pennautier
contact@lorgeril.com   www.vignobles-lorgeril.com
Tel 04 68 72 65 29
GPS 43.244304 2.317294

MAP 1
Open 10.00-18.00 (July and August until 23.00) Closed Sunday and (except in July and August) Friday and Saturday evenings.

The château, which has been described as a Languedoc version of Versailles, dates back to the days of the construction of the Canal du Midi, with which the ancestors of the present owners were well connected. The taxes raised to pay for the canal were in a small part no doubt creamed off by the King's Lorgeril tax-gatherers to finance the construction of the château. Today this is the best-known and most commercially orientated of all the Cabardès properties, with interests in other vineyards locally (Chx de Caunettes, de Garille and La Bastide Rouge Peyre), as well as properties in Faugères, Minervois, and Roussillon (Mas des Montagnes where the red is easy and good value). There is a wine bar and restaurant on the spot, and they run gîtes too. The wines are readily available in the UK and the US among other countries, and are well-made, particularly in the upper ranges, although the size of the enterprise can hardly merit the description of terroir-driven. For export markets, wine is often sold simply under the name of the château, but in fact there are four different ranges. 'Collection Fruitée' (A), is a range which includes varietals from chardonnay, viognier, syrah and merlot as well as AOP Cabardès. As the name implies, these wines are easy, simple and drinkable either as an aperitif or with light meals or picnics. 'Collection Gourmande' (A) adds muscat and pinot noir to the list of varietals as well as a number of two-wine blends; a range which is a bit fuller than the 'Fruitée. 'Collection d'Altitude' (A/B), as the name implies, comes from the best terroirs on the higher ground of the estate and comprises wines with more finesse and bottle age. Finally, the top 'Collection Grands Vins' (B/C) is more ambitious and for special occasions.

CHÂTEAU LA BASTIDE ROUGE PEYRE

Dominique de Lorgeril Régisseur: Jacques de Lépinau
11610 Pennautier
Tél 04 68 72 51 91
GPS 43.273638 2.327449
chateaudelabastide@wanadoo.fr   www.rougepeyre.com

MAP 2
Appointment recommended but not essential.

Once a fortified farm and a refuge for the Cathars, this property (in the same ownership as Château de Pennautier, see above) has a wine history going back several generations. Their rosé (A) is quite a big wine with a wild red fruit

Ventaillole label

character, and is best with food (Asian cuisine, stuffed aubergines etc.). The red 'Tradition' (A) is unoaked but aged for two years in tank, generous, with good fruit and some spiciness. 40% of the 'Prestige' (B) is raised in oak, and it is recommended by the growers to accompany a cassoulet: it will keep and decanting is advisable. 'L'Esprit' (B) is made only in the best years, and is given 30 days' maceration and 18 months in new oak. There is also a range of IGPs, unoaked and raised in tank for eight months from chardonnay, merlot, syrah and malbec.

B **CHÂTEAU DE BRAU** Wenny et Gabriel Tari

11620 Villemoustaussou
Tel 04 68 72 31 92
Mobile 06 64 31 48 65
GPS 43.257784 2.377081
chateaudebrau@aliceadsl.fr   chateaudebrau.wixsite.com

MAP 7
Appointment preferred.

Château Pennautier

This property has been fully organic for over 20 years, having originally been planted by Gabriel's father. Gabriel was planning to be a lawyer but, as so often, the lure of the family vineyard proved irresistible. Gabriel works alongside his wife Wenny, a qualified architect. They produce from 40 hectares a large range of wines, some using unorthodox grapes, including their pink 'Domaine de Brau ZE' and a red IGP 'Cité de Carcassonne' (both containing some egiodola*, from which there is a varietal IGP de l'Aude), varietals from petit verdot and pinot noir as well as more conventional Cabardès grapes. All (A) so far. There is a fine pure oaked chardonnay (B), and an unoaked blend of that grape with roussanne. The three AOP Cabardès reds are called 'Cuvée Chateau' (A), half Atlantic, half Mediterranean grapes. The 'Cuvée Exquise' (B) is from the same grapes and raised in old barrels, and the top 'Suc de Brau' (C) is a chunky wine from syrah and cabernet sauvignon only, one third of which is given new barrels.

*Egiodola is a cross between fer servadou and abouriou, both being grape-varieties particular to SW France. It is also the basque word for "pure blood."

O'VINEYARDS Joe, Liz and Ryan O'Connell
885 Avenue de la Montagne Noire, 11620 Villemoustassou
Mobiles 06 30 18 99 10 or 06 88 91 60 56
GPS 43.259622 2.340387
ovineyards@gmail.com   www.ovineyards.com

MAP 8
Said to be ever open, but prior phone call may be wise.

Purists may turn up their noses at the style of this 17-hectare property, run on modern New World lines since 2005 by this team of iconoclasts. But the public seem to love it all, and certainly the owners can teach their neighbours something about marketing. The prices are mostly (C), (B) if you're lucky. 'O'Syrah (100% rich, spicy and peppery, and very Californian) is a good example. 'Trah Lah Lah' is a merlot/cabernet blend in the Bordelais manner (with New World overtones), good fruit, crisp and with medium weight body, but not cheap. 'Les Américains' is dense with big chunky tannins, and manages to combine richness with some austerity. 'Proprietor's Reserve' is distinctly Californian in style, rich, with perfumes of spice and dried fruits. 'Mediterranean Mojo' has plenty of upfront fruit with good acidity, perhaps because the blend is Atlantic-orientated. Liz O'Connell is also a fine cook and runs cookery classes, while Ryan is the author of a small but useful book on the wines of Cabardès and Carcassonne.

B ✳✳✳DOMAINE DE CAZABAN

Clément et Claire Mengus
11600 Villegailhenc
Tel 04 68 72 11 63
Mobile   06 58 06 22 74
GPS 43.285485 2.353714
clement.mengus@orange.fr   www.domainedecazaban.com

MAP 5
Prior appointment recommended.

Young newcomers started this promising and adventurous domaine with only four hectares of syrah and merlot, which they are extending to grow other grapes. They have land further east at Limousis, where they are growing grenache blanc and gris soon to come on stream. They must have spent all their savings and more besides on the spanking cellars and tasting room. They already make a white 'Coup de Foudre' (B), which manages to combine zing with *gras*. A cinsault/grenache rosé (A) makes a good start to a visit here. 'Jours de vigne' (A) is a tank-raised blend and makes a fine introduction to the range of reds. A merlot/syrah mix called 'Les petites Rangées' (B), after four weeks *cuvaison*, is given nine months in Burgundian barrels. The wine is intensely fragrant with aromas from the garrigue, fennel and eucalyptus. 'Demoiselle Claire' (B) is another syrah/merlot blend, of which most is raised in tank and made without any additives, except a tiny amount of sulphur at the moment of bottling. Domaine de Cazaban' (C/D), from the same grapes, is vinified and aged in barrels, some new, others one year old.

B ✳✳PRIEURE DU FONT JUVENAL

Georges et Colette Casadesus
11600 Conques sur Orbiel

Clément Mengus, Domaine de Cabazan

Tel   04 68 79 15 55
GPS   43.297854 2.342534
scea.cgaf@orange.fr   www.font-juvenal.com

MAP 12
Appointment strongly recommended.

As well as being in the business of plant-nurserymen, the owners are often busy at wine-salons. They have 15 hectares of vines, surrounded by garrigue, which affords an interesting eco-system. The vineyards are in a hollow of the slopes of the Black Mountain, near the village of Aragon. The red wine grapes are given a cuvaison of 25-30 days, with regular pigeage. There is a speciality sweet wine called '?' (C), for which muscat and viognier grapes are picked young and then stored on trays under glass or plastic to protect them from moisture. After careful selection, the grapes are then barrel-fermented for eight months, drawn off their lees and put back into wood for a further year. More conventional dry wines (B) are made from the same grapes, sometimes with chenin and chardonnay added. The red wines (from merlot, cabernet and grenache) start with 'Jeanne' (A), a *vin de soif,* followed by 'Fontaine de Jouvence' (B), which has a bit of malbec added, then 'L'Asphodèle' (B), which is matured for 18 months in tank and is rather more serious. The top wine is called 'Le Sauvage' (C) and is in the modern style, raised a year in oak before a further month's maturing in tank.

***DOMAINE CABROL   Claude Carayol
11600 Aragon
Tel   04 68 77 19 06
Mobile   06 81 14 00 26
GPS 43.3103630 2.3308321
cc@domainedecabrol.fr   www.domainedecabrol.fr

MAP 13
Visits Mon-Sat 11.00-12.00 and 15.00-19.00 (but only from 17.00 out of season). Sunday by appointment.

The postal address may be Aragon, but this domaine is some way away from the village, just about the last on the main road to Mazamet before the Black Mountain takes over the landscape. The estate is large: it runs to 125 hectares, but the vines occupy only 21, the remainder being given over to garrigue, woodland, olive and almond trees. Two easy-drinking reds are called respectively 'Requieu' (from young vines and for enjoyment on its fruit) and 'Blue Note' (often to be found locally in wine bars), both (A). The two best-known wines, both (B), are 'Vent d'Ouest' (featuring largely the Atlantic cabernet sauvignon) and the 'Vent d'Est' (the mediterranean syrah and grenache). All those wines are denied barrels, but there is a top wine called 'La Dérive' (C), which is raised for two years in large 600-litre casks which avoids an excessive oaky flavour. The range is completed by a viognier/grenache blanc (B), also given some time in wood, and a directly-pressed rosé (A) from cabernet and grenache which sells out instantly. A little carignan and the

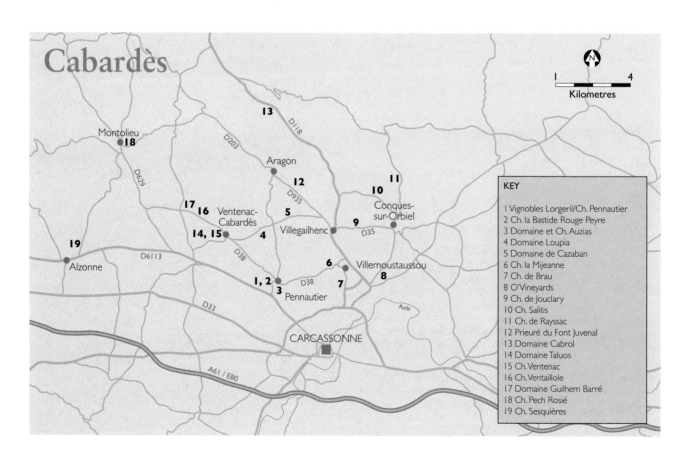

Cabardès

Kilometres

KEY
1 Vignobles Lorgeril/Ch. Pennautier
2 Ch. la Bastide Rouge Peyre
3 Domaine et Ch. Auzias
4 Domaine Loupia
5 Domaine de Cazaban
6 Ch. la Mijeanne
7 Ch. de Brau
8 O'Vineyards
9 Ch. de Jouclary
10 Ch. Salitis
11 Ch. de Rayssac
12 Prieuré du Font Juvenal
13 Domaine Cabrol
14 Domaine Taluos
15 Ch. Ventenac
16 Ch. Ventaillole
17 Domaine Guilhem Barré
18 Ch. Pech Rosié
19 Ch. Sesquières

despised aramon go into their bargain Bag-in-Box red along with the other red wine grapes, by no means to be scorned. These wines are often considered to be among the finest of all Cabardès.

**DOMAINE TALUOS   Eric Soular
6 bis Avenue de la Viale, 11610 Ventenac-Cabardès
Tel   06 86 49 84 32
domaine.taluos@gmail.com

MAP 14
Appointment essential.

This newcomer has only 2.8 hectares of vines, but the attention given them is worthy of the best Bordeaux. Picking is done by hand and the grapes are carried to the *chais* in small *cagettes* weighing not more than 10 kilos. Soular has been winning medals with his rosé, 60% grenache, 20% cabernet sauvignon and 20% cinsault, noted for its freshness and the flavour of summer fruits. It is (A) too, compared with the red AOP which is well into (C) but worth every euro. Because the property is so small, the wines are hard to get hold of; the French call them "*confidentiels.*" Quite clearly a grower to watch.

B **CHÂTEAU VENTAILLOLE
Robert and Marie-Claude Curbières
11610 Ventenac-Cabardes
Tel   04 68 24 92 74
Mobile 06 81 00 72 93
GPS 43.280147 2.293728

Map 16
curbieres.bio@gmail.com   www.domaine-ventaillole.fr

Robert, though on the point of retirement before handing over to his daughter, is determined to find out who was guilty and why of setting fire to his chais in November 2013, destroying all his barrels and almost all his recent vintage. He is the local representative of the *Confédération Paysanne*, which give him a platform to fight tirelessly against the use of pesticides and chemical fertilisers. Was the arsonist perhaps someone bent on stopping his propoganda? In 2014 and 2015, while restoring his buildings, he sold his grapes off to dealers, resuming his own production in 2016. He still has a few bottles of the wine he managed to rescue from the fire which he calls 'L'Inattendue'. 'Huppe' is the name he gives to the modern version, based on cabernet franc, grenache and fer servadou, a grape grown to please his aveyronnais wife and from which he makes a varietal low-alcohol wine. He rounds off his range with a sweet wine from chardonnay. He hopes to resume his practice of using special labels printed on a paper made at a nearby mill from the *rafle* of his grapes. His courage fully entitles him to the support and encouragement he has received from his local colleagues. All the wines are A/B and tremendous value.

**CHÂTEAU VENTENAC SARL
Les Vignobles A.Maurel
1 Place du Chateau, 11610 Ventenac-Cabardes
Tel   04 68 24 93 42
GPS 43.266238 2.282152
accueil@maisonventenac.fr   www.vignoblesalainmaurel.net

MAP 15
Avoid Sundays and public holidays.

This is a large and important estate making some of the best wines in the Cabardès, for which the makers do not hesitate to use the latest technology in the chais (oxidative and reductive methods for their chardonnay (A), which has a little gros manseng mixed in with it). Their chenin-colombard blend (B) is more than a nod in the direction of the Côtes de Gascogne, but with impressive and powerful notes of lemon and grapefruit. The pure syrah (A) is peppery but, largely because of the altitude of the vineyard, not hot or jammy, while the rosé (A) (from a cocktail of all their red grapes) they describe as "intense pleasure reduced to its purest simplicity." The AOP reds are headed by 'Réserve' (A) and 'Grande Réserve' (B), respecting the need to blend the Atlantic and Mediterranean grapes. Of the first of these, 10% is raised in new American wood, the remainder in tank. The second is wholly barrel-aged for 12 months before being put back to tank for a further 12 months. Finally, the de luxe wine of the property, 'Mas Cabardès' (C), comes from the finest of the parcels of vines and is aged for 12 months in various sizes of new French barrels, then given further time in bottle before being released.

OTHER GOOD GROWERS IN CABARDÈS

*DOMAINE ET CHÂTEAU AUZIAS
Nathalie and Dominique Auzias
Paretlongue, 11610 Pennautier
Tel   04 68 47 28 28
GPS 43.236293 2.332706
auzias@auzias.fr   www.auzias.fr
MAP 3
Visits without appointment Mon-Sat 9.00-17.30, otherwise by arrangement. Groups can have a pre-booked 45-minute tour and tasting.
The fact that the owners have offices in Paris and China, and a château also in China, says much for their achievement as well as their ambition.

Cabardès

Robert Curbières, Château de Ventaillole, p123

B *DOMAINE LOUPIA   Philippe et Nadine Pons
Les Albarels, 11610 Pennautier
Tel   04 68 24 91 77
GPS 43.264675 2.30155
domaineloupia@orange.fr   www.domaineloupia.com
MAP 4
Visits by appointment, Monday to Friday 11.00-12.30 and 18.00-19.30, Saturday mornings. Music-lovers may find they are able to hear piano recitals here.

*CHÂTEAU LA MIJEANNE   contact Sylvie Benzal,
Route de Villalier, 11620 Villemoustassou
Tel   04 68 33 32 22
Mobile   06 78 88 69 66
lamijeanne@gmail.com
MAP 6
Open every day from 9.00.

**CHÂTEAU DE JOUCLARY   Pascal Gianesini
11600 Conques sur Orbiel
Tel   04 68 77 10 02
Mobile   06 80 28 51 03
GPS 43.273086 2.370659
chateau.jouclary@orange.fr
www.chateaujouclary.over-blog.com
MAP 9
Cellars open Monday to Saturday 11.00-19.00

*CHÂTEAU PARAZOLS-BERTROU
Jean-Marie et Béatrice Bertrou
Domaine de Parazols, 11600 Bagnoles
Tel   04 68 77 06 46
vinsparazolsbertrou@orange.fr   www.domaine-parazols.com
see under Minervois
Appointment advisable.

*CHÂTEAU SALITIS
Anne Marandon-Maurel and Frédéric Maurel,
11600 Conques-sur- Orbiel
Tel   04 68 77 16 10
Mobile   06 32 39 06 49
GPS 43.284262 2.37381
salitis@orange.fr
MAP 10
Monday to Friday usual hours. Closed Saturdays. Appointment needed for Sundays.

*CHÂTEAU DE RAYSSAC   Marc Delsuc
11600 Conques sur Orbiel
Tel   09 62 05 87 42
GPS 43.286861 2.389878
chateau.rayssac@orange.fr   www.chateau-rayssac.com
MAP 11
Appointment advisable.

B **DOMAINE GUILHEM BARRÉ
Guilhem Barré
11610 Ventenac
Tel   06 32 38 72 55
guilhem.barre@voila.fr
www.domaineguilhembarre.over-blog.com
MAP 17
Visits by appointment.
Guilhem Barré arrived in Cabardès in 2008 where he acquired a mere five hectares. He had just finished a stage with Alain Brumont at Madiran.
Another property to watch.

* CHÂTEAU PECH ROSIÉ
Anne Capdevila-Séguier and Jean-Marc de Crozals
11700 Montolieu
Tel   04 68 78 10 51
jm.decrozals@free.com   www.domainnedeshoms.com
MAP 18
Appointment required.

*CHÂTEAU SESQUIERES   Gérard Lagoutte
Route de Montolieu, 11170 Alzonne
Tel   04 68 76 00 12
GPS 43.288642 2.188025
lagouttegerard@wanadoo.fr chateau-sesquieres.fr
MAP 19
Prior appointment suggested.

MINERVOIS
and St Jean de Minervois

Minerva was the Roman goddess of wisdom – an inspiration for the invading legions to bring their native vines from Italy and create vineyards in their new colony in the Midi. She continues to lend her name today to the wine-growing area called Minervois, an area north of the river Aude and between Carcassonne and Narbonne.

When the Romans left, the vineyards were cherished by the Church, which evangelised the region, taking the vines to the foot of the Black Mountain. The vines thrived, even as the zeal of the Church was also shamefully devoted to the suppression of the Cathar heresy. The town of Minerve was the scene of a particularly brutal massacre, and today the crumbling ruin of the rebel castle glows red in the spectacular sunsets of the region as a reminder of the bigotry and intolerance of the medieval Establishment.

The Minervois vineyard may be imagined as an amphitheatre on a vast scale: the Canal du Midi its southern boundary as the stage, Carcassonne and Narbonne as the wings, while the auditorium rises in terraces to the north. Rivers running off the Black Mountain are the stairways which connect the upper and lower levels, dividing the vineyard into a mosaic of varied *terroirs* and producing a patchwork of wine-styles. Sometimes the *terroir* is made up of seemingly polished pebbles, like those to be found in dried-up river beds, or of sandstone, chalk or even marble. This is a subtle landscape of gentle, rolling contours, though the arid vineyards in the north can reach a height of 450 metres above the sea.

There are variations in the climate too. The prevailing winds are the 'Marin', from the sea, humid and often the harbinger of rain. From the northwest, the 'Cers' is dry and cooler. Breezes coming off

Jean-Baptiste Senat, p.132

the Black Mountain help to determine the northern limits of viticulture, where only the most sheltered sites are cultivated in pockets of red soil nestling between the rocks or sometimes pure chalk. The *appellation* is cleanly divided into five climatic zones: the Cotes Noires in the far northwest, located on the coolest, most Atlantic-influenced foothills of the Montagne Noire; La Clamoux, on alluvial terraces and flatter land in the southwest towards Carcassonne; La Zone Centrale, in the middle of the *appellation*, at an altitude of around 1,200ft (400m); La Causse, on high land and poor, dry soils in the northeast, where yields are lowest; and Les Serres, in the warmest, most Mediterranean southeast.

Further inland, the humidifying influence of the sea is less marked and the climate becomes more arid. Between Trausse and Olonzac the rainfall is exceptionally low. Further west there are Atlantic influences. The combination of soil variation and micro-climate will determine which grapes grow where, and even the way the vines are trained.

The predominant grape varieties used in AOC Minervois wines are grenache, syrah and mourvèdre, which must collectively make up at least 60% of the blend, possibly complemented by carignan and cinsault. Older varieties such as aspiran or piquepoul noir sometimes take on a minority role. The *appellation*'s white wines, which vary considerably in quality and style, are made from

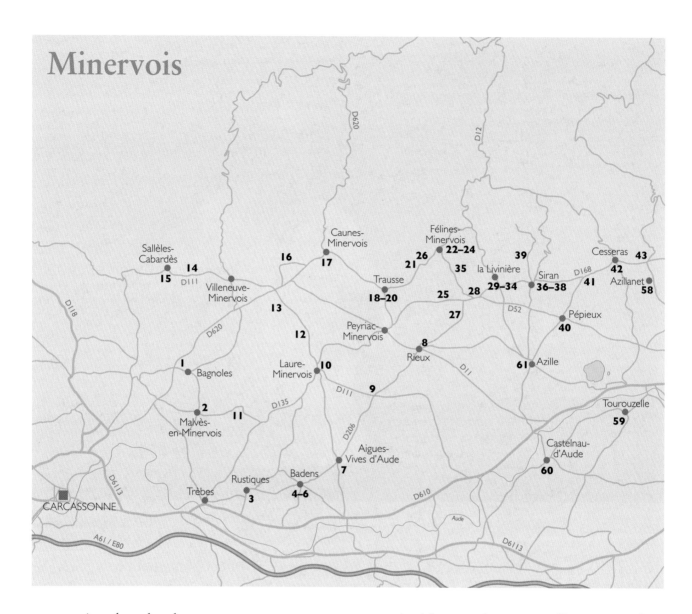

vermentino, bourboulenc, roussanne, marsanne, grenache blanc and occasionally terret. White Minervois is developing, becoming increasingly aromatic and refined. In addition to dry red and white wines, the area has a historical sweet-winemaking tradition. Minervois Noble, as it is known, does not have its own *appellation*. It is made from the same white grapes as its dry counterparts. The grapes are picked when they have reached a high level of sweetness, either as a result of noble rot or by being dried out naturally after picking.

Minervois, for a long time the only Languedoc name (apart from Corbières) known outside the region, became an *appellation* area in 1985, but more recently a score or so of independent growers and a few *coopératives* have developed the internal *appellation* Minervois La Livinière for making wines which they say have more complexity, quality and ageing potential. There is an elaborate self-regulating system of analysis and tasting before a wine may use the Livinière name.

The growers listed below start at the gates of Carcassonne and then follow a northerly and eastern route until turning back towards Carcassonne.

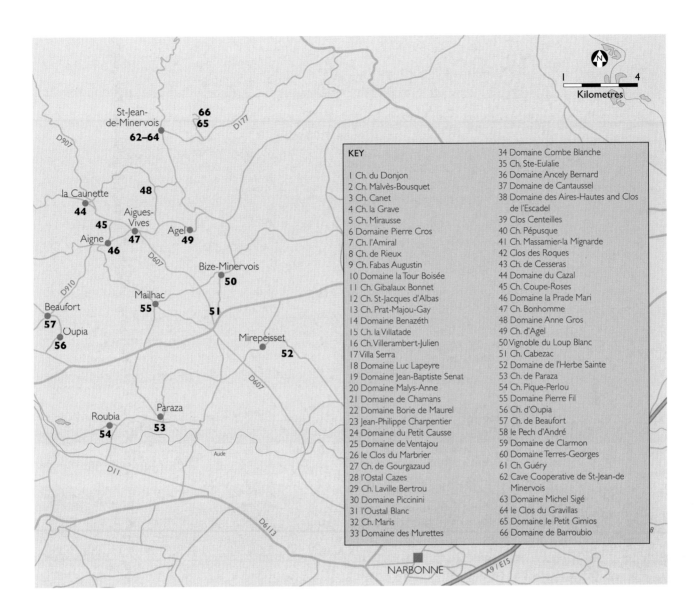

KEY

1 Ch. du Donjon
2 Ch. Malvès-Bousquet
3 Ch. Canet
4 Ch. la Grave
5 Ch. Mirausse
6 Domaine Pierre Cros
7 Ch. l'Amiral
8 Ch. de Rieux
9 Ch. Fabas Augustin
10 Domaine la Tour Boisée
11 Ch. Gibalaux Bonnet
12 Ch. St-Jacques d'Albas
13 Ch. Prat-Majou-Gay
14 Domaine Benazéth
15 Ch. la Villatade
16 Ch. Villerambert-Julien
17 Villa Serra
18 Domaine Luc Lapeyre
19 Domaine Jean-Baptiste Senat
20 Domaine Malys-Anne
21 Domaine de Chamans
22 Domaine Borie de Maurel
23 Jean-Philippe Charpentier
24 Domaine du Petit Causse
25 Domaine de Ventajou
26 le Clos du Marbrier
27 Ch. de Gourgazaud
28 l'Ostal Cazes
29 Ch. Laville Bertrou
30 Domaine Piccinini
31 l'Oustal Blanc
32 Ch. Maris
33 Domaine des Murettes
34 Domaine Combe Blanche
35 Ch. Ste-Eulalie
36 Domaine Ancely Bernard
37 Domaine de Cantaussel
38 Domaine des Aires-Hautes and Clos de l'Escadel
39 Clos Centeilles
40 Ch. Pépusque
41 Ch. Massamier-la Mignarde
42 Clos des Roques
43 Ch. de Cesseras
44 Domaine du Cazal
45 Ch. Coupe-Roses
46 Domaine la Prade Mari
47 Ch. Bonhomme
48 Domaine Anne Gros
49 Ch. d'Agel
50 Vignoble du Loup Blanc
51 Ch. Cabezac
52 Domaine de l'Herbe Sainte
53 Ch. de Paraza
54 Ch. Pique-Perlou
55 Domaine Pierre Fil
56 Ch. d'Oupia
57 Ch. de Beaufort
58 le Pech d'André
59 Domaine de Clarmon
60 Domaine Terres-Georges
61 Ch. Guéry
62 Cave Cooperative de St-Jean-de Minervois
63 Domaine Michel Sigé
64 le Clos du Gravillas
65 Domaine le Petit Gimios
66 Domaine de Barroubio

***CHÂTEAU LA GRAVE

Jean-Pierre, Josiane and Jean-François Orosquette
11800 Badens
Tel   04 68 79 16 00
Mobile   06 81 32 15 25
info@chateau-la-grave.net   www.chatea-la-grave.com

MAP 4
Visits all year, Monday to Friday, 8.00 -12.00 and 14.00 -17.30

The Orosquette family have gradually built up this vineyard and its chais over a period of nearly 40 years. There are now some 70 hectares, of which one third is given over to a range of varietal IGPs, mostly from non-Languedoc grapes (A). Today, Jean-François has 'taken over' from his parents who, nevertheless, are always on hand for advice ("a true vigneron never retires"). The micro-climate here is exceptionally dry and the soil arid, but there are parcels of more hospitable ground where the family's beloved maccabeu produces one of the best white wines of the entire region. It comes in unoaked (A) and oaked (B) versions, always with good acidity and freshness of fruit, rare to find in this part of Languedoc. 'Expression' is the name given to their attractive syrah/grenache rosé (A), as well as to their traditional un-oaked red (also A), which has some old vine carignan in the mix. A very attractive quaffer called 'Tristan et Julien' (A) is named after the younger members of the family; a wine full of black fruits and wild flowers. There is a grenache-dominated red called 'Ô Marie' (C), raised in tank but with an assured long life, and made only in limited quantities. The 'Privilège' red (B) is the only one aged in oak. It has a little mourvèdre in the blend and is very dark in colour, with a bouquet of preserved fruits.

Polyculture is still a way of life for many

CHÂTEAU MIRAUSSE Raymond Julien
11800 Badens.
Tel   04 68 79 12 30
Mobile   06 87 77 81 53
julien.mirausse@wanadoo.fr

MAP 5
Prior telephone call advised.

This 18-hectare estate is a lovely château with a colourful proprietor not far from Carcassonne. His reds include 'l'Azerolle' (A), which in 2009 was from carignan, syrah and grenache, serious and with sweet fruit and aged in *cuve*; a pure carignan given one month's cuvaison; 'Le Grand Penchant' from syrah and grenache, with scents of the garrigue and blackcurrant fruit; and 'Le Cendrous', with rather more syrah, dark, sweet fruit, with some oak in the modern manner. These last wines are (B/C). They are not as well-known as some, but display a quiet excellence and finesse. Well worth supporting.

***DOMAINE PIERRE CROS** Pierre Cros
20 rue du Minervois, 11800 Badens
Tel   04 68 79 21 82
Mobile   06 74 47 25 80
dom-pierre-cros@sfr.fr   www.pierrecros.fr

MAP 6
Appointment recommended.

This must be the driest part of the Languedoc, where the old traditional grapes (before the arrival of the 'upstarts' syrah and mourvèdre) thrive so well: carignan, of course, but also alicante, aramon and piquepoul noir, which all go to make up a Vin de France called 'Les Mal-Aimés' (B), a reference to the low esteem in which these old grapes are held by those who should know better. The Minervois blanc (B) comes from old varieties too: grenache blanc, vermentino, muscat and white piquepoul (none of your chardonnay or roussanne), and manages to be fruity and floral while retaining perfect balance. Under the disguise of Vin de France comes a surprising 100% pinot noir (C), dark but still managing to be brilliant, spicy on the nose and with bags of fruit and more spices on the palate. The oaking is discreet, but note the 14.5% alcohol. Another interesting experiment is the pure nebbiolo called 'La Liberté' (B), a grape which Cros has been wanting to try for some years. Grenache makes an appearance under the name of 'Pierre Henri', a wonderfully rich, plummy wine, but which still manages to avoid heaviness. Again, note the 14.5 degrees of alcohol. Carignan is the star of the 'Vieilles Vignes' (C), a splendid example of the grape from its favourite kind of terroir. 'Tradition' (B) allows a little syrah into the grenache/carignan blend, while 'Les Aspres' (C) marks a final surrender to syrah. These wines are unmistakably among the best from the Minervois, made by a winemaker who, while in so many ways devoted to tradition, is not afraid of experimenting or of making modern wines from the 'modern' grapes.

**CHÂTEAU FABAS AUGUSTIN

Roland, Yann and Loïc Augustin,
Domaine de Fabas, 11800 Laure-Minervois
Tel 04 68 78 17 82
chateaufabas@wanadoo.fr
www.vinsdusiecle.com/chateaufabas

MAP 9
Visits every day, 8.00 -12.00 and 14.00 -19.00.

One would expect good wines to come from a former director of Moët & Chandon, and customers are not likely to be disappointed. For the 58 hectares of vines (45 of which are AOP), Roland and his two sons exploit three different terroirs: chalky clay on the highest ground, then sandstone, leading down to silex on the lower terraces. The other 13 hectares are devoted to the production of a sauvignon, typical of its grape and noted for its fresh coolness; a red blend of syrah and petit verdot, aromatic and weighty; and a pure carignan. The white AOP Minervois (A) is especially admired: a blend of vermentino, maccabeu, roussanne and bourboulenc, it shares its name, 'Serbolles' (A), with a red from syrah, grenache and very old mourvèdre, a wine which features fresh summer fruits on the palate, with some smoky and mineral elements. 'Le Mourral' (B), from the same grapes, has more flesh and is aged in oak, its flowery nose giving way to peppery and prune flavours. The top red is called 'Cuvée Seigneur Fabas' (B/C) and is altogether more solid, more extracted and is also, of course, given oak-ageing.

B **DOMAINE LA TOUR BOISÉE

Marie-Claude and Jean-Louis Poudou
11800 Laure-Minervois
Tel 04 68 78 10 04
Mobile 06 47 08 15 12
info@domainelatourboisee.com
www.domainelatourboisee.com

MAP 10
Appointment advisable.

The Poudous have built up an impressive holding of over 80 hectares from which they make a large range of wines. The family goes back a long way; an ancestor having won medals in Paris as long ago as 1897. Jean-Louis is himself self-taught and untrained, and has an innate fear of technique as it is taught in college. "Man should not impose a programme on his grapes. A winemaker's job is simply to make the best wine he can – sales will follow." His wines range from the simple (nice IGPs from chardonnay and from the usual merlot / cabernet blend) (A), to the eccentric.

'Une Histoire de Famille' is a name given to a blend of just about every white grape there is in Languedoc, while the very traditional red version is raised in vat from grenache, carignan and cinsault. Don't forget to ask about his Rosé (A) – one of the best to come out of Minervois, which Jean-Louis is too shy to mention on his website. A pure unoaked carignan, which is a bargain (A), leads into their classique red Minervois 'Cuvée Marielle et Frédérique' (A), mostly from grenache and cinsault with a little syrah and old carignan. From here on we're into barrels, although Jean-Louis believes that the wood is there to give roundness and not flavour. 'Cuvée à Marie Claude' (B) is a blend of equal quantities of syrah, grenache and carignan, while 'Jardin Secret' (D) is the flagship blend to which Jean-Louis adds a little mourvèdre. For the adventurous there is a curiosity called 'Plantation 2005' (B), made from over 20 ancient grape varieties, some forgotten, others still just holding on like alicante bouschet and morrastel. Finally, there is a honeyed sweet marsanne, 'Minervois Noble Blanc', late-picked in November and fermented and aged in wood for four or more years. There's something for everyone here.

***CHÂTEAU ST-JACQUES D'ALBAS

Beatrice Graham and Andrew Nutter
11800 Laure-Minervois
Tel 04 68 78 24 82
info@chateaustjacques.com   chateaustjacques.com

MAP 12
Open throughout the summer during usual hours.

This English family have been making wines at this elegant domaine since 2001 and share winemaking expertise with Domaine Bégude at Limoux (q.v.). There are IGPs in all three colours and all (A): a white from vermentino, viognier and roussanne; the pink a blend of syrah and grenache, with a touch of mourvèdre; and the red from cabernet sauvignon and grenache. The first AOP red is called 'Domaine Saint Jacques', and at (A) is one of the best buys in Languedoc. Syrah usually dominates the blend at 60%, with 20% each of grenache and mourvèdre. 'Château Saint Jacques' (B) is again syrah-dominated – increasingly so as the years have gone by – and is raised in wood for 12 months. 'La Chapelle' (C) is a virtually pure syrah (with just a touch of grenache to ensure compliance with the rules which require AOPs to be blends) from the best vines, made only in small quantities and given 18 months in the wood. There are two gîtes available to rent, and in summer there are classical and jazz concerts.

***CHÂTEAU   VILLERAMBERT-JULIEN

Bonfils Group
11160 Caunes- Minervois
Tel 04 68 78 00 01
Mobile 06 07 87 48 22
infos@villerambert-julien.com   www.villerambert-julien.com

MAP 16

From June 1 to September 30, the property is open every day from 9.30-11.30 and from 13.30-18.30. Out of season, visits are possible Monday to Friday and at weekends by appointment.

The 76 hectares of vines include some recent plantings of white grapes – roussanne and viognier, the blend from which (A) makes a fine aperitif or accompaniment to exotic food. Apart from some recent experiments with mourvèdre, the reds are all made from syrah and/or grenache. Syrah can suffer from hydric stress in the hottest summers, so it is ideally suited by the clay-ish soils to the west of the estate, while to the east, the slate, schist and marble in the ground are perfect for the grenache. A rosé, well-named 'Pleasure'(A), combines a little of the new mourvèdre, as well as some old carignan, and is a powerful example of the style with a long finish. Nearby Caunes-Minervois is famous for its quarries of red marble, which went into the building of the Trianon Palace at Versailles and the Palais Garnier opera house in Paris. It is not surprising, therefore, that two of the reds reflect this peculiarity. 'L'Incarnat' (A) is usually (but not necessarily) mostly grenache with a little syrah and aged in tank, and is suited to all occasions, informal or grand. 'Opera' (A/B) is a bit more ambitious, half the grapes (2/3rds syrah, the rest grenache) being given ageing in four-year-old barrels. Another red, bottled simply under the name of the château (B) and made only in the best years also has a mixed *élevage*, partly in tank and partly in a combination of new and old barrels. 'Ourdivieille' (B) is mostly grenache and only a small percentage is raised in barrel – its peculiarity is that the grapes are raised on schist. The wines here all tend to be big and generous, but they have elegance and style too.

B ** VILLA SERRA Claude and Anne Serra
vineyards at 11160 Caunes-Minervois.
Business at 3 Impasse des Acanthes, 34070 Montpellier
Tel   04 11 65 54 47
villaserra.minervois@gmail.com

MAP 17
Phone a good while ahead.

A tiny two-hectare family domaine in the heart of Caunes, fully organic (Ecocert) from 2011 onwards. Claude lectures in winemaking at Montpellier University, so the wines get good exposure in the restaurants and bars of that city. A little grenache blanc, grown on chalk, gives an IGP of good quality, and there is an AOP rosé too made from grenache, cinsault and mourvèdre (both A). Surprisingly there is no syrah grown here, so the reds manage without. 'Que Serra Serra' (B), in which the 60% majority grape is cinsault, gives a fine expressive account of itself, and is understated and elegant, with jammy fruit, spices and hints of bay leaves. The wine is aged 80% in tank and 20% in old barrels. 'Pinabo' (C) is mostly from grenache with just a little mourvèdre, and is given a long cuvaison before being aged in wood, half one-year-old and the rest in 500-litre barrels. 'Villa Serra' (C), sometimes called 'Le rouge', is a blend of all four grapes,

aged in wood of which a maximum of 15% is new and 40% aged in demi-muids.

*** DOMAINE LUC LAPEYRE
Luc and Jean-Yves Lapeyre
17 rue Marcellin Albert, 11160 Trausse
Tel   04 68 24 73 70
Mobile   06 71 59 72 92
luc.lapeyre@wanadoo.fr   www.domaineluclapeyre.fr

MAP 18
Appointment strongly recommended.

Jean-Yves has just about taken over the reins from his father at this much admired Minervois estate. Wine has been in their blood for many generations of growers, coopers and merchants. For some years now, free from the ties of the *coopérative*, Luc and his son have been making some of the most attractive wines of the region from their 35 hectares of vines. Luc is an ebullient and entertaining host – he could be mistaken for one of his own barrels were it not for the once raven-black hair, eyes and beard which top his rugby-player's frame. His AOP white, 'L'Amourier Blanc' (B), is roussanne-based with just a touch of muscat to give a typically scented hint to the wine. His main red is also called 'L'Amourier' (A/B), and is a blend of 50% syrah, 25% grenache and 25% mourvèdre, given just a touch of old oak. Two good-value wines for everyday drinking are the AOP 'San Brès' (A), mostly grenache, and an IGP (because it has some merlot in there with the carignan and grenache) called Le Vin à Boire de Luc Lapeyre', also (A). Every grower these days has his 'Tête de Cuvée' (C), and here it is called 'Les Clots de l'Amourier'. It is a blend of mourvèdre and grenache, which Luc says will keep for 10 years.

B *** DOMAINE JEAN-BAPTISTE SENAT
Jean-Baptiste et Charlotte Senat
12 rue de l'Argent Double,
11160 Trausse
Tel   04 68 79 21 40
Mobile   06 08 41 27 47
charlotte.senat@gmail.com
www.domaine-jeanbaptistesenat.fr

MAP 19
Visits during usual times – normally someone is available. If you want to be sure of meeting J-BS, phone in advance.

In 1995, Senat came back to Trausse with his wife Charlotte ("the soul of the *domaine*") to take over the family's abandoned vineyards, which included some centenarian vines and a dilapidated *chais*. Parisian by birth and education, he twisted the arms of loyal friends to help him over the first few difficult years. Today his has become one of the top Minervois spots, famous for its wines which are neither pretentious nor overbearing. Senat has all the Minervois

Jean-Philippe Charpentier

His rosé (A) may be a blend of syrah and marsanne, while his white 'Aude' (B) is also marsanne, this time with a little muscat. But it is the reds that have made the name of this property: 'Esprit d'Automne' (A) will usually be a blend of syrah, grenache and carignan, and has a distinctly mushroom character (Michel says it is matured "according to an ancient local method"); 'Féline' (B) is called "feminine" by Michel, though it has 70% peppery syrah and is partly aged in barrel; 'Rêve de Carignan' is just what it says on the label (B); 'Belle de Nuit' (C) is all grenache; 'Maxime' (C) is all mourvèdre; and, finally, 'Sylla' (D) is all syrah by macération carbonique. All the reds here benefit from – in fact, they require – ageing in bottle, and are some of the most highly esteemed of all Minervois wines. Visit the tasting bar called 'Chiavari', which the Escandes started in 2008. In times gone by, the chais was out of bounds even to his wife, but maybe Michel is less shy these days.

✳✳✳ JEAN-PHILIPPE CHARPENTIER
Place du Château 34210 Félines-Minervois
Tel 04 68 71 20 96
Mobile 06 81 83 37 85
jpcvins@voila.fr

MAP 23
Appointment please.

In 1998, Jean-Philippe Charpentier, originally from the Champagne area, gave up teaching to follow his wife Laurence to Languedoc. After working in Carcassonne, he became a Blanquette producer in Limoux. In 2003, he purchased his first five hectares of vineyard at the heart of the Minervois-La Livinière *appellation*. He then created his own cave at Félines with new plant, much of it buried underground to protect from the summer heat. His wines range from the relatively easy 'Le Paysan' (A), with its ripe fruits, through to 'Les Trois Cailloux' (A/B), well-balanced and with a lively freshness, some pepper and more complexity. 'In Vino Libido' (A/B) and 'La Friponne' (B) are syrah-based, chocolatey and spicy, and are given some time in used barrels. There follows his top La Livinière wine called 'L'Intégrale' (D), dense, highly aromatic, the fruit and spice well integrated with the oak in which it is raised. This small *domaine* relies on word-of-mouth reputation, rather than pushy marketing. It has already created a big impression and will go on increasing its renown.

grapes, although his syrah is grown some distance away because the soil in the old family vineyards at Trausse is too sandy. He is living proof that you don't have to be at La Livinière to make top class Minervois. He offers no rosés, and only one white, 'Aux Armes de Ma Soeur', mostly from grenache gris. There are four reds: 'Arbalète et Coquelicots' (B), mostly grenache with 20% cinsault, fermented for just 12 days and raised in a mix of tank and barrel; 'La Nine' (B), Senat's best-known and best-selling wine, being a blend of all five AOP grapes and again aged in a mix of vats and barrels; 'Mais où est donc Ornicar' (B), described by Senat as "playful and lively, fruity yet supple and with a hint of liquorice," mostly mourvèdre and raised in barrel for six months to clarify the juice; and finally 'Le Bois des Merveilles' (C), the *tête de cuvee* from the very oldest vines, given 14 months in wooden vats. Senat says this wine knows how to show its maturity without ever letting the barrel get the upper hand. He uses only old barrels which he gets from Burgundy.

✳✳✳ DOMAINE BORIE DE MAUREL
la Famile Escande
Rue de la Sallèle , 34210 Félines-Minervois
Tel 04 68 91 68 58
Mobile 06 03 25 03 87
contact@boriedemaurel.fr www.boriedemaurel.fr

MAP 22
You could try pot luck.

Michel Escande and his two sons, starting with only five hectares, now run a considerable enterprise of 35 hectares, all worked with the aid of their two horses, Luna and Ni-non, and harvested by hand. Michel, a former mariner, abandoned the sea for this rugged part of Languedoc and took a leading role in the creation of the La Livinière *cru*. The soil here is partly argilo-calcaire, but with glacial limestone on some of the steeper slopes. Michel made a name for himself as the 'Sorcerer of Félines' towards the turn of the millennium, hitting the headlines with a range of top-class Minervois which remains substantially unchanged today.

✳✳ DOMAINE DE VENTAJOU
Thierry de Marne
Bel Soleil, 34210 Félines-Minervois
Tel 04 30 16 65 75 Mobile 06 33 05 37 93
thierry.demarne@sfr.fr

MAP 25
Visits by appointment. Because of the remote situation, pot luck inadvisable.
You'll need a sturdy vehicle and a sense of adventure to

Terraces near La Livinière.

negotiate the road to get there. Quirky, natural wines, well worth a go. Remote, so best to book ahead

**CHÂTEAU DE GOURGAZAUD
Chantale Piquet and Annie Tiburce (contact Laetitia Chabbert)
Hameau de Gourgazaud, 34210 La Livinière
Tel   04 68 78 10 02
contact@gourgazaud.com   www.gourgazaud.com

MAP 27
Visits Monday to Friday, 09.00 to 17.00, Saturday and Sunday by appointment.

This beautiful, improving and good-value property, rather lost in the countryside with its 100 hectares of vine, has been in the Piquet family for generations. The current owners are the daughters of Roger Piquet, who, having started off as a négociant, replanted the vineyard at Gourgazaud mainly with syrah and mourvèdre, varieties which he pioneered in the region in the 1970s. Nowadays, they have some grenache too, a grape which father used to frown on. 2012 was their first vintage with it, 'La Vigne de mon Père' (B). There is as well a range of whites – note especially their pure viognier, with understated peach and apricots and not at all heavy. There is a viognier blend with chardonnay, too (both B). Chardonnay appears as a varietal in both oaked and unoaked versions, again, both (B). The oaked viognier is a cultivated taste but the pure sauvignon (A) is a good-value delight. The salmon-coloured rosé (A) is all syrah and is full of red fruits, while the reds start with a 'Tradition' (A), which has a hint of carignan in the syrah/mourvèdre blend. Those two grapes make up the 'Cuvée Mathilde' (A/B), deep purple, prunish and even sometimes truffly, but without oak, whereas the 'Réserve' (B) is given 12 months in new barrels. The flagship 'Quintus' (C) is made only in the best years, again from syrah/mourvèdre, concentrated, with long élevage and Parker written over it. It has been recently joined by a pure old-vine Grenache called 'Pater Familias' (C).

***CHÂTEAU LAVILLE BERTROU
Gérard Bertrand
34210 La Livinière commercially based at L'Hospitalet, route de Narbonne Plage, 11104 Narbonne Plage
Tel 04 68 42 68 68 (Narbonne tel 04 68 45 36 00)
vins@gerard-bertrand.com

MAP 29
Tasting recommended at L'Hospitalet, otherwise try by appointment at the château.

This is where Gérard Bertrand started his meteoric rise to eminence in the Languedoc, and where he still makes what is probably his best wine. The château comprises 50 hectares of south and south-east-facing vineyards of La Livinière, and nowadays all the wines (B) seemingly carry the Livinière name. Gérard Bertrand purchased the estate in 1997 from the Bertrou family who had owned the property for approximately 100 years. The grapes from here are syrah, grenache and old-vine carignan, all hand-picked. Yields are 35 hl/ha. The carignan and syrah grapes are vinified for 15-20 days by macération carbonique. The grenache grapes are vinified separately in the traditional way for rather less time. In February, the wine is transferred to French barrels for up to a year. Unfiltered, the wine (B) is bottled and then aged further prior to release. It is dark ruby with an elegant bouquet, ripe black and red fruit prominent on the palate with woody flavours. Peppery too, with a long finish.

***DOMAINE PICCININI
Jean-Christophe Piccinini
14 Route des Meulières, 34210 La Livinière
Mobiles 06 87 04 48 47 and 09 61 21 07 80
domainepiccinini@orange.fr   domainepiccinini.com

MAP 30
Appointment not necessary, but advisable.

The Piccinini family have been pillars of the Minervois, more especially La Livinière, for many years. Jean-Christophe's father founded the local *coopérative* and was a leading light in the establishment of La Livinière as a cru of the Minervois. Jean-Christophe has been an independent grower since 1997, and his wines are some of the best references in the *appellation*. Not only his reds; his white 'Réserve' (B), a blend mostly of grenache blanc but also containing roussanne, muscat, maccabeu and bourboulenc, is among the top whites in the area. Given six months in old wood, the oaking is very discreet and in no way masks the delicious citrus fruit and almond flavours. There are three reds. Firstly, the 'Tradition' (A) is everything that a first wine should be, mostly syrah which gives peppery and liquorice character. 'Clos d'Angely' (B) is from the oldest vines, again mostly syrah. Raised only partly in old barrels, the oaking is again very sensitive. The top red is diplomatically called 'Line et Letitia' (B/C) after Jean-Christophe's wife and his sister, both pillars of the enterprise. It is a blend of mourvèdre (40%) with grenache and syrah. The mourvèdre is usually matured in new oak, the other grapes in used barrels. Elegant, plummy on the nose with some liquorice, the tannins are fine with red fruits prominent. Great value for money here.

***CHÂTEAU SAINTE-EULALIE Isabelle Coustal
34210 La Livinière
Tel   04 68 91 42 72
Mobile   06 03 89 13 41
info@chateausainteeulalie.com
www.chateausainteeulalie.com

MAP 35
Visits from June through September every day, 10.30-12.30 and 15.00-18.30. October through May Monday to Friday, 10.30-12.00 and 15.00-17.00. Weekends by appointment.

Isabelle and her *oenologue* husband have 40 hectares of vines with an able and enthusiastic team to help them. Their vines are mostly on chalky clay soil, but covered with pebbles which protect the land from drying out and reflect back on to the grapes the heat of the midday sun. Isabelle makes a little white wine as an IGP from pure sauvignon (A), which she leaves on its lees for a couple of months. It is pale in colour, but with plenty of exotic fruits, lively and with good weight. Her rosé, 'Printemps d'Eulalie' (A), is *saigné* from all the Languedoc grapes bar mourvèdre, typically with strawberry and liquorice notes. It is delicate and dangerously quaffable. The reds, though, are the backbone of this vineyard. 'Plaisir d'Eulalie' (A) has a bit more carignan than either grenache or syrah. It is given a short maceration of only 10 days, but nevertheless the colour is dark and brilliant, and dark fruits on the nose give way to plenty of grip on the palate, the tannins silky and smooth. Not a long-keeper, though it will last for three to five years. The 'Cuvée Prestige' (A/B) is nearly half syrah, backed by grenache and rather less carignan, given a little longer maceration and aged partly in old barrels, while 'Cantilène' (B/C) is the much-admired top wine with 55% syrah, 25% carignan and 20% grenache, this time aged for 12 months in a mix of old and new wood. In exceptional years, Isabelle makes a few bottles of almost pure carignan which she calls 'Le Grand Vin' (D), and which she macerates for 20 days and bottles early to preserve the fruit. No wood. An explosion of fruit on the nose gives way to fullness on the palate, with silky and well-integrated tannins. Long, this has class and harmony.

***DOMAINE ANCELY BERNARD
Bernard and Nathalie Ancely
4 Place du Soleil d'Oc, 34210 Siran
Tel   04 68 91 55 43
domaineancelybernard@wanadoo.fr
www.domaine-ancely-minervois.fr

MAP 36
Appointment advisable.

The family has had vines in the area for many years, but Bernard decided to start up on his own in 2001 with 30 hectares of old vines, low-yielding and manually harvested. This is something of a cult estate, the wines not being easy to find on the market. Of the two reds, 'La Muraille' (B) is a familiar blend of 40% Grenache, 40% syrah and 20% carignan, while 'Les Vignes Oubliées' (C) is more ambitious, dropping the carignan and adding substantial extraction, oak-ageing and developing 15% alcohol, with a black fruit and violet nose, stiff tannins and needing some ageing in bottle. A domaine well worth seeking out.

Patricia Boyer Domergue, Clos Centeilles

****CLOS CENTEILLES Patricia Boyer Domergue
Chemin de Centeilles, 34210 Siran
Tel   04 68 91 52 18
Mobile   06 11 65 15 81
GPS   43 19 45 N 2 39 10 E
contact@closcenteilles.com   www.closcenteilles.com

MAP 39
Visits better by appointment, but you could take pot luck.

Patricia bought what was then a tumbledown '*campagne*' (the local equivalent of château) in 1990, when there were already 13 hectares of old vines, including notably a plantation of cinsault. Amazed at the success of this grape in her first year, it has become the hallmark of Patricia's production. Her experience is that most people find it difficult to use, so they tend to reserve it for making rosés. She finds it develops fullness and real stature with age. For example, 'Campagne de Centeilles' (B) is almost 100% cinsault but with a little syrah to add structure, and 'Capitelle de Centeilles' (C) is a pure varietal from old vintages. Patricia says this is her favourite wine. More conventionally, syrah, grenache and mourvèdre are at the base of 'Clos Centeilles' (C), which has the benefit of the 'La Livinière' label. This should not be confused with 'C de Centeilles rouge' (B), a thoroughly unorthodox blend of forgotten grapes such as piquepoul noir, riveirenc noir, morrastel and oeillade. Piquepoul is also a third of the blend with carignan for a light wine like 'clairet' called 'La Part des Anges' (B). Patricia makes a pure pinot noir which she claims is as traditional to Languedoc as any other grape variety: it is called 'Guigniers de Centeilles' (C). Another delight is

'Carignanissime' (B), pure carignan, or, as Patricia prefers to describe it, 60% carignan and 40% carignan. Note also her two whites – a pure grenache gris shrivelled on the vine until November called 'L'Erme de Centeilles' (D), and 'C de Centeilles Blanc' (C), from the ancient grapes carignan blanc, riveirenc blanc and gris. Some of Patricia's *cuvaisons* are very long, except for her carignan which is made by *macération carbonique*. On the other hand, no new wood is used, only mature small old barrels from Hungary. This is one of the most original of all Minervois estates, where the emphasis is on elegance and finesse, rather than power. The wines are a refreshing antidote to the blockbuster school.

***CHÂTEAU PÉPUSQUE Renée et Benoît Laburthe
7 rue du 11 novembre 1918, 11700 Pépieux
Tel   04 68 91 41 38
chateau.pepusque@orange.fr   www.chateau-pepusque.fr

MAP 40
Rendezvous recommended.

The present generation (Benoît was once a chartered accountant) took over from their grandfather in 1986, and the first vintage they bottled themselves was 2005. They have quickly built a reputation for producing Minervois of high quality from two distinct *terroirs*, one at Pépieux itself and the other in La Livinière. The rosé, called 'Perle de Rosée' (A), is wholly from cinsault and shows elegance as well as richness. There are four reds (no whites), the first three from Pépieux: 'Les Terres Rouges' (A/B depending on age), based on carignan, is easy on the palate, but with good bite; 'Les Gravettes' (B) is largely grenache with some syrah, dense in colour and texture, and with hints of blackcurrant and liquorice; and 'Les Terres Fines' (B) is the top Pépieux red, aged for six months of its life in old barrels and benefiting from a blend of 80% mourvèdre and 20% syrah. It is very deep and M. Laburthe describes it as "my St. Emilion." From La Livinière comes the *tête de cuvée*, 'Les Cailloux Blancs' (D), powerful, rich and barrel-aged. In some years, the bouquet suggests fresh and preserved fruits, tapenade and grilled almonds. On the palate, it is chewy and firmly structured.

***CHÂTEAU MASSAMIER-LA-MIGNARDE
Frantz Vénès
11700 Pépieux
Tel   04 68 91 64 55
Mobile   06 10 29 39 33
massamier-la-mignarde.com
www.massamier-la-mignarde.com

MAP 41
Visits April-October inclusive, Monday - Saturday, 9.00-12.15 and 14.00-19.15. Sundays and holidays, 15.00-19.15. November - March inclusive, Monday - Saturday, 9.00-12.15 and 14.00-18.00. Sundays and holidays, 15.00-18.00.

Frantz and his parents recovered their rightful ownership of this domaine only after a long court case. They then set out to restore the vineyard and the chais. The latter remains within the walls of the old building but is entirely re-equipped. Having won an award for the best red wine in the world in 2005, Frantz Vénès has demonstrated what a quiet revolution he has wrought at this 70-hectare property, which was badly damaged by the floods in 1999. The estate is named after a Roman legionary Maximus and a M. Mignarde who modernised it in the 18th Century, and on it Vénès grows all the Languedoc grapes and, for IGPs, including 'Oliviers Rouge' (A), some cabernet sauvignon, as well as a sauvignon blanc for a white aperitif. At the 'Tradition' level (A/B), the white AOP is all grenache blanc, flowery and aniseedy, and with enough body to support spicy food. The red is nearly half carignan, grenache and syrah, completing the blend with just a touch of cinsault. The rosé is a multi-medal winner, half cinsault, the rest syrah and grenache. Old barrels are used to age 'Cuvée Aubin' (B), a name lent also to a pure cabernet IGP. Among the most attractive wines are the 'Expression' varietals (B) from carignan and cinsault respectively, while the two top reds 'Domus Maximus' (D), the world prize-winner, and 'Tènement es Garouilhas' (D+) are generously treated to new wood. Frantz is also the leading light behind a project called 'Laurbauzil', which comprises just under six hectares of mourvèdre, grenache and carignan, and which is open to subscription to 99 'partners'. 'Laurbauzil' will offer for auction a demi-muid of the wine for the benefit of children in hospital.

**CHÂTEAU DE CESSERAS
Pierre-André Ournac
Chemin de Minerve, 34210 Cesseras
Tel   04 68 91 15 70
Mobile   06 08 88 60 17
pierreandre.coudoulet@wanadoo.fr

MAP 43
Phone ahead.

Strictly for those Parker-followers who like fruit-bombs with plenty of extraction and oak and who might be rather more lavish with stars than the author. 'Cuvée Olric' (A) is powerful and muscular with 60% syrah dominating some old carignan and mourvèdre. The 'La Livinière' cru (B/C) is more ambitious with some grenache thrown in. Viscous and smoky, but long with a peppery and slightly bitter finish. It has been described as both "a flagship blend from a flagship property" and "the horrifying over-cocacolaisation which has overtaken the wine world." Cesseras divides opinion, but those who like the wines are very enthusiastic.

Storm near Siran

**CHÂTEAU COUPE-ROSES

Françoise and Pascal Frissant
4 Rue de La Poterie, 34210 La Caunette
Tel   04 68 91 21 95
Mobile   06 75 21 88 18
GPS   43 20 57 54   2 47 12 58
coupe-roses@wanadoo.fr   www.coupe-roses.com

MAP 45
The fairly remote situation means that the growers here are worth a phone call ahead of a visit.

The 40-hectare property is largely on the north side of the 'Petit Causse' and is on relatively high ground between 250 and 400 metres above sea-level. This ensures cool nights, late harvests and good acidity. The makers enjoy the services of François Serre, consultant at Château Rayas in Châteauneuf du Pape, but there is nothing overweight about the wines here. The top soil is chalky, with a good clay sub-soil and a deal of manganese which accounts for both its red colour and the name of the property. Viognier is at the base of their first white IGP (A), delicate and best as an aperitif, or perhaps with ungarnished fresh shellfish. It is floral rather than fruity and thus atypical of the grape. Another white, 'Cuvée Champ du Roy' (A), is a blend of all their white grapes, easy drinking and a real party wine, while their AOP white, mostly Roussanne and still (A), is more substantial and sometimes partially oak-aged, its vivacity reinforced by a slight sensation of fizz. It will keep well. A fresh spring-like orangey rosé with a deal of mourvèdre heralds the range of AOP reds, starting with the earthy 'Bastide de Coupe-Roses'

(A), a carignan-dominating wine, thirst-quenching and to be enjoyed on its fruit. 'Les Plots' (A/B) is their *classique;* a fine mainstream Minervois which can be held up as an example to all. It is not difficult to guess that 'Granaxa' (B) is based on grenache and aged in old barrels, while 'Cuvée Orience' (C) is an oak-fermented-and-aged syrah, warm and generous and to be cellared for a good few years.

**CHÂTEAU BONHOMME
(DOMAINE DES DEUX BONHOMMES)

Jean-Noël Bousquet and Patrick Granier
11800 Aigues-Vives
Tel   04 68 76 99 64
dfrederic@chateau-bonhomme.com

MAP 47
Appointment advised.

This 93-hectare domaine was recently taken over by its present owners (Bousquet is also the owner of the well-known Grand Moulin in Corbières q.v.), following the retirement of Jean-Pierre Aymar who, in turn, had rescued the vineyards and the château from falling into decay as recently as 1997. A fine reputation was and is enjoyed by the red 'Les Alaternes' (the local name for a particularly spiny wild bush). Results from the new régime awaited with interest.

***DOMAINE ANNE GROS
Anne Gros and Jean-Paul Tollot
Rue du Couchant, Cazelles, 34210 Aigues-Vives
Tel 03 80 61 07 95
domaine-annegros@orange.fr   www.anne-gros.com/en.minervois

MAP 48
Telephone the proprietors in Burgundy (as above) to arrange visits. No sales from the cellar, only from shops.

These famous Burgundian growers from Vosne-Romanée (with holdings in Richebourg) are relative newcomers to Minervois, building their own state-of-the-art *chais* and making their first wines here in 2008. They have 12 hectares under vine with more land yet to plant. There are no white wines – yet. For them, one of the great discoveries was the virtue of carignan, with which they have fallen in love, not surprisingly since they have some centenarian vines. The juice from these and from their syrah is often vinified and raised in wood, but not so their grenache and cinsault (another grape they love and compare with pinot noir). The wines are much admired for their finesse and elegance, but they have good structure too and will improve with age. '50/50' is what they call a "true table wine" (B), a blend of some of their younger carignans with cinsault and a touch of grenache. No wood here, just refreshing fruit and a very more-ish result. 'Les Fontanilles' (C) is another tank-raised wine, a blend of all their red varieties, a thoroughbred atypical wine, showing its Burgundian pedigree. This wine is grown on north-facing plots, unlike 'La Ciaude' (C), for which the vines face full south, with equal quantities of old carignan and syrah, with some grenache too to give fullness. Restrained power is perhaps the hallmark of the top red, 'Les Carrétals' (C/D), lively but elegant, fine and long. These wines are top-class Minervois, even if the style derives from further north.

B ***VIGNOBLE DU LOUP BLANC
Carine Farre and Nicolas Gaignon   (contact Julien Losada)
Hameau de la Roueyre, 11120 Bize Minervois
Tel 04 67 38 18 82
Mobile 06 21 31 70 93
contact@vignobleduloupblanc.com
www.vignobleduloupblanc.com

MAP 50
Visits preferably by appointment.

This property is where the *appellations* of Minervois, St Chinian and St Jean de Minervois meet. The vineyard was created by a family of restaurateurs in Canada who then spread their wings to Bize-Minervois. The unusual *encépagement* includes alicante and tempranillo, which join with carignan and grenache in their red IGP, 'Les 3 C's' (B), powerful but well-balanced and calling for strongly-flavoured food. They also do another quaffer called (appropriately) 'Le Soif du Loup' (A), to be drunk at cellar temperature, light and fruity, not at all serious but quite delicious. The first of two AOP Minervois is 'Le Régal du Loup' (B), a mainly grenache/carignan blend raised in concrete tank. The second is 'La Mère Grand' (C) from the same grapes, given, like the IGP, 20 months in barrel. Not to be missed is their rosé, 'Rosé Petit Chaperon' (A/B), an unusual blend of cinsault and chenanson. There are some eccentric reds too: a pure carignan called 'Méchant Loup' (C), raised in demi-muids and made only in small quantities; as is their dessert Grenache, 'Péché du Loup' (C), aged for many years in barrel and having a good deal of residual sugar in the bottle. Something of a connoisseur's property.

**DOMAINE DE L'HERBE SAINTE
Famille Greuzard
Route de Mirepeisset, 11120 Mirepeisset
Tel 04 68 46 30 37
herbe.sainte@wanadoo.fr   www.domaine-herbe-sainte.com
MAP 52
Appointment advisable.

Originally from Burgundy, this family of winemakers moved into this domaine in 2001 and produced their first Languedoc wines. They had already bought a small plot of carignan vines in nearby Sallèles. Now they have 60 hectares of vines with another 20 ready to be planted when permitted. There are white IGPs (all A) from colombard, sauvignon, viognier and chardonnay (both oaked and unoaked), pink (A) from cinsault, and reds (A) from syrah, cabernet sauvignon and merlot. From their oldest syrah they make a speciality called 'Artemisia' (A), dense, opaque and unoaked, it boasts black pepper and olives as well as liquorice and divers spices. Three grades of AOP Minervois begin with their 'Tradition' (A), a syrah/carignan blend, leading to 'Prestige' (also A), from the same grapes, which is spicy too. The top red is called 'Ambroisie' (B) and adds grenache to the mix, which is made after the *cuvaison* but before it is put in barrels for eight to 12 months. The wood gives it characteristic toasty cedar flavours. 'Noble Gold' (C) is a white dessert wine presented in 50-centilitre bottles, made from late-picked grapes and offering up aromas of dried figs and exotic fruits.

***DOMAINE PIERRE FIL Jérôme Fil
12 impasse des Combes, 11120 Mailhac
Tel 04 68 46 13 09 or 09 67 19 40 24
jeoffrey@domaine-pierre-fil.fr   www.domaine-pierre-fil.fr

MAP 55
Visits by appointment.

This 25-hectare vineyard is in the south-east corner of the appellation, and has been in the same family for seven generations. The speciality is the mourvèdre grape, which is the mainstay of the top wines here. The grapes are mostly hand-harvested and vinified by *macération carbonique*. Quaffing wines include a rosé, mostly saigné from grenache and carignan, and a red IGP with some merlot in it. For the less exacting, there is also BIB presentation. The AOP wines start with 'Heledus' (A), from equal quantities of carignan, grenache, mourvèdre and syrah, raised 60% in *cuve*, 40% in used barrels for 12 months. The wine can show cassis and flowers, with good fruit on the palate, soft and round. Next up the scale is 'Orebus' (B), 60% mourvèdre, 30% grenache, 10% syrah, aged as to 40% in tank, 60% in French oak for 18 months. It is deeper in colour, with a spicy bouquet and notes of the garrigue and liquorice. More spice and vanilla on the finish from the wood. Finally, there is 'Dolium' (C), the same grapes but with more mourvèdre, all raised in wood for two years, powerful and complex. Exceptionally good value for the quality throughout the range.

**CHÂTEAU D'OUPIA Marie-Pierre Iché
34210 Oupia   Tel   04 68 91 20 86
chateau.oupia@aliceadsl.fr

MAP 56
Appointment advisable.

Marie-Pierre is the daughter of André Iché, who inherited this impressive ancient estate and made wines sold *en négoce* until a visiting Burgundian persuaded him to make his own. Now his daughter carries on the tradition which André started. Apart from a rosé (A) from syrah/grenache/cinsault, the wines commonly on the market are red, starting with a pure carignan called 'Les Hérétiques' (A), half made by *macération carbonique*, the other half the traditional way. The 'Tradition' (A) also contains 60% carignan, the rest mostly grenache. Aromatic and deeply fruity, the wine can be drunk young or kept for some years. The top reds are the 'Cuvée des Barons' (B) and 'Nobilis' (C), and are made from 60% syrah and 40% carignan, all coming from the best plots. These wines are aged in Bordeaux barrels for 20 months, so are slower to mature and aim higher, retaining dark berry flavours and good spice on the bouquet.

OTHER GOOD GROWERS IN THE MINERVOIS

*CHÂTEAU DU DONJON   Jean Panis
11600 Bagnoles,
Tel   04 68 77 18 33
jean.panis@wanadoo.fr   www.chateau-du-donjon.fr
MAP 1
Appointment recommended.

*CHÂTEAU MALVÈS-BOUSQUET
Christian and Jean-Louis Bousquet
7 Avenue du Château, 11600 Malvès-en-Minervois
Tel   04 68 72 25 32
malves-bousquet@wanadoo.fr   http://www.les-freres-bousquet.fr
MAP 2
Visits Monday to Friday, 9.00-12.00 and 14.00 -18.00. Weekends by appointment.

A large estate fairly close to Carcassonne, where the brothers Bousquet, whose winemaking traditions go back four generations, make a large range of good-value IGPs as well as red and white AOP Minervois.

**CHÂTEAU CANET   Floris and Victoria Lemstra
11800 Rustiques
Tel   04 68 79 28 25
Mobile   06 84 54 23 10
info@chateaucanet.com
MAP 3
Visits during normal hours, Monday to Saturday.
45 hectares of vines at this traditional 19th Century estate (90% of which are AOP Minervois) are complemented by a substantial olive grove and other farming activities, all within striking distance of Carcassonne. You can also rent adjoining cottages, formerly the homes of vineyard-workers.

*CHÂTEAU L'AMIRAL   Bénédicte Gobe
14 Avenue de l'Amiral Gayde, 11800 Aigues-Vives d'Aude
Mobile   06 83 51 68 88
contact@chateaulamiral.fr   www.chateaulamiral.fr
MAP 7
June, July and August; visits Monday to Friday from 17.00-20.00, Saturdays and Sundays from 10.30-12.30. Otherwise Saturdays from 10.30-12.30 or by appointment. Wine-tasting workshop every Monday at 18.00 by reservation only.

**CHÂTEAU DE RIEUX   Emmanuel de Soos
11160 Rieux
Mobile   06 86 45 53 63
emmanuel@chateauderieux.com   www.chateauderieux.com
MAP 8
Appointment advisable.

**CHÂTEAU GIBALAUX BONNET
Olivier Bonnet 11800 Laure-Minervois
Tel   04 68 78 12 02
la-presse-des-arcades@orange.fr
MAP 11
Appointment avoids frustration.

B *CHÂTEAU PRAT-MAJOU-GAY
Géraldine Gay and Guilhem Pédréno
Lieu-dit Prat-Majou, 11800 Laure-Minervois
Tel   04 68 78 08 57
prat-majou.gay@wanadoo.fr   www.pratmajougay.com
MAP 13
Appointment advised. An exceptionally good value 40-hectare *domaine*. If you want better, you'll need to pay more.

**DOMAINE BENAZÉTH   Franck Bénazeth
16 rue de la Condamine, 11160 Villeneuve Minervois
Tel   04 68 36 57 56
GPS 43 19 1N 2 27 15E
moulin.11@free   www.moulin-benazeth.fr

Unweeded grenache vineyard

MAP 14
Visits April 14.00-17.00, May to September 10.00-17.30. October through March by appointment.
This property features a working windmill close beside the *caveau de dégustation*. Exceptionally good value for money, surprisingly so in view of the many medals which Frank Bénazeth has won.

**CHÂTEAU LA VILLATADE

Denis et Sophie Morin
11600 Sallèles-Cabardès
Tel   04 68 77 57 51
villatade@wanadoo.fr   www.villatade.com
MAP 15
Visits during normal hours except Sunday.
This extensive estate is on the Cabardès borders and reaches up into the forests and *garrigue* of the Black Mountain.

**DOMAINE MALYS-ANNE

Caroline Froc, Jacques Gury and Philippe Recoulles
11160 Trausse
Tel 04 68 78 01 83
Mobile   06 30 89 09 76
GPS 43 18 58.0N 02 33 00.0E
contact@domaine-malys-anne.com   www.domaine-malys-anne.com

MAP 20
Visits by appointment only. The *cave* has moved from Caunes-Minervois to Trausse.

BD **DOMAINE DE CHAMANS

Sir John Hegarty and Philippa Crane
11160 Trausse
Tel   04 68 78 46 21
Mobile 06 08 02 65 60 (ask for Jessica)
chamans@wanadoo.fr   www.hegartychamans.com
MAP 21
Telephone for appointment.
The style here is very southern and appeals to the huge number of fans which the makers enjoy. Generous extraction and loads of dark fruit are the hallmarks. Not for the faint-hearted.

**DOMAINE DU PETIT CAUSSE

Philippe et Maguy Chabbert
Rue de la Sallèle, 34210 Félines-Minervois
Tel   04 68 91 66 12
Mobile   06 71 13 09 68
chabbertphilippe@orange.fr   www.domainedupetitcausse.com
MAP 24
Best to phone ahead.

B **LE CLOS DU MARBRIER** Irène Prioton
Hameau de Camplong, 34210 Félines-Minervois
(cave de vinification at 28 rue des Remparts
11160 Caunes-Minervois)
Tel   04 68 43 85 79 Mobile 06 85 91 27 57
leclosdumarbrier@wanadoo.com www.leclosdumarbrier.com
MAP 26
Appointment required.
Visitors can taste from the tanks, tour the vineyards, even rent a few vines themselves and take part in the harvest and make their own blends. There is a *gîte* and some *chambres d'hôte* too.

** L'OSTAL CAZES** Jean-Michel and Jean-Charles Cazes
(Maître de chais Fabrice Darmaillacq)
34210 La Livinière
Tel   04 68 91 47 79
contact@lostalcazes.com www.jmcazes.com
MAP 28
Cellars open Monday to Saturday.
One would expect these owners of Château Lynch-Bages in Bordeaux to have made a grand success of their venture in the Minervois, and so they have.

L'OUSTAL BLANC Claude and Isabel Fonquerle
Chemin des Condamines, 34210 La Livinière
Tel   04 67 26 93 84
Mobiles   06 03 61 02 31 and 06 10 50 41 23
earl.fonquerle@wanadoo.fr www.oustal-blanc.com
MAP 31
Visits by appointment.
There are distinct echoes of Châteauneuf-du-Pape here, but the owners claim also inspiration from Burgundy. Most people may however have to search hard for this below the layers of richness and sweet fruit which are the features of the top wines here.

BD ** CHÂTEAU MARIS
Grandes vignobles en Méditerranée (Robert Eden)
34210 La Livinière
Tel   04 68 91 42 63
Mobile 06 82 78 39 13
robert@chateaumaris.com www.chateaumaris.com
MAP 32
Appointment strongly recommended.
All the wines here are big, smoky, dark and packed with fruit. If you like the style you won't mind paying the money.

DOMAINE DES MURETTES Jean-Louis Bellido
3 rue des Ecoles, La Livinière
Tel   04 68 91 62 84
Mobile 06 87 40 27 21
domaine.murettes@orange.fr
MAP 33
Visits best by appointment. Back on form after a difficult patch.

DOMAINE COMBE BLANCHE
Guy Vanlancker
3 ancien chemin du Moulin Rigaud, 34210 La Livinière
Tel   04 68 91 44 82
Mobile   06 80 43 40 61
contact@lacombeblanche.com www.lacombeblanche.com
MAP 34
Rendezvous recommended.
Guy is keen on experiment, so the blends and the styles may change from year to year, depending on the characteristics of the vintage.

B ** DOMAINE DE CANTAUSSEL
Claude and Jean-Luc Bohler
Lieu-dit Cantaussel, 34210 Siran
Tel   04 68 91 46 86
Mobiles   06 12 10 85 79 and 06 21 14 20 55
jbohler@pt.lu www.cantaussel.fr
MAP 37
Appointment recommended.
The vineyard has been overhauled. It is not often that one finds a 100% vermentino wine, but here it is made as an IGP (A).

DOMAINE DES AIRES-HAUTES and **CLOS DE L'ESCANDIL** Gilles Chabbert
10 Chemin des Aires, 34210 Siran
Tel   04 68 91 54 40
Mobile 06 11 17 54 27
Gilles.chabbert@wanadoo.fr
www.aires-hautes.pagesperso-orange.fr
MAP 38
Appointment advisable.
This 28-hectare domaine goes back to 1938. Gilles is the grandson of the founder and his father mayor of Siran. Gilles took over the reins here in 1995 and has since been building a reputation for high-class Minervois.

B **CLOS DES ROQUES Nelly and Laurent Gastou
Chemin du Tribi, 34210 Cesseras
Tel   04 68 91 28 70
closdesroques@yahoo.fr www.closdesroques.fr
MAP 42
Rendezvous recommended.
The growers used to send their grapes to the *coopérative*, but now they are advised by Claude Serra (q.v.) in the making of their own wines.

DOMAINE DU CAZAL Claude et Martine Derroja
Route de St Pons de Thomières, 34210 La Caunette.
Tel   04 68 91 62 53
info@lecazal.com
MAP 44
Open daily, 9.00-12.00 and 13.30-18.30.

*DOMAINE LA PRADE MARI Eric Mari
34210 Aigne
Tel   04 68 91 22 45
Mobile   06 87 33 58 13
domainelaprademari@wanadoo.fr   www.laprademari.com
MAP 46
Visits by appointment.

*CHÂTEAU D'AGEL
Christian Berger and his colleagues
Lotissement Les Crozes, 34210 Agel
Tel   04 68 91 37 74
Mobile   06 31 29 27 98
contact@chateaudagel.com www.chateaudagel.com
MAP 49
Phone ahead.

**CHATEAU CABEZAC
Gontran et Stéphanie Dondain
23 Hameau de Cabezac, 11120 Bize Minervois
Tel   04 68 46 23 05
info@chateaucabezac.com   www.chateaucabezac.com
MAP 51
Appointment required.

** CHÂTEAU DE PARAZA Annick Danglas
11200 Paraza
Tel   09 64 33 37 43
chateaudeparaza@gmail.com   www.chateau-de-paraza.fr
MAP 53
Appointment recommended.

**CHÂTEAU PIQUE-PERLOU Serge Serris
12 Avenue des Écoles, 11200 Roubia
Tel   04 68 43 22 46
Mobile   06 16 57 14 61
GPS 43 14 51 N 2 47 58 E
chateau@pique-perlou@wanadoo.fr
MAP 54
Open usual hours but appointment safer.
Once a member of the local *coopérative*, Serge Serris set up his own winery in 1993 and has since been making wines of serious quality.

*CHÂTEAU DE BEAUFORT
(DOMAINE D'ARTIX) Jerôme Portal
34210 Beaufort Tel ; 04 68 91 28 28
ch-beaufort@wanadoo.fr
MAP 57
Visits Monday to Saturday during usual hours.
A large 110-hectare property where there is a predominance of syrah and a handful of good-value reds.

*LE PECH D'ANDRÉ Mireille Remaury
334210 Azillanet
Tel   04 68 91 22 66
Mobile   06 87 34 67 04
contact@lepechdandre.fr

MAP 58
Visits every day from 10.00 -20.00.

B **DOMAINE DE CLARMON
Frédérique and Denis Josserand
16 Place du Château, 11200 Tourouzelle
Tel   04 68 41 60 12
Mobile   06 15 87 19 75
domaine@clarmon.fr www.clarmon.fr
MAP 59
Visits during normal hours (not Sundays).

DOMAINE TERRES-GEORGES
Anne-Marie and Roland Coustal
2 rue des Jardins, 11700 Castelnau d'Aude
Tel   04 68 43 79 39
Mobile   06 30 49 97 73
info@domaineterresgeorges.com
www.domaineterresgeorges.com
MAP 60
Disappointment best avoided by rendezvous.

*CHÂTEAU GUÉRY René-Henry Guéry
4 Avenue du Minervois, 11700 Azille
Tel   04 68 91 44 34
Mobile   06 75 74 33 45
rhguery@chateau-guery.com   www.chateau-guery.com
MAP 61
Visits during usual business hours, Monday to Saturday. Prior appointment might save anguish.

ST JEAN DE MINERVOIS

This separate *appellation* is for wines from the muscat grape, although growers within it may also produce conventional Minervois wines and, of course, IGPs. The vineyards are situated on chalky soil high up in the hills at the eastern end of the Minervois area, the kind of *terroir* which seems to suit the muscat grape to perfection. Of all the muscat wines made in the South of France, many people hold these to be the finest, the cooler climate – particularly at night – providing more elegance and finesse than you find in the lower and hotter areas of Languedoc or Roussillon. There are two styles: the one dry and unfortified, the other sweet and fortified as in Frontignan or Rivesaltes.

**CAVE COOPÉRATIVE DE ST JEAN DE MINERVOIS
34360 St Jean de Minervois
Tel   04 67 38 03 24
www.muscat-saintjeanminervois.com

MAP 62
Visits Monday to Friday, Saturday and Sunday in summer.

An outstanding *coopérative*, two thirds of whose effort is given over to the making of red Minervois wines, the other third to its better-known Muscat de St Jean. For example, its 'Muscat Petit Grains' (B), with its eye-catching gold label, can be widely found in all kinds of retail outlets. It is also of course available to purchase on the spot. It is remarkable for its perfume of grapes freshly picked off the vine, with aromas of citrus fruits and exotic apricots, quince, mandarin and honey. Another wine called 'Domaine les Roumanis' (B) shows similar qualities and gets many medals. There is also a tiny production of an ultra-sweet wine, 'Vendanges d'Automne' (C), from only eight hectolitres per hectare of grapes, and with a concentration of 350 grams of sugar per litre. Four months in oak complete its maturity.

**DOMAINE MICHEL SIGÉ   Michel Sigé
34360 St Jean de Minervois
Tel   04 67 38 03 07
muscatsige@free.fr   www.muscatsige.free.fr

MAP 63
Ring before visiting.

Sigé believes the secret of the muscat from Saint Jean is in the control of temperature. Unfashionably, he does not shun the rapid freezing of the wine (B) just before bottling because he does not like the formation of crystals in the bottle. Freshly picked fruit is once again the hallmark of these wines, the fresh acidity being an essential complement to the sweetness of the product after being fortified with alcohol. The wine is required to attain a degree of sugar equal to 125 grams per litre, and is bottled only after a year and a half of élevage. Sigé also makes a *moëlleux* from his muscat (A), as well as a small amount of red Minervois (A).

B ****LE CLOS DU GRAVILLAS
Nicole and John Bojanowski
34360 St Jean de Minervois
Tel   04 67 38 17 52
Mobile   06 07 90 09 67
contact@closdugravillas.com   www.closdugravillas.com

John Bojanowski, Le Clos du Gravillas

MAP 64
Prior appointment advisable.

This is undoubtedly one of the most original, inventive and thoroughly principled pair of winegrowers in the Languedoc. John landed in this remote spot from the US via Spain, Nicole from a wine-trade background in Bèziers. They built much of their small nine-hectare vineyard themselves by clearing away several hectares of scrub and boulders, as well as nurturing precious old vines such as carignan, one of their present mainstays. They now also have syrah, grenache in all three colours, muscat, terret gris and noir, cabernet sauvignon, cinsault, mourvèdre, counoise, maccabeu, roussanne, marsanne and viognier. The house style prefers elegance rather than power, and care over the use of oak. Although within the special AOP of St Jean (and they do make lovely muscats (B)), these are but a small part of their production. So where to start? With 'Mademoiselle Lily' perhaps (B), from viognier, roussanne and terret, aromatic and well-balanced, in apéritif style? Or a pure terret (B) from 50-year old vines, light, floral and refreshing? Or 'L'Inattendu' (C) perhaps, a grenache blanc/maccabeu blend, rich and mineral, fermented and raised in barrel on its lees? Or straight to the reds:

'Sur la Lune' (B), half carignan, half syrah and exhaling the garrigue; 'Lo Vielh Carignan', one of the best varietals from this grape to be found in Languedoc (C); its eccentric relative 'From the Dark side of the Moon' (C), sometimes loaded with cassis; or the IGP, 'Sous les Cailloux des Grillons' (B), from a cocktail which includes non-AOP grapes such as cabernet sauvignon and counoise? Otherwise, 'Rendez-vous au Soleil' (B/C) from carignan, cabernet and syrah, sweetish on the tongue, but with a lot of body and longing for partnership with a magret de canard? And do you start or finish the tasting with 'Oxytan' (C), a dry white oxidised wine from grenache blanc, raised under a *voile* like sherry for five years? A visit here is very special.

BD ***DOMAINE LE PETIT GIMIOS

Anne-Marie and Pierre Lavaysse, Gimios
34360 St Jean de Minervois
Tel   04 67 38 26 10

MAP 65
Appointment strongly advised.

Madame Lavaysse started in 1993 the work of re-establishing this tiny boutique vineyard of four and a half hectares, working biodynamically in the vines and, more recently, without enzymes or sulphur in the cellar. Yields are absurdly low, hence the price (D, rather than C), but they have a real character to make them at once distinguishable. Her dry muscat 'Des Roumanis' will seem less muscaty and paler than other wines you are used to, and there is a touch of sweetness deriving from a small amount of residual sugar left in the wine, which is vat-fermented and matured in bottle. It is quite deliciously different, and sometimes with a slight prickle on the tongue. Then there is her 'Moëlleux', which, like all good wines of this style, has a nice touch of acidity at the end to balance the round sweetness on the palate. Madame also makes a *vin de table* rosé from a cocktail of old Languedoc varieties including aramon and Alicante, as well as the more familiar carignan, grenache, cinsault and muscat. Her range ends with her *vin doux naturel*, which comes in 50-centilitre bottles and which is so unusual that Madame is sometimes refused the right to put St Jean de Minervois on the label. It is not as sweet as some wines of this style, and even after ten years or so in bottle can seem even older. These wines are entirely out of the mainstream: no better reason for sampling them.

****DOMAINE DE BARROUBIO

Laurent Miquel
34360 St Jean de Minervois
Tel   04 67 38 14 06
Mobile   06 10 63 67 44
barroubio@barroubio.fr   www.barroubio.fr

MAP 66
Visits in theory at usual hours, but prior notice advisable because of the remoteness of the domaine.

The Miquel family have been here since the 15th Century, in a moonscape of chalk with only occasional flecks of red sandstone lining a road that seems to lead to nowhere. This is a high-altitude vineyard of 27 hectares, where the winds blow and at night the cool breezes mitigate the heat of the sun that reflects off the bare stone during the day. Laurent makes a white IGP from sauvignon and chardonnay grapes (A), which are grown near Pézenas and brought here for the cooler night climate. There is a rosé under the Minervois AOP from syrah and Grenache (A) and two reds (both A/B) raised in barrel for 14 months. Firstly, a carignan/syrah/grenache blend which he makes partly by macération carbonique and partly by traditional methods, and secondly a wine which has much more carignan. These are good Minervois wines indeed, but it is the muscat petit grains wines that have attracted worldwide attention. First there is a dry version of wonderful freshness and fruit (A/B), but above all, his range of *vins doux naturels*, of which he makes no fewer than five. 'Classique' (B) is pale with scents of dried flowers, pears and citrus fruits; 'Dieuvalle' (B) is a step up if one were needed; 'Cuvée Bleue' (C) is given more ageing on its lees; 'Cuvée Nicolas' (C) is made by *macération carbonique* and is recommended to accompany foie gras or a good cigar; and finally 'Grain d'Automne' (C/D) is from super-ripe grapes, half of which are fermented and aged in oak. The distinguishing feature of these wines is that the alcohol used to stop the fermentation is not as strong as that which most growers use, and the extreme richness of the wine is balanced with just the right touch of acidity. These wines are the ultimate in this style, and they have been called the finest, most elegant and "most spiritual" of their kind in France.

SEE ALSO UNDER SAINT CHINIAN; CLOS BAGATELLE, DOMAINE SACRÉ COEUR.

SAINT-CHINIAN

Saint-Chinian was a famous vine growing area long before it was granted VDQS status in 1951 and, eventually AOC (AOP) classification for the red and pink wines in 1982. The wines became popular long before those of many other areas in Languedoc that have since become fashionable and much sought after. The district is somewhat shut away from the rest of Languedoc, the hills to the east separating it from the immediately adjoining Faugères, the Cévennes to the north acting as a natural barrier, and the chalky hills of Saint Jean de Minervois making access from the west quite tricky. To the south, the countryside opens up a bit and most people would approach Saint-Chinian from Béziers or Narbonne. There are 3,300 hectares of vines planted in the region. AOP status was accorded the whites in 2004.

There are two quite distinct *terroirs*; a continuation of the Faugères schist to the north, and a more conventional *argilo-calcaire* ground to the south. Despite this there is a certain homogeneity of style throughout the area, although some say that the schist wines are finer and more elegant, while the wines from further south have more power and fruit. Some growers have ground in both *terroirs* and so make wines which might suggest a hybrid style. Generally speaking the wines of Saint-Chinian balance well their fruit, tannin and spicy flavours, and are sometimes easier to drink than those from many other areas east and southwards.

This is a wonderful area to visit. The spectacular countryside offers open views to the mountains in the north, in particular 'Cebenna', the name given by locals to a mountain they say has the form of a sleeping woman. The mountains give protection from the cold north wind and the atmosphere is unusually clear. A mild springtime usually enables mimosas to bloom wild, and orange trees need no particular protection. The *arbousier*, sometimes called the strawberry tree, offers its yellow flowers and red fruits in autumn, and many species of cistus adorn the hillsides.

The grapes grown here are the same as those generally used throughout Languedoc, the old carignan, cinsault, grenache and lledoner pelut surviving alongside the newly imported syrah and mourvèdre. These two so-called *améliorateurs*, along with grenache, must comprise at least 60% of an AOP vineyard. Whites are made mostly from roussanne and grenache blanc, and cinsault, as often, is the mainstay of many of the rosés.

The area being so straggly, the following is an attempt to list the best-known vineyards in an order which makes a tour of the region as easy as possible in the circumstances. But it is a good idea to start at the Maison des Vins in Saint-Chinian itself, housed in the former family home of Charles Trenet in the centre of town. It is open Monday to Friday all the year round, Saturday mornings (afternoons too in season) and on Sunday mornings in July and August. You can telephone 04 67 38 11 69, otherwise email maisondesvins@saint-chinian.com. The website is www.saint-chinian.com. Here you will find not only good advice but the opportunity to taste and buy a wide range of the local wines at cellar prices.

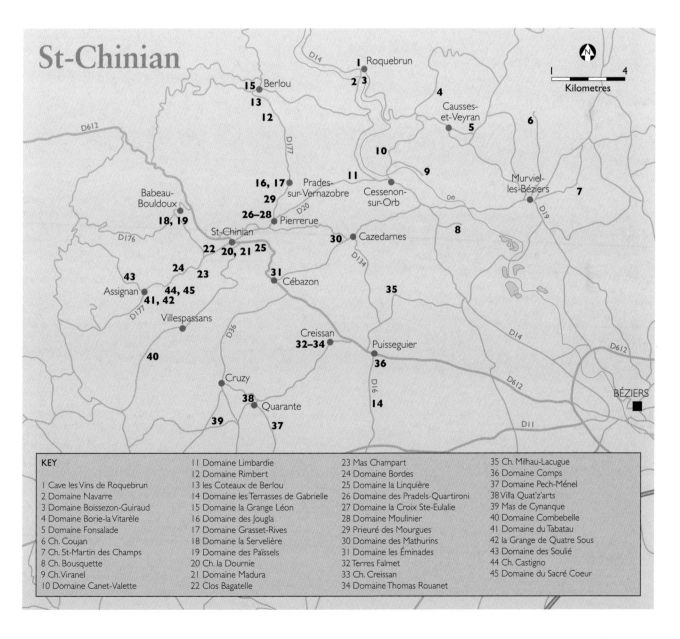

KEY
1 Cave les Vins de Roquebrun
2 Domaine Navarre
3 Domaine Boissezon-Guiraud
4 Domaine Borie-la-Vitarèle
5 Domaine Fonsalade
6 Ch. Coujan
7 Ch. St-Martin des Champs
8 Ch. Bousquette
9 Ch. Viranel
10 Domaine Canet-Valette
11 Domaine Limbardie
12 Domaine Rimbert
13 les Coteaux de Berlou
14 Domaine les Terrasses de Gabrielle
15 Domaine la Grange Léon
16 Domaine des Jougla
17 Domaine Grasset-Rives
18 Domaine la Servelière
19 Domaine des Païssels
20 Ch. la Dournie
21 Domaine Madura
22 Clos Bagatelle
23 Mas Champart
24 Domaine Bordes
25 Domaine la Linquière
26 Domaine des Pradels-Quartironi
27 Domaine la Croix Ste-Eulalie
28 Domaine Moulinier
29 Prieuré des Mourgues
30 Domaine des Mathurins
31 Domaine les Éminades
32 Terres Falmet
33 Ch. Creissan
34 Domaine Thomas Rouanet
35 Ch. Milhau-Lacugue
36 Domaine Comps
37 Domaine Pech-Ménel
38 Villa Quat'z'arts
39 Mas de Cynanque
40 Domaine Combebelle
41 Domaine du Tabatau
42 la Grange de Quatre Sous
43 Domaine des Soulié
44 Ch. Castigno
45 Domaine du Sacré Coeur

Thierry Navarre, Domaine Navarre

ROQUEBRUN

The wines of Roquebrun, all made from grapes grown on the schist, have the right to add the name of their commune to the AOP Saint-Chinian, provided the yield from the wines is more limited, the grapes are picked by hand, and the wines are aged until the end of the year following the vintage.

* * CAVE LES VINS DE ROQUEBRUN
Avenue des Orangers, 34460 Roquebrun
Tel   04 67 89 64 35
cave@cave-roquebrun.fr   www.caveroquebrun.fr

MAP 1
Visits Monday to Friday during normal hours

Often considered to be the best of the *Caves Coopératives* at Saint-Chinian, ranking on a par with all but the best independent growers. There is a huge range of wines, even though the members combined have only 650 hectares of vines between them. Everything here is of reliable quality and many bottles are better than that. There are four whites alone, ranging from the basic 'Col de l'Orb' (A); through 'Terrasses d'Aupenac' (B) which is all-viognier and partly raised in oak; 'Les Fiefs d'Aupenac' (C) which is essentially roussanne and given 9 months in barrel; and 'Seigneur d'Aupenac' (D) from grenache blanc and roussanne, and which is vinified as well as aged in barrel. The one rosé, 'Col de l'Orb' (A), is two parts syrah, one grenache, a deepish colour, very fruity and quite big on the palate, suggesting it is a wine to go with food. There are at least eight reds (and you may be offered others as well), ranging in price from (A) to (D): the basic 'Col d'Orb' (A) ("*pour un moment simple et convivial*"); 'La Grange des Combes' (B), with a touch more class and depth of flavour; 'Roches Noires' (B), largely syrah made by *macération carbonique*; 'Prestige' (B), from mourvèdre made the same way; 'Les Fiefs d'Aupenac' (B/C), 60% syrah and raised in oak; 'Sir Roc de Brun' (B/C), its mourvèdre counterpart; 'Seigneur d'Aupenac' (C) spicy and leathery and aged for 14 months in barrel; and lastly 'Baron d'Aupenac' (C), mostly syrah and even longer oak-aged. An *embarras de choix*.

* * * DOMAINE NAVARRE Thierry Navarre
Avenue de Balaussan, 34460 Roquebrun
Tel   04 67 89 53 58
thierry.navarre@orange.fr   www.thierrynavarre.com

MAP 2
Appointment advisable

Thierry operates organically but without making a fuss about it, or being officially registered. He comes from a long line of winemakers, and on his 12 hectares of brown schist he grows not only the usual AOP grapes, but a variety of others as well. These include oeillade (a cousin of cinsault from which Thierry makes a light, deliciously fruity wine (B) for drinking slightly chilled and young); ribeyrenc (one of the oldest *cépages* of the Languedoc, aka aspiran noir); terret, from which he makes a varietal dry wine 'Issu de terret gris' (B), with hints of amber and a slightly oxidised taste which points up the flavour of the fruit. His first AOP is called 'Le Laouzil' (B), spicy with soft tannins and a blend of carignan, grenache, cinsault and a little syrah. Then there is 'Cuvée Olivier' (B/C), another spicy wine with plenty of red fruit flavour from old vine-syrah grenache and carignan, and aged in 500-litre *fûts*. You can also taste a sweet grenache for drinking either as an aperitif or perhaps with chocolate desserts (B/C), and a sweet dessert wine from Muscat (B/C). Thierry has recently acquired more vineyards up in the hills to be planted with Bordeaux grapes(!), fearing that the climate at Roquebrun will get too hot for the kind of wines he likes to make.

CAUSSES-ET-VEYRAN

BD * * * DOMAINE BORIE-LA VITARÈLE
Mme Cathérine Izarn
34490 Causses-et-Veyran
Tel   04 67 89 50 43
Mobile   06 83 75 10 22
contact@borielavitarele.fr

MAP 4
Appointment recommended

The whole of the wine world in Languedoc and beyond was shocked to hear of the tragic death of Jean-François in a tractor accident in the spring of 2014. His widow Cathy, in whose family many of the vines have been for several generations, is nevertheless confidently carrying on with some help from other growers and the consultant Claude Gros – every wine-lover will wish her well. She has 18 hectares under biodynamic cultivation since 1998, and by common consent has been making some of the best wines, not only in Saint-Chinian, but in the whole of the Languedoc. Jean-François described his wines as "the pleasure of sun in the glass". They are full-bodied, well-built and generous. Yields from the vines are low and in the cellar macerations are long with frequent *pigeages*. Barrel-ageing is careful, only some of the wood being new. No filtering or fining of course. After a white from clairette, vermentino and bourboulenc called 'Le Grand Mayol' (B), raised in tank apart from a small 10% in new wood, the range (otherwise all red) starts with an IGP Hérault called 'Cuvée des Cigales' (A) from equal quantities of merlot and grenache. The fruit from the one and the garrigue from the other combine to give a *vin de plaisir* at a very reasonable price. AOPs include 'Les Terres Blanches' (B), a grenache/syrah blend grown on causse-type soil surrounded by pines and garrigue, very Mediterranean, but quite elegant. 'Les Schistes' (C) is from old vines grown

Roquebrun

on high-altitude ground, surrounded by cystus and heather, aromatic, spicy and elegant. 'Les Crès' (C) means 'big round pebbles', the wine's specific *terroir*, where syrah and mourvèdre combine to make a powerful wine designed 'to confront the years'. 'Midi rouge' (C) is Cathy's own challenge to the future. With syrah from two different *terroirs*, carignan and mourvèdre, which are all vinified and aged in *demi-muids*, this is a wine which is intense yet fresh and refined.

**DOMAINE FONSALADE Julien Peltier
34490 Causses-et-Veyran
Tel   05 62 88 13 35 or 04 67 24 42 71
christinegent@btinternet.com   www.fonsalade.com

MAP 5
Visits by appointment.

This delightful estate enjoys a variety of *terroirs*: not only the usual schist (Faugères is nearby), but a generous dose of *graves*, pebbles and chalk. 'Fonsalade' means 'salt spring', and indeed there is such a spring which gives water to the *chais*, but it is only for washing the glasses, not drinking. The 27 hectares of grapes are largely syrah and grenache, but there is some carignan too and a little mourvèdre.

White wine, called 'La Lyre' (B) is also being made nowadays here, from chardonnay, chenin, viognier, roussanne and muscat, a cocktail of grapes which produces a wine of as many flavours. The rosé here used to be all syrah, but now 'Le Petit Bonheur' (A/B) is a blend of the other grapes (but no cinsault) and the wine is kept three months on its lees. There are four reds: 'Tradition' (A) from syrah, grenache and carignan, for drinking young; 'Cuvée Frédéric' (B), a syrah/grenache blend named after the son of a previous owner, Madame Maurel, who died tragically in an avalanche; 'Vieilles Vignes' (B/C) mostly from old-vine grenache, given long macerations and a year or so in barrel; and finally (but only in good years) 'Felix Culpa' (C/D), mostly syrah, vinified in open vats and given long oak-ageing.

B **CHÂTEAU COUJAN Florence Guy
34490 Murviel–lès-Béziers
Tel   04 67 37 80 00
chateau-coujan@orange.fr   www.chateau-coujan.com

MAP 6
Visits weekdays during normal hours.

Be greeted by flocks of free-range peacocks at this historic

Saint-Chinian address. Other unique features include a restored Romanesque chapel and one of the finest collections of old *foudres* you are ever likely to see. Note also the bed of fossilised coral on which the 56 hectares of vines are planted. These include pinot, merlot and cabernet, as well as the more traditional varieties. Florence's father was probably the first to plant Bordeaux varieties in Saint-Chinian. The result is a parallel range of AOP wines and equally successful IGPs, all fantastic value for money. There is a deal of further ground now prepared for organic farming. The IGP white is a rare 100% vermentino (A), aged three months on its lees. Its AOP counterpart 'Cuvée Bois Joli' (B) is more conventionally grenache blanc, roussanne with just 12% vermentino and fermented in *demi-muids*. The AOP rosé (A) is almost all *saigné* from mourvèdre. An IGP red, 'Cuvée Kenza Marie' (B/C) from merlot, cabernet and a little mourvèdre enjoys 25 days' maceration followed by 26 months in barrel. There are three AOP reds: a 'Tradition' (A), easy and well-balanced; 'Cuvée Gabrielle Spinola' (A), named after a former feudal landlady who took her rent in wine; and 'Cuvée Bois Joli rouge' (B), from nearly equal quantities of old syrah and mourvèdre. The family also produces high-grade oil from an orchard of Lucques olives.

CESSENON-SUR-ORB

**CHÂTEAU VIRANEL

Nicolas and Arnaud Bergasse-Milhé
Route de Causses-et-Veyran, 34460 Cessenon
Tel 04 67 90 60 59
contact@viranel.fr   www. viranel.com
GPS 43 27 06 2N 3 04 14.5E

MAP 9
Open weekdays during normal hours, but an appointment still desirable.

This important estate, reliable and good-value, has been in the same family for generations, and today they pursue the old house plan of principally serving the restaurant trade. The wines are thus full-bodied without being overweight, made to drink earlier rather than later and therefore with less accent on acidity. There are three distinct *terroirs*: alluvial terraces close to the river (cabernet and mourvèdre); a mixture of marls and chalk around and above the château (syrah, carignan and some grenache); and more acidic higher ground (grenache blanc, viognier and more grenache). Curiosities include 'Gourmandise' (C) a blend of alicante-bouschet with eau-de-vie, to be drunk *en apéritif,* and 'Folies d'Automne' (B/C) a sweet Grenache dessert wine. Alicante-bouschet is a speciality grape of the house, part of the blend for 'Trilogie Rouge' (A/B) and offered on its own as a *mono-cépage*, 'Aromes Sauvages' (B/C). There is a white viognier varietal kept for four months on its lees (B), and a rosé (A/B). With some cabernet in the blend, pale and by-the-side-of-the-pool style. The white 'Cuvée

Tradition' (A/B) is pure grenache blanc (three months on lees but no wood). The two AOP reds are predominantly from syrah and grenache: 'le V de Viranel' (A/B) and the partly oak-aged 'Tradition' (A/B).

B ***DOMAINE CANET-VALETTE

Marc Valette
Route de Causses-et-Veyran, 34460 Cessenon
Tel 04 67 89 51 83
Mobile 06 07 95 68 95
contact@canetvalette.com   www.canetvalette.com

MAP 10
Appointment advisable

It would be difficult to find a grower who is more sincere or self-confident. His wines will inspire either huge enthusiasm, or regret that so much talent is dissipated in producing wines of such huge extraction and alcoholic degree. For some, five stars would be awarded with acclamation, for others perhaps two would be too many. What you can't dispute is the actual quality of Marc's work. He started with just two reds and they are still on his books: 'Mille et Une nuits' (B), dark garnet, with cherries and flowers on the nose and palate, with an élevage of 30 months, half in tank and half in wood, and 'Le Vin Maghani' (D), half syrah half mourvèdre, and almost a caricature of extremity in technique – 90 days' maceration followed by three years in *demi-muids*. In recent years Marc has made some concessions to moderation. 'Antonyme' (A/B) can just about be called a '*vin des copains*', and is spared long *cuvaisons* and ageing, and 'Ivresses' (C), has a charming red-fruit character. Although its *cuvaison* lasts for 90 days, it is raised in stainless steel. None of this can really be called typical Saint-Chinian but you have to admire the chutzpah.

BERLOU

This commune, along with Roquebrun (q.v.) is entitled to add its name to those of its Saint-Chinian wines which come from its best *terroirs*. It is an old place: the Romans called it "ver luporum" – springtime of the wolves. It is small too, about 180 inhabitants these days. The winning of its sub-*appellation* has brought a lot of attention to the area, and a number of growers have set up on their own on the back of the Berlou name.

Vieussan, north of Roquebrun

B ***DOMAINE RIMBERT

Jean-Marie Rimbert
1 Rue de l'Aire, 34360 Berlou
Tel   04 67 89 74 66
domaine.rimbert@wanadoo.fr   www.domainerimbert.com

MAP 12
Open for tastings every day, but prior appointment suggested.

Jean-Marie has gradually built up his holdings from an initial four hectares to a present 28, split among 40 parcels within a radius of 10 kilometres of the village. Thus there is a diversity of soil types as well as the usual schist. Jean-Marie stands out among Saint-Chinian growers for two reasons.Firstly, because of his passion for the carignan grape, which appears sometimes as a varietal in his wines and sometimes as a substantial part of the blend. Secondly, because he uses only really old barrels for his *élevages*. His belief that wine is for pleasure, not for intellectual debate shines through all the wines, whether *vins de table* such as his all-cinsault 'Cuvée Oscar' (A), his 'Grenachator' (B), his 'Cuvée Q' (a blend of carignan syrah and grenache) or 'Petit Cochon Bronzé' a delightful quaffing rosé. The all-carignan wines include 'Carignator' (C) from 10-year-old wood, and a tank-raised 'Chant de marjolaine' (A/B). His AOPs (by law required to be blends) include a syrah/cinsault rosé, perfect with exotic foods, and a 'Blanc' (A/B) from 35% clairette, 15% roussanne, 25% vermentino and 25% grenache blanc, a wine which has subtlety in with its *gras*. There are three reds: 'Travers de Marceau' (A/B) for drinking on its fruit, though Jean-Marie says it will keep and is the best-value wine from his *domaine*; 'Le Mas du Schiste' (B/C), again with a deal of carignan; and finally his Berlou wine (C), once more with the accent on carignan, powerful and redolent of cherries and prunes.

***DOMAINE LA GRANGE LÉON

Joël Fernandez
3 Rue du Caladou, 34360 Berlou
Tel. 06 73 83 37 61
fernandez.berlou@wanadoo.fr   lagrangeleon.fr

MAP 15
Rendezvous required.

Joël's father and grandfather Léon had been *vignerons* here for many years, sending their wines to the *coopérative*. Joël decided in 2008 to make his own wine, so this *domaine* came into being. It has rapidly become quite fashionable, with a Coup de Coeur Guide Hachette for its top red in 2013. Joël offers a rosé (A) suggesting cherries, made from 50% cinsault, the rest syrah and grenache, well balanced between body and freshness. There are three reds: 'L'Insolent' (A), to be drunk cool and enjoyed young on its fruit; 'L'Audacieux' (B), with its 40% carignan, bright garnet colour, black fruit character, chewy palate and charm too; and the top 'D'Une Main à l'Autre' (C), with just a little

more syrah than grenache and carignan. 2/3rds of this wine is aged six months in one-year-old barrels. It is big, with plenty of minerality and garrigue and a long peppery finish. Needs ageing. A property with a bright future.

SAINT-CHINIAN

In and around the town of Saint-Chinian itself, some of the best-known growers of the *appellation* are to be found.

**CHÂTEAU LA DOURNIE Véronique Étienne

Route de St Pons, 34360 Saint-Chinian
Tel 04 67 38 19 43
chateau.ladournie@wanadoo.fr   www.chateauladournnie.com

GPS 43 4221915 2 9414226

MAP 20
Open Monday to Saturday during normal hours 9.00-12.00 and 14.00-18.00. Sundays by appointment.

This is one of the oldest Saint-Chinian estates, the Étienne family going back to 1870. The vines are all in one piece ("*dans un seul tenant*", as they say) and run to 52 hectares, shared between schist and sandy clay. They make one red and two white IGPs, the first of the latter being a lemony white fruit blend of roussanne, viognier and vermentino (A), the second a pure roussanne called 'Marie' (A). Both are raised in tank. The red (A) is a cabernet franc/merlot blend. There is an AOP rosé (A) from grapes grown on the schist and a red *Tradition*-type blend (A) dominated by syrah with some carignan and grenache, 20% of which is given some ageing in oak. 'Étienne' (B) is from the same blend as the rosé. Each variety is vinified separately, then after the *assemblage* given a year in barrel. The top wine is 'Élise' (C), a much admired, mostly low-yielding syrah with some grenache and, like 'Étienne', raised in wood for 12 months. The value here is as warm as the welcome.

***DOMAINE MADURA

Cyril and Nadia Bourgne
12 Rue de la Digue, 34360 Saint-Chinian
Tel   04 67 38 17 85
info@lamadura.com   www.lamadura.com

MAP 21
Pot luck may work, but rendezvous safer.

These are incontestably some of the best wines of the area. The *cave* used to be in the middle of town, but the Bourgnes have built a new one on the heights overlooking the contryside. The 12 hectares or so of vines are dotted around the countryside in a number of parcels on different soils; no cinsault but all four of the other usual AOP grapes, and sauvignon for the IGPs. After several years' experience at Château Fieuzal in the Graves, Bourgne has learnt to keep his range conveniently small, like they do in Bordeaux. There is the 'Classic' (B) in both colours (no rosé here), matured in tank, matched by two 'Grands Vins' (C), the white fermented and aged in barrel (a process which entirely changes the character of the sauvignon grape), the red aged in barrels at least three years old. A *domaine* for the short list.

* * CLOS BAGATELLE
Christine Deluze and Luc Simon
Route de Saint Pons, 34360 Saint-Chinian
Tel 04 67 38 04 23
closbagatelle@wanadoo.fr   www.closbagatelle.com

MAP 22
Open Monday to Saturday during usual hours, Sunday mornings in July and August.

In addition to their vines at Saint-Chinian, this brother and sister team whose family have been growing vines here for many generations also have plantations on schist at the hamlet of Donnadieu, where they make a pink and a red wine both under the name of 'Camille et Juliette' (A), largely from old carignan. They also have vines at St Jean de Minervois, not far away over the border from Saint-Chinian, where they make a delicious sweet Muscat (B). At the home *chais*, they make a big and often changing range of IGPs and AOPs. Look out for the 'Bagatelle Blanc' (A/B), as well as their good line in rosés, one mostly from cinsault and the other from grenache, syrah and just a little cinsault (both A). The reds range from good value inexpensive wines (e.g. 'Tradition Rouge' (A)) right through to 'Je Me Souviens' (D+), a huge modern style wine where the oak manages not to obtrude. Something for everyone here.

* * * MAS CHAMPART
Isabelle and Mathieu Champart
Bramefan, Route de Villespassans, 34360 Saint-Chinian
Tel 04 67 38 20 09 or 04 67 38 05 59
mas-champart@wanadoo.fr

MAP 23
Rendezvous required.

Of the 16 hectares of vine, the grapes from four still go to the *Coopérative* at Saint-Chinian. Nevertheless, the wines made at home are some of the finest, most unusual and acclaimed wines of the area, very personal and not necessarily typical. Mathieu is largely in charge of the vineyards, which are divided into a number of parcels that play all variations of the argilo-calcaire repertoire (no schist here, we are south of the town and up in the hills). Meanwhile Isabelle is in charge

of the cellar and the paperwork. Your visit may well start with a delightful, though modest IGP from cabernet franc and syrah (A). The rest of the wines are all AOP: a white (B) from roussanne, marsanne, bourboulenc and grenache blanc redolent of blossom, white fruit and lemon, with a touch of barrel and good weight; then 'Côte d'Arbo' (A/B), the *entrée-de-gamme* red, silky but with good body and with southern hints of herbs and figs. 'Causse du Bousquet' (B/C) is syrah-dominated and their best-seller, half made and aged in tank, the other half in a mix of old and new barrels. Finally, on no account should you miss the much-admired 'Clos de la Simonette' (C/D) based on mourvèdre, a big wine raised as one might expect in barrel. The last two wines need keeping to show their best.

B * * DOMAINE BORDES
Emma and Philippe Bordes
Hameau de Tudéry, 34360 Saint-Chinian
Tel 04 67 38 26 37
Mobile 06 66 60 85 10
p.bordes@wanadoo.fr

MAP 24
Appointment advisable.

This 10-hectare *domaine* goes back to 2001 and is now fully authentic in its organic approach. There are vines on schist at Babeau-Bouldoux, and on chalky clay at Saint-Chinian itself, in Assignan and Villespassans. Some carignan is more than 100 years old. The wines are all vinified in *cuve* and aged in a stone cellar at the foot of the hills. Here they do not distinguish between their AOPs and their IGPs, so why should anyone else? Their rosé (A) is from a mix of the two *terroirs*, comprising cinsault, grenache and mourvèdre – what the French call *vineux*. Grenache gris goes to make their *mono-cépage* 'Les Grèzes' (B), aged 12 months in barrel but deliciously fresh. 'Les Narys' (A/B) is their best known red, syrah, carignan and grenache aged 12 months in used barrels. 'Les Peyroulières' (B) is all mourvèdre, very southern in style and requiring a certain ageing. 'La Plage' (B) features the old carignan with some syrah, and one third of the wine is aged in new wood. 'Elles' (C/D) is their top wine, syrah from the best parcels, given a long ageing for two years in new barrels. To finish there is a sweet wine from ugni blanc (B/C), shrivelled on the vine until November, peppery, spicy and reminiscent of quince.

PIERRERUE

Here we are back on the schist. The next grower's family originally came from Faugères, so the *terroir* is not strange to him.

**DOMAINE DES PRADELS-QUARTIRONI

la Famille Quartironi
Hameau de Priou, 34360 Saint-Chinian
Tel   04 67 38 01 53
Mobile 06 59 25 24 01
quartironi-radels@gmail.com   www.vins-quartironi.com

MAP 26
Telephone for appointment.

This is a less well-known 16-hectare estate which has been in the same family for three generations. They make astonishingly inexpensive but good quality wines, which have attracted some plaudits in French magazines. The vines are grown organically but they do not claim the official bio label. It is the reds rather than the whites that command attention. 'Cuvée Quartironi de Sars' is a blend of old carignan, syrah and grenache, uncomplicated but undeniably attractive, while 'Cuvée Campanil' is from older vines and raised in *demi-muids*. All the wines here are (A).

**DOMAINE LA CROIX SAINTE-EULALIE

Agnès Gleizes and Philippe Giarardi
Avenue de Saint-Chinian, Combejean, 34360 Pierrerue
Tel   04 67 38 08 51
croix-sainte-eulalie@neuf.fr   www.croixsainteeulalie.isasite.net
GPS 43 25 N 2.58E

MAP 27
Rendezvous recommended

Agnès has been in charge of this long-established estate since 2000, making a large range of wines of high quality. There is a white Vermentino (A), a traditional AOP from roussanne and grenache as well as vermentino; a pure viognier (A), floral and lemony rather than apricots and peaches; and 'Cuvée Clémence' (C) an oak-vinified and -aged blend of the two grenaches, roussanne and a little terret. Their 'Tradition Rosé' (A) is largely syrah, with some grenache and cinsault, raised conventionally in tank. The reds start with a syrah-cabernet IGP (A) for early drinking; then the 'Tradition Rouge' (A), a four-way blend (no cinsault) raised in tank; 'Cuvée Jade' (C), named after Agnès' daughter, which is 80% mourvèdre, aged for 6 months in old barrels; and 'Espéranto' (A), 70% syrah and no barrel-ageing. Syrah also dominates 'Cuvée Baptiste' (B), aged in barrels which are renewed on a four-year cycle, and 'Cuvée Armandélis' (B), which has 80% syrah and 20% mourvèdre. It is a real keeper.

**DOMAINE MOULINIER

Guy and Stéphane Moulinier
34360 Pierrerue
Tél 04 67 38 03 97
Mobile 06 07 96 71 58
domaine-moulinier@wanadoo.fr   domaine-moulinier.com

MAP 28
Open for visits every day from 10.00-12.00 and 14.00-18.00

The Moulinier family have twenty-two hectares of vines spreading over many parcels and encompassing all types of *terroir*: schist, sandstone and argilo-calcaire. Apart from the viognier from which they make a peachy *blanc* (A), allowed two months on its lees and free from wood, they have only syrah, which comprises most of their plantations, grenache and mourvèdre. Guy says he was the first to plant syrah in Saint-Chinian (in 1981). A large part of their production is given over to *vin rosé*, of which they make two (both A), one wholly from syrah and the other a blend of all three grapes. The first of their four reds is a quaffer, oddly called 'Homo Erectus' (A), to be drunk young and with food such as *charcuterie*. The 'Tradition' (A) is another blend of all three grapes, while 'Sigillaires' (B) is mostly syrah, aged in old barrels. The top wine 'Les Terrasses Grillées' (C) is virtually all syrah and aged in barrels, about half of which are new. This wine is somewhat in the New World manner, which no doubt explains why Parker was attracted by it as he was passing by, just as the Mouliniers were starting out (a bit of luck for them). The family also have an excellent wine-shop called 'L'Espace du Vin' in the town of Saint-Chinian, where they sell a large variety of wines, not just their own, which is well worth a visit.

CÉBAZAN

B **DOMAINE LES ÉMINADES

Patricia and Luc Bettoni
Rue des Vignes, 34360 Cébazan
Tel 04 67 36 14 38
Mobile ; 06 72 89 04 40
contact@leseminades.fr   www.leseminades.fr

MAP 31
Visits by rendezvous.

These growers have a great variety of soils including red sandstone, limestone and schist, divided between the communes of Cébazan and Villespassans. On these they grow largely carignan (very old vines), some old grenache too and a little syrah and oeillade. For their whites they have grenache blanc, marsanne and an hectare of sauvignon. From the latter they make 'Cuvée Silice' (B/C) as an IGP, which has an unusual freshness and subtle influences of citrus and exotic fruits. A second white is the AOP 'Cuvée Montmajou' (B) from grenache blanc and marsanne, planted on limestone, fresh and elegant, minerally with hints of white fruits. The first red 'Cuvée la Pierre Plantée' (A) is described as a *vin de bistro,* mostly from old oeillade and grenache. It has good acidity and is refreshing and more-ish. 'Cuvée Cébenna' (B) is syrah/mourvèdre/grenache, garriguey and red fruit in character. 'Sortilège' (C) is from some of the oldest vines in the vineyard, yielding barely 20 hl/ha. 'Les Vieilles Canailles' (D) is their homage to carignan, with plenty of wild flowers and fruits to show on the nose and on the palate, well-balanced and long in the finish. A fine example of the grape.

CREISSAN

***TERRES FALMET Yves Falmet
10 Avenue de la République, 34370 Creissan
Mobile 06 20 90 60 84
terres.falmet@sfr.fr   www.domaine-terres-falmet.fr
MAP 32
Visits not encouraged, but you could try by appointment. The wines are available at Espace des Vins in Saint-Chinian and at Caves Paul Riquet in Béziers.

Falmet arrived in 1995 to take over this abandoned vineyard, badly in need of rescuing from oblivion. There are 20 hectares, mostly facing north, which is a challenge for a start, but has its advantages for a grower who prefers cooler conditions for making cooler wines. With one exception, he does not use barrels, not even for his 'L'Ecume des Jours' (C), pure viognier raised in tank on its lees. His red grapes, except his syrah, are grown *en gobelet*, even the mourvèdre, which is at the base of his Rosé (A), and which does not necessarily need to be drunk young. Reds tend to be almost pure varietals (not quite pure because of the rules): 'Cinsault' (A), supple and flavoursome; 'Carignan' (A), tannic but fruity and made traditionally and not by *macération carbonique*; 'Mourvèdre' (A), spicy, peppery and garriguey, and capable of lasting 20 years or more. The one blended mainstream red is 'L'Ivresse des Cîmes' (A/B), from syrah, mourvèdre and grenache, aged in tank for three years. A real curiosity is a red *vin de voile* from old carignan and grenache, left to age in barrel without topping up for eight years or so, oxidised and rejected by most so-called professionals, but loved by 'natural' wine fans. Falmet says, "It is a wine which I created for true wine-lovers, those who have not succumbed to uniformity of taste, stereotyped standardised wines".

PUISSERGUIER

***CHÂTEAU MILHAU-LACUGUE
Jean Lacugue
Route de Cazedarnes, 34620 Puisserguier
Tel 04 67 93 64 79
milhau-lacugue@wanadoo.fr   www.milhau-lacugue.com

MAP 35
Rendezvous required.

Marie-Françoise and Elisabeth Poux
Domaine Pech-Ménel

Over 100 hectares make up this estate and half are under vine, so the range of wines (no difference being accorded between the AOPs and the IGPs) is large. Among the best known are the simple white AOP and the rosé (both A), an easy quaffing red called 'Cuvée Magali' (A), and a syrah/grenache blend called 'Cuvée des Chevaliers'. Then there is the much-praised 'Les Truffières' (C) and a long-keeper called 'Les Curées' (C), these last two being in a particularly pronounced southern style, with plenty of deep fruit and chocolate. Note also a *moëlleux* chenin blanc called 'Grain d'Automne' (B). The available range will include many wines from earlier vintages.

QUARANTE

**DOMAINE PECH-MÉNEL
Marie-Françoise and Elisabeth Poux
Route de Creissan, 34310 Quarante
Tel 04 67 89 41 42 or 04 68 65 09 49
Mobile 06 07 96 50 01
pech-menel@wanadoo.fr   www.pech-menel.com

MAP 37
Appointment requested.

This 20-hectare vineyard, planted in the heart of the garrigue and mostly one continuous plot, and part of a *domaine* three times the size, has been worked by the two Poux sisters for many years. One of the pleasures in visiting them is that they have a good stock of older, mature vintages, which show off the potential of Saint-Chinian wines to age gracefully. Their white, grown on grapes down towards the Canal du Midi is due soon to come on stream (viognier, chardonnay and vermentino). Meanwhile they have a rosé called 'Demande en Mariage' from syrah and grenache. But the accent is on

Famille Franssu, Mas de Cyranque

the reds, of which there are five, ranging from the easy-going 'No Name' (B), which has a hefty dose of cinsault in its five-way blend, to the traditional-style 'Château Pech-Ménel' (C), mainly syrah and carignan with a little grenache (the carignan here is almost always made by *macération carbonique*). Older vintages of this wine may be purchased as a six-year vertical (e.g. 1999 to 2004). As you might expect, the older vintages offered are more expensive. In addition to the Pech-Ménel wines there are wines bearing the name Château Vallouvières (up to 2/3rds carignan) and 'La Villa-Pech-Menel' (B) which is 2/3rds mouvèdre.

CRUZY

B ***MAS DE CYNANQUE
Violaine and Xavier de Franssu
Route d'Assignan, 34310 Cruzy
Tel   04 67 25 01 34
Mobile ; 06 20 08 37 57
contact@masdecyranque.com   www.masdecyrenque.com

MAP 39
Appointment recommended.
These talented winemakers came to Saint-Chinian and made their first wines in 2004, but their *chais* dates only

from 2006 and they have just built another brand new one. They have 15 hectares on a mostly sandstone soil. Xavier is experienced in the Midi because he was at Château D'Or et des Gueules in the Costières de Nîmes (q.v.) for some years. They make a smallish quantity of white wine under the name of 'Althea Blanc' (B/C) from roussanne, grenache blanc and vermentino, and a good value rosé, 'Cuvée Fleur de Cynanque' (A), with plenty of red fruit flavours as well as citrus. Rather more interest centres around the reds: 'Plein Grès' (A/B), spicy, fruity and some meaty character, aged in tank; 'Acutum' (C), a four-way blend (no cinsault), and with a well-balanced strucure, its syrah aged partly in barrel; 'Amicytia' (C), mostly grenache, chocolatey and toasty; and its syrah-based brother 'Nominaris' (D). There is also a pure carignan called 'Carissimo' (C) with a delightfully austere charm.

VILLESPASSANS

BD **DOMAINE COMBEBELLE
Catherine Wallace and Patrick Keohane,
Combebelle le Haut, 34360 Villespassans
Tel 04 67 38 09 86
Mobile 06 25 24 64 37
wine@combebelle.com   www.combebelle.com

MAP 40
Visits May to October Thursday to Sunday, 16.00-19.00, otherwise by appointment.

You can, if you like, book a wine-tasting dinner (local Languedoc chef) and/or stay in Catherine's *gîte*. Catherine (ex-Majestic, Adnams and Lay & Wheeler) took over this 17-hectare *domaine* from Robert Eden in 2005, and it has been fully organic for more than 30 years. It is on the frontier with Minervois and has red clay soils as well as schist. Catherine has just the two red grapes, rather less grenache than syrah, whose juice she ages in a mix of old and new wood. So far there is an award-winning rosé (A/B) and just two reds, one oaked (C) the other not (A/B). Both are in a very southern style and easy to drink. Catherine also plans to plant white grapes which she thinks should produce fine wine on her *terroir* and at her altitude of 300 metres.

ASSIGNAN

***DOMAINE DU TABATAU Bruno Gracia
Rue du Bal, 34360 Assignan
Tel 04 67 38 19 60 or 09 60 38 89 73
domainedutabatau@wanadoo.fr

MAP 41
Appointment strongly advised.

Bruno's forbears had the *tabac* in Salvetat-sur-Agout, and he has named his vineyard after the local word for the son of a *tabac*-proprietor. He was once *régisseur* at Mas de Daumas Gassac, no less, so came to Saint-Chinian with a heavy bag of expertise to exercise over the six hectares of vines which he acquired, including some old aramon (since ditched). Still something of a boutique vineyard, the wines are nevertheless well-known and much admired. Their apparent simplicity belies the technique behind their making. His rosé (A) for example, redolent of cherries and redcurrants, or his white Geneviéve (B), an IGP from chardonnay and grenache blanc, given 11 months in barrels between one and six years old. His opening red 'Camprigou' (A) is a copybook example of style from a blend of everything but cinsault, and aged 10 months in *cuve*, while 'Tabataire' (B), a syrah/ mourvèdre/ grenache blend is accorded 14 months in a mix of used barrels up to 10 years old. Finally, 'Les Titous' (C) is a nod in the direction of a weightier style, hand-harvested from low-yielding grapes and given up to six weeks' *cuvaison* followed by 18 months in new *demi-muids*, bottled without fining or filtering. A chocolatey, jammy wine, rich and well-balanced and quite different from Bruno's other wines.

B ***LA GRANGE DE QUATRE SOUS
Hildegard Horat, and Alioune Diop
34360 Assignan
Tel 04 67 38 06 41
info@quatresous.eu   www.quatresous.eu
GPS 43.394787 2 894810

MAP 42
Appointment requested.

Hildegard's independent spirit and her refusal to be constrained by rules have made her one of Languedoc's best stars: she is nearly the only *vigneron* in Saint-Chinian to eschew the *appellation* altogether. She left her native Switzerland in 1983 to settle in Assignan, where today she has a vineyard of eight hectares, planted on clay and limestone with Malbec, the two cabernets and some viognier. She has even tried petite arvine, a Swiss grape. Her buildings are very old and probably belonged to the Knights of St John of Jerusalem, but when she found them they were almost a ruin, hence the name 'Grange de Quatre Sous'. Her range of white wines includes 'Le Jeu du Mail' (B), a viognier/marsanne blend, made and aged for at least a year in 500-litre barrels; 'Bu N'Daw' (B) from petite arvine; and a chardonnay varietal (B). Le Rosé' (A/B) is from a conventional Languedoc blend (although with no carignan). The reds, all given long macerations of up to 30 days, include 'Les Serrottes' (C) from syrah and malbec; 'Le Molin' (C) from the two cabernets; and 'La Grange de Quatre Sous' (C) from syrah, malbec and the cabernets. They are all aged in *foudre* and barrel for two years. The house style is therefore quite powerful and the wines need keeping to show their best. An outstanding and original producer.

B **DOMAINE DES SOULIÉ Rémy Soulié
Carriera de la Teulliera , 34360 Assignan
Tel 04 67 38 11 78
remy.soulie@wanadoo.fr   www.domainedessoulie.fr

MAP 43
Visits in principle during normal hours weekdays, but rendezvous might be wise.

The organic nature of this vineyard goes back many years. Rémy's father refused to use chemicals when they first became widespread, so the present vines have never been anything but chemical-free. In fact, the family tradition here goes back to 1610, though the *chais* is new, built by Rémy and his father with their own hands (to a design by the architect responsible for the *chais* at Mas Jullien). Today there are 27 hectares of vines all on argilo-calcaire soil, and Rémy makes both AOP and IGP wines. The white lemony 'Cuvée Mathilde' (A) is mostly grenache gris with just a little marsanne and roussanne. You may be lucky enough to find 'Cuvée Nord et Sud', a blend of sauvignon and marsanne, but little of this is made and it sells out quickly. The Rosé (A) is a traditional AOP blend, suggesting raspberries and red-currants. A large range of reds starts with the astonishingly cheap cinsault-based 'Cuvée Rémy' (A), followed by the 'Tradition' (A), a conventional blend raised in tank. Then there are varietal IGPs from grenache (A) and merlot (B) in *barriques*, and Malbec (A), the latter light, quaffable and cherry-like. 'Cuvée de Rémy' (B) is tank-raised from syrah and grenache, while the top red is 'Château Soulié des Joncs' (B/C), almost all syrah and raised for 24 months in *foudres*.

OTHER GOOD GROWERS AT SAINT-CHINIAN

**DOMAINE BOISSEZON-GUIRAUD
Michel and Pompilia Guiraud
34460 Roquebrun
Tel 04 67 89 68 17
Mobile 06 87 04 55 52
gaec.guiraud@wanadoo.fr   www.michel-pompilia-guiraud.com
MAP 3
Visit by appointment.

**CHÂTEAU SAINT MARTIN DES CHAMPS
Pierre (*oenologue*) and Michel (*vigneron*) Birot
Route de Puimisson, 34490 Murviel-lès-Béziers
Tel 04 67 32 92 58
domaine@saintmartindeschamps.com
www.saintmartindeschamps.com
MAP 7
A fine *château* and a thoroughly modern *chais* (including an underground barrel-store) make this an attractive visit. The easier wines are reasonably priced too.

B **CHÂTEAU BOUSQUETTE
Isabelle and Eric Perret
34360 Cessenon
Tel 04 67 89 65 38
labousquette@wanadoo.fr   www.chateau-bousquette.com
MAP 8
Visits every day from 8.00-18.00 (but avoid Sunday)

**DOMAINE DE LIMBARDIE
Henri Boukandoura
Grange Neuve-Limbardie
34460 Cessenon-sur-Orb
Tel 04 67 89 61 42
limbardie@orange.com
MAP 11
Appointment advised.
At this 13-hectare domaine (whose name translates as 'lizard') you will find only IGPs and no AOPs, but the wines are good and exceptionally good value for everyday drinking.

**CHÂTEAU MOULIN DE CIFFRE
Nicolas Lorgeril
34480 Autignac
Tel 04 67 90 11 45
info@moulindeciffre.com   www.moulindeciffre.com
See under Faugères.
MAP Faugères map 1

*LES COTEAUX DE BERLOU
Avenue des Mimosas, 34360 Berlou
Tel 04 67 89 58 58
contact@berloup.com   www.berloup.com
MAP 13
Open daily.
An excellent starting-point for the discovery of the wines of Berlou. The *Cave* is a member of the giant *coopérative* Val d'Orbieu.

**DOMAINE LES TERRASSES DE GABRIELLE
Olivier Pascal
9 Avenue Emile Loscos, 334310 Capestang (business address)
Tel 04 67 93 38 23
Mobiles 06 31 77 11 38 and 06 07 30 41 93
www.lesterrassesdegabrielle.fr
MAP 14
Telephone as to where to visit ; at Capestang or Berlou.
Pascal has vines not only in Saint-Chinian, but in various other parts of the Midi where he makes a range of IGPs.

B **DOMAINE DES JOUGLA Laurence Jougla
34360 Prades-sur-Vernazobre
Tel 04 67 38 06 02
info@domainedesjougla.com   www.domainedesjougla.com
MAP 16
Cave open Monday to Saturday usual hours. By appointment on Sundays.
Since Laurence has taken over here, the *domaine* seems to have stepped into the 21st century.

*DOMAINE GRASSET-RIVES Vincent Grasset
rue Moulin à l'Huile, 34360 Prades-sur-Vernazobre
Tel 04 67 38 10 14 / 09 83 80 10 14
Mobile 06 68 22 16 64
grassetrives@aol.com
MAP 17
Rendezvous requested. An inexpensive good-value *domaine*.

**DOMAINE LA SERVELIÈRE Joël Berthomieu
1 rue des Cèdres, 34360 Babeau-Bouldoux
Tel 04 67 38 17 08
Mobile 06 10 48 79 61
joel.berthomieu@orange.fr
MAP 18
Visits by appointment

**DOMAINE DES PAÏSSELS
Vivien Roussignol and Marie Toussaint
Rue des Cèdres, 34360 Babeau
Tel   06 22 74 24 51
contact@paissels.fr   www.païssels.fr
MAP 19
Visits by appointment.
This is an old family property but only recently has the vineyard started to be reconstructed. It is named after the stakes used to support young vines.

**DOMAINE LA LINQUIÈRE Pierre Salvestre
12 Avenue de Béziers 34360 Saint-Chinian
Tel ; 04 67 38 25 87 or 04 67 38 04 57
liniquiere@neuf.fr www.linquiere.fr
MAP 25
Cellars open daily during business hours except Sunday afternoons.

**PRIEURÉ DES MOURGUES Jérôme Roger
34360 Pierrerue
Tel 04 67 38 18 18
prieure.des.mourgues@wanadoo.fr
www.prieuredesmourgues.com
MAP 29
Rendezvous advisable.

B **DOMAINE DES MATHURINS
Nicolas et Émilie Pistre
22 Avenue de St Bauléry, 34460 Cazedarnes
Tel 04 67 38 08 33
Mobile 06 80 53 22 65
contact@domainedesmathurins.com
www.domainedesmathurins.com
MAP 30
Arrange rendezvous

*CHÂTEAU CREISSAN Bernard Reveillas
3 Chemin du Moulin d'Abram, 34370 Creissan
Tel 04 67 93 84 80
bernard.reveilllas@orange.fr
MAP 33
Visits Wednesday and Saturday from 17.00 to 19.00 (18.00 to 20.00 in July and August). Otherwise by appointment.
This estate, is notable for probably the best value for money in the region, all the wines being (A).

**DOMAINE THOMAS ROUANET
1 bis Rue de la République, 34370 Creissan
Tel 06 16 81 36 95
domainethomasrouanet@gmail.com
domainethomasrouanet.wordpress.com
MAP 34
Appointment recommended.

*DOMAINE COMPS Jean-Pierre Comps
23 Rue Paul Riquet, 34620 Puisserguier
Tel   06 73 30 00 30 / 06 08 75 77 38
www.domainecomps.com
MAP 36
Visits : Wednesday, Friday and Saturday 9.00-12.00 and 15.00-18.00. Otherwise by appointment.

**VILLA QUAT'Z'ARTS
directeur Michel Rémmondat,
chais at 3 rue Moulin à Vent , 34330 Quarante.
Office ; 3 rue de Sauret, 34170 Castelnau-le Lez
Tel   06 20 26 28 40
villaquatzarts@gmail.com
MAP 38
Arrange rendezvous

B **CHÂTEAU CASTIGNO
Tine and Marc Verstraete
2 rue des Écoles, 34360 Assignan
Tel   04 67 38 05 50   Mobile   07 61 96 30 00
village@chateaucastigno.com   www.chateaucastigno.com
MAP 44
Rendezvous required through Carolien Calleweir.

**DOMAINE DE SACRÈ COEUR Luc Cabaret
route de Saint-Chinian, 34360 Assignan
Tel   04 67 38 17 97
Mobile   06 62 32 17 76
geacsacrecoeur@wanadoo.fr www.domainedusacrecoeur.com
MAP 45
Appointment advisable.

Faugères

The *appellation* area Faugères is just north of Béziers and on the southern edge of the first foothills of the Cévennes. It is defined by its topsoil, which isn't soil at all but schist (or shale). Schist is everywhere in this district, with only a few pockets of chalky clay in between. Growers claim that the grapes ripen during the night because the shale keeps the subsoil below warm – a protection against the cool night breezes. (It is strange that in other areas, Pic St Loup for example, the same cool night breezes are so highly prized.)

Faugères may come from growers in any one of seven villages, and the growers are listed this way below in a sequence which, it is hoped, would facilitate a tour of the region. There are also two *coopératives*, which together supply the market with about half of the total production of Faugères. These are the wines which are more likely to be found in the *grandes surfaces*, because they are mostly cheaper than the wines from the independent growers. While the *coopératives'* wines are of good quality, the independents, of whom there are upwards of 50, generally make the more characterful wines. About half of them are organic growers, or in the process of being converted – perhaps the highest proportion of any AOP in Languedoc-Roussillon.

Wines of all three colours enjoy AOP, the whites only since 2005. In the bad old days, Faugères wines were no more distinguished than the poor wines then made all over Languedoc. In fact, the district was more famous for its brandies. Manufacture of the latter died out some years ago, but the tradition has been revived and the results are just about coming on stream. A travelling still (a double still in the Cognac style) visits about a dozen growers, and the resulting spirit they bottle themselves. It will cost retail about 30/35€ per 50-cl. bottle.

The rapid metamorphosis of the red table wines won Faugères its *appellation* status in 1982, and since then improvement has continued unabated. Their characteristic is a rich round smooth-

Dry schist wall near Faugères

ness, gained usually after relatively long ageing, though really mature examples are fairly hard to come by. Some say that the quality is attributable to the 'importation' of syrah and mourvèdre to 'improve' on the more traditional grenache, cinsault and carignan. Others maintain that Faugères is not Faugères without a good dose of carignan. Today carignan may not represent more than 40% in any blend, nor cinsault more than 20%, while syrah, grenache and mourvèdre must contribute at least 20% each. As elsewhere, cinsault is reserved mostly for rosés. Carignan and cinsault have been gradually squeezed during recent years, but there appears to be some flexibility in the application of the rules, as people have come to realise that carignan is not such a bad grape after all.

The white wines are from blends of any two or more of roussanne, marsanne, vermentino and grenache blanc. Roussanne must constitute at least 40%. Other traditional grapes such as bourboulenc, carignan blanc, clairette and macabeu are also allowed, pending their gradually being phased out by natural wastage as the old plants die off. Modern plantations of these will not qualify for AOP.

Wines of IGP status may be found from growers who have some schist-less soil not qualifying for AOP. This category also includes wines which would otherwise qualify for AOP but for the fact that they do not comply with the *encépagement* rules.

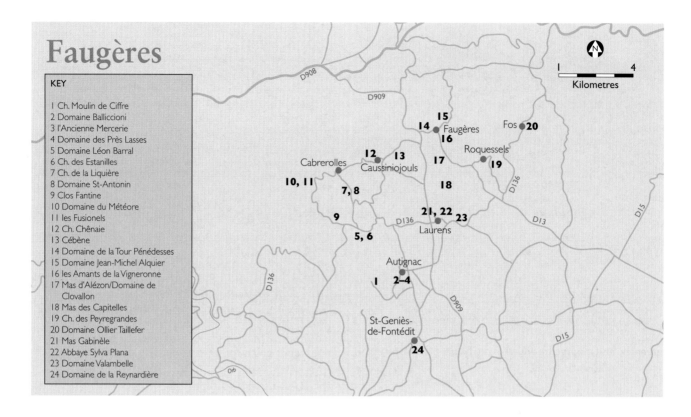

Faugères

KEY

1 Ch. Moulin de Ciffre
2 Domaine Balliccioni
3 l'Ancienne Mercerie
4 Domaine des Près Lasses
5 Domaine Léon Barral
6 Ch. des Estanilles
7 Ch. de la Liquière
8 Domaine St-Antonin
9 Clos Fantine
10 Domaine du Météore
11 les Fusionels
12 Ch. Chênaie
13 Cébène
14 Domaine de la Tour Pénédesses
15 Domaine Jean-Michel Alquier
16 les Amants de la Vigneronne
17 Mas d'Alézon/Domaine de Clovallon
18 Mas des Capitelles
19 Ch. des Peyregrandes
20 Domaine Ollier Taillefer
21 Mas Gabinèle
22 Abbaye Sylva Plana
23 Domaine Valambelle
24 Domaine de la Reynardière

The total area under vine is about 21,000 hectares, and the total production reaches 224,000 hectolitres, of which 80% is red.

Growers are listed in a roughly west-to-east course, starting on the Saint-Chinian borders.

**CHÂTEAU MOULIN DE CIFFRE

Nicolas Lorgeril, winemaker Bernard Durand
c/o Château de Pennautier (q.v.), 11610 Pennautier
Tel 04 68 72 65 29
contact@lorgeril.com   www.lorgeril.com

MAP 1
Telephone for appointment.

This 35-hectare property is on the boundary between Faugères and St. Chinian, making wines under both *appellations*, as well as IGPs and AOP Coteaux de Languedoc on non-schistous soil. The property was bought in 2007 by the Lorgeril family (see Ch. Pennautier in Cabardès) after the sad death of the former owner, Jacques Lésineau, who had died in a car accident. Lésineau had links back to Château de Fieuzal in Bordeaux. The influence of Bordeaux lingered on for some while, but the wines currently being made here in Faugères have more of an emphasis on fruit, with softer tannins but still a capacity to age. The more ambitious growths from St. Chinian and Faugères are aged for a year in a mix of old and new barrels. Of the Faugères, note particularly a barrel-aged wine called 'Terroirs d'Altitude' (B) and 'Le Causse' (D). These are matched by the St Chinians, the 'Tradition' (A), raised in tank and another (B) in wood. The top red is called 'Les Pins' (D). There is also a St. Chinian rosé, largely from cinsault. A viognier (B) is made and matured in barrel.

**DOMAINE BALLICCIONI

André et Véronique Balliccioni,
1 Chemin de Ronde, 34480 Autignac
Tel 04 67 90 20 31
Mobile 06 11 12 02 41
ballivins@aol.com   www.ballivin@sfr.fr

MAP 2
Rendezvous required.

André is Corsican by origin (they have a lot of schist in Corsica too), but there is nothing to fear, at least from his entry-level wines: a charming, easy and fruity rosé (A) and his red 'Tradition' (A), which is soft, silky and with just a touch of spice. 'Orchis' (B/C) is a grenache/mourvèdre blend reminiscent of cherries. 'Kallisté' (C), meaning 'very beautiful' in Greek, is usually given part-ageing in barrel, which some find obtrusive, others not. A touch of grenache plumps up the syrah and carignan. This is a small seven-hectare estate but it nevertheless has a keen following.

B ***L'ANCIENNE MERCERIE
Nathalie and François Caumette
6 rue Egalité, 34480 Autignac
Tel   04 67 90 27 02
Mobile   06 31 32 96 20
ancienne.mercerie@free.fr   www.anciennemercerie.fr

MAP 3
Worth phoning ahead.

A 16-hectare estate at the western end of this *appellation*, but still entirely on the Faugères schist. Former *coopérateurs*, the owners made their own wine for the first time in 2000. The property was a former haberdashery shop with winemaking facilities at the rear, and the owners' grandparents carried on both occupations. The rosé of the house is a cinsault-mourvèdre blend called 'Frou Frou' (A/B), sometimes showing, when young, evidence of the residual fizz from its fermentation. From a parcel of vines off the schist comes an AOP Languedoc from grenache and mourvèdre called 'Bonheur des Dames' (B). The first of the two AOP reds here is 'Les Petites Mains' (A), based, like its older brother, on carignan but with grenache and mourvèdre added in the blend. Straightforward, dependable and most agreeable. The other red, 'Couture' (C), is raised in mostly old barrels, some of which have seen 10 years' service, so the wood influence is in the gentle aeration rather than the flavour of barrels. This is bigger and more backward than its unoaked sibling, and needs a bit of time to come around.

CABREROLLES

BD ****DOMAINE LÉON BARRAL
Didier Barral
Lenthéric, 34480 Cabrerolles
Tel   04 67 90 29 13
www.domaineleonbarral.com

MAP 5
Visits by appointment for tasting, but rarely is any wine available to purchase on the spot.

Barral, who started this vineyard in 1993 in memory of his grandfather, is one of the pillars of the biodynamic movement in France, and enjoys huge respect not only for his methods but his results. He has almost 30 hectares facing mostly full south on steep sloping schist. All the vines are grown *en gobelet* to protect the grapes from burning by the fierce Midi sun. The vineyards are patrolled by cattle, pigs and goats, effectively balancing the growth and suppression of weeds, and the ecology with the insects and other small beasts which they attract to the surface. The vines are sulphured only once a year against oidium, otherwise no sulphur is used either in the vinification or the bottling. It is the red Faugères which have made Barral's reputation, though there is a white IGP (B/C), mostly from the white and 'grey' versions of terret. The reds start with the Faugères Tradition

(C), half carignan, with grenache and cinsault, then 'Jadis' (C/D), where the cinsault is replaced by syrah, and finally 'Valinières' (D), which is mostly mourvèdre. All three are substantial and very serious, and rank among the top wines of Languedoc. None of them is racked, fined or filtered.

B *** CHÂTEAU DES ESTANILLES
Julien Seydoux
Lenthéric, 34480 Cabrerolles
Tel   04 67 90 29 25
contact@chateau-estanilles.com   www.chateau-estanilles.com

MAP 6
Sales and tasting at the cellar 10.00-12.30 and 14.00-18.00. Not Sundays.

Unlike his neighbour, Didier Barral, Seydoux's vines are all trained on wire, because he sees advantages in the grapes getting the maximum of sunshine and heat. There are 35 hectares of them, all at about 300 metres above sea level, and the estate is now wholly organic, with about a third of its produce going for export. For the flinty white wine (B) – part of the range called 'L'Impertinent' – he uses mostly roussanne and marsanne. For the first rosé (B), mainly cinsault and grenache, and for the reds, all five of the standard varieties, with syrah dominating (an inheritance from the previous owners, the Louison family, who have since moved to Limoux). 'L'Impertinent' (B/C) is aged in tank, while 'Inverso' (C), with plenty of mourvèdre, 'Clos du Fou' (C/D), mostly syrah, and 'Raison d'Être' (D), a three-way syrah, grenache and mourvèdre blend, are all aged in oak. There is too an oak-aged rosé mostly from mourvèdre (C). Excellent quality but no bargains.

B ** CHÂTEAU DE LA LIQUIÈRE
La Famille Vidal-Dumoulin
La Liquière, 34480 Cabrerolles
Tel   04 67 90 29 20
Mobiles   06 36 38 66 74 or 06 36 38 66 75
info@chateaulaliquiere.com   www.chateaulaliquiere.com

MAP 7
Open weekdays during usual hours. Saturdays by appointment.

This is one of the oldest winemaking families in the region, and they have had an important influence on the development and improvement of Faugères wines over the last 30 years. The tasting room is in the heart of La Liquière, though the wines are actually made in other cellars, one old underground one (gravity fed) and the other modern and high-tech. Their 60 hectares of vines enable them to make a range of 10 or so wines, the reds coming from the five usual grape varieties, the whites from terret, bourboulenc, viognier and clairette, as well as the more usual roussanne and grenache blanc. Every parcel is vinified separately, giving no fewer than 50 different *cuvées* from which to blend the wines. 'Les Amandiers' (A) comes in all three colours, and is a range intended for early drinking. A second rosé called 'L'Unique Gaz de Schist' (B) is a slightly

Arielle Demets-Villaneuva, Les Fusionels

off-dry sparkler from mourvèdre and grenache. 'A mi-chemin' (A) is the name of two more tank-raised easy-drinking wines, the red largely from carignan (part only made by *macération carbonique*) and cinsault. There are four further reds, their ambitiousness in ascending order: 'Vieilles Vignes' (B), mostly carignan and grenache, raised in tank; 'Nos Racines' (B), an almost pure carignan with just a touch of grenache to give it AOP legality; 'Cistus' (C), syrah-based with long *cuvaisons* and part raised in *demi-muids*; and finally 'Tucade' (D), largely mourvèdre and raised in barrel for at least a year before being finished in tank. Benchmark wines, whose characteristics are well-rounded fruit and very good value.

**DOMAINE SAINT ANTONIN
Frédéric Albaret
La Liquière, 34480 Cabrerolles
Tel 04 67 90 13 24
Mobile 06 10 19 17 46
stantonin@wanadoo.fr www.domainesaintantonin.fr

MAP 8
Rendezvous necessary.

Frédéric has moved out of the hamlet of La Liquière, building himself a spanking new cellar on the road to Lenthéric to house the wines from his 26 hectares. He started from scratch with a mere 13 in 1994, and was joined by his wife Fabienne in 2001. Frédéric believes in the simplest possible vinification, with the gentlest extraction so as to show off the character of the schist. Of the four wines, the name 'Les Jardins' is shared by a rosé (A), which is half cinsault, the rest mourvèdre and Grenache, and a red (A) (corresponding to the style of a 'Tradition'), made typically from equal quantities of syrah, grenache and carignan. This wine carries its 14.5 degrees of alcohol remarkably well, because of its fine balance. 'Lou Cazalet' (B) adds mourvèdre to the *assemblage*, and comes from old vines in the neighbouring villages of Antugnac and Laurens as well as Cabrerolles. It is aged in tank, not wood. The top red is called 'Magnou' (B/C) and is largely (70%) syrah, aged in a mix of *foudres* and *demi-muids* before being finished for a year in tank. The oak here is therefore never prominent, and the wine benefits from keeping. Frédéric brings a high degree of consistency to his wines year after year.

BD ***CLOS FANTINE
Carole, Corine and Olivier Andrieu
La Liquière, 34480 Cabrerolles
Tel 04 67 90 20 89
corine.andrieu@laposte.net

MAP 9
Prior rendezvous could avoid disappointment.

The Andrieu siblings are 'natural wine'-makers. There is no precise definition of a 'natural' wine, but here it means no chemicals, filtering or fining, no sulphur at any stage of the vinification or bottling, and the banning of all but the

natural wild yeasts. Their vines are spread over 28 hectares, and their willingness to depart from tradition shows in their one white wine, made entirely from terret, called 'Valcabrières' (B/C), surprisingly dry in view of its deep colour and showing mineral acidity. You might also describe their 'Lanterne Rouge' (B) as quirky, made from aramon and cinsault as a *vin de table*, fresh, spicy and more-ish despite a certain toughness. More conventionally, their AOP red 'Tradition' (B) has a good percentage of carignan and usually shows wild fruits from the garrigue and spiciness. Finally, 'Courtiol' (C) is made predominantly from what they consider their best *cépage* of the year. Often this is mourvèdre, but it may as well be carignan. None of the wines here see wood. These are among the most interesting of all 'natural wine'-makers in the Midi.

B **DOMAINE DU MÉTÉORE
Geneviève et Guy Libes,
Route d'Aigues Vives, 34480 Cabrerolles
Tel 04 67 90 21 12
domainedumeteore@wanadoo.fr

MAP 10
Rendezvous recommended.

Two features distinguish this 19-hectare property: a particularly large and noisy dog, and a large hole in the ground truly made by a meteor. The lively welcome of Mme Libes, who makes some of the best value Faugères of all, is another defining characteristic. Her red 'Tradition', called 'Léonides' (A), is everything an entry-level wine should be: fruity, lively, unoaked and needing little cellarage. Barrel ageing marks her 'Les Orionides' (A/B), a mourvèdre-syrah blend which does on the other hand need keeping a few years. Her 'Réserve', sometimes also called 'Les Perséides' (B), has rather more syrah than her other wines, which tend to balance equally the four main red wine grapes of the area. There's an unoaked white from roussanne and marsanne called, like her first red, 'Les Léonides' (A), fully up to the quality of the red, as well as a late-harvested viognier wine called 'Ballade d'Automne' (C) to round off a tasting, or indeed any meal with a worthy dessert. Madame also owns vines in St. Chinian, on schist soil as in Faugères.

***LES FUSIONELS Arielle Demets-Villaneuva
Route d'Aigues Vives, 34480 Cabrerolles
Tel 04 67 93 63 58
Mobile 06 07 03 56 16
arielledemets@outlook.fr www.vignoblesfusionels.com

MAP 11
Visits by appointment.

Arielle's wines are so good that she will not allow her career as a wine-grower in Faugères to be influenced by the romantic ballyhoo which surrounded her film-star-like arrival in Faugères in 2007. With some support from her family in Champagne, she has built an entirely modern *chais* in the hills above Cabrerolles, where she is making some of the most impressive of all wines from this *appellation*. It has not taken her long to decide what she can do best in this Languedoc world of Faugères. Having recently added four hectares, all mourvèdre to her original 12, she will want to consolidate what she has achieved since her first year. There are just four wines for the moment. Firstly, an aptly named rosé, 'Coeur de Fraise' (B), mostly cinsault with a touch of grenache, which she says goes well with fish and shellfish as well as more usual fare, with good acidity to balance the strawberry character. Then follows an opening red, 'Le Rêve' (B), largely syrah but with grenache and carignan, too, with strawberry and wild flowers in style, a kind of super *'vin des copains'*. 'In Tempus' (C) is more ambitious with plenty of mourvèdre in its make-up, silky and reminiscent of dark fruits, aged in mostly old barrels. Finally, 'Renaissance' (D) has even more mourvèdre (80%) and is raised in new *demi-muids*, but with little hint of the wood. It is silky but with good grip and is beautifully balanced. The three stars are more than fully deserved.

CAUSSINIOJOULS

B ***CÉBÈNE Brigitte Chévalier
Route de Caussinniojouls ,34600 Faugères   Business; Ancienne Route de Béziers, 34600 Bédarieux
Tel   06 74 96 42 67
bchevalier@wanadoo.fr   www.cebene.fr

MAP 13
Cellars open Saturday mornings and Wednesday afternoons. Otherwise by appointment.

A relative newcomer in 2007, after working for 10 years with Jean-Luc Thunevin in Bordeaux, Mme Chevalier has vines elsewhere in Languedoc, from which she makes, for example, a red IGP from Grenache, 'Ex Arena' (B/C), which is the nearest she gets to an entry-level wine. But it is in Faugères on the schist, in full view of the mountain of Cebenna the sleeping lady that she has made a real stir. Her ambition is to make Midi wines in the northern style, so she says. Many of her vines face north too, adding coolness to her output. Her three red AOP Faugères have given her a passport to the top. 'Les Bancels' (C), a syrah/mourvèdre/grenache blend, she recommends with grilled meats or a risotto with truffles, while 'Belle Lurette' (C) is mostly from old-vine carignan. Her top red, 'Felgaria' (D) is a real mourvèdre keeper and has won countless medals and awards. Not the cheapest wines, but there's no mistaking the quality.

***DOMAINE JEAN-MICHEL ALQUIER
Jean Michel Alquier
4 route de Pezènes-les-Mines, 34600 Faugères
Tel   04 67 23 07 89
contact@jmalquier.com or jmalquier@malquier.com
www.jmalquier.com

MAP 15
Appointment strongly advised, though strictly not necessary.

There is a long family history to the Alquier family in Faugères. In recent times, Jean-Michel and his brother Fréderic decided to go their separate ways, and Jean-Michel set himself up with 11 hectares of vines, of which one is dedicated to white grapes. Today he ranks among the most admired, as well as pricey, of all Faugères producers. His vines are densely planted and the yields are low – 30 hectolitres to the hectare on average. A certain predilection for the wines of the Rhône is reflected in the *encépagement*: syrah, mourvèdre and grenache for the reds, roussanne, marsanne and grenache blanc for the whites. Jean-Michel doesn't mind if a bit of the stalk is left in the pressing, because it gives a certain austerity which he finds attractive. The AOP wines are all more or less aged in wood, renewed every other year. There are two whites: an IGP from sauvignon, fresh and spared oak (B), and the white AOP 'Les Vignes du Puits' (B/C), nowadays made in wood but aged in tank without a second fermentation to keep the fruit fresh and lively. The rosé (A/B) is all grenache and bottled in December following the vintage. There are three reds. 'Les Premières' (C) is mostly from young vines, its 14 months' ageing including some time in wood. 'Maison Jaune' (C) is mostly from grenache which is not destalked, and the barrels are 10% new. Jean-Michel being a stickler for quality, this *cuvée* was not made in 2002, 2008 or 2012. Nor was the top red, 'Les Bastides' (D), made in 2002 or 2008. It is an ambitious wine, largely syrah and destined to be kept some years. Time will tell whether Jean-Michel commercialises an experimental 'Les Grandes Bastides', in which some of the grapes are left for a late harvesting. The cuvaison lasts 50 days and there is more new wood in the *élevage*.

***LES AMANTS DE LA VIGNERONNE
Christian and Régine Godefroid
Route de Pézenas, 34600 Faugères
Tel   04 67 95 78 49
info@lesamantsdelavigneronne.com
www.lesamantsdelavigneronne.com

MAP 16
Retail cellars open every day 10.00-19.00, but phone for rendezvous from April to October.

Apart from running a busy Bed and Breakfast, and selling wine from a *caveau* at which they offer no fewer than 120 different wines (mostly, but not exclusively, Faugères), Christian has recently added the profession of winemaker to his portfolio with eight hectares of vines yielding on average a mere 30 hl/ha. The wines have gradually gained a considerable reputation. They include a white mostly from rousaanne (B), barrel-fermented and aged for six months on its lees, and five reds from varying blends of syrah, grenache and mourvèdre, ranging in price from (B) to (C). All are aged in barrels, some second-hand and others new. The style goes well with the well-seasoned cooking of Régine, who serves meals on request to her Bed and Breakfast customers, while Christian shows off both his own wines and those of other Faugères growers. This is by far the best haven if you are staying in the area.

Young mourvèdre plantation

BD ***MAS D'ALÉZON/
DOMAINE DE CLOVALLON Cathérine Roque

1 Route de Pézenas, 34600 Faugères
mas@alezon.fr   www.alezon.fr
domaine@clovallon.fr   www.clovallon.fr

MAP 17
Rendezvous necessary.

Mme Roque has the highest vines in the *appellation*, just on the southern side of the road tunnel leading to Bédarieux where she also has her well-known Domaine Clovallon, and where her daughter Alix makes wonderful pure pinot noir wine. Here in Faugères (just), Cathérine has syrah, mourvèdre and grenache from which she makes classy wines which she raises in barrel. As befits a biodynamic producer, the vines are allowed plenty of grass with which to compete between the rows. Picking is by hand and inferior matter is rejected both on the vine and at the cellar. No chemical yeasts are used. There are just two AOP reds. First, 'Le Presbytère' (B), named after the former vicarage of Faugères where Mme Roque once had her *cave*. It is mainly derived from grenache, and is floral, spicy and blackfruity. Then there is 'Montfalette' (C), which is mostly mourvèdre, chocolatey and laden with fruit and spice. These wines need opening well ahead of consumption and can do with some ageing. They are among the 'biggest' of the region. Try also the white 'Cabretta' (C) from roussanne, clairette and grenache blanc. Cathérine also proposes a new-style *Fine*. And, of course, you must visit Domaine de Clovallon or at least taste the lovely wines, especially the famous pinot noir (B). There is also an AOP Clairette (B) from here, a style which is getting rarer by the day. Although outside the official *appellation* area for Clairette, Cathérine has a dispensation to make and label this wine under the AOP. She is very keen on it, especially because of its slightly bitter Seville orange character.

BD **MAS DES CAPITELLES

Jean et Cédric Laugé et leur Famille
Route de Pézénas, 34600 Faugères
Tel   04 67 23 10 20
Mobile   06 82 91 54 02
mas.des.capitelles@laposte.net   www.masdescapitelles.com

MAP 18
Open daily between 9.00-19.00.

The family has a long history in Faugères, having for many years been enthusiastic *coopérateurs*. Jean's father was a president of the local one. In 1999 they decided to revert to their original independent status. The 24 hectares of vines include a large proportion of carignan, described by Jean as making powerful, generous wines, in direct relation to their *terroir*. They also have a deal of mourvèdre, which they like for its leathery, peppery blackcurrant flavours, as well as its keeping qualities. 'Cuvée Loris' (C) shows off both these varieties, raised largely in barrel, whose flavour they are not ashamed to feature. 'Cuvée No.1' (C) is mostly mourvèdre, again aged in oak for two years. 'Cuvée Vieilles Vignes' (B) also has a deal of this variety, backed up with old carignan and some syrah, and only partly barrel-aged. Cuvée 'La Cateide' (A) is the one wine aged in tank, half carignan, fruity on the nose and round on the palate with notes of leather and citrus. Wines here should be opened well ahead of time as they are preserved by carbon dioxide instead of sulphur.

ROQUESSELS

B **CHÂTEAU DES PEYREGRANDES

Marie-Geneviève Boudal-Bénézech
Chemin de l'Aire, 34320 Roquessels
Tel   04 67 90 15 00
info@chateaudespeyresgrandes.com
www.chateaudespeyregrandes.com

MAP 19
Visits Monday to Saturday afternoons, but not Saturday during winter.

Heir to this 27-hectare *domaine* since 1995, long established by the Bénézech family, Madame is making what must be some of the best-value wines in Faugères. She vinifies her 70-year-old carignan by *macération carbonique* and the other four red-wine-grapes by traditional means. Yields are low, reflecting her determination to pursue quality rather than quantity. Her white Faugères (B) is a blend of marsanne and roussanne which she planted herself. Of her two rosés (both A), one is largely cinsault, the other syrah/grenache and given just a touch of oak-ageing. There are five reds, of which the first two (both A) are aged in tank, the difference being the length of *cuvaison*. The other three are given more or less oak, the Prestige (B) being made entirely by *macéra-*

tion carbonique before transfer to barrels for up to a year. Syrah dominates 'Cuvée Charlotte' (B), named after Marie-Geneviève's grandmother, and some of the barrels will be new, while 'Marie Laurencie' (C) is intended for long keeping after extended *cuvaison*.

FOS

B ***DOMAINE OLLIER TAILLEFER
Françoise and Luc Ollier
34320 Fos
Tel   04 67 90 24 59
Mobile   06 15 61 56 72
GPS 43 568 3 246
ollier.taillefer@wanadoo.fr   www.olliertaillefer.com

MAP 20
Cellars open from Easter to the end of October every day except Sundays and public holidays, 11.00-12.00 and 14.30-18.00. Otherwise by appointment.

This was one of the pioneering Faugères estates, one which did perhaps more than any other to secure *appellation* status for Faugères blanc. Then there are the wines of course, which are tremendously good value. Though the vineyards were hit by hail just before the 2008 vintage (which affected not only the wines of that year, but those of the succeeding year as well), the wines today are just as good, if not better than they ever were. The white 'Allegro' (B), if there is any left in the cellar here, is by common consent probably the best of all Faugères whites, while 'Les Collines' (A) is the archetypal *vins des copains*. 'Grande Réserve', despite its name, is not the top red, but a delicious middle weight Faugères from carignan, grenache and syrah, and raised without the benefit of wood. 'Castel Fossibus' (C) is more ambitious and stars the syrah which grows so well on the schist here. There are also two rosés, one dry (A) and one sweet, the latter making a wonderful aperitif with its strawberry bonbon character.

***MAS GABINÈLE   Thierry Rodriguez
1750 chemin de Bédarieux, 34480 Laurens

Tel   04 67 89 71 72
Mobile   06 07 11 14 45
info@masgabinele.com   www.masgabinele.com

MAP 21
Cellars open Monday to Saturday during usual hours, but closed Sundays. On Saturdays in summer, make an appointment.

Rodriguez is a highly admired perfectionist. He has only 10 hectares of vines, but he believes in making small quantities of top class wines, fruity and which avoid over-extraction and hard tannins, but which are round and age well. There are just two AOP reds, 'Mas Gabinèle Rouge' (C), which combines power with subtlety, and 'Rarissime' (D), given an ambitious oak *élevage*, with a long finish redolent of fruits in eau-de-vie. There is also a white from grenache gris (A/B), an IGP de l'Hérault made entirely from carignan (C), and a sweet grenache red (C/D) from very late-picked grapes. Generally speaking the wines need keeping so that the oak becomes fully integrated. The quality here is quickly recognisable.

OTHER GOOD GROWERS IN FAUGÈRES

B **DOMAINE DES PRÈS LASSES
Boris and Denis Feigel
26 Avenue de la Liberté, 34480 Autignac
Tel   04 67 90 21 19
Mobile   06 03 40 27 75
info@pres-lasses.com or boris.feigel@pres-lasses.com
www.pres-lasses.com
MAP 4
Rendezvous necessary.

**CHÂTEAU CHÊNAIE   André and Eric Chabbert
2 rue des Noyers, 34600 Caussiniojouls
Tel   04 67 95 48 10 or 04 67 95 30 29
Mobile   06 23 77 11 94
chateauchenaie@orange.fr   www.chateau-chenaie-vins.fr
MAP 12
Rendezvous advised.
The price range here means there is something for all tastes and purses. In terms of value this property is one of the most attractive.

B **DOMAINE DE LA TOUR PÉNÉDESSES
Alexandre Fouque
2 rue droite (Place de la Mairie), 34600 Faugères
Tel   04 67 95 17 21
Mobile   06 98 28 75 15
info@latourpenedesses.com
domainedelatourpenedesses@yahoo.fr
www.domainedelatourpenedesses.fr
MAP 14
Open during normal hours Monday to Saturday.

B **ABBAYE SYLVA PLANA
Henry Bouchard and Cédric Guy
Ancienne Route de Bedarieux, 34480 Laurens
Tel   04 67 93 43 55
Mobile   06 77 14 82 10
info@vignoblesbouchard.com   www.vignoblesbouchard.com
MAP 22
Open Monday to Friday usual hours.
The headquarters of this organisation are at Alignan du Vent (Domaine Deshenrys), where the wines of the *Abbaye* may be tasted along with many others. The Faugères establishment (open during normal hours) includes a restaurant and *chambres d'hôte*.

B **DOMAINE VALAMBELLE
La Famille Abbal
25 Avenue de la Gare, 34480 Laurens
Tel   04 67 90 12 12
Mobile   06 77 36 60 21 and 06 84 00 42 40
 m.abbal@aliceadsl.fr   or domamine.valambelle@outlook.fr
www.domaine-valambelle.com

MAP 23
Prior appointment advisable.

*DOMAINE DE LA REYNARDIÈRE
Pierre and Jean-Michel Mégé
7 Cours Jean Moulin, 34480 Saint Génies de Fontédit
Tel   04 67 36 25 75
contact@reynardiere.fr   www.reynardiere.fr
MAP 24
Open Monday to Saturday usual hours.

La Clape

The region called La Clape (Occitan for 'heap of stones'), today on the doorstep of Narbonne, was once an island when the Romans first planted vines here. They sought to link it to the mainland by diverting the waters to Gruissan, forming a series of lagoons to give Narbonne direct access to the sea, and these are still a feature of the present landscape. In the 14th century, La Clape became permanently attached to the mainland by an accumulation of deposits of the river Aude. It was largely deforested during the Middle Ages, giving the area its present desert-like aspect in the higher, wilder parts of the region. It is basically a chalky mountain rising to some 214 metres above sea level, enjoying a particularly dry climate, tempered from time to time by the sea mists rising off the Mediterranean. Technically the area around Gruissan is part of the Corbières (q.v. for growers), but may declare wines as La Clape also.

La Clape, today Narbonne's vinous appendage, has its own AOP, while being a recognised *cru* of Languedoc. There are 30 or so independent producers growing the usual range of Languedoc grapes, but a local speciality is the bourboulenc, which by law must form 40% of the *encépagement* of the white wines claiming the AOP La Clape. From it the growers make a tangy, sometimes slightly salty white, which enjoys an excellent reputation for its freshness. Whether or not this character derives from the area's long relationship to the sea is debatable, but certainly the lowest-lying areas separating mainland and island were once a salt-marsh.

Bourboulenc (known also in parts of the Midi as malvoisie or tourbat) may be grown as a *monocépage* but, if blended, there must be a minimum total of 60% bourboulenc and/or grenache blanc. Viognier is frowned on (maximum 10%). Growers not complying with these requirements

Historic remains near Armissan

may declare their whites as Languedoc AOP, IGP or *Vins de France*. There are no unusual rules in relation to the red or pink wines, save that cinsault and carignan may not together exceed 70% of the *encépagement*.

The sequence of listings starts just outside Narbonne, continues southwards and then eastwards along the coast and finally north to rejoin the Narbonne-Béziers motorway.

B *** CHÂTEAU PECH-REDON

Christophe Bousquet
Chemin de la Couleuvre, Route de Gruissan, 11100 Narbonne
Tel   04 68 90 41 22
Mobile   06 08 62 33 97
chateaupechredon@orange.fr   www.pech-redon.com

MAP 3
Appointment strongly recommended.

"The wine-producer is only an artisan who strives to polish what nature has given him." So says M. Bousquet, the owner of this hilltop *domaine* and president of the *syndicat* of La Clape growers. His wines reflect the importance which he accords to his work in the vineyard. To get there you need to travel three kilometres off the main road up a winding country track which leads nowhere else. The journey pays off, because this is considered by many people to be the best vineyard in the region. Given the quality, prices are very fair. The wines are not textbook (they include IGPs from cabernet sauvignon and alicante), and even the AOPs are distinctive – sometimes on the wild side and truly *terroir*-driven. There are three wines in the 'L'Épervier' range: a white (B) from grenache blanc as well as bourboulenc (a grape which is particularly well-suited by the altitude of the vineyard and its exposure to the sea); a Rosé (A) from syrah and grenache, simple yet fruity and managing to avoid 'bonbons anglais' flavours; and the red (B/C), 60% syrah and 40% grenache, some of the syrah being given a little oak. This is Bousquet's best seller. Other reds include 'Les Cades' (B), which has a deal of both carignan and cinsault, and is raised in tank, 'Lithos' (B/C), sometimes all tank, sometimes with light oak ageing, and the *tête de cuvée* 'La Centaurée' (C) from the same assemblage as 'L'Épervier' but aged wholly in *demi-muids* for 24 months. There is a plump IGP white called 'Les Genéts' (B/C) from chardonnay and viognier, barrel-fermented and aged two years in wood on its lees.

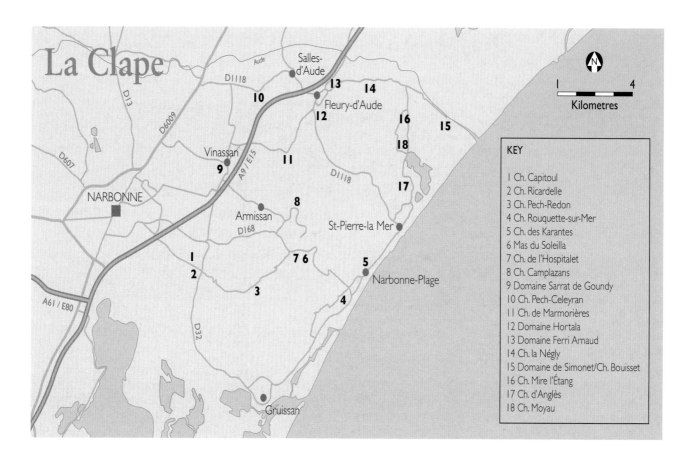

La Clape

KEY

1 Ch. Capitoul
2 Ch. Ricardelle
3 Ch. Pech-Redon
4 Ch. Rouquette-sur-Mer
5 Ch. des Karantes
6 Mas du Soleilla
7 Ch. de l'Hospitalet
8 Ch. Camplazans
9 Domaine Sarrat de Goundy
10 Ch. Pech-Celeyran
11 Ch. de Marmorières
12 Domaine Hortala
13 Domaine Ferri Arnaud
14 Ch. la Négly
15 Domaine de Simonet/Ch. Bouisset
16 Ch. Mire l'Étang
17 Ch. d'Anglès
18 Ch. Moyau

***CHÂTEAU ROUQUETTE-SUR-MER

Jacques Boscary and family
Route Bleue, 11100 Narbonne-Plage
Tel   04 68 65 68 65
chai@chateaularouquette.com   www.chateaurouquette.com

MAP 4
Cellars open seven days a week 9.30-12.30 and 15.00-19.00.

The present buildings, dating from the 1880s, stand alongside a ruined fortress going back to the 13th century. The 62 hectares of vines, planted within shouting distance of the sea, are on a variety of soils: hard white chalk, pebbly red Mediterranean stones, large white pebbles, offering the chance to produce a variety of different styles of raw material. For example, there is the bourboulenc based 'Arpège' (B), light and with good acidity but with some *gras*, two rosés, both *saignés*, the light and easy 'Cuvée Marine' (A), and the more serious 'Adagio' (B) with its strawberry notes. Among the reds are the 'Esprit Terroir' (B), a fruity thoroughbred, and the more complex oak-aged 'Amarante' (B). There are two wines named after Henry Lapierre, Jacques Boscary's grandfather, a rich white (C) with plenty of roussanne and raised in new wood, and a plump red (C), raised in oak from syrah, carignan and mourvèdre. 18 months in new wood gives 'Cuvée Clos de la Tour' (D) the chance to show off the oldest vines from syrah and mourvèdre, while 'L'Absolu' (D++) is the top wine from here which manages to combine delicacy with power, especially on the finish. You can spend a lot of money here, but the less expensive wines are very good value, the bag-in-box versions being a big attraction. The family is planning further plantings.

B **MAS DU SOLEILLA

Peter Wildbolz and Christa Derungs
Route de Narbonne Plage, 11100 Narbonne
Tel   04 68 45 24 80
Mobile   06 20 80 40 37
GPS 43.10.11   3 07 20
vins@mas-du-soleilla.com   www.mas-du-soleilla.com

MAP 6
Cellars open Monday to Saturday, 9.00-19.00 (18.00 October to March) and by appointment only at weekends.

Carved out of L'Hospitalet (q.v.) before the latter was sold to Gérard Bertrand, this 22-hectare *domaine* is one of the top La Clape properties, especially if you like your wines dark and powerful. Peter Wildbolz, a wine-lover all his life, is an oenologist and agricultural engineer, so the transition to winemaker was not difficult. Though his wines are not cheap, the medals keep coming. Bourboulenc and roussanne are the mainstays of the two whites, 'Rupture' (B) and 'Réserve Blanc' (C/D), the latter being quite a big, fat wine raised in barrel, substantial enough to accompany scallops or poultry. The first red, 'Les Chailles' (C), is mostly from old grenache, with just a bit of syrah to give it spice, and

Jacques Boscary, Château Rouquette-sur-Mer

Susan Close, Château Complazens

is raised in tank for 12 months. 'L'Intrus' (C) is the only wine here which sports some carignan, along with the usual grenache and syrah, a garriguey wine with wild berries, serious tannins and a fruity, spicy finish. 'Les Bartelles' (C) is another garriguey blend with good attack and some oak, a partner for serious meat eating. Apart from an IGP blend of cabernet franc and merlot called 'Terre du Vent' (C/D), dark, big, rounded and looking for game, the top red is 'Clôt de l'Amandier' (D) from 60-year-old vines, a hefty wine which needs keeping to shrug off the vanillin oak and absorb its 14.5 degrees of alcohol. There are no rosés here, but there are some very attractive *chambres d'hôte*, which are the special province of Christa.

***CHÂTEAU CAMPLAZENS
Peter and Susan Close
11110 Armissan
Tel   04 68 45 38 89
GPS 43.112996   3.7 36 83
wine@camplazens.com   www.camplazens.com

MAP 8
Rendezvous advisable.

Peter and Susan acquired this 45-hectare *domaine*, three

kilometres from the sea as the bird flies and at a height of 150 metres, in 2001, and have since made quite a splash, particularly with the international market. Their vineyard is half syrah, the rest divided between grenache, marselan, carignan and viognier. There is a range of IGP varietals from viognier and every red grape other than carignan. The AOPs start with 'La Garrigue', a light wine showing off the fruit from the syrah and only 20% of which sees wood. Next comes 'Prestige' from the same grapes with a bit of carignan too. 'Premium' (C) is from selected parcels of those grapes, all raised in barrel, and 'Julius' (D) is one of the top wines, all from syrah and something of a blockbuster for those who like that sort of thing, as is 'Livia' (D). The red wines are all given their malo in barrels, renewed on a three-year cycle, in which half the wines are aged for 12 months before assemblage and bottling. The wines here manage to be both popular and artisan in style, and are commercially very successful. Except where mentioned, the wines are all (B).

***DOMAINE SARRAT DE GOUNDY
Olivier Calix
46 Avenue de Narbonne, 11110 Vinassan
Tel   04 68 45 30 68
oliver@sarratdegoundy.com   www.sarratdegoundy.com

Olivier Calix, Domaine Sarrat de Goundy

MAP 9
Cellars open every day except Sundays and public holidays, 9.30-12.30 and 14.30-19.00.

This 70-hectare *domaine* was created by Olivier's parents in 2000. His father was formerly president of the *cave coopérative* at Armissan, and as an expert in the planting of vines had plenty of experience in the vineyard, if not so much in the *chais*. Olivier, who incidentally has an English History of Art degree which got him working with the Guggenheim Foundation in Spain, has created a range of wines dedicated to his father. 'Cuvées du Planteur' (B) is the name for a spicy red and a slightly oxidised white (roussanne/bourboulenc), both raised in barrel, as well as a sprightly mineral rosé. He has added marselan to the traditional black grape varieties of Languedoc, while macabeu and viognier add something different to his bourboulenc and roussanne. On the lowest ground, he grows IGP *cépages* such as merlot, cabernet, chardonnay, muscat and sauvignon, from which he makes a three-colour range of easy drinking quaffers (A). The AOP range starts with a bourboulenc-based white (B), sometimes suggesting almonds and honey with a touch of aniseed. The rosé (B) is a swimming-pool affair, all wild strawberries and cherries. The red (B) has spice from syrah, roundness from grenache and bite from some carignan. 'Cuvée Sans titre' is the name given to a wine which is different each year:

in 2012 it was all-cinsault. Olivier finishes with a range he calls 'Spécialités', comprising a late-harvested roussanne (B/C) raised in barrel for 18 months, a sulphur-free mourvèdre-based wine called 'La Combe aux Louves', aged in *demi-muids* for 14 months (C), and a couple of Cartagènes (B/C), one red and one white. The *chais* is as striking as the wines and it houses a number of terracotta *cuves*, which Olivier is experimenting with as an alternative to *fûts*. An interesting *domaine*; *à suivre*, as they say.

✳✳CHÂTEAU PECH-CELEYRAN
Nicolas and Ombline de Saint-Exupéry,
11110 Salles-d'Aude
Tel 04 68 33 50 04
saint-exupery@pech-celeyran.com   www.pech-celeyran.com

MAP 10
New tasting room open daily except Sundays and public holidays.

This was the Languedoc home of the mother of Toulouse-Lautrec, celebrated in the painter's many paintings and posters in the museum of his works at Albi, just two hours' drive away. It came to the Saint-Exupéry family in 1902 by marriage, and the present winemakers are the fifth genera-

Cave at Château Camplazens

tion to live here. There are 94 hectares of vines, about half of which are in the AOP La Clape, the other half, for some unaccountable reason, outside it, and from the latter come a fine range of IGPs D'Oc and Côtes de Pérignan based on a mix of Languedoc and Bordeaux grape varieties. Most of the wines are stored in huge old *foudres*, though the top reds are aged in more modern barrels. The IGPs, in a range called 'Cuvée Ombline' (A) come in all three colours, the white from 80% chardonnay and 20% viognier, the rosé from 80% merlot and 20% mourvèdre, and the red from merlot, cabernet and cot. A range of varietals are sold as IGPs d'Oc (B), from merlot, syrah, cot, cabernet, chardonnay and viognier. The La Clape AOPs come in two ranges: 'Cinquième Génération' (A/B), all three colours raised in tank, and 'Céleste' (B) (no rosé), the red aged for eight to 12 months in barrel, the white left five months on its lees before being transferred to oak. Under the name 'Grands Fûts' there are *mono-cépages* from pinot noir (B) with 12 months' barrel-age, and Alicante (B), a rare experience not to be missed. Sign off (or on) with their Cartagène (B/C), which makes a fine marriage with chocolate. This is one of the most interesting visits in La Clape, for its historical associations, for its magnificent *caveau* and, of course for its wines, which are exceptional value.

***CHÂTEAU LA NÉGLY Jean Paux-Rosset
Routes des Cabanes, 11150 Fleury d'Aude
Tel   04 68 32 41 50
lanegly@wanadoo.fr   www.lanegly.fr

MAP 14
Cellars open Monday to Friday, 10.00-12.00 and 15.00-18.00. Saturday 9.30-12.30 and 15.00-18.30.

One of the star vineyards of La Clape, indeed of the Languedoc. The high proportion of sunny days and the southern position close to the sea gives these wines richness, depth and a very Mediterranean feel. The range is large. It is easy to overlook 'Oppidum Sauvignon' (A), a 100% IGP with exotic fruits, pomelo and lychee, and another IGP called 'Oppidum' (B) from 40% chardonnay, 55% muscat and just a touch of sauvignon. But 'La Brise Marine' (B) is a proper La Clape, with 70% bourboulenc and 30% grenache blanc, virtually all raised in tank. 'La Falaise Blanc' (C) is a roussanne/marsanne blend, raised in oak for 10 months with due *bâtonnge*. Two rosés have disappointed some: 'l'Ecume' (A) is designed as an apéritif or for summer grills, 'Les Embruns' (B) has some cinsault. Passing to the big range of reds you might pick a cinsault-based 'Le Pavilion' (B), with its 20% syrah aged five months in wood, or their best-selling 'La Falaise' (C), half syrah vinified in wood, 40%

Typical La Clape *terroir*

grenache and 10% mourvèdre, made in tank, but the whole *assemblage* aged in wood for 12 months. This is regularly a concentrated and hugely impressive wine, typically showing liquorice and toast flavours, it keeps astonishingly well; the 1998 is still superb. 'Le Grès' (C) is from syrah and grenache vines grown on particularly stony soil, given 40 days' *cuvaison* with *pigeage* twice a day. Then we move into the stratosphere (D++) with three top *cuvées*: 'L'Ancely', mostly mourvèdre with a lot of chocolate and spice developed after 20 months in *demi-muids*, 'La Porte du Ciel' and 'Clos des Truffiers', grown from grapes far away in the Hérault in a vineyard shared with truffle oaks. Try to pick out the truffles, if you are lucky enough to get your host to pour you some of this treasure.

***DOMAINE DE SIMONET / CHÂTEAU BOUISSET** Christophe and Claude Barbier

Route des Cabanes, 11560 Fleury-sur-Aude
Tel   04 68 33 60 13
Mobile   06 10 21 79 05

MAP 15
Visits every day from 9.00-12.00 and 14.00-18.00.

Simonet is a tiny seaside vineyard planted with bourboulenc

and a little merlot, where Barbier produces two IGP Côtes de Pérignan wines, 'Bourboulenc' and 'Terres Salées'. The vines were once a marsh, and Barbier continues to flood them in winter to prevent the return of the salt. It is this same salt which protected the wines from phylloxera so the vines are ungrafted. 'Bourboulenc' (A/B) is given a mere eight days in barrel while 'Terres Salées' (B) gets eight months, and this wine should be stored away to let the wood integrate itself. The wines, though completely dry, even salty, recall apples and honey. Do not be afraid if there is some reduction, and open the bottle well ahead of time. Perhaps, unusually, the wines would keep well. They are quirky but quite delicious. The merlot (A) is easy, round and even a bit salty, too. Barbier also produces wines from the family base at Château Bouisset, including a red called 'Les Bécassines' (A), fair enough but not as characterful as the bourboulenc wines. The top red (B) is given its malo in barrel.

***CHÂTEAU D'ANGLÈS** Eric Fabre

Rivière le Haut, 11560 Fleury d'Aude
Tel   04 68 33 61 33
info@chateaudangles.com

MAP 17
Visits daily (except Sunday) from 9.00 -19.00.

Eric Fabre was at Ch. Lafite Rothschild for eight years, so there's not much he doesn't know about winemaking, and it is not surprising that the wines at Anglès have achieved a considerable international reputation. There are just two whites, a rosé and two reds. The flamingo-coloured rosé (B/C) is 80% directly pressed mourvèdre, with just 10% each of *saigné* syrah and grenache. Fruity and floral, it is a 'food' rosé and, unlike most, it will keep a few years. The whites and reds both come in two grades, 'Classique' and 'Grand Vin'. Of the whites, the 'Classique' (B/C) is half bourboulenc and raised in tank, the 'Grand Vin' (C) oak-fermented and aged for six months in used barrels. It is pale in colour but rich on the palate. The red 'Classique' (B/C) is a standard syrah/grenache/mourvèdre blend, deep in colour and with plenty of red and black berry fruits. The 'Grand Vin' (C) is more than half mourvèdre and has a touch of carignan to bring bite to the syrah and grenache also in the blend. It is a complex wine in which you may detect spice, tobacco, liquorice and mint, according to the vintage, and will keep a long time. The wine is aged in old barrels, except for its grenache which is aged in tank prior to the *assemblage*.

OTHER GOOD GROWERS AT LA CLAPE

*CHÂTEAU LE CAPITOUL Bonfils group,
Route de Gruissan, 11100 Narbonne
Tel 04 68 49 23 30
GPS 43.127846 3.055864
contact@chateau-capitoul.com
MAP 1
Visits by rendezvous.
Formerly the property of the Mock family, this 64-hectare *domaine* was acquired by the Bonfils group in 2011.

**CHÂTEAU RICARDELLE
Bruno Pellegrini (régisseur Eric Français)
Route de Gruissan, 11100 Narbonne
Tel   04 68 56 21 00
ricardelle@orange.fr   michel.jousseaume@yahoo.fr
www.chateau-ricardelle.com
MAP 2
Visits 9.00-19.00 Monday to Friday. 10.00-19.00 Saturdays and Sundays. Guided tours Thursdays from 17.30-19-30.

**CHÂTEAU DES KARANTES Nicolas Laverny
Karantes-le-Haut, 11100 Narbonne-Plage
Tel 04 68 43 61 70
chateaudeskarantes@karantes.com   www.karantes.com
MAP 5
Visits by appointment Tuesday to Friday, 9.00-13.00. Saturday 9.00-13.00 and 14.00-18.00.
It is said that Gérard Bertrand has his eyes on buying this estate from its present American owners and may well have done so by the time this book comes out. Meanwhile, it seems that the winemaking is suspended pending a possible sale.

B **CHÂTEAU DE L'HOSPITALET
Gérard Bertrand
Route de Narbonne Plage, 11100 Narbonne
Tel   04 68 45 57 27
vins@gerard-bertrand.com   www.chateau-hospitalet.com/fr/
MAP 7
Open for visits seven days a week.
This huge estate of 1,000 hectares is the headquarters of Gérard Bertrand, one of the most important figures on the Languedoc-Roussillon scene. A visit is as fascinating as it is awe-inspiring. A bit of Napa Valley transported to the Languedoc.

**CHÂTEAU DE MARMORIÈRES
Jéhan et Sabine de Woillemont
Route de Fleury, 11110 Vinassan
Tel 04 68 45 23 64
marmoriereres@orange.fr   www.marmorieres.com
MAP 11
Appointment recommended.
This is one of the largest (over 100 hectares of vines) as well as the oldest of estates in La Clape. The family De Woillemont founded the *syndicat* of La Clape growers, leading to the recognition of AOP in 2005.

*DOMAINE HORTALA   S.C.E.A. Hortala
10 place du Languedoc 11560 Fleury d'Aude
Tel   04 68 33 37 74
www.domaine-hortola.fr
MAP 12
Appointment advisable.

*DOMAINE FERRI ARNAUD
Joseph and Richard Ferri
Avenue de l'Hérault, 11560 Fleury d'Aude
Tel   04 68 33 89 77 or 04 68 33 62 43
Mobile 06 75 73 54 92
catyferri-domaineferriarnaud@wanadoo.fr
MAP 13
Appointment advisable.

**CHÂTEAU MIRE L'ETANG
la Famille Chamayrac
11560 Fleury d'Aude,
Tel 04 68 33 62 84
mireletang@wanadoo.fr   www.chateau-mire-letang.com
MAP 16
Cellar open every day except Sundays and public holidays, 9.00-12.00 and 15.00-19.00 (14.00-18.00 from 1/11 through 28/2).

**CHÂTEAU MOYAU Bernhard Köhler
11560 St Pierre la Mer
Tel 06 83 28 27 00
info@moyau.com www.moyau.com
MAP 18
Appointment recommended.
Winemaker Peter Munday ex-Corbières

Béziers/Pézenas

This section covers a wide and heterogeneous range of wines grown in the area east of Faugères and north-east of La Clape. It goes from Béziers in the south, almost to Clermont-l'Hérault in the north, taking in the AOP area of Languedoc Pézenas, the tiny district of Cabrières, the rather rare Clairette de Languedoc, and a mass of properties simply entitled to the generic Languedoc *appellation*. There are as many IGPs/Vins de France as AOPs. The former represent two quite different kinds of winemakers: those who prefer to make wine outside of the AOP rules (perhaps because they do not wish to be limited in their choice of grape varieties), and those who prefer to make wines beyond the authorised yield limits prescribed by the AOP rules. The first category show, in general, much better than the second. But, in any case, this area demonstrates above all why the distinctions between AOP production and IGPs/Vins de France are becoming more and more blurred, and how many non-AOP producers are making wines which go to the top of the class in Languedoc.

The order of growers begins in the south, going to the far north and then back again, ignoring boundaries, in the hope that this will suggest a convenient method of visiting growers in a sensible sequence, avoiding too much unnecessary travel.

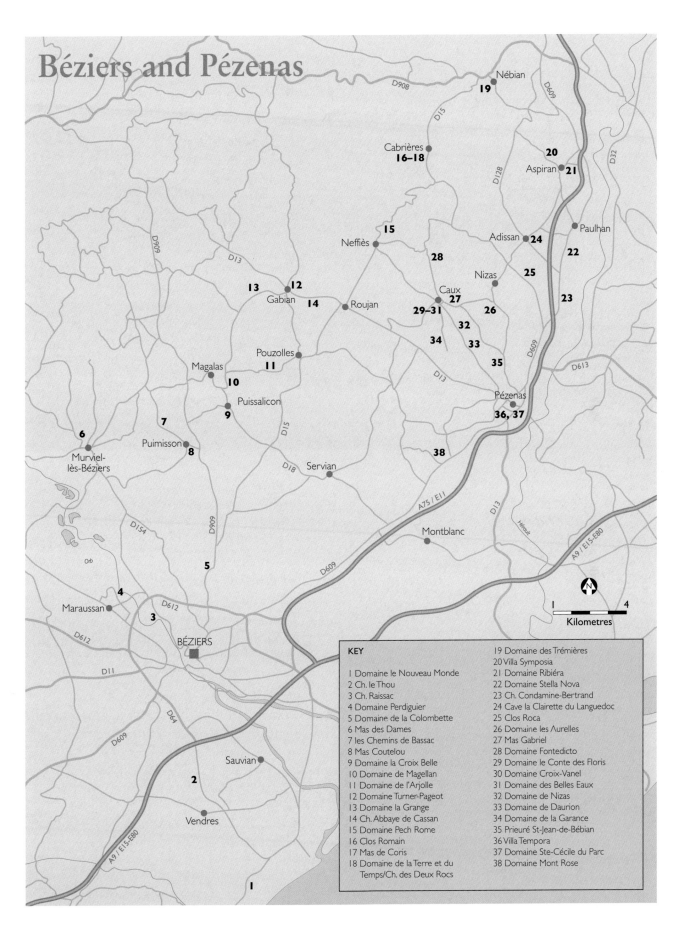

Béziers and Pézenas

KEY

1 Domaine le Nouveau Monde
2 Ch. le Thou
3 Ch. Raissac
4 Domaine Perdiguier
5 Domaine de la Colombette
6 Mas des Dames
7 les Chemins de Bassac
8 Mas Coutelou
9 Domaine la Croix Belle
10 Domaine de Magellan
11 Domaine de l'Arjolle
12 Domaine Turner-Pageot
13 Domaine la Grange
14 Ch. Abbaye de Cassan
15 Domaine Pech Rome
16 Clos Romain
17 Mas de Coris
18 Domaine de la Terre et du
  Temps/Ch. des Deux Rocs

19 Domaine des Trémières
20 Villa Symposia
21 Domaine Ribiéra
22 Domaine Stella Nova
23 Ch. Condamine-Bertrand
24 Cave la Clairette du Languedoc
25 Clos Roca
26 Domaine les Aurelles
27 Mas Gabriel
28 Domaine Fontedicto
29 Domaine le Conte des Floris
30 Domaine Croix-Vanel
31 Domaine des Belles Eaux
32 Domaine de Nizas
33 Domaine de Daurion
34 Domaine de la Garance
35 Prieuré St-Jean-de-Bébian
36 Villa Tempora
37 Domaine Ste-Cécile du Parc
38 Domaine Mont Rose

Cave at Pouzolles

**CHÂTEAU LE THOU

Managers la Famille Valéry
Route de Béziers, 34410 Sauvian
Tel   04 99 41 02 74
GPS 43.29 573N 3.25 789E
contact@chateaulethou.com   www.chateaulethou.com

MAP 2
Tastings etc. at neighbouring Domaine des Deux Ruisseaux, same address. Usual hours.

The Valéry family have been big players for many years in the vineyards around Sauvian, which are on terraces between the mouths of the rivers Orb and Aude, but they raised their game in 2003 when they took a lease on the Château le Thou, a property which had been acquired and much improved by a consortium of sportsmen only two years before. The top wine of the property is today still named after two of their landlords, 'À George et Clem' (B), and has acquired a considerable reputation for its modern but elegant style. Basing it on 70% syrah, 30% grenache, the Valérys have not really changed this wine at all. It has a white partner (B), largely from roussanne, with some marsanne and grenache blanc. These are the top wines, both given some oak-ageing that contributes to their contemporary character, unlike a range of tank-raised wines, mainly from the same kind of *assemblages*, called 'Cuvée Collection' (A/B). Finally, there

is a quaffing red called 'Le Petit Thou' (A), tank-raised from syrah, cabernet sauvignon and petit verdot. At the tasting shop you will no doubt be encouraged to try the other products of the Valéry family, fair enough but which even they would not claim to be in the same class as from le Thou.

***DOMAINE PERDIGUIER   Jérome Feracci

34370 Marausssan
Tel   04 67 90 37 44
Mobile   06 22 42 86 51
GPS Lat.43.367143 Long 3.1706099
perdigui@terre-net.fr   www.domaineperdiguier.com

MAP 4
Cellar open 7/7 10.00-12.00 and 14.00-18.30

Jean Perdiguier was a medieval tax collector who met a sticky end at the hands of assassins in Montpellier in the 15th century. HMRC, please note. The Feraccis have owned the property for 60 years or so, and have made it into a delightful home, being careful to preserve some frescoes discovered in the spiral staircase of the southern tower of the *château*. The vines, grown on 25 hectares mostly surrounding the *château* are mainly red, though there is one white chardonnay varietal, and a rosé deriving from syrah and the two cabernets. All the wines here are IGPs, the two main reds being largely from merlot and cabernet sauvignon, for example their first 'Domaine' wine (A/B). The top *cuvée*, 'En Auger' (B/C), concentrated and long on the palate, is named after a fortification demolished some hundreds of years back, and is indeed 85% cabernet and 15% merlot. A recent innovation is a cabernet franc-based 'Cuvée des Filles de Perdiguier' (B), which has a touch of grenache to give it local character. The wines here have a cedary, rather Bordeaux style, not surprising in view of the grapes grown. Impressive and good value.

B ***DOMAINE DE LA COLOMBETTE
François et Vincent Pugibet
Ancienne Route de Bédarieux, 34500 Béziers
Tel 04 67 31 05 53
contact@lacolombette.fr   www.lacolombette.fr

MAP 5
Cellars open 8.00-12.00 and 13.30-18.00 except Sunday, but it might be worth an appointment, and in any event allow plenty of time for a visit.

This *domaine*, which extends to 72 hectares, is like no other. Passionate believers in reducing the level of alcohol in wine, father and son have a range of wine in all three colours called 'Plume' (A/B), in which the alcohol has been reduced to nine degrees. They are devotees of the screwcap, though recognising that red wines need to breathe more than whites, they have devised a modified capsule to let in just that bit more oxygen. Practitioners of drip-by-drip irrigation, both in summer and spring, they are now experimenting in the creation of new *cépages* with a view to mitigating the risk of disease in the vineyard, thereby reducing the need for the use of sprays, even copper and suphur. Both harvesting and pruning is done by machine, and this is being developed in such a way that eventually the vines will, they say, need little if any pruning at all. Meanwhile, the 'Colombette' range (nothing above B and mostly A/B) includes a charmingly delicious sauvignon, a chardonnay raised in *demi-muids*, a white from the experimental cabernet jura and cabernet blanc, two rosés from grenache, one from the bio vineyard, and a big range of reds, from which one might pick out the pinot noir, raised in small barrels with regular *pigeage* and aged in old wood. There is also a pure lledoner pelut, a biggish wine (the only one they make where the alcohol level rises above 12.5) with bags of red fruits and herby flavours from the surrounding vegetation. Vincent Pugibet says "some may call us iconoclasts. We may seem atypical, but we think of ourselves as avant-garde" – an understated self-assessment.

B ***MAS DES DAMES   Lidewij Van Wilgen
Route de Causses et Veyran, 34490 Murviel-lès Béziers
Tel 04 67 37 26 63
Mobile 06 60 88 00 17
GPS 43 27 233 3 07 847
mas.desdames@orange.fr   www.masdesdames.fr

MAP 6
For information about visits and tastings, phone 06 60 88 00 17.

Lidewij was formerly a publicity consultant in Amsterdam before moving to Languedoc in 2002, where she undertook training in viticulture and oenology. "When you give up everything for a new life, you are even more motivated," she says. Since restructuring the vineyard and the cellars, she has become a much-admired winemaker in the region, helped by her three young daughters and winemaking neighbours, M. et Mme Huc. To the alicante bouschet, carignan and grenache she found on arrival, she has added some mourvèdre and grenache blanc. She also has syrah, which she ages in *demi-muids* for her top red, 'La Diva' (C), to give it complexity before transferring it back into concrete. There is another very herby red called 'La Dame' (B), a white (B/C) where the grenache blanc is vinified and aged in barrel, as well as a charming rosé (A/B). This is a serious and improving *domaine*, and Lidewij is one of the Vinifilles (q.v.)

B ***MAS COUTELOU
Jean-François (Jeff) Coutelou
6 rue de l'Escarède, 34480 Puimisson
Tel 04 67 36 19 17
Mobile 06 64 62 12 57
www.mas-coutelou.vinsnaturels.fr

MAP 8
Appointment advisable.

Jeff was once a teacher at a hotel school in Paris (he is a great cook apparently), but returned in 1987 to take over the family vines, which he cultivated organically from the word go. Furthermore, his 14 hectares produce 'natural' wines, with minimum sulphur, sometimes none. He has been making wines in this style since 1987, and they manage to remain firm in structure, dry and fresh despite the absence of sulphur. Try, for example, the tasty, zingy blend from maccabeu and grenache gris (B). The reds include two pure cinsault wines, 'Les Copains' (B), which is a revival of a wine last made in 2003, and 'Cinsault Simple' (B), a quaffer. 'Classe' (B) is a syrah/grenache/carignan blend, 'Les Vins des Amis' (B) is mostly grenache, while 'Flambadou' (B/C) is an excellent pure carignan. Syrah is featured in '7 rue de la Pompe', a dry north Rhône-ish style wine, and the top 'Paf La Syrah' (C), which is surprisingly light and stylish.

**DOMAINE DE L'ARJOLLE
La Famille Teisserenc
7 bis rue Fournier, 34480 Pouzolles
Tel 04 67 24 81 18
domaine@arjolle.com   www.arjolle.com

MAP 11
Cellars open Monday to Saturday, 9.00-18.00.

Landscape near Roujan

The extended Teisserenc family give visitors one of the warmest welcomes in Languedoc. For over 30 years they have enjoyed the flexibility the Côtes de Thongue give their growers in the choice of grape varieties, which they cultivate on their 80 hectares of vineyard. Here you will find not only the cabernets, merlot, sauvignon, viognier, muscat and even carmanère, but also possibly the only zinfandel vines in France. The range of products is never-ending (21 at the last count), and liable to change from year to year, so any attempt to list them is bound to quickly go out of date. It is unlikely though that their varietals from muscat: 'Allegria (A); chardonnay (A) from 'Domaine de Bargon', a property which they bought a few years back; their regular cabernet-merlot blend (A); a pure cabernet (B); and a sauvignon-merlot blend called 'Equilibre' (A) are anything but permanent fixtures. You may also find 'Equinoxe' (B/C), from muscat, sauvignon and viognier, and an oaked chardonnay (B/C), as well as more sophisticated reds based on the Bordeaux grapes, then, of course, their tiny production of zin.

BD ****DOMAINE TURNER-PAGEOT

Karen Turner and Emmanuel Pageot
3 Av. De la Gare, 34320 Gabian,
Tel 04 67 00 14 33
Mobiles 06 77 40 14 32 and 06 32 23 60 14
contact@turnerpageot.com www.turnerpageot.com

MAP 12
Visits by appointment only.

A small vineyard (with nevertheless a large variety of 17 *terroirs* on its different parcels) aiming at the highest level. Both partners have wide experience in all parts of the new and old world. Karen has to devote most of her time to St Jean de Bébian (q.v.), but also works here when she can, leaving much of the burden at home to Emmanuel. His experience has taken him all over the world, as a sommelier in Edinburgh, as a manager at Oddbins and then a spell with Johnny Hügel in Alsace, where he learnt his winemaking skills. The current production includes a pure sauvignon, 'La Rupture' (C), admired for its mineral liveliness, while a carefully oaked roussanne-marsanne blend, 'Le Blanc' (B), combines spice and citrus notes on the bouquet with honeyed flowers on the palate. The first red, called 'Carmina Major' (C), is a syrah-mourvèdre blend, an object lesson in combining finesse and concentration, while 'Le Rouge' (B) is in a more orthodox Languedoc style with good tannins. Then there is an all-grenache called 'B8 15', which is very good indeed and rare as an example of unblended grenache. And don't forget the *clairet* (B), produced by popular request, which Emmanuel says aims to combine the *apéritif* and food styles, whereas in fact it provides a serious mouthful. And, if you are a keen cook, buy the verjus, difficult to obtain elsewhere.

***DOMAINE PECH ROME

Mary and Pascal Blondel
17 Montée des Remparts, 34320 Neffiès
Tel 04 67 59 42 05 Mobile 06 08 89 58 11
contact@domainepechrome.com
www.domainepechrome.com

MAP 15
Visits by appointment.

Mary comes from Ireland, but Pascal is pure Languedoc, and they were both once pharmacists. In 2001, submitting to their passion for wine, they set up with 10 hectares of vines of which 8.5 are AOP Pézenas, the remainder in nearby Caux from which they make IGPs. The Pezenas vines are mostly on Faugères-type schist, being just beyond the eastern extremity of that region. The house style is for fruity elegant wines which can be drunk for pure pleasure and when young. The first AOP Pézenas called 'Clemens'(B) is mostly grenache, with the other usual grape varieties playing a varying role according to the vintage. 'Florens'(B), the second, largely based on mourvèdre, is for early drinking. The top red is called 'Opulens' (C), mostly syrah, kept in the cellar for 24 months before bottling and is a hefty bottle. The IGP Tempranillo (B) is intended for open-air food and enjoyment as an aperitif. There is a rosé, too, from the same grape and made for the same purpose. Finally, there is a sweet grenache (B), called 'Suavité, recommended to accompany Roquefort cheese or foie gras. This *domaine* makes stylish but elegant wines, most of them a long way away from the old-fashioned blockbusters.

B ***CLOS ROMAIN

Céline Beauquel and Romain Cabanes
Route de Clermont, 34800 Cabrières
Tel 04 67 96 97 60 Mobile 06 11 37 05 01
romaincabanes@hotmail.fr

MAP 16
You could take pot luck, but it would be better to phone ahead.

Romain Cabanes trained as a lawyer in Paris, but his family came from Clermont l'Hérault, so it was not surprising that one day his father bought up some vines and a lot of *garrigue* nearby at Cabrières. Soon Romain and Céline found themselves running the family farm, from which the grapes went to the local *coopérative*. They decided to leave and go organic in 2007, so the three years' process of conversion is well up by now. The fact that the vines are in the heart of garrigue not only gives the wines a certain herby character, but ensures that they are protected from 'contamination' by other non-organic producers. To the usual Languedoc varieties, these growers have added some pinot noir, and a tentative plantation of viognier and roussanne, the only white grapes they grow. The accent is for the moment mainly on the reds: 'Paranthèse' where a little of the viognier is added to the syrah (B), a carignan-based 'Rêves Enclos'(B) aged in

Emmanuel Pageot, Domaine Turner-Pageot

Deborah Gore, Mas Gabriel, p.189

tank, a cinsault-based 'Soir d'Hiver' (B), 'Patience' raised in old barrels (B/C) and 'Phidias'(C) from syrah and grenache and made unusually in an amphora. Romain finds that wine matures more quickly in this kind of container. He gets his from Terres d'Autan, a pottery just outside Castlnaudary.

B ***MAS DE CORIS   Jean and Véronique Attard
34800 Cabrières   (their office is at 3 rue du Dauphiné, 34170 Castelnau le Lez).
Tel 06 74 14 88 91 and 06 14 41 06 44
jeanattard54@hotmail.com   byvero34@gmail.com
www.mascoris.com

MAP 17
Phone ahead

This young domaine, just 4 hectares of vines and the same of garrigue and woodland, was acquired and established in 2009 by a couple a little less young, searching for a new life in semi-retirement. Under the inspiration of Jean Natoli, they have taken six different parcels in the lee of the Pic de Vissou, all on pinkish schist, sometimes mixed with a little sandstone. For the moment there are just two reds, both (C); 'Atout Pic', a syrah-cinsault blend and 'Bouteilles à la Mer' (C) to which grenache is added to syrah and the dominant cinsault. Grenache blanc, roussanne, viognier and a deal of vermentino (50%) go to make up the sole white (C/D) (named after the Pic), but the holding includes also a parcel of clairette. The rosé, 'La coulee Douce' (B) is 70% cinsault. The cave is in the centre of the village of Cabrières, where the Attards have retained two huge old cement cuves, relics of former days when wines from the village went to the *coopérative*. No evidence of wood so far. The wines here are cultish but not cheap.

**DOMAINE DE LA TERRE ET DU TEMPS (CHÂTEAU DES DEUX ROCS)
Jean-Claude Zabalia
Route des Crozes, Le Mas Rouch, 34800 Cabrières
Tel 06 85 42 92 35
contact@laterreletemps.com   www.laterreletemps.com

MAP 18
Wines available either from the *domaine* or from Zabalia's shop which bears the domaine's name at 10 rue La Foire in Pèzenas, open from April to September.

Zabalia who has vineyards also at Aniane and Pinet, grows syrah, grenache and carignan on schist in this remote valley north of Cabrières. From his 17 hectares he makes a single red wine (B)which is given six months ageing in tank after the assemblage, deliciously peppery and spicy. There are also a white based on Muscat and viognier and a delightful rosé from cinsault (60%), syrah and grenache (both B).

BD ***VILLA SYMPOSIA
Eric Prissette and Jean Pierre Lebaindre
Rue Saint-Georges, 34800 Aspiran
Tel 09 98 66 90 32
Mobile 06 30 35 91 48
reservations@villasymposia.com   www.villasymposia.com

MAP 20
Appointment required.

An ambitious partnership who have 18 hectares of vines, of which 12 are in production. They are mostly planted with syrah, including a substantial area of younger vines. There are currently four reds of varying degrees of sophistication: 'Petite Sieste' (B), which is nearly all cinsault with just a touch of mourvèdre, raised in tank and intended as a *'vin des copains'*. 'Amphora' (B) is largely from the younger syrah vines and is also made in stainless steel. 'Équilibre'

Lieuran-Cabrières

(B/C) has some carignan but is mostly syrah, and is given up to a year in barrels, mostly once used. The top red is more ambitious and highly praised by critics who go for a '*boisé somptueux*' – it is called 'Origine' (D) and is nearly all syrah, accorded 16 months or so in wood. Despite its price, there is good value to be had among the other *cuvées*.

✶✶CHÂTEAU CONDAMINE-BERTRAND
Bernard Jany and Bruno Andreu
2 Avenue Wladimir d'Ormesson, 34230 Paulhan
Tel   04 67 25 27 96
Mobile   06 11 48 15 48
chateau.condamineber@free.fr

MAP 23
Open Monday to Friday during usual hours.

Father and son-in-law have been running this 40-hectare estate since 2000, dividing their production roughly 50/50 between AOP wines and IGPs. 70% of the production is red and 30% white (apart from their rosés). Among the host of grape varieties to be found here are clairette (in whose area of production they are) and petit verdot, an essentially Bordelais grape but of which they have some forty-year-old plants. Under the brand 'Baron de Montgaillard' they produce from their younger vines an easy-drinking range in all three colours, the white a blend of sauvignon and roussanne, the pink of syrah and grenache, and the red a blend of old merlot and young syrah, while under the *château* label there are varietals of merlot, syrah, cabernet sauvignon and syrah. All these wines (A) are to be enjoyed on their young fruit while fresh. There is also a pure Clairette (A). This one is pale, with exotic fruits and flowers on the nose and hints of aniseed and white fruits on the palate, to be drunk young. Another white (B) has clairette too, but this time blended with roussanne and a little viognier. The red in this range exists in oaked (B) and unoaked (A) form, from blends of syrah, grenache and mourvèdre. The 'Grandes Cuvées' range has the 'Petit Verdot' (C) with its nice curranty finish, a grenache/syrah blend produced under the Pézenas *sub-appellation*, and a mainly syrah wine called 'Elixir' (B), with a little cabernet sauvignon to give structure to an already fleshy, concentrated and oaked wine. Reliable wines all.

****DOMAINE LES AURELLES
Basile et Caroline Saint Germain
8 Chemins des Champs Blancs, 34320 Nizas
Tel 04 67 25 08 34
bsg@les-arelles.com   www.les-aurelles.com

MAP 26
By appointment only.

The local basalt forms the base of this eight-hectare vine-yard, beneath a sandy-gravelly soil covered with *galets roulés*. Such a *terroir* provides distinguished, classy wine reminiscent of Burgundy, even though the founders of this vineyard were Bordeaux-trained! The white wine is made entirely from tiny yields of roussanne, is called 'Aurel' (D+), and is one of Languedoc's best, possibly *the* best. It is aged in new wood, unlike all the reds which are made and matured in enamelled steel vats, where the wines are kept for up to four years before bottling. 'Déella' (B) is their entry red, largely from grenache, and intended as a wine to be enjoyed on simple food. It has a good spicy bouquet and is easy to drink. 'Solen' (B) has 60% old carignan and grenache and is altogether more ambitious, deeper in fruit than 'Déella', the carignan giving good bite to balance. The top red wine, called like the white 'Aurel' (C), is 75% mourvèdre and a real keeper, in great years the tannins need time to resolve themselves and to integrate into the fruit. It is nevertheless a really fine and elegant wine. One of the top estates of this area.

BD ***MAS GABRIEL Peter and Deborah Gore
9 Avenue de Mougères, 34720 Caux
Tel 04 67 31 20 95
Mobile 07 88 22 94 40
info@mas-gabriel.com   www.mas-gabriel.com

MAP 27
Visits on Saturdays during June, July and August, 11.00-18.00. Otherwise by appointment.

This English couple, Peter once a finance director, Deborah a lawyer, have only a little over six hectares of vines, mostly in Caux (where there is an unusual quantity of volcanic basalt to the *terroir*), otherwise at St Jean de Bébian, where there are a lot of Chateauneuf-type *galets*. Following work experience in New Zealand, they are biodynamic converts and are ECO certified. Their vines, the first of which they acquired in 2006, are mostly syrah and carignan with some grenache for the reds and carignan blanc for the white. They are uncloned, and therefore, it is said, less prone to disease, and because the yields are lower (15-25 hectolitres per hectare), they give more concentrated fruit character to the juice. At this level of production, *vendanges vertes* are unnecessary. Their pure white carignan is called 'Clos des Papillons' (C). Only 1,500 bottles or so are produced each year and the wine has achieved a certain renown. 'Les Fleurs Sauvages' (A/B) is the name of their rosé from carignan and cinsault, pale and full of summer fruit. There are just two reds: 'Les Trois Terrasses' (B), mostly carignan (raised in tank) with some syrah and grenache, a garriguey wine with black-currants on the nose and more delicious fruits, balanced by the typical carignan firmness and acidity; then 'Clos des Lièvres' (C), mostly syrah, with complex dark fruits and spices, soft tannins and a long finish.

BD ***DOMAINE FONTEDICTO
Cécile and Bernard Belhasen
34720 Caux
Tel 04 67 98 40 22
fontedicto@tele2.fr

MAP 28
Appointment recommended.

Your ideas about viticulture will never be the same after a visit here. You are greeted at this property in the middle of nowhere by broad smiles, as the music of Pergolesi plays within the small *cave* in the middle of a field. The choice of grapes which the Belhasen family grow on their tiny four-hectare *domaine* says it all: carignan, grenache, terret and clairette, even a little aramon. No so-called '*améliorateurs*'. Nor do the family believe in *vendanges vertes*, which they say interrupt the development of the vines – severe pruning while the vine is dormant is all that is needed. All the work in the vineyard is done by hand and horse, the horse is fed on home-grown hay, bio of course, and the flour is used to make bread which the family bake in their home-built bread oven and sell at the local bio markets. You would not expect a large range of wines from such small producers, nor would you expect them to be cheap, but they give you a fascinating experience of what natural winemaking is all about. 'Pirouette' (C) is all carignan, thirst-quenching, elegant but powerful at the same time. 'Promise' (D) sees the carignan blended with grenache, a real keeper which needs decanting well ahead of drinking. In poorer vintages, 'Promise' is replaced by 'Coulisse', not a second wine, but Belhasen reserves the name 'Promise' only for the best. Finally, the most extraordinary of all is 'Clair de Terre' (D), mostly 60-year-old terret with a little clairette, together yielding just 8/10 hectolitres per hectare, pure gold in colour, with plenty of fat, while remaining completely dry with an everlasting finish. Bernard has had sight problems which once nearly persuaded him to sell up; that would have been a sad day indeed.

B ***DOMAINE LE CONTE DES FLORIS
Daniel Le Conte
7 rue Victor Hugo, 34720 Caux
New cellar at 19 Avenue Émile Combes, 34120 Pézenas
Tel 06 16 33 35 73
Mobile 06 16 34 43 91
domaine.floris@gmail.com www.domainelecontedesfloris.com

MAP 29
Phone for rendezvous and ask where, i.e at Caux or Pézenas

This is a tiny *domaine* of seven and a half hectares which Daniel, once a journalist on *La Revue du Vin de France*, bought in 2000. His first vintage was the following year. The production is only 2,000 cases all told. The vines are spread over the communes of Caux, Gabian and Pézenas, though the cellar is in Pézenas itself. Burgundian by inclination and training, his reds include a carignan-based 'Basaltique', the percentage varying from 50% to 80% according to vintage (B). The entry-level wine, 'Six Rats Noirs' (B), is 75% syrah, of which a quarter is oak-aged, the remainder raised in tank. 'Villefranchien' (C) is largely Grenache, given a long *cuvaison* and aged in oak for 12 months before being given another six in tank. 'Carbonifère' (C) is a long-lasting, big and tannic wine, given long extraction and ageing in one-year-old barrels for three years. The last red is 'Homo Habilis' (D), a syrah/grenache/mourvèdre blend, aged for two years in once-used barrels from Clos de Tart. The whites are, if anything, more distinguished than the reds, particularly 'Lune Blanche' (D), almost all white carignan and one of the most unusual, as well as the best of all Languedoc whites. Its sister, 'Lune Rousse' (D) is also largely carignan, but also half roussanne. 'Arès Blanc' (C) is an unusual blend of marsanne, terret bourret and white carignan and is aged in slightly younger barrels.

B *** DOMAINE CROIX-VANEL
Jean-Pierre Vanel
41 Boulevard du Puits-Allier, 34720 Caux
Tel 04 67 09 32 39
Mobile 06 81 72 07 74
contact@domainelacroix-vanel.com
lacroix-vanel@wanadoo.fr www.domainelacroix-vanel.com

MAP 30
Appointment advisable.

Vanel used to have a restaurant in Sète, so is no stranger to good wine, but in 1998 he bought this *domaine*, whose vines are just a kilometre outside the village of Caux (his *cave* is in the village). Today he has 10 hectares with all the grape varieties you would expect to find in a Languedoc vineyard, plus one or two others as well, e.g. oeillade. The house style is very much aimed at wines for keeping, food wines. But Vanel does not believe in allowing the fruit to over-ripen, nor does he go in for long extraction or indeed (for his reds) any oak-ageing. His white, called 'E Blanc' (C), is mostly from grenache blanc with some roussanne,

and is fermented and raised in barrel for 18 months. The wood is very discreet. There are four reds: a grenache-dominated 'Fine Amor' (B), 'Melanie' (C), named after Vanel's grandmother and based 70% on syrah; 'Natura rerum' (C), another syrah wine from a very particular syrah vineyard; and a 90% mourvèdre called 'Ma Non Troppo' (C). Vanel is interesting to visit because of his rejection of the modern trends to over-sweet fruit, long *cuvaisons* and excessive use of oak. At the same time, the wines give no hint of being old-fashioned.

B ***DOMAINE DE LA GARANCE
Pierre Quinonéro
Hameau de Sallèles, 34720 Caux
Tel 04 67 09 30 74
Mobile 06 30 42 97 46
GPS 43 498657N 3.397062E
quinonero-pierre@wanadoo.fr www.domainelagarance.com

MAP 34
Cellar open from September to June on Fridays from 10.00-12.30 and 14.00-18.00. Otherwise by appointment.

Garance is a yellow wild flower whose roots make the powerful red dye we know as madder. There's plenty of it chez Quinonéro. He has always been a bio producer since he started in 1991, and recently he has gone over to ploughing with animals. His family was Spanish and they fled the Franco regime and eventually settled in Languedoc after a spell in the mines at St-Etienne. Nowadays he has just eight hectares of vines. His production is as eccentric as he, individual and quite out of the mainstream. The wines are unfiltered and sulphur-free. A basic range called 'Aclara' (B) comes in all three colours, including his first white, a chardonnay, usually given some new oak and a malolactic fermentation. This is more conventional than 'Les Claviers' (C/D), which is largely from old ugni blanc with some centenarian grenache gris and just a touch of clairette, sometimes chardonnay. The wine is matured in old *demi-muids*, which are not completely filled so as to give a *noisette* flavour to the wine. A fully developed version of this wine is called 'In Fino Blanc', a homage to his Spanish origins and more than reminiscent of sherry. Fresh cherry fruit is the best way of describing his pinot noir, which he calls 'Kaze le Vent' (B/C), while his *tête de cuvée* is called 'Les Armières' (C) and boasts 90% carignan from vines over 50 years old, the rest syrah. Some of the blend spends two years in oak, and the result is dense and very cassis, sumptuous, chocolatey and somewhat out of the local norm, the wood showing on the nose. A much admired and somewhat cult estate, an example of the "opposite of technology," as Pierre has said. He is serious and very good fun at the same time.

Pierre Quinonéro, Domaine de la Garance

✳✳✳✳PRIEURÉ ST JEAN DE BEBIAN

La famille Pumpyanskiyi Manager Karen Turner
Route de Nizas, 34120 Pezenas
Tel   04 67 98 13 60
info@bebian.com   www.bebian.com

MAP 35

Sales and tastings six days a week during usual hours; by rendezvous on Saturdays and Sundays from October to April.

The owners today are Russian, but as the proprietors of this 32-hectare *domaine*, whose history goes back to Roman times, they have sensibly confided the making of their wines to Karen Turner, (see Domaine Turner-Pageot). Bought by Maurice Roux in 1954, then taken over by his grandson Alain, and later sold to the ex-editors of *La Revue du Vin de France*, the estate has gone from strength to strength. While retaining the old Languedoc *cépages*, there have been successive plantings of syrah, grenache and mourvèdre. Some of their new syrah is bred from vines from Chave at Hermitage and Beaucastel at Châteauneuf. They have grenache from Château Rayas and mourvèdre from Domaine Tempier at Bandol. For the whites, they have roussanne and grenache

blanc of course, but also the local bourboulenc and piquepoul. The *encépagement* at the *domaine* is under regular scrutiny and analysis, perhaps because in the old days they grew all 13 Chateauneuf varieties. This has been one of the top *domaines* in Languedoc since the renaissance of the 1980s. The grapes are hand-picked by a regular team who know the vineyard well. Vinification is traditional, the malolactic fermentation for the syrah is in barrel, and for the other grapes in tank. The syrah and mourvèdre are aged in lightly toasted barrels, renewed on a three-year cycle. There are two whites: the 'Prieuré' (C/D), aged in wood with 60% roussanne, aided by piquepoul, grenache blanc, clairette and bourboulenc; and 'La Chapelle' (B/C), (only partly oaked) from grenache blanc and roussanne with a touch of clairette. There are three reds, the lightest of which is 'La Croix' (B), from young grenache and cinsault, 'La Chapelle' (B/C) from grenache and syrah with a touch of cinsault, and finally the top 'Prieuré' (C/D), 45% syrah, 30% grenache and 5% mourvèdre. Nowadays there is also an IGP from merlot and cabernet (C), fully worthy of the *domaine*, and which promises to age well.

OTHER GOOD GROWERS IN THE BÉZIERS AND PÉZENAS AREA

**DOMAINE LE NOUVEAU MONDE
Anne-Laure and Sébastien Borras-Gauch
34530 Vendres
Tel   04 67 37 33 68
Mobile   06 18 41 03 33
domaine-lenouveaumonde@wanadoo.fr
www.nouveaumonde.com
MAP   1
Appointment advised.

*CHÂTEAU RAISSAC   Marie and Gustave Viennet
Puech Cocut, Route de Murviel, 34500 Béziers
Tel   04 67 28 15 61
info@raisssac.com   marie.viennet@raissac.com
www.raissac.com
MAP   3
Cellars open Monday to Friday all the year from 9.00-12.00 and 14.30-18.00. Saturday by appointment. Closed Sundays and public holidays.
Do not be put off by the fact that the enterprise here is quite obviously 'commercial', because the wines are good, and good value too.

B ***LES CHEMINS DE BASSAC
Rémi and Isabelle Ducellier
9 Place de la Mairie, 34480 Puimisson
Tel   04 67 36 09 67
Mobile   06 07 59 51 67
cheminsdebassac@orange.fr   www.cheminsdebassac.com
MAP   7
Phone ahead.
Note ISA (A), a fine red 7-variety IGP.

**DOMAINE LA CROIX BELLE
Jacques and Françoise Boyer
34480 Puissalicon
Tel   04 67 36 27 23
information@croix-belle.com   www.croix-belle.com
MAP 9
Open Monday to Saturday during usual hours.

B **DOMAINE DE MAGELLAN
Bruno Lafon and Sylvie Legros
467 Avenue de la Gare, 34480 Magalas
Tel   04 67 36 20 83
contact@domainemagellan.com
MAP 10
Open Monday to Friday usual hours. Saturdays by appointment. Lafon is a Burgundian from Meursault, a brother of the well-known Dominique.

**DOMAINE LA GRANGE   Sandrine Jugeux
Route de Fouzilhon, 34320 Gabian
Tel   04 67 24 69 81
Mobile   06 43 71 93 24
info@domaine-lagrange.com   www.domaine-lagrange.com
MAP 13
Appointment suggested.
There is no lack of resources behind this recently developed 30-hectare estate, nor presentation nor marketing skills. The oenologist is Jean Natoli.

*CHÂTEAU ABBAYE DE CASSAN
la Famille Lebel
Route de Gabian, 34320 Roujan
Tel   04 67 24 52 45
contact@chateau-abbaye-cassan.com
www.chateau-abbaye-cassan.com
MAP 14
Visits in July and August from 11.00-19.00, April, May, June and September 14.00-19.00 and in October weekends only from 14.00-19.00. (Tour of *château* is not free).
This huge and unmissable edifice, classified as a historic monument, has developed during the last few years a serious interest in winemaking.

**DOMAINE DES TRÉMIÈRES
Bernardette Rouquette
Route de Fouscaïs, 34800 Nébian
Mobile   06 16 79 30 28
GPS   43 605131 3 437519
tremieres@gmail.com
MAP 19
Appointment advised.
Bernardette, a *vinifille* (q.v.) is one of those winemakers who, having once escaped to make another career, was lured back by the fascination of the vine to take over the family vineyards.

**DOMAINE RIBIÉRA   Régis and Christine Pichon
22 Avenue de la Gare, 34800 Aspiran
Tel   04 67 44 16 83
Mobile   06 11 10 09 38
ribiera@wanadoo.fr
MAP 21
Rendezvous advisable.
Régis, ex-wine buyer, and Christine, store-manager, both for Hédiard, the high-end *épiciers*, changed tack and bought this six-hectare *domaine* in 2005.

BD **DOMAINE STELLA NOVA
Philippe Richy
546 Route d'Usclas, 34230 Paulhan
Tél   04 67 00 10 76
Mobile   06 20 14 53 87
GPS   43.509257 3.369502
stellanova@wanadoo.fr
MAP 22
Open every day by appointment.
Richy now has 10 hectares of vines, all cultivated biodynamically, and the wines are ultra-natural (no sulphur). Fair value for money and much recommended.

*CAVE LA CLAIRETTE DU LANGUDOC

director   Jean Renaud
2 Avenue Général de Gaulle, 34230 Adissan
Tel   04 67 25 01 07
info@clairette-adissan.fr   www.clairette-adissan.fr
MAP 24
Cellars open all year from Monday to Friday during usual hours,
and Saturday mornings.
The small but distinctive AOP area for Clairette de Languedoc
(not to be confused with Clairette de Bellegarde in the Costières de
Nîmes area) extends over a handful of villages: Adissan, Aspiran,
Le Bosc, Cabrières, Ceyras, Fontès, Lieuran-Cabrières, Nizas,
Paulhan, Péret and Saint-André-de-Sangonis. Clairette is also made
at Château la Condamine Bertrand (q.v.), Domaine de Clovallon
(q.v.), and at Croix Chaptal (see Terrasses du Larzac).

B *CLOS ROCA   Louis Aleman

Domane du Clos Roca, 34320 Nizas
Tel   04 67 25 19 43 or 06 74 73 84 02
GPS lat 43.513595, long 3.431926
closroca.nizas@gmail.com   www.closroca.com
MAP 25
Appointment recommended.

**DOMAINE DES BELLES EAUX

Grands Chais de France
Plan du Château, 34720 Caux
Tél   04 67 09 30 96
Mobile   06 26 74 33 42
GPS lat 43.500318 long 3.341926.
contact@mas-belleseaux.com
MAP 31
Cellar open all year Monday to Friday 9.00-12.00 and 14.00-
18.00. Otherwise by appointment.
This property, until recently in the hands of Axa Millésimes (the In-
surance Group), has been sold to the big négociants Grands Chais
de France.

**DOMAINE DE NIZAS   John Goelet

Hameau de Sallèles, 34720 Caux
Winery at Usclas L'Hérault a few kilometers away
Tel   04 67 90 17 92
contact@domaine-de-nizas.com   www.domaine-de-nizas.com
MAP 32
Cellar open Monday to Friday 9.00-17.00 non-stop.
This *domaine*, which now extends to 60 hectares plus, was bought
in 1998 by John Goelet, the owner of Clos du Val in California and
famous vineyards in Victoria and Tasmania.

**DOMAINE DE DAURION

Isabelle Cordoba-Collet and Laurent Braujou
34720 Caux
Tél   04 67 98 47 36
Mobile   06 62 31 89 41
info@daurion.fr   www.daurion.fr
MAP 33
Cellar open Thursday, Friday and Saturday, 10.00-18.00.
Into the third generation here, these Languedoc growers are pio-
neers of the chardonnay grape, and one of the few makers of a
white sparkling wine in the Languedoc outside Limoux.

B **VILLA TEMPORA

Serge Schwartz and Jean-Pierre Sanson
17 rue Marcelin Albert, 34120 Pézenas
Tel   09 52 54 14 79
Mobile   06 60 75 11 21
contact@villatempora.com
MAP 36
Appointment advisable because the vines are out of town at Caux
and Neffiès.

B **DOMAINE STE-CECILE DU PARC

Christine and Stephane Bertoli
34120 Pézenas
Tel   04 67 94 85 88
Mobile   06 79 18 68 56
cmb@stececileduparc.com   www.stececileduparc.com
MAP 37
Worth phoning ahead.
Former *coopérateurs* who only bought their vines in 2005, these
owners have 10 hectares of mixed *cépages*. They have planted olives
too to create biodiversity.

*DOMAINE MONT ROSE

Bernard and Olivier Costes
Tourbes, 34120 Pézenas
Tel   04 67 98 63 33
contact@domaine-montrose.com
www.domaine-montrose.com

MAP 38
Visits Monday to Saturday during normal hours.
A good value, no frills estate, which has the virtue of a long tradi-
tion and authenticity.

Terrasses du Larzac

Larzac is the name given to the extensive chalk plateau to the north of Lodève, subject of the celebrated local fight against the occupation of the plateau by the military. To the south of it, the terrain drops into Languedoc through woods and well-drained stony ground, punctuated by streams and ancient churches. The region has been baptized 'Terrasses du Larzac' by the wine authorities seeking to draw into one *appellation* the vineyards of Salagou, Saint Saturnin, Montpeyroux and Aniane, home to some of the finest of all Languedoc wines, as evidenced by the abundance of stars accorded here to the producers. The reputation of the district has grown quickly, the prices of the wines even more so.

The *terrasses* extend eastwards until separated from Pic Saint Loup only by the main road leading north from Montpellier to Ganges. The unifying feature of this heterodox area is the climate, with big swings in temperature from noon to dawn, the cool nights bringing welcome relief to the vines after the severe heat of the midday sun. There is also more rainfall here than further south, and that helps the syrah vines resist the effects of hydric stress during the summer months.

Perhaps because there is such variation in wine styles, the distinction between *appellation* wines and IGPs is blurred, with some producers making wines under both *régimes*, and some even forsaking the formal rules of the AOP system altogether. The region is also home to many organic winemakers whose boutique *domaines* are sometimes among the finest (and most expensive) of all, particularly those who realise that the *terroir* lends itself less to big, heavy wines than those showing elegance, finesse and better-balanced fruit.

Bruno Peyre, Mas du Salagou

BD ***DOMAINE DE LA MALAVIEILLE

Mireille and André Bertrand
Hameau de Mérifons,
34800 Clermont l'Hérault
Tel   04 67 96 34 67
Mobile   06 72 11 72 19
domainemalavieille.merifons@wanadoo.fr
www.domainedemalavieille.com

MAP 1
Cellars open Monday to Friday from 14.00-19.00.

M. Bertrand claims a substantial Anglo-Saxon clientèle at the doors of his caveau. They must have good taste because they not only enjoy the beautiful area round Lake Salagou, but the wines here are very good too, whether they come from the vines close to the *domaine* or from other vineyards in Montpeyroux. A full range of white and red wines go from (B) to (C).

***BRUNO PEYRE (MAS DU SALAGOU)

Bruno Peyre
Chemin des Landes, 34800 Octon
Tel   04 67 96 26 01
mas.salagou@yahoo.fr   www.masdusalagou.com

MAP 3
Phone ahead

The vineyards have been in the family for generations, Bruno's grandfather having owned 11 hectares of vines that are now mostly submerged by the creation of the Lac du Salagou. But Bruno Peyre has come back to restore what is left of them after long service for the house of Advini (Jeanjean), duties to the *Comité Interprofessionel* of the wines of Languedoc and INAO. A man of passion, which he fully communicates, and as atypical as his wines, Bruno has in a short space of time became famous for his carignan wines; he is perhaps the loudest evangelist for the grape in this part of Languedoc. Beginning with only 2.3 hectares which he inherited from his blacksmith grandfather, and from which he made a mere 4,000 bottles for his first vintage (2004), he has now doubled the size of his tiny holding, but hopes perhaps to grow it to seven hectares. 'Clos des Capisses' is the name of his range of carignans: one white (B), one rosé which Bruno calls 'gris', the other red, (all B/C). Under the name of the Mas, the red is called 'Ruffe' (B). 'Cinerite' (D++) is completely atypical, a blend of all five Languedoc grapes, raised in barrel and rising to 14.5 degrees of alcohol. Bruno says he makes this as a challenge to himself. A visit here is as unusual as the wines themselves. Allow plenty of time.

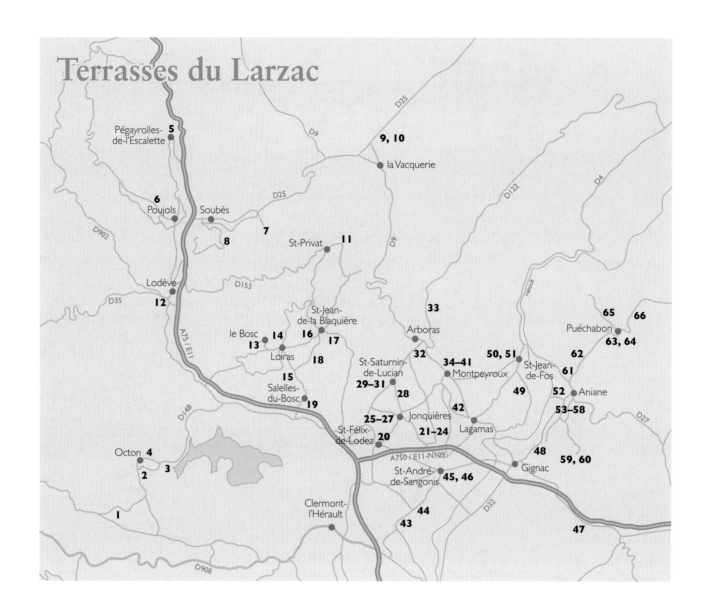

B ***MAS DES CHIMÈRES Guilhem Dardé

26 rue de La Vialle, 34800 Octon
Tel   04 67 96 22 70
mas.des.chimeres@wanadoo.fr   www.masdeschimeres.com

MAP 4
Cellars open weekdays 17.30-18.30, Saturday 15.00-18.30
and Sunday 10.00-12.00. Rendezvous nevertheless advisable,
especially off season. Wines for sale on the village square
July and August every day (not Sunday afternoon) 10.00-
12.00 and 17.00-19.00.

Guilhem is as good value for money as his wines. His
arboreal jet black moustache and eyebrows, twinkling eyes
and mischievous sense of humour guarantee a remarkable
visit. With his more infamous general, Bové, he was a leading
light in the *Confédération Paysanne*, which successfully
fought off government efforts to take over entirely the
Causse de Larzac for military purposes. He also managed
to fight the campaign to prevent a moto-cross circuit and
property development around the lake Salagou. Today,
enthusiastically aided and abetted by his wife Palma and
daughter Maguelone, he concentrates on his 12 hectares of
vines, whose grapes he takes in and out of *appellations* as he
wishes. His 'Oeillade' (A) for example, a pure neo-cinsault
with its delicious flavour of bitter cherries, charm and good
acidity, or his more or less pure carignan (sometimes with
a touch of syrah) called 'Marie et Joseph' (A), beautifully
flowery and not at all astringent. With the recognition of the
Terrasses as a cru of Languedoc, Dardé makes two. There
is a syrah/grenache/mourvèdre blend which perpetuates his
traditional red, so loved by so many over the years. Today
it is called 'Nuit Grave' (B). There is then 'Caminarèm' (C)
a blend of all five grapes made to 'push a little further the
identity of our wines' he says. And don't neglect 'l'Hérétique'
(B), an IGP from merlot and cabernet which needs keeping
to ensure a blend of the tannins with the lovely fruit. Round
off your visit with a taste of his late-harvested muscat (B),
kept for two years in barrel.

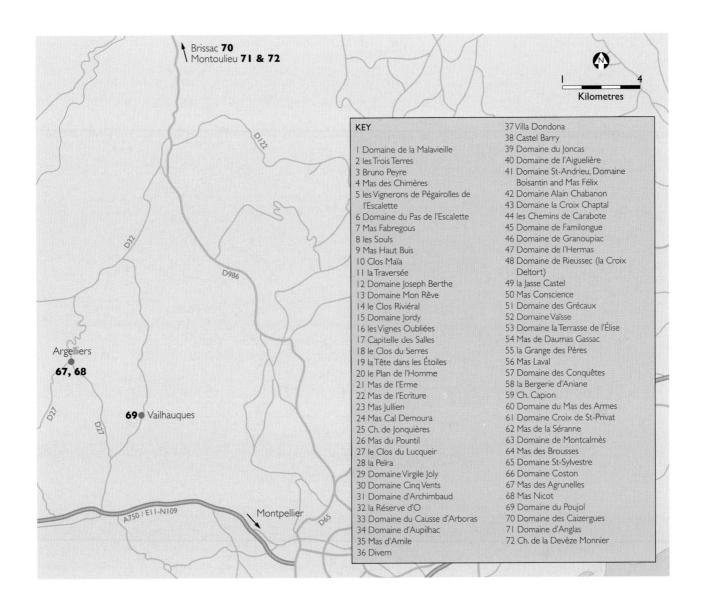

KEY

1 Domaine de la Malavieille
2 les Trois Terres
3 Bruno Peyre
4 Mas des Chimères
5 les Vignerons de Pégairolles de l'Escalette
6 Domaine du Pas de l'Escalette
7 Mas Fabregous
8 les Souls
9 Mas Haut Buis
10 Clos Maïa
11 la Traversée
12 Domaine Joseph Berthe
13 Domaine Mon Rêve
14 le Clos Riviéral
15 Domaine Jordy
16 les Vignes Oubliées
17 Capitelle des Salles
18 le Clos du Serres
19 la Tête dans les Étoiles
20 le Plan de l'Homme
21 Mas de l'Erme
22 Mas de l'Ecriture
23 Mas Jullien
24 Mas Cal Demoura
25 Ch. de Jonquières
26 Mas du Pountil
27 le Clos du Lucqueir
28 la Peïra
29 Domaine Virgile Joly
30 Domaine Cinq Vents
31 Domaine d'Archimbaud
32 la Réserve d'O
33 Domaine du Causse d'Arboras
34 Domaine d'Aupilhac
35 Mas d'Amile
36 Divem
37 Villa Dondona
38 Castel Barry
39 Domaine du Joncas
40 Domaine de l'Aiguelière
41 Domaine St-Andrieu, Domaine Boisantin and Mas Félix
42 Domaine Alain Chabanon
43 Domaine la Croix Chaptal
44 les Chemins de Carabote
45 Domaine de Familongue
46 Domaine de Granoupiac
47 Domaine de l'Hermas
48 Domaine de Rieussec (la Croix Deltort)
49 la Jasse Castel
50 Mas Conscience
51 Domaine des Grécaux
52 Domaine Vaïsse
53 Domaine la Terrasse de l'Élise
54 Mas de Daumas Gassac
55 la Grange des Pères
56 Mas Laval
57 Domaine des Conquêtes
58 la Bergerie d'Aniane
59 Ch. Capion
60 Domaine du Mas des Armes
61 Domaine Croix de St-Privat
62 Mas de la Séranne
63 Domaine de Montcalmès
64 Mas des Brousses
65 Domaine St-Sylvestre
66 Domaine Coston
67 Mas des Agrunelles
68 Mas Nicot
69 Domaine du Poujol
70 Domaine des Caizergues
71 Domaine d'Anglas
72 Ch. de la Devèze Monnier

***DOMAINE DU PAS DE L'ESCALETTE

Delphine Rousseau and Julien Zernott
Le Champ des Peyrottes, 34700 Poujols
Tel 04 67 96 13 42
Mobiles Julien 06 73 84 35 89   Delphine 06 08 93 13 26
contact@pasdelescalette.com   www.pasdelescalette.com

MAP 6
Appointment recommended in view of the remote location. The *caveau* is on the road to Laurou after the village of Poujols (turn left not right after the bridge), 2 kilometres off the autoroute north of Lodève.

Before the modern roads were built, access from the plateau to the valley at Lodève below was by ladder only, the rocks were so steep and impenetrable. Hence the name 'escalette' (the modern French word is 'échelle'). This wild landscape is a far cry from the gentle *coteaux* at Ménétou-Salon where Julien Zernott trained under Henry Pellé. In 2002 he and his partner Delphine found this high-altitude 15-hectare vineyard, its widely-located vines going back some 60 years or more and naturally irrigated by the streams flowing off the plateau. Its *terroir* and climate offer them the opportunity to pursue their preference for elegance and finesse in wine. In this they were assisted by the fact that the vines face either due east or due west, thereby escaping the fiercest heat in summer, and ensuring a freshness and tension in the fruit. In winter there is no sun after 3pm. (2pm GMT). The *chais* was formerly in a *bergerie* in the village, but in 2009 Julien built a spanking new one which now houses his elegant Austrian *foudres*. The *cépages* are mostly grenache and carignan for their reds (though they have some syrah and cinsault too) and carignan blanc and terret for the whites. From the latter they make 'Les Clapas Blanc' (C/D), highly admired for its mineral and delicate quality. 'Ze Rosé (B)' is a syrah/cinsault blend, directly pressed, cool, elegant and thirst-quenching with raspberry notes, and sometimes rated among the best of all French rosés. 'Les Petits Pas' (B) is a wine for everyday pleasure, blended from all their red grapes,

Lac du Salagou

with raspberry notes, and sometimes rated among the best of all French rosés. 'Les Petits Pas' (B) is a wine for everyday pleasure, blended from all their red grapes, while 'Ze cinsault' (B) is a mono-cépage a little in the same style (B). Old carignan, grown *en gobelet* gives freshness to 'Les Clapas rouge' (C), while the other varieties add fruity and floral qualities with more than a hint of the garrigue. 'Le Grand Pas' (D) represents for Delphine and Julien the essence of their adventure in Languedoc. Grenache is the star here in a wine which is at once silky, deep, cool and intensely elegant. It is vinified and aged in old barrels for 6 months.

BD ***MAS FABREGOUS   Philippe Gros
Chemin d'Aubaygues, 34700 Soubès
Tel   04 67 44 31 75
Mobile   06 21 99 65 71
masfabregous@free.fr   www.masfabregous.com

MAP 7
Appointment requested, but not Saturday afternoons or Sundays.

No newcomers these: the family ownership goes back to 1610, but Philippe only became an independent winemaker as recently as 2004. Today there are 16 hectares divided into 20 or so plots scattered around the village of Soubès. Over the years Philippe Gros has been converted to biodynamic philosophy, but without signing up officially. His mother gives her name to his 'Rosé de Juliette' (A), mostly grenache and very widely praised. Philippe makes two whites: a pure chenin (B) with a character of flowers and fruit, clean, restrained and with nice acidity; and a blend called 'Sentiers Botaniques' (B/C) from roussanne, marsanne, vermentino and a little muscat. Philippe's ambition is to make one of the great white wines of Languedoc, and this is a good start in the right direction. 'Croquignol' (A) is a bestselling *vin de copains*, mostly alicante bouschet, and pressed directly like a pink wine so as to avoid too dense a colour. Drink slightly chilled. Of the reds, 'Jardin de Grégoire' (A) is largely oeillade (a favourite cépage for Philippe) and another wine to be drunk cool in summer. 'Trinque Fougasse' (B), named after a local rocky outcrop (which is a favourite local picnic spot) is a merlot/grenache blend, firm and tannic following a part-ageing in wood. The same treatment is given to the red version of 'Sentiers Botaniques' (B/C), a more conventional wine from syrah, grenache and carignan, and a contrast to the lighter wines mentioned above. 'Le Centaur' (D), a red which spends two years in new wood, is a sudden uprush of ambition and price, the kind of blockbuster which so many growers feel they have to make. Otherwise astonishing value here and the quality is uniformly high throughout the range.

B ***MAS HAUT BUIS   Olivier Jeantet
Route de Saint Maurice, 34520 La Vacquerie
Tel   04 67 44 12 13
Mobile   06 13 16 35 47
mashautbuis@hotmail.fr   www.mashautbuis

MAP 9
Rendezvous advised.

Olivier Jeantet, nowadays known for his excellent wines, was formerly a famous motor rally driver. In 1999 he bought 12 hectares of vines (he now has 20), 650 metres high up towards the Larzac plateau, and taught himself the art of winemaking. The vines were already old (they include some pre-phylloxera carignan) but he himself added some roussanne and chardonnay, and more recently some extra grenache. His style is very much inclined to finesse and elegance, and he eschews heavier over-extracted and over-oaked styles. The altitude, cooler climate and a reasonable supply of rain all help him to this end, as does his preference for large wooden containers such as demi-muids and foudres over the smaller traditional barriques. Olivier's aesthetic is reflected in his two easy-drinking reds: 'Glouglou' from syrah (A/B) and 'Les Carlines', a traditional Languedoc blend, which Olivier no longer ages in wood. 'Costa Caoude' (C) is from grenache and carignan, and is an altogether bigger wine, though still retaining balance and elegance, while his single white wine 'Les Agrunelles' (C) is from the vines he planted himself.

B ***CLOS MAÏA   Géraldine Laval
34520 La Vacquerie

MAP 10
Rendezvous advised (see also Mas Haut Buis above)

Géraldine is the *compagne* of Olivier Jeantet, and they share some of the wine-making facilities at Mas Haut Buis. But Géraldine, who trained with Chave at Hermitage and later with Olivier Jullien, has her own four hectares of vines where she grows, in addition to the usual grapes, some oeillade and terret blanc. Her astonishing terret-based white (C) is raised in *barriques* and the red 'Clos' (C) in the *foudre*, but her other wines, a charming *vin de soif* called 'Le Petit clos' (B) and her lively pale thirst-quenching 'Rosé' (B) are made and aged in *tronçonnique* concrete tanks. Since Olivier has three stars, Géraldine must obviously have them too, and deservedly. Géraldine plans to build herself a new *chais* and to acquire a bit more carignan, cinsault/oeillade, but does not want to be burdened with more than six hectares.

B ***LA TRAVERSÉE   Gavin Crisfield
6 rue des Deux Ponts, Les Salces, 34700 St Privat
Tel   04 67 88 11 07
Mobile   06 11 23 72 73
info@latraversee.fr   www.latraversee.fr

MAP 11
Appointment required.

Gavin, *en route* from Belfast, stopped off for some while as winemaker at La Sauvageonne, and he has taken the style with him to this boutique vineyard of only four and a half hectares. Cinsault, carignan, grenache and syrah are each grown on separate parcels of vines, and the grapes from each are vinified separately in concrete egg-shaped tanks, and aged in *tronçonnique* French oak and oval *foudres*. Gavin believes that the form and material of these vessels is essential to the overall quality and expression in the finished wine. The eponymous red (D) is admired particularly by those who have the patience to wait for the wood to melt into the wine, which is at once powerful and unctuous, loaded with sweet red and black fruit. The finished wine has however considerable finesse and always good acidity. Fermentations are long (up to two months) with no additional yeasts added. The quality is reflected in the price.

**DOMAINE JOSEPH BERTHE

Jean-René Berthe
9 rue Paul-Dardé, 34700 Lodève.
Tel 06 33 12 01 67
Mobile 06 33 12 01 67
j.berthe@laposte.net

MAP 12
Rendezvous required. The vines are at Usclas-du-Bosc, 8 km. away to the east.

This must be one of the tiniest *domaines* on the Terrasses; just 1.5 hectares of syrah and grenache (with a little mourvèdre too) grown on schist near the village of Usclas. M. Berthe produces a mere 1,000 bottles of wine a year, but has attracted some of the most perceptive of connoisseurs who share his passion and dedication. The French call this scale of output 'confidentiel'. There are just the two reds: an AOP Languedoc called 'La Légende de Faliadous' (B) and the Terrasses wine 'De l'Éternité' (B/C). Excellent quality if you can persuade M. Berthe to let you taste, or better still to go round his mini-vineyard. The wines are rarely seen in commerce, but you should grab a bottle if given the chance.

B ***LES VIGNES OUBLIÉES

Jean-Baptiste Granier
3 rue de la Fontaine, 34700 St Jean-de-la-Blaquière
Tel 06 72 77 38 88
lesvignesoubliees@gmail.com   www.lesvignesoubliees.com

MAP 16
Phone ahead.

Son and grandson of growers (Mas Montel near Sommières q.v.), Granier studied at Montpellier, which involved a *stage* with Olivier Jullien (q.v.), who became a sort of viticultural godfather. These forgotten six hectares of vines at Saint Privat would have been abandoned, their owners, clients of the *Coopérative*, not being able to make a go of them. Today Granier works with some of them as quasi-partners, having along the way converted to organic production. He has also built a *cave* nearer to the vines at St Jean,

having previously relied on hospitality from Jullien, who has now sent Granier out into the big wide world on his own. At Saint Privat the vines, grenache predominating supported by syrah and carignan, enjoy a variety of terroirs: chalky clay, schist and sandstone. Partial de-stalking and *cuvaisons* from 15-20 days lead to most of the one red wine (C) being aged in barrel. The aim is to preserve the fruit and freshness, supported by fine tannins. The wine can be drunk with pleasure when young, but decanting improves its appreciation, and no doubt it would be better after some cellarage. Watch for the results of experiment in white wine (clairette, roussanne and grenache blanc).

B ***LE CLOS DU SERRES

Béatrice and Sébastien Fillon
Route de Viala, Les Condamines
34700 St Jean de la Blaquière
Tel 04 67 88 21 96
Mobiles Béatrice 06 88 35 90 07 Sébastien 06 85 36 43 78
contact@leclosduserres.fr
www.leclosduserres.fr

MAP 18
Rendezvous required.

Sébastien, originally from the Loire, gave up his job as an engineer in Lyon to become a vigneron in 2001, gaining experience in winemaking in the Beaujolais and later in Languedoc. In 2006 he bought 10 hectares at le Serres (the local word for hills) by subscription (75 investors of all ages and walks of life). Béatrice, an indigenous *languedocienne* joined him in 2008. They have a brand new cellar, equipped with concrete *tronçonnique* tanks. The vineyard now extends to 12 hectares split over 15 parcels (it seems rare in this part of Languedoc for a *domaine* to have large adjoining areas under vine). Each parcel is vinified separately. There is no mourvèdre, but all the other usual Languedoc varieties are present. The *domaine* makes mainly red wines, though there is a tiny quantity of a minerally white called 'le Saut du Poisson' (C). The star of the reds is a blend including carignan from 80-year-old vines called 'Humeur Vagabonde' (C/D). But before that, try a syrah-dominated blend 'La Blaca' (C), of which only 10% sees any wood, and 'Les Maros' (B/C), which largely features vat-aged grenache. Oeillade is to the fore in a rosé called 'En Terrasse' (B) and in the red 'Le Clos' (B). In both these wines the cinsault is backed up by grenache and a little syrah. Sébastien is becoming more and more convinced that he can do without barrels. An outstanding *domaine* which is doing much to promote the fame of the Terrasses.

B **PLAN DE L'HOMME Rémi Duchemin

15 avenue Marcellin Albert, 34725 St Félix de Lodez
Vines at 34700 St Jean-de-la-Blaquière
Tel 04 67 44 02 21
Mobile 06 89 33 40 64
contact@plandelhomme.fr www.plandelhomme.fr

Terrasses du Larzac

MAP 20
Rendezvous required.

Formerly a partner in the creation of Domaine Mortiès at Pic Saint Loup (q.v), Duchemin set up in 2009 on his own at the foot of Larzac. His 15 hectares of vines are mostly very old, with 40-year-old grenache and carignan and 50-year-old cinsault, but the syrah is a mere 20 years of age. Yields here are very low; 15/20 hl/ha. Rémi also has some more recently planted roussanne which, with some grenache blanc, is transformed into 'Sapiens' (B), handsomely bright and clear with a bouquet of flowers, apricots and perhaps a little aniseed; and a bigger, slightly oaked 'Alpha Blanc' (C). Of the reds try 'Flores' (B), with its jammy fruit and a touch of spice, 'Habilis' (C), complex and round on the palate, with firm but silky tannins, or 'Évolution' (C), a tougher proposition from syrah and grenache which rewards patience.

B ***MAS DE LÉCRITURE Pascal Fullà
5 rue de la Font du Loup, 34725 Jonquières
Business address 93 Chemin de la Frigoule, 34200 Sète
Tel 04 99 57 61 54
Mobile 06 80 15 57 72
pascal.fulla@masdelecriture.fr   www.masdelecriture.fr

MAP 22
Rendezvous necessary.

At the age of 42, Pascal Fullà abandoned the world of business to fulfil his dream of becoming a *vigneron*. He bought some vines at Jonquières (today he has 10 hectares), built his own *chais*, installed the best equipment and made his first wines in 1999. They follow an entirely personal pattern. Pascal describes himself as an artisan not an artist, but creativity remains at the heart of his life. He is today joined by his daughter Léa. Pascal is accepted as a top grower. His wines are on the lists of the Fat Duck in England and Michel Guérard in Gascony. The yields are small and the cultivation of the vineyards and the handling of the grapes are all to the highest standard. So it is not surprising that he commands high prices for his wines, all red, like his opening wine (his best-seller incidentally) called 'L'Émotion' (C), made to be drunk among friends for pleasure and happiness. It is in principle an equal blend of syrah, grenache, cinsault and carignan, and it represents 60% of his output in volume. The wines' 'elder sisters' are 'Les Pensées' subtle and complex, based on grenache, an elegant and nuanced wine (D), while Pascal's *vin de garde* is 'L'Écriture' (D), the only one of his wines to contain mourvèdre, along with the syrah and grenache. There are just the three wines, but all represent class. Even their colour stands out from that of other growers' wines; a deep plummy red.

Amélie d'Hurlaborde, Mas d'Amile, p.205

BD ****MAS JULLIEN Olivier Jullien
4 Chemin de Mas Jullien , Route de St.André-de-Sangonis, 34725 Jonquières
Tel 04 67 96 60 04
masjullien@free.fr

MAP 23
Rendezvous strongly recommended.

Olivier was only 20 when, in 1985, he decided to start his own vineyard next door to that of his father, Jean-Pierre. This was not because they didn't get on, quite the reverse, but because he was able to see that his future as a grower lay in learning how to make and bottle his own wine, rather than sending his grapes to the *coopérative* as the family had always done. (His father went independent too in 1993 when he took over Mas Cal Demoura q.v.). He also needed to learn how to reconcile his often-conflicting ideas with the rapidly changing scene in the Languedoc. His volatility created him as a star from day one, and he has remained that ever since. The conflict within Olivier has always been his pursuit of absolute quality, while at the same time resisting the tag of elitism and remaining one of the lads (which nearly 30 years on he still is). To this end he has always adopted an improvisatory attitude to his vineyard; the modern idea of a business plan would be abhorrent to him. He has, for example, switched back and forth on his perception of new wood, sold some parcels of his land and bought others, the total area under vine varying between 12 and 15 hectares. He has also tended to reduce the number of different *cuvées* he makes at any one time to as few as possible. Readers should be warned therefore that, if they get to visit Olivier, everything may have changed yet again. Currently however, you may expect to find a white that will almost certainly rely on carignan blanc and grenache blanc, but may well contain other varieties too. The main red from the Mas can be expected to be a blend of syrah, mourvèdre and carignan, while grenache is the mainstay of 'Carlan Terrasses de Larzac'. The wines here are all (D), but worth every euro if you can lay your hands on them.

✳✳✳MAS CAL DEMOURA
Isabelle and Vincent Goumard,
Route St André, 34725 Jonquières
Tel   04 67 44 70 82
 Mobile   06 85 09 38 74 or 06 85 09 72 26
info@caldemoura.com   www.caldemoura.com

MAP 24
Cellars open July and August, Monday to Saturday 10.30-12.30 and 14.30-18.30. Otherwise by appointment.

Isabelle and Vincent took over this property in 2004 from Jean-Pierre Jullien, Olivier's father, who had in turn left the *coopérative* a decade earlier and turned this *domaine* into one of the most interesting in the area. Vincent was the *locommotif* in the establishment of the Terrasses du Larzac as an AOP in its own right, and is still a leading voice in the syndicate of growers. 'Cal Demoura' means 'You must stay', originally an exhortation to possibly deserting *vignerons*. Today Vincent, qualified in oenology at the University of Dijon, follows in the Jullien tradition by making you very welcome. He and Isabelle have enlarged the seven hectares they acquired from Jullien *père* by buying some more from Jullien *fils*, as part of the latter's continual vineyard-swapping. Today half their holdings (totaling 14 hectares) are in red wine grapes (the invariable five), the other half in white. The red wines are put in barrel, parcel by parcel before being blended twelve months later. The whites are partly vinified in tank (viognier and muscat), part in barrel (chenin, grenache blanc, roussanne and even petit manseng) with no malolactic fermentation. The whites are chenin-dominated. There are two of them, 'L'Étincelle' (C) and 'Parole des Pierres' (C), both expressing a northern-style minerality inherent in the grape-variety, here matched by the micro-climate of the *Terrasses*. 'Qu'es aquo', meaning "What is it", or "*qu'est-ce que c'est,*" is the name given to the rosé (B), a title they inherited from Jullien and a continuing of his choice of the cinsault and syrah grapes. 'L'Infidèle' (C) is an homage to Jullien, all syrah blended from two different terroirs, reflecting his iconoclastic attitude to winemaking, encouraged no doubt by his son. Here all five grape varieties are aged in barrel (mostly *demi-muids*) for 18 months.

The wood is well handled and lets the fruit show through clearly. 'Mas des Amours' (B) is a syrah/mourvèdre blend, more affordable than the remaining reds. 'Les Combariolles' (C/D) is another five-way blend from grapes grown on the vines bought from Jullien *fils*, and aged in barrel like 'L'Infidèle'. There is also a limited production of the oldest vines of syrah, grenache and carignan called 'Feu Sacré' (D).

✳✳✳CHÂTEAU DE JONQUIÈRES
Charlotte de Béarn-Cabissole
Place de l'Église, 34725 Jonquières
Tel   04 67 96 62 58
Mobile   06 66 54 22 66 or 06 50 96 56 54
vin@chateau-jonquieres.com   www.chateau-jonquieres.com

MAP 25
Cellars open Monday to Friday, 17.00-19.00 and Saturday 10.00-19.00. Sunday by appointment. A modest charge for a guided historical tour at 6pm (not Sundays) includes a tasting of the wines. Phone ahead for this.

Charlotte and her husband Clément have taken charge of the Cabissole vineyards at this beautiful château, one of the few worthy of the name in the region. The family goes back, albeit in broken line, for hundreds of years, and the architecture bears witness to a remarkable history. The double renaissance staircase and the *folie* of an arch in the park which leads to nowhere and which nobody seems able certainly to explain are but two remarkable features. The four *chambres d'hôte* and the *gîte* are the most comfortable in the region and the welcome from Isabelle de Cabissole could not be warmer. Meanwhile, the eight hectares of vines, which until 1992 provided grapes for the *coopérative*, produce two ranges of wine (B), vinified and aged in the old *chais*: 'Lansade', in white, pink and red tank-aged versions; and the more serious 'La Baronnie', white and red, both given some oak. With her combined business and wine qualifications, Charlotte is already taking this vineyard far.

✳✳✳✳LA PEÏRA   Rob Dougan,
Manager Audrey Bonnet-Koenig, Oenologist Claude Gros
Domaine St Dominique, 34725 Jonquières
Tel   04 67 44 79 48
Mobile 06 12 27 94 13
www.la-peira.com

MAP 28
Rendezvous required.

This is the unlikely story of an ex-Australian, now London-based composer Rob Dougan and his wife Karine, who together, after holidaying in the Languedoc, bought two parcels of vines in 2004 and set up house and *chais* between Daumas Gassac and Grange des Pères. So they were aiming high from the beginning. Luck smiled on them when the vines they had bought turned out to be on deep, well-

Liausson village

draining gravels. The *chais* became too small and cramped, so in 2007 they moved to Jonquières, aided by famous winemaker Jérémie Depierre and consultant Claude Gros. Yields are tiny, which means that Dougan does not rely on the revenue from them for a living. His expenses are high because his standards are demanding. This also means the prices are often C, mostly D. Let us hope he has the stamina to stick it out. If he does, the fourth star is richly deserved, because there has been more ballyhoo about this *domaine* than any since Daumas Gassac. Presently there is just one white, the exotic 'Deusyls', which has a little clairette in the blend. 'Les Obriers' is a dark cherry-toned carignan-cinsault affair. 'Las Flors' drops the carignan but adds syrah, grenache and mourvèdre. The serious 'La Peïra' is mostly syrah. A varietal mourvèdre, 'Matissat', rounds off a fascinating range, much praised by famous judges as being among the top wines from Languedoc.

B ✱✱✱DOMAINE VIRGILE JOLY   Virgile Joly
22 rue Portail, 34725 Saint Saturnin
Tel   04 67 44 52 21
Mobile   06 60 93 68 93
virgilejoly@orange.fr   www.domainevirgilejoly.com

MAP 29
Cellars open every day except Sunday, 9.00-12.00 and 14.00-18.00

Virgile, who comes from a family of Rhône Valley *vignerons*, had already worked making wine for ten years in Chile, as well as France, before setting up with a single hectare in 2000. Within the year it had grown to four and a half, and today he has 15. He is much admired by local colleagues, and is chairman of the committee behind 'Millésimes Bio,' the influential annual organic wine fair in Montpellier. His vines are scattered between Saint Saturnin, Jonquières and Arboras, a common feature in the patchwork which goes to make up the Terrasses du Larzac. This is one of only two Languedoc vineyards (the other being Mas de Daumas Gassac) to have had a whole book devoted to it, in this case Patrick Moon's *Virgile's Vineyard, A Year in the Languedoc Wine Country*. In addition to IGP varietal wines from merlot and sauvignon (both B) from other growers, there are three pairs of table wines. 'Joly Blanc' (A/B) is mostly grenache blanc with just a touch of roussanne, while 'Joly Rouge' (A) can be drunk slightly chilled. Both are for easy drinking. 'Saturne White' (B) is again grenache, aged in tank and a medium-term wine, while the red sibling (B) is also aged in tank, a blend of all the usual grapes except mourvèdre. 'Virgile White' (D) is from grenache blanc, aged 18 months in wood after 12 in tank. 'Virgile Red' (C), being a roughly equal blend of carignan, syrah and grenache, and given a second year in barrel after a first in tank is obviously a wine for keeping. Virgile also makes a 'Carthagène' (B), as well as an *eau de vie* (C).

BD ***LA RÉSERVE D'O

Marie and Frédéric Chauffray
Rue du Château, 34150 Arboras
Tel 06 76 04 03 88
GPS 43 710860 3 485363
contact@lareservedo.fr   www.lareservedo.fr

MAP 32
Rendezvous advisable, but pot luck may be…just that.

Marie and Frédéric used to have a wine shop, and Frédéric played guitar in a band. In 2004 they decided to chuck everything and find a vineyard. Not only that, but to do things biodynamically from the word go. Marie, part of the organisation of lady winemakers called Vinifilles (q.v.), does most of the wine-making. Frédéric does the pruning and a lot of other vineyard work (disbudding, manuring etc). They have 12 hectares or so on limestone pebbles at 400 metres above the sea, overlooking the valley leading to Montpeyroux and Saint-Saturnin. Plenty of wind here, and variation in temperatures between night and day. Picking is often done in the morning to avoid the possibility of oxidisation in the heat. The syrah is pruned only on a falling moon, to give better protection against disease. Best practice includes the use of already-recycled label material and degradable vegetable inks. Treatment of the vines (even with Bordeaux mixture) is reduced to a minimum, and no sulphur at all is used at the vinification stage. They built their *chais* in 2006 and immediately became a hit. Their use of barrels is limited and confined to neutral wood and a mix of old and new containers. Their one white is a blend of grenache blanc, chenin and roussanne (B/C) and the principal red 'Réserve d'O' (B/C) is from syrah and grenache, the latter often left with its stalks. Speciality reds include a grenache-based 'Bilbo' (B), 'Hissez O' (C) with rather more syrah than grenache, and a new-style 'Sansoo' (C), which has a good dose of cinsault mixed in with the syrah (no sulphur even at the bottling stage). And, if the wild boar have not got to the vines first, there is a sweet red grenache to round off the tasting. Outstanding.

****DOMAINE D'AUPILHAC

Sylvain and Désirée Fadat
28 rue du Plô, 34150 Montpeyroux
Tel 04 67 96 61 19
Mobile 06 11 94 74 57
GPS 43.66967946 3.5038278
aupilhac@wanadoo.fr   www.aupilhac.com

MAP 34
Phone ahead

The Fadat family have been making wine for over five generations, but it was Sylvain who launched the *domaine* as an independent vigneron in 1989, and he has fought to secure for Montpeyroux the right to its own label since then. Sylvain owes his four stars to his skill in combining a fine balance between fruit and tannin, between elegance and muscular strength, and his consistency in producing fine wines year after year. He has gradually expanded his operation, building a splendid underground cellar to house the barrels and casks. The site, called 'Aupilhac' (13.5 hectares), is home mainly to mourvèdre and carignan, while 'Les Cocalières' (eight hectares) is syrah-based and also bears white grapes – the usual Languedoc varieties with some grenache and mourvèdre. 'Cocalières' is the name of a basin formed in the crater of an old volcano, from which Sylvain created an amphitheatre of vines. The vines at Cocalières are grown on steep terraces, which Sylvain built and maintains himself. More recently he has leased two and a half hectares of cinsault adjoining Cocalières. So he has 24 hectares in all. Of his two whites, one is a blend (B) of clairette, ugni blanc and grenache blanc, mostly matured in old barrels and allowed a malolactic fermentation. 'Les Cocalières blanc' (C) is from equal quantities of roussanne, marsanne, grenache blanc and vermentino, blended prior to fermentation; a wine which again is in old barrels. The single 'Rosé' (B) is 1/3rd mourvèdre 1/3rd cinsault and 1/3rd grenache, matured in tank and given a second fermentation before bottling. Sylvain prefers direct pressing to *saignage*, which he says unsettles the rest of the juice from which such wines are drawn, though he does bleed off the cinsault. It is invidious to pick from his range of no fewer than seven or eight reds, but do not miss his pure carignan (C), made from vines which are so old that they do not need to have their yield limited by *vendanges vertes*, or his mainstream AOP (C) from all five red grapes. 'Le Clos' (D) veers towards mourvèdre and carignan with just a little syrah and will appeal to those who like oak-aged wine. 'Lou Maset' (A/B) has a touch of alicante for a change, to back up the grenache and cinsault. 'Les Servières' (B) is pure cinsault (or is it oeillade?), dominated by sharp red fruit, fresh and clean on the finish.

***MAS D'AMILE

Amélie d'Hurlaborde and Sébastien Carceller
Chemin de Careneuve, 34150 Montpeyroux
Cellar at 2 Chemin des Combettes
Tel 04 99 91 78 07
Mobile 06 03 32 75 78
contact@masdamile.fr   www.mas d'amile.fr

MAP 35
Appointment more or less essential.
Amélie, who started making her own wine as recently as 2007, has been aided and abetted by her brother Sébastien, who works for Alain Chabanon, and her husband Jérôme, one of the export managers for Advini (Jeanjean). Amélie started with just one hectare of carignan on the road south to Lagamas, but has gradually expanded her holdings. She now has three and a half under vine with a further similar

Vincent Goumard, Mas Cal Demoura, p.203

M. Morrot's *domaine* is but four and a half hectares in area, and the yields are tiny, between 10 and 15 hl/ha. The Languedoc grapes are all grown *en gobelet*, so as to minimise damage from the mistral, and to protect the fruit from being grilled in the high summer. Grenache is dominant in the two parcels Morrot has between the villages of Montpeyroux and Arboras, while on the soil at Fontcaude which has more clay (only 65 ares), he grows merlot, the wine from which Morrot likens to a fine Pomerol. It will be seen that he is aiming high. Nevertheless, there is a wine he makes from the young Languedoc varieties called 'Initiales de Divem' (B), which is immediately attractive. The other two reds (he makes reds only), 'Divem' (D) and the merlot-dominated 'Carpe Divem' (D+) are more ambitious, being raised two years or more in Taransuad barrels and with a long period of ageing ahead. The latter is not sold by vintage; the wine is an *assemblage* of perhaps three years. Eccentric indeed, these wines are to be found in some of France's top restaurants.

*** VILLA DONDONA (DOMAINE LYNCH ET SUQUET) Jo Lynch and André Suquet

L'Hopital le Barry, 34150 Montpeyroux
Tel 04 67 96 68 34
Mobile 06 09 18 43 46
villadondona@wanadoo.fr   www.villadondona.com

MAP 37
Phone for appointment.

Jo, an English artist and her husband André bought 15 hectares of wild *garrigue* in 1998 just below the ruined castle of le Castellas. Nowadays they have just short of 10 hectares, having originally planted five with mourvèdre and syrah in 2000. As *débutants* in 2004, they won medals and haven't looked back. Today they make a white wine ('Espérel') from vermentino, roussanne and white grenache. This too won medals. Then there is an all-cinsault rosé 'Esquisse' (B). The reds include an all-grenache quaffer called 'Que de grenache' (B); a carignan IGP 'Chemin des Cayrades' (B/C); a straight vat-aged silky Montpeyroux under the Dondona name called 'Oppidum' (C), rather more mourvèdre than syrah and aged for 12 months in *Tronçais* oak; and finally, an all-mourvèdre 'Dame Mourvèdre' (C), made only in the best years, and in tiny quantities at that.

area about to be planted. As well as her carignan, she has a parcel of terret so tiny that you will be lucky to get to taste the wine, as well as some syrah and grenache with which she has started making an AOP Languedoc Montpeyroux (first vintage being 2013 and due to come on stream as this book appears). For the moment, until the AOP gets established, her star wine is her carignan (B), raspberry-perfumed, beautifully balanced and not at all dried out by a partial ageing in American oak. Up until recently, Amélie has been making her wine in her grandfather's garage on the outskirts of Montpeyroux, but she plans a brand new *chais* and tasting room to house her expanding production.

B *** DIVEM Gil Morrot

21 rue des Lions , 34150 Montpeyroux
Tel   04 67 96 56 59
Mobile   06 06 61 67 81
gil.morrot@divem.fr   www.divem.fr

MAP 36
Appointment required.

BD **** DOMAINE ALAIN CHABANON /DOMAINE FONT-CAUDE Alain Chabanon

Chemin de Saint-Étienne, 34150 Lagamas
Tel   04 67 57 84 64
Mobile   06 95 82 17 70
domainechabanon@gmail.com   or   domainechabanon@free.fr
www.alainchabanon.com

MAP 42
Phone ahead to ensure Alain is going to be there.

A native of Languedoc, though part of his family comes from nearby Aveyron, Alain took agricultural training in Montpellier and Bordeaux before working for two years with Alain Brumont in Madiran; an education which has left a mark in his penchant for long *élevages*. He was an overnight star when he started in 1995, his wines selling out so fast that he actually discouraged visits to the *domaine* by not putting up any signposts. Some of his wines are not cheap, so perhaps one might start with two that are within most peoples' reach: a 'Rosé Trémier' (B) from mourvèdre and carignan, deep in colour and definitely a wine for the table rather than the swimming-pool; or his best-selling 'Campredon' (B), which expresses his love for freshness, a concept which is, he points out, a comparatively new word in Languedoc vocabulary. The chenin grape has always been a feature of his whites. Nowadays he balances it with vermentino to produce his one *blanc sec* called 'Trélans' (C/D). It is made from tiny yields and aged for three years, of which one is spent in barrel (none of his wood is new). The other white, 'Le Villard' (D+) is pure chenin and *moël-leux*, and enjoys no less than 30 months in cask. Going up the scale of reds, 'Petit Merle aux Alouettes' (B) is an all-merlot inox-raised quaffer, one which sells well by the glass in top hotels, while its elder brother 'La Merle aux Alouettes' (D) has mourvèdre in with the merlot, and after two years in barrel has a certain rigidity which calls for cellarage. 'L'Esprit de Font Caude' (D) is an exuberant syrah/mourvèdre blend and one of Alain's most admired wines. 'Les Boissières' (C/D) shows off his grenache and is exempt from barrel-ageing, while 'Saut de Côte' (D), mostly mourvèdre, is fashionably raised in egg-shaped concrete tanks for three years and Alain is proud of its finesse and elegance.

Charlotte de Béarn-Cabissole
Château de Jonquières, p.203

B ✳✳✳LES CHEMINS DE CARABOTE

Jean-Yves Chaperon
Mas de Navas, 34150 Gignac
Tel   04 67 55 50 27
Mobile   06 07 16 76 13
contact@carabote.com   www.carabote.com

MAP 44
Appointment essential.

Another family of *ex-coopérateurs* created this domaine, named after a former mill which has since disappeared. They built a smart new gravity-fed *chais* in 2006. Operating initially from Paris (they now live in Gignac), they had to revise entirely their techniques in the vineyard, reshaping the method of pruning, remaking the system of wires supporting the vines, reducing the yields by three-quarters and starting *vendanges vertes*. Organic status was a logical development. Jean-Yves still has time to continue as a jazz presenter on RTL, and jazz concerts are a regular feature of the *domaine* in summer. There are just under eight hectares of vines, from which they make a pure carignan (B), a real *vin des copains*, which Jean-Yves calls "carignan's revenge on the world." 'Chemin Faisant' (B), is their first blend: syrah, grenache and carignan, supple and fresh. 'Promenade en Novembre' (C) is a pure grenache, pruney, with figs and quinces too, and 'Les Pierres qui Chantent' (C/D) is also grenache-dominated and raised in barrel for 18 months. Jean-Yves describes it as 'wild and elegant.' This small *domaine* is yet again proof that personal control and supervision is the secret of a success often more difficult to achieve in a larger enterprise.

✳✳✳DOMAINE DE FAMILONGUE

Martine and Jean-Luc Quincarlet
3 rue Familongue, 34725 Saint-André-de-Sangonis
Tel   04 67 57 59 71
Mobile   06 10 29 52 18
contact@domainedefamilongue.fr
www.domainedefamilongue.fr

Towards the hilltop village of Olmet

MAP 45
Probably open during usual hours Monday to Saturday, but a call ahead would do no harm.

Martine has retired from working for *La Poste*, while Jean-Luc now devotes more attention to his vines than to his dental practice in Saint André. He left the *coopérative* in 2002 to become an independent winemaker, and has grown his land-holding to 25 hectares. Self-taught, he and Martine have benefited from the advice and help of experienced colleagues and oenologists. They are virtually bio, but as yet without certification. They have created distinctive labels featuring a red macaw, reflecting their other passion: breeding exotic birds, and the specimens to be found in the garden will keep visitors' children amused. The Quincarlets have vines to the north and south of the village on completely different terroirs: one with chalky pebbles mixed in with argilo-calcaire, the other a mix of *galets roulés* and sandy soil. Even within these there are subtle differences that have persuaded Jean-Luc to make a relatively large range of different wines, all at extremely good value. Under the Familongue banner, their dry white is called 'L''Envoi' (A), bottled without ageing in wood, while at the other end of the spectrum there is a late-picked clairette (B/C) from grapes yielding a mere 6 hl/ha. There are two rosés: 'Trois Naissances' (A), where the syrah and cinsault are *saignés*, and the grenache and carignan directly pressed; and 'Èté à Fami-

longue' (A), whose blending is done while the grapes are still undergoing their different vinifications. The reds include varietals from carignan, a particular love of the Quincarlets: 'Le Carignan de Familongue' (A), and cinsault 'Mas de Vignals' (A). There are also blends such as 'L'Ame' (A/B) and 'Les Trois Naissances' (B/C), the latter being the only one aged in barrel after being vinified there too, with the benefit of *microbullage*. There is a second range called 'La Bastide des Oliviers' offering four more reds, dry and sweet whites and rosé. A visitor will be kept busy here and would do well also to take away with him/her some of their delicious olive oil.

B ***DOMAINE DE L'HERMAS
Matthieu Torquebiau
Lieu-dit Mas de Ratte, 34150 Gignac
Tel   06 64 89 20 29
mt@lhermas.com   www.lhermas.com

MAP 47
Rendezvous required.

Torquebiau, *maître de chais* at Domaine d'Aupilhac (q.v.) now has six hectares of vines of his own at this new *domaine*. He started work here in 2003 and planted his first vines the following year. There are two more hectares recently planted. The grapes are grown *en gobelet* with low *palissage*. His first vintage was 2009 and the wine was made at Aupilhac, so 2010 was the first vintage he made in his own *chais*. At present he makes just three *cuvées*. There is a white (B/C) from 70% vermentino, with roussanne and just a little chenin, which shows flowers and exotic fruits and good acidity. The grapes are assembled before fermentation and are all crushed together. Even though the *cépages* ripen at different parts of the cycle, somehow they balance each other out. It has considerable aromatic power, which is why Torquebiau suggests you taste his red first. There is a pale pink rosé (A/B), showing tart red fruit and with good fruit on the palate. The red (C) is from syrah and mourvèdre. Torquebiau has just the two varieties (he is no fan of carignan, which is surprising for a Fadat pupil). The wine is aged in 700-litre *demi-muids*, some old cast-offs from Aupilhac, some more recent. Ruby-red in colour, the wine is all fruit-iness and garrigue, with soft tannins. Good though these wines are now, they will surely get even better.

B ***LA JASSE CASTEL   Pascale Rivière
Le Cross, route de Gignac, 34150 St Jean de Fos
Tel   04 67 88 65 27
Mobile   06 09 90 18 58
jasse-castel@orange.fr   www.jasse-castel.com

MAP 49
Visits by rendezvous (mobile).

Pascale (another 'Vinifille' q.v.) was once a journalist, a teacher and writer, but in 1998 her urge to have a vineyard was satisfied when she bought these seven hectares and a former

Arnaud Sandras, Domaine des Grécaux, p.210

sheepfold ('Jasse') from M. Castel, the former owner. Pascale, with a vivacious and bubbly personality, is in love with her new profession; she says that 'culture' has found its roots again. She has centenarian cinsault at Arboras, old carignan at Les Olivettes and syrah on the edge of a nearby oak forest. There is grenache too, and a mix of white grapes more recently planted. These include some carignan blanc which she sometimes uses to give added kick to her white 'L'Égrisée' (B). Her rosé (mostly from the first grenache pickings) she calls 'Tutti Frutti' (A/B). Grenache is also at the base of 'Les Combariolles' (D), the top red, with a little oak-aged syrah added. It is "a gourmet wine and serious at the same time." 'Pimpanella' (B) is a blend of all Pascale's red grapes, which she says can be drunk lightly chilled in summer. 'Bleu Velours' (B) is mostly syrah and carignan and raised in old barrels for a year. Finally, there is 'La Jasse' (C), nearly all syrah, aged for 18-24 months partly in tank and partly in barrel.

The *cave coopérative* at Octon

BD ✳✳✳ MAS CONSCIENCE

Eric and Natalie Ajorque
Route de Montpeyroux, 34150 St Jean de Fos
Tel   04 67 57 77 42
Mobile   06 76 78 56 14
masconscience@gmail.com   www.mas-conscience.com

MAP 50
Rendezvous advisable.

Eric and Nathalie acquired this top *domaine* with the help of 40 'partners' from Laurent and Geneviève Vidal in 2014. So it is early days to assess their skills. The Vidals had in turn built a fine winery when they moved here in 2003, the grapes up to that time having been sent to the *coopérative*, who were not willing to reward the Vidals for the extra expense and quality of their organic production. The Ajorques, having spent some time doing social work in Pondicherry, built a business off their own back in France, sold it and no doubt used the proceeds towards the acquisition of this vineyard. They were particularly attracted by the bio certification which the *domaine* enjoyed. They have followed the Vidals down this road and maintained the range of wines the former owners made, although no doubt in future they will develop their own wine style. For the moment there are the white 'In' (B), half grenache blanc, the rest roussanne and vermentino with just a hint of viognier; 'Pure' (B) a mono-cépage from petit manseng and raised in tank; 'La Petite Prise' (B) a red syrah/grenache blend; 'Cieux', a pure cinsault light in alcohol (B); and 'Le Cas' (B) a pure carignan. So far no wood, but 'As' (C), mostly from syrah and grenache with just a touch of carignan, is given two years in large barrels, while 'Mahatma' (D), pure mourvèdre, is aged in a fashionable egg-shaped amphora.

B ✳✳✳ DOMAINE DES GRÉCAUX

Sophie and Arnaud Sandras
4 Avenue du Monument, 34150 St.Jean de Fos
Tel   04 67 57 38 83
Mobile   06 38 25 14 89
contact@domainedesgrecaux.com
www.domainedesgrecaux.com

MAP 51
Cellars open April-September, Tuesday and Thursday, 17.00-19.00, otherwise by appointment (mobile no.). Parking by the *Maison de la Poterie* (50m.)

The Sandras took over this seven-hectare domaine in 2012

at a point when it was considered one of the top *domaines* in Languedoc. Even with their short history, the Sandras are proving worthy successors. They have added a pure chardonnay (B/C) raised half in tank, half in barrel to the repertoire of their predecessors, which they have otherwise retained. The vines are scattered over the communes of Montpeyroux, Aniane and Lagamas. Those who find many of the wines from the Rhône just too much of a good thing will be bowled over by the fresher, lighter styles of the Sandras' wines, which manage to combine a southern richness with good freshness and acidity. They make just two reds. 'Terra Solis' (C) is from 60% grenache, 30% carignan and 10% mourvèdre, and is a blend from all their parcels. It has dark blackcurrant and blackberry character, but its mineral freshness ensures elegance and finesse. The other is 'Hêméra' (C), mostly syrah, finished with some grenache, the grapes coming from the *causse* above the village of Montpeyroux. The wine is fine and elegant, a shade bigger than 'Terra Solis'. A small plot of chardonnay near Lagamas should by now be producing a white, the only one from this *domaine*, which is to be half raised in tank, half in barrel. The rosé has been going for some time now and is called 'La Farandole' (B), entirely from grenache and deliciously spring-flowerish.

✻✻✻DOMAINE VAÏSSE   Pierre Vaïsse
12 route d'Aniane, 34150 Puechabon.
Tel   04 67 57 28 86
domaine.vaisse@free.fr

MAP 52
Appointment required. The *chais* is just outside Aniane on the road to St Guilhem-le-Désert.

Pierre Vaïsse counts among his friends, and indeed his teachers, Laurent Vaillé and Frédéric Pourtalié, and his wines are on the point of earning a fourth star. He is almost everywhere tipped for the top. He started in 2007 with a mere two hectares of vines, but he now has six. His contract with the *coopérative* still runs to 2017, but meanwhile he is making a superb viognier called 'Hasard' (D), raised surprisingly not in wood but in tank, nor does he allow it a malolactic fermentation. The price is accounted for by the tiny quantity made. There are just two reds. 'Les Aphyllants' (C/D) is virtually a mourvèdre varietal, which sometimes suggests cherries and/or tapenade. Pierre has learned to tame his youthful exuberance with oak, so that it is not discernible except for the complexity which it adds in this wine. The second red is 'Galibaou de Russe', named after a kind of oak tree. The wine is half syrah, half mourvèdre and spends two years in barrel. It is a smoky, fresh and fine wine, rather more restrained than 'Les Aphyllants'. Pierre is definitely a *vigneron à suivre*, as they say.

B ✻✻✻ DOMAINE LA TERRASSE D'ÉLISE
Xavier Braujou
Lieu-dit Le Causse, RD 32 E2, 24150 Aniane
Tel   04 67 57 24 47

la famille Ajorque, Mas Conscience

Mobile   06 22 91 81 39
terrassedelise@club-internet.fr   terrassedelise@gmail.com

MAP 53
Rendezvous advisable.

In the space of a decade, Braujou has become incontestably one of Languedoc's finest winemakers. He started building this *domaine* in 1998, having had some training at Daumas-Gassac (to whom nevertheless he declined to sell two hectares of vines which they would like to have had) and before that in Alsace, but he is essentially self-taught. Originally a forester (an occupation which he kept going until 2008 when the vineyard called for all his attention), he settled down with 12 hectares of vines, relying on observation and study so as to understand and get the best from his *terroir*. He reproduces his own stock by *sélection massale* and stays away from the rigidity of the *appellation*, making his wines as IGPs or even *Vins de France*; this largely because so many of his wines are *mono-cépages* and would not qualify anyway. For example, his cinsault wines 'Le Pradel' (C), pink and red, with their cherry style and raised in new barrels; or the tank-raised 'XB' (A/B), all syrah; or the pure carignan ' Le Pigeonnier' (B), aged a year in used barrels; or again the pure merlot 'Mas de Blanc' (C). 'Elise' (D) is exceptionally a syrah/mourvèdre blend, named in honour of Xavier's great aunt, and thus favoured with two years in old wood. For such exceptional quality the wines are fairly priced, almost bargains.

Frédéric Pourtalié, Domaine de Montcalmès

***MAS DE DAUMAS GASSAC

Samuel and Roman Guibert
Haute Vallée du Gassac, 34150 Aniane
Tel   04 67 57 88 45
contact@daumas-gassac.com   www.daumas-gassac.com

MAP 54
Shop open Monday to Saturday (except public holidays)
10.00-12.00 and 14.00-18.00

This is the daddy of all Languedoc wine-estates, to which there has been devoted an entire book, *Daumas Gassac; the Birth of a Grand Cru*, Seagrave Foulkes (London 1995). It tells how Aimé Guibert, a lawyer from Millau, was advised by the geologist Henri Enjalbert, and later by the oenologist Émile Peynaud, not only that his newly purchased country property at Aniane was a suitable place to grow vines, but that it was also an ideal site for cabernet sauvignon, a grape which in the 1970s was virtually unknown in Languedoc. Today it constitutes 80% of the *assemblage* of the *grand vin* here. The rest is history; how the family, with their flair for marketing and public relations, and the courage and know-

how to see off predators such as Robert Mondavi, made this estate into by far the most famous vineyard in the Midi. Alas, it is difficult to lead from the front, and today there are many challengers to the Guiberts' crown. Perhaps it is the need of the family to ensure a succession and future for the four sons of the family that has driven them towards a more frankly commercial approach to their enterprise, to the extent that they have also developed a business taking in grapes from other growers and making and marketing the resulting wine. The artisanal character of the *domaine* has rather fractured in the process. If some of the shine has gone off their grand cru red (D), their inox-raised white (D) is excellent (a blend of viognier, chardonnay, petit manseng and a host of other grape varieties), and the 'second' wines sold as 'Moulin de Gassac' are also attractive and extremely good value (B/C). A visit is an experience in itself, perhaps not unlike a trip to Mondavi.

****LA GRANGE DES PÈRES   Laurent Vaillé

34150 Aniane
Tel   04 67 57 70 55

MAP 55
Appointment required, but difficult to obtain. No *caveau de dégustation*; tasting will be done in the *chais*.

Although in a sense following in the footsteps of Aimé Guibert, the contrast between Daumas Gassac and this *domaine* could not be greater. Not because of the choice of grapes grown (though Vaillé does have some cabernet sauvignon), but because the whole operation here has retained its artisanal feel. Before settling in Aniane, Vaillé (once a physiotherapist) did *stages* with Chave in Hermitage, Comtes Lafon in Burgundy and Trévaillon in Provence. He says that, like a composer, you must study the works of the masters, but then follow your own path without copying them. Whereas Guibert is a past master at marketing, this is an activity which Vaillé seems to disdain. With Vaillé it is the quiet pursuit of perfection which counts, and which has spread to the whole family like an infection. Unlike Guibert, Vaillé has no interest beyond his own twelve hectares; the vines are grown *en gobelet*, almost touching the ground, which makes the work on them extremely hard. The yields are tiny. Not surprisingly, he makes just two hard-to-get wines. The red (D+), to which syrah and mourvèdre are added to give richness, and fruit and spice to balance the freshness of the cabernet, are aged in a mix of new and old wood and then matured in tank before bottling two and a half years after the vintage. The style is aristocratic and modern, without being 'New World'. The even rarer white wine (D+) is mostly roussanne, barrel-fermented in *demi-muids* rather than *barriques*. It explodes in the mouth without being in any way vulgar, and the finish is long indeed. These wines are as difficult to find as the money with which to pay for them, but they should be tasted at least once in a lifetime.

*** MAS LAVAL Joël and Christine Laval
26 rue Jean Casteran, 34150 Aniane
Tel   04 67 57 79 23
contact@maslaval.com   www.maslaval.com
MAP 56
Rendezvous required.

This is very much a family operation; Joël's brother and father are still part of the enterprise. This is a fair-sized *domaine* (30 hectares of vines, including those whose grapes still go to the *coopérative*). The property itself has been in the family a long time. Grandfather kept bees here. Joël has kept some aramon, and has some of both cabernets too, though you would need to ask him what he does with them as they do not feature on his public list. From the more mainstream grapes he makes two whites: 'Les Pampres' (B) and 'Les Souls' (B/C), the latter being partly raised in barrel though the viognier is aged in tank to keep its aromatic freshness. A fairly rich and fruity rosé (A/B) derives from equal quantities of syrah and mourvèdre, while there are just two reds, both of which are syrah-based. 'Les Pampres' (B), is given 6-8 months in used barrels, and the 'Grande Cuvée' (C) rather longer. The wines here have a disarming lightness of character, and perhaps more acidity than usual. Excellent value from an improving *domaine*.

B *** MAS DE LA SÉRANNE
Isabelle and Jean-Pierre Venture
Route de Puechabon, 34150 Aniane
Tel. 04 67 57 37 99
Mobile 06 82 19 36 56
mas.seranne@wanadoo.fr   www.mas-seranne.com

MAP 62
Cellars open Monday to Saturday, 10.00-12.00 and 15.00-19.00 (18.00 in winter). Sundays and public holidays by appointment.

Although Isabelle was a native of nearby St Guilhem-le-Désert, she and Jean-Pierre worked in Toulouse for 20 years, he making pâtisseries and she as a nurse. Nowadays they are full-time *vignerons* ("Vigneron, ce n'est pas le gateau," quips Jean-Pierre). They settled in Aniane in 1998, starting with just five hectares of vines, but over the years the addition of various parcels has increased the total to 16. After a trip down a long lane seemingly leading to nowhere, your welcome will be of the warmest sort, charm mingled with a certain modesty, for make no mistake, these are wines of real quality. The house style can be summed up in two words: finesse and spice. The reds, justly famous, should not overshadow two excellent whites in different style; 'Sous les Camisses' (A/B), sauvignon-based; and 'Les Ombelles' (A/B), an AOP raised half in tank and half for six months in *fûts*. Nor should you overlook the charming red-fruited rosé 'Sous les Micocouliers' (A/B), with its hints of aniseed, liquorice and ground pepper. For an *entrée-de-gamme* red, the very cinsault 'A l'Ombre du figuier' (A) will come as quite a shock with its burst of fruit. 'Les Griottiers' (B), with its strawberry and cherry bouquet has a longer *cuvaison* and would keep a few years. Finally there are two *Terrasses* wines: 'Clos des Immortelles' (C), usually a traditional syrah/grenache/mourvèdre blend and aged in old barrels; and 'Antonin et Louis' (C/D), named after a great-uncle and grandfather, largely syrah, a very dark wine, and aged for 13 months in a mix of new and one-year-old wood. The top red 'Bonaventura' (D), a tiny production, will appeal to oak-lovers.

B ****DOMAINE DE MONTCALMÈS
Frédéric and Muriel Pourtalié
Chemin du Cimetière , 34150 Puechabon
Tel   04 67 57 74 16
gaecbh@wanadoo.fr   www.domainedemontcalmes.fr

MAP 63
Visits by appointment only. Cellar on the village square.

Undoubtedly this is one of the finest *domaines* not only of the region, but of the whole of Languedoc. It is named after an abandoned hamlet, which was once the family home. Frédéric gets, perhaps unfairly, most of the credit, because this is a brother-and-sister enterprise. He has worked in the past with distinguished teachers, including Vaillé at La Grange des Pères, from whom he still gets cast-off barrels. There are today about 25 hectares of vines; syrah and grenache on a north-facing chalky plateau at Puechabon, and mourvèdre at Aniane on *galets roulés*. They are now converted to organic production, 2015 being their first year of official certification. They are already bottling on the old moon. Apart from some *vins de cépage*, chardonnay and viognier, which he makes from bought-in grapes (partly to soothe the disappointment of customers who find he has sold out of his mainstream wines), Frédéric makes just one white (C/D) from equal quantities of roussanne and marsanne, pressed and vinified together and fermented and aged for 24 months in barrels that have seen at least one year's use. The reds (all D) include a quite oaky grenache, a grenache-dominated blend called 'le Géai' which is rather more complex, and a Larzac from syrah (60%), grenache and mourvèdre (20% each), vinified separately (they ripen at different times). It is a wine of great delicacy, complex and with considerable length.

***MAS DES BROUSSES** Géraldine Combes
2 Chemin du Bois, 34150 Puechabon
Tel 04 67 57 33 75
combesgeraldine@orange.fr   www.masdesbrousses.fr

MAP 64
Appointment advisable.

Xavier is a grandson of Lulu and Lucien Peyraud of the famous Domaine Tempier in Bandol, from where he has no doubt brought his love and a selection of cuttings of the mourvèdre grape. Together with his wife Géraldine, he has taken over the latter's family vines, stretching over more than 20 hectares. Not officially certified as bio growers, they are better organic practitioners than many who are, working manually in the vineyard without pesticides or herbicides and with a plough rather than machinery. To emphasize the nature of their *terroir* they do not filter their wines. Their one white (B/C) is big and from nearly as many grapes as the Daumas Gassac white. Their tank-aged IGP 'Chasseur des Brousses' (B) is a merlot/grenache blend, sometimes with a little cinsault, pumped over daily throughout the four-week *cuvaison* to give a wine with more than a hint of Bordeaux. The 'Terrasses de Larzac' (C) is 60% syrah and 40% mourvèdre, with a bouquet of dark black fruits, peppery on the palate and with a long finish. The top cuvée 'Mataro' (D) (an alternative name for mourvèdre) is nearly all from that grape and raised in new barrels. In grandfather's footsteps, indeed.

***DOMAINE SAINT-SYLVESTRE
Sophie and Vincent Guizard
Rue de la Grotte, 34150 Puechabon
Tel 09 60 50 30 15
domaine-st-sylvestre20@orange.fr
www.domaine-saint-sylvestre.com

MAP 65
Rendezvous required.

This is the oldest vineyard in Puechabon, planted round the eponymous country church. Vincent learnt about winemaking from his grandfather when he was a child, and then from Oliver Jullien. Subsequently he worked alongside his cousin Pourtalié for seven years. With Sophie, they together created this eight-hectare *domaine* as recently as 2010. Sophie too had learnt about wine from her family, and worked in the trade for a while, including spending a year in London marketing the wines of the Loire. Their first joint vintage was in 2011, and they are certainly on the way to joining their distinguished neighbours at the top of the class. Their main white wine (C), 'Languedoc Blanc' is a blend of marsanne and roussanne with just a little viognier and, though raised in barrel (old wood), it can be drunk young as well as kept a while for improvement. There is also a small production of a chardonnay-based blend called 'Le coup de calcaire' (C). Their main red wine (C) is mainly syrah, with some grenache and mourvèdre. But note too a pure carignan called 'Les vignes des Garrigues' (C), aged for a year in barrel. Another *domaine* to be followed.

OTHER GOOD GROWERS ON THE TERRASSES DU LARZAC

B **LES TROIS TERRES   Alice and Graeme Angus
Rue de la Vialle, 34800 Octon
Tel 04 67 44 71 22
Mobile 06 15 16 92 68
contact@trois-terres.com   www.trois-terres.com
MAP 2
Cellars open Friday from 17.00-19.00 and Saturday from 15.00-19.00. Also in July and August on Thursday evenings from 18.00-20.00. Otherwise by arrangement.
In 2000 Graeme forsook his full-time life as a doctor in London to go and learn about winemaking in Australia, finally ending up with his wife Alice in this small, less then four-hectare *domaine*.

*LES VIGNERONS DE PÉGAIROLLES DE L'ESCALETTE
Rue de la Mairie
34700 Pégayrolles de l'Escalette
Tel 04 67 44 09 93

Near Clermont-l'Hérault

GPS 43. 48'03" N 3.19'24E
vigneronspegairolles@mcom.fr
www.vigneronsdepegairolles.com
MAP 5
Cellars open Fridays 8.00-12.00 and 14.00-17.30.

**LES SOULS Roland Almeras

Chemin de Rochegude, Route de Fozières, 34700 Soubès
Tel 04 67 44 21 56
roland.almeras@sfr.fr
MAP 8
See Mas Laval (Aniane); Alméras is in partnership there to produce white wine from his vines in Soubès, 'Les Pampres Blanc' (A/B).

B **DOMAINE MON RÊVE Sébastien Rouve

Cartels du Bosc, _34700 Le Bosc
Tel 06 82 28 67 97
sebastienrouve@hotmail.fr
MAP 13
Cellars open June, July and August, Monday to Friday, 10.00-12.00 and 13.30-19.00, and on Saturday and Sunday afternoons. The rest of the year Monday to Friday, 17.30- 19.00, and 14.00-18.00 on Saturdays and Sundays. Otherwise by appointment.

B **LE CLOS RIVIÉRAL Olivier Bellet

6 rue du Riviéral, 34700 Loiras-du-Bosc
Tel 04 67 44 72 71
Mobile 06 72 22 38 68
contact@leclosrivieral.fr www.leclosrivieral.fr
MAP 14
Appointment advisable.

**DOMAINE JORDY Frédéric Jordy

9 route de Salelles, 34700 Loiras
Tel 04 67 44 70 30
Mobile 06 27 30 10 69
frederic.jordy@orange.fr www.domaine-jordy.fr
MAP 15
Cellars open every day Monday-Saturday, 8.00-20.00. Sundays by appointment.

**CAPITELLE DES SALLES

Estelle and Frédéric Salles
6 route de Rabieux, 34700 St Jean de la Blaquière
Tel 04 67 72 02 50
Mobile 06 86 93 33 48
estelle@capitelle-des-salles.com
www.capitelle-des-salles.com
MAP 17
Sales from the *domaine* everyday by appointment. Visits to vineyard free from 17.30 every day, but confirmation required before 14.00 on the day of visit. Also there are oenology tutorials on Saturday and Sunday evenings at 30€ a head, refundable on purchase of more than 80€ of wine.

B **LA TÊTE DANS LES ÉTOILES

Luc Jourdan,
1 bis rue du Cayre, 34700 Salelles du Bosc
Tel 06 47 04 05 35 _
latetedanslesetoiles@orange.fr
www.latetedanslesetoiles.com
MAP 19
Rendezvous required.

B **MAS DE L'ERME Florence and Fabien Milési

7 route de Saint-André, 34725 Jonquières
Tel 04 67 88 70 63
Mobile 06 87 81 32 35__
contact@masdelerme.fr www.masdelerme.fr
MAP 21
Pot luck could pay off; better to phone.

B **MAS DU POUNTIL Brice and Bernard Bautou

10 bis rue du Foyer Communal, 34725 Jonquières
Tel 04 67 44 67 13
Mobile 06 07 82 07 27
mas.du.pountil@wanadoo.fr
www.mas-du-pountil.com
MAP 26
Cellars open Monday to Saturday, 10.00-12.30 and 15.00-18.30, but a call on the mobile would do no harm.

*LE CLOS DU LUCQUIER

Nicole and Claude Panis
Rue de la Font du Loup, 34725 Jonquières
Tel 04 67 44 63 11
Mobile 06 11 55 80 89
contact@leclosdulucquier.com
www.leclosdulucquier.com
MAP 27
A very reliable and good value *domaine* without frills, but producing wines of consistent quality.

B **DOMAINE CINQ VENTS

Christopher Johnson-Gilbert
34275 St Saturnin
Tel 04 67 44 52 21
CJG@D5V.fr www.montpeyroux-tco.fr
MAP 30
There is a new winery also built in 2009 to serve Virgile Joly (q.v.) and this property. Phone ahead.

**DOMAINE D'ARCHIMBAUD

Marie-Pierre Cabanes
12 Avenue du Quai, 34725 St Saturnin_de Lucian
Tel 04 67 96 65 35
MAPß 31
Rendezvous advisable.

Galets roulés - a favourite *terroir* for vines

B **DOMAINE DU CAUSSE D'ARBORAS
SCEA du Causse d'Arboras (Jeanjean)
34380 Arboras
Tel   06 11 51 08 41
causse-arboras@wanadoo.fr
www.jeanjean.fr/en/causse-arboras
MAP 33
Rendezvous required.

**CAVE COOPÉRATIVE DE
MONTPEYROUX   (CASTEL BARRY)
Place François Villon, 34150 Montpeyroux
Tel   04 67 96 61 08
www.montpeyroux.org
MAP 38
Shop open Monday to Saturday, 9.00-12.00 and 14.00-18.00. Sundays and public holidays, 10.00-12.00 and 15.30-18.00
This is the biggest employer of the region and produces wines of excellent quality and at prices which rarely cross the A barrier.

BD **DOMAINE DU JONCAS
Pascal and Christiane Dalier
670 Chemin des Saumailles, 34150 Montpeyroux
Tel   04 67 88 57 00

Mobile   06 09 43 29 61
contact@domaine-du-joncas   www.domaine-du-joncas.com
MAP 39
Rendezvous requested.

**DOMAINE DE L'AIGUELIÈRE
Christine Commeyras
2 Place Teysserenc, 34150 Montpeyroux
Tel   04 67 96 61 43   Mobile   06 23 47 26 00
christine@aiguiliere.com   auguste@aiguiliere.com
www.aiguiliere.com
MAP 40
Open everyday, 9.00-18.00, but *rendezvous* preferred.
The top reds 'Côte Dorée' and 'Côte Rousse' (both D) have attracted Parker attention in their time and are given the full new barrel treatment.

**DOMAINE SAINT-ANDRIEU,
DOMAINE BOISANTIN AND MAS FÉLIX
Charles Giner and Anne Jeffroy
La Dysse, 34150 Montpeyroux
Tel   04 67 96 61 37
saintandrieu-boisantin.com
www.saint-andrieu-montpeyroux.com

MAP 41
Cellars open daily (9.00-18.00) except Sunday.
The operation was extended by the creation of Domaine Boisantin and later in 2003 by Mas Félix, achieved by his partnership with his daughter, Mme Jeffroy. The cellars are in the heart of the village, two storeys underground in what might be the catacombs of Montpeyroux, and which by themselves make any visit memorable.

** DOMAINE LA CROIX CHAPTAL
Charles-Walter Pacaud
Hameau de Cambous, 34725 Saint André de Sangonis
Tel   04 67 16 09 36
Mobile   06 82 16 77 82
lacroixchaptal@wanadoo.fr   www.lacroixchaptal.com
MAP 43
Cellars open from 10th July to 28th August (approx) from 10.00-12.00, otherwise by appointment.

**DOMAINE DE GRANOUPIAC
Claude Flavard
34725 Saint-André de Sangonis
Tel   04 67 57 58 28
cflavard@iinfonie.fr   domaine.granoupiac@gmail.com
MAP 46
Cellars open Monday to Friday and Saturday afternoons. Saturday mornings at Gignac market.
The queues of cars here attest to the popularity of the wines with the locals. He no longer sells *en négoce*, but does sell *en vrac*.

**DOMAINE DE RIEUSSEC (LA CROIX DELTORT)   Marie-Hélène Deltort,
Route d'Aniane, 34150 Gignac Correspondence address ; 16 rue Ségurane, 06300 Nice
Tel   04 67 57 54 11
contact@domaine-de-rieussec.com
marie-helene.deltort@libertysurf.fr
www.domaine-de-rieussec.com
MAP 48
Visits by rendezvous. Find time for a visit to the lovely gardens.

**DOMAINE DES CONQUÊTES
Philippe Ellner, Chemin des Conquêtes
34150 Aniane
Tel   04 67 57 35 99
Mobile   06 98 30 94 27
domainedesconquetes.vin@outlook.fr
www.domainedesconquetes.fr
MAP 57
Cellars open Tuesday to Saturday, 9.00-12.00 and 15.00-19.00. Otherwise by appointment.
The IGP from this property is called 'Guillaume les Conquêtes', though the real name of the place is 'Conquettes', meaning small shells; an example of French humour which doesn't translate.

**LA BERGERIE D'ANIANE
Jean-Claude Zabalia
Business address Route des Crozes, Le Mas Rouch, 34800 Cabrières
Tel   06 85 42 92 35
contact@laterreletemps.com   www.laterreletemps.com
MAP 58
Because Zabalia has three quite distinct vineyards (the other two being at Cabrières and in Picpoul country) special arrangements would be needed to visit one or the other.

**CHÂTEAU CAPION   Frédéric Kast
34150 Gignac
Tel   04 67 57 71 37
chateau.capion@wanadoo.fr   www.chateaucapion.com
MAP 59
Cellars open Monday to Friday, 09.00-18.00, Saturdays by appointment.

***DOMAINE DU MAS DES ARMES
Marc and Régis Puccini
Route de Capion, 34150 Aniane
Tel   04 67 29 62 30
GPS 43.670122 3.581414
masdesarmes@orange.fr   www.lemasdesarmes.com
MAP 60
Visits by rendezvous, but not encouraged, nor are non-trade sales at the door. Fine wines though.

B **DOMAINE CROIX DE SAINT PRIVAT
Olivier Ferrie
Route de Saint Guilhem, 34150 Aniane
Tel   04 67 57 21 66
Mobile   06 82 91 51 17
GPS ; 43.6902008 3.5836254
olivier-ferrie@orange.fr
MAP 61
Cellars open daily 9.00-20.00. It is a relief to find in Aniane a grower whose wines one is not frightened to open on account of price.

B **DOMAINE COSTON
Joseph and Marie-Thérèse Coston
3 route de Montpellier, 34150 Puechabon
Tel   04 67 57 48 96
Mobile   06 17 35 64 80
GPS 43.42..52N 3.37.10 E
domainecoston@yahoo.fr   www.domainecoston.fr
MAP 66
Appointment advisable.
The story of how Phiilip Coston, one of Joseph's brothers, managed to acquire some of the land which had been denied to Robert Mondavi 10 years earlier, is a classic tale of the kind of political wheeling and dealing which they are so good at in the South of France. It is worth a book, or even an opera, on its own account.

*MAS DES AGRUNELLES

Frédéric Porro and Stéphanie Ponson
1501 Chemin de Fontméjane, 34380 Argelliers_
Tel   04 67 55 67 44
Mobile   06 14 55 54 7
contact@masdesagrunelles.com   www.masdesagrunelles.com
MAP 67
Remotely situated, so appointment advised.

BD *MAS NICOT   Stéphanie Ponson

Le Mas de Perry, 1471 Chemin de Fontméjean, 34380 Argelliers
Tel   04 67 55 67 44
stephanie@masnicot.com   www.masnicot.com
(see also Mas des Agrunelles above)
MAP 68
Appointment advisable.

* *DOMAINE DU POUJOL

Robert and Kim Cripps
1067 route de Grabels, 34380 Vailhauques
Tel   04 67 84 47 57
poujol.Cripps@sfr.fr   www.domainedupoujol.com
MAP 69
Visits every day, but appointment suggested to avoid disappointment.

* *DOMAINE LES CAIZERGUES

Jean-Luc and Brigitte Fallet
34190 Brissac
Tel   04 67 73 71 83
Mobile   06 07 88 41 14
falletjl@orange.fr   www.domainelescaizergues.com
MAP 70
Cellars open July and August, Monday to Saturday, 9.30-12.00 and 15.00-19.00. Rest of the year Saturdays only, 8.30-12.00 and 14.00-18.30.

B *DOMAINE D'ANGLAS

Carole and Roger Gaussorgues34190 Brissac
Tel   04 67 73 70 18
Mobile   06 24 33 28 08
contact@domaine-anglas.com   www.camping-anglas.com
MAP 71
Shop open on the *domaine*'s campsite from mid-April until the end of September every day, 9.00-12.00 and 14.00-19.00 from April to September. Not Sunday. Otherwise by appointment and go to the *domaine* itself.

*CHÂTEAU DE LA DEVÈZE MONNIER

Laurent Damais
34190 Montoulieu
Tel   04 67 73 70 21
domaine@deveze.com   www.deveze.com
MAP 72
Cellars open weekdays and Saturday mornings.
This is a huge estate. The wines are sure to give everyday pleasure.

Torrential storms had punctuated an already late harvest,

and it was getting on towards the second half of September before Sylvain Fadat could resume picking. He had yet to harvest half of his red wine grapes when his team of pickers assembled in his yard at 7.30 one Monday morning. The vines had been given the chance over the weekend to re-balance themselves after a complete drenching of their roots.

Sylvain knows from long experience how to run a *vendange*. He had enlisted a score or so of pickers from all over the place: an artist from Ireland who had settled in Montpeyroux some years back; a jack of all trades from Marseille who proved himself able to speak as fast as he could pick; an Ecuadorian, a Spaniard, three *stageaires* who had come to spend a few weeks with Sylvain learning about the work in the *chais*; and an assorted crowd from Montpeyroux, some younger than others.

In the Midi, punctuality is not always observed, so it was surprising to find the entire troupe arriving at base on time. Wine-harvesting is an all-day job, so, perhaps because Sylvain does not believe in midnight picking, it was important for everyone not to be late. Sylvain is a firm but popular leader, but he is not slow in admonishing those who do not do what is expected of them. He directs operations from his tractor, behind which a large *benne* is attached to receive the grapes from the pickers as and when their buckets are filled. He manages to manoeuvre the vehicle between the rows so as to be just ahead of the pickers, who work about five rows of vines at a time. Simple arithmetic suggests there are four pickers per row, two each side of the plant, armed with sécateurs, some of which are sharper than others.

On this occasion, there was still some grenache to be picked at the vineyard nearest to the village, the parcels called Aupilhac, the name Sylvain gives to his *domaine*. They are north of the village, just below the ruined castle called 'Le Castellas'. Most of the grapes had survived the bad weather, and no time was lost in attacking them. The swaying of the pickers' bodies as they emptied their buckets into the *benne* was quite like a ballet to watch. Idle bystanders might reflect while savouring this spectacle that this was the climax of a *vigneron*'s year, the result of punishing hard work and the emotional stress of fighting the weather, disease in the vineyards, the ever-present possibility of mistakes or disasters in the *chais*. But Sylvain seemed to treat the occasion as just another day's work.

He is accompanied by his wife Désirée, whose time is mostly occupied by driving the full *bennes* back to the *chais*, then bringing them back empty. It is vital, if oxidisation of the juice is to be avoided, that no time is lost between the loading of the *bennes* and the delivery of the grapes to be destalked and lightly crushed at home, then swiftly pumped to the tanks for fermentation.

The work at this vineyard was soon finished and the team split into two groups. The first, about eight pickers, travelled to Aniane, where Sylvain has a parcel of very old carignan he is determined not to forget, even if there is only a third of a hectare of grapes. He wouldn't refuse an offer from someone to buy this parcel, because it is some way away from the village of Montpeyroux and hardly worth the expense and effort of looking after. Perhaps this explains why the weeds between the rows had grown to dwarf the plants. Nevertheless, old carignan is old carignan and much to be prized. It was sad that so much of the crop here had suffered first

Vendanges at Montpeyroux

from oidium during the spring and summer and then from rot following the storms. The year had been *compliqué*…

The other team travelled to the vineyard called 'Cocalières'. This was once the crater of a now extinct volcano, so it has a very particular *terroir*, especially suitable for white grapes. Sylvain had himself fashioned a vineyard in this amphitheatre, covering 10 hectares or so of steep terraces, where the vines are grown not horizontally but in up-and-down rows (*de haut en bas*). The white grapes had already been picked and the mourvèdre and grenache were recent plantings, not yet yielding grapes for winemaking. There was however a substantial parcel of cinsault, which needed all the pickers, including those returned from Aniane, and took the rest of the day to tackle.

Soon after eleven o'clock, thoughts begin to turn to lunch, conversation in the vines increasingly speculating on menus. Sylvain does not let them go however until well after 12.30, with instructions that they were to be back by two o'clock sharp. Presumably they complied, but Sylvain allowed himself a longer break, partly to entertain his guests and *stageaires*, and partly to make sure that the fruit of the morning's work was safely bubbling away in the vats back at home.

The preparation of the midday meal is down to Sylvain's mother-in-law, Marie, who has been spending most of the day making tomato sauce; there would eventually be at least 100 *bocaux*. Any surplus finds its way into the lunch, delicious, but modest. Growers do not have huge midday feasts however hard they may have worked in the morning. They are no doubt worried about falling asleep over their *sécateurs* during the afternoon. Nevertheless, precious bottles from Sylvain's cellar find their way to table and, though much appreciated by all present, are not wholly emptied.

Back to work at Cocalières. Towards five o'clock, the pickers had reached the bottom of a group of rows, and it required transport to take them back up the hill to start on the next batch. However, the pickers thought they had enough. The afternoon had turned out to be unexpectedly hot and energy was flagging. So, everyone decided it was time to stop. For Sylvain, it was time once again to go home and inspect the result of the day's work, and to taste some of the juice from the *cuves*.

It would not be long before the *vendange* was over. The following weekend there was to be a big fête in the village to celebrate the end of the wine year. No doubt wine would flow freely, the bars in the village would do a roaring trade and there would be dancing in the streets. Work would not have finished in the *chais*, however. The new wine will have to be nursed over the coming months if it is to justify all the hard work that has gone into making it. The cycle begins once again.

Grès de Montpellier

This *appellation* covers a variety of different *terroirs* and growers surrounding the city of Montpellier; no fewer than 46 communes in all. The section deals with those growers to the west and north-west of the city, the remaining producers (including those from the sub-*appellations* of Saint-Christol, Saint-Drézéry, Vérargues and La Méjanelle) being dealt with in a later section covering the area north and east of the town.

The soils vary from sandstone, from terraces created by alluvial erosion, to large pebbles, hard chalk, as well as layers of sand and fine stones. Grenache must make up at least 20% of any *assemblage* here, and that grape, syrah and mourvèdre or any combination must make up 70%. The remainder may or may not contain carignan and/or cinsault. These restrictions persuade many growers to make wine outside the *appellation* if they wish to profit from parcels of carignan, cinsault or other unpermitted varieties. AOP yields may not exceed 45 hl/ha.

As in many parts of Languedoc, the distinctions between the classifications and between IGPs and even *Vins de France* is becoming more and more academic as far as the consumer is concerned. The important factor is the grower rather than what appears on their labels.

In this section, we start at the western end of the Grès, taking in the area of St Georges d'Orques as far as the suburbs of Montpellier. Generally speaking, the wines of this area are exemplified by an abundance of red fruits and herby hints of the surrounding garrigue. Most growers aim for soft tannins.

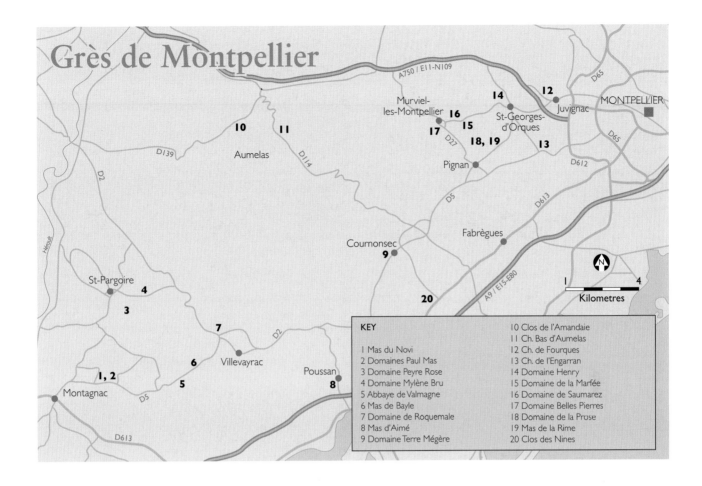

Grès de Montpellier

KEY

1 Mas du Novi
2 Domaines Paul Mas
3 Domaine Peyre Rose
4 Domaine Mylène Bru
5 Abbaye de Valmagne
6 Mas de Bayle
7 Domaine de Roquemale
8 Mas d'Aimé
9 Domaine Terre Mégère
10 Clos de l'Amandaie
11 Ch. Bas d'Aumelas
12 Ch. de Fourques
13 Ch. de l'Engarran
14 Domaine Henry
15 Domaine de la Marfée
16 Domaine de Saumarez
17 Domaine Belles Pierres
18 Domaine de la Prose
19 Mas de la Rime
20 Clos des Nines

B ****DOMAINE PEYRE ROSE

Marlène Soria
34230 St. Pargoire
Tel   04 67 98 75 50
peyrerose@orange.com

MAP 3
The wines are not sold at the *domaine*, and a visit calls for prior appointment.

The *domaine* is hard to find, but if you turn up a track opposite the fire station in Saint-Pargoire and follow the telephone posts for four kilometres, you eventually get there: a delightful spot surrounded by the protective *garrigue* and always full of flowers. Mme Soria and her husband first came here in 1973. The local stone glowed pink, and the pink cistus was in full bloom. Everything seemed pink so she called her new home Peyre Rose, 'pink stone'. The stars indicate her standing as one of the most revered growers in France. They also explain the high price (D+) which she manages to achieve for her wines, which is partly also due to the fact that she does not market them until the fourth year after the vintage. They are given a long period of ageing in large *foudres*. Syrah is at the basis of her wines, so far all red. 'Clos Ciste' has some grenache, is deep, complex and quite garriguey, while 'Cuvée Léone' has some mourvèdre which gives it a meaty, leathery quality. 'Marlène no. 3' has

nearly as much grenache as syrah and there is some carignan too in the blend, making for rich red fruit and firm tannins. These wines are quintessential Languedoc.

B **DOMAINE MYLÈNE BRU

Mylène Bru Aubun
34230 St. Pargoire
Business address and *caveau* at 23 Quai Noël Guignon
34200 Sète
Mobile   06 83 08 97 30
mylene@free.fr

MAP 4
Appointment essential.

Mylène, spurned by her family in the Corbières because she was a woman, left home and eventually settled in this wild region north of Pézenas. Her vines are almost as difficult to find as those of Marlène Soria. She nowadays has five hectares and grows some unusual grapes including aubun from the Rhône Valley. Many vines are left *en gobelet* to avoid the strength of the wind which can be fairly fierce hereabouts. Mylène makes a rare wine from pure chasselas called 'Lady Chasselas' (B), surprisingly dry and quite minerally, and her reds include a pure tempranillo called 'Karm Rouge' (B) and 'Rita' (B), a straight carignan which she has named

Near Aumelas

Thierry Hasard, Domaine de la Marfée, p.236

after her grandmother. Another unblended wine is 'Monts et Merveilles' (B/C), which is all syrah. Blends include 'Les Moulins de Mon Coeur' (B/C), from carignan, cinsault and syrah, and 'Far Ouest' (B/C), a mix of just about everything she has. None of her wines are filtered, and they have little if any added sulphur. For the most part, they boast low alcohol and a pleasant quaffability and lightness; dare one say femininity? No barrels either. Much of her wine finds its way to Japan.

***MAS D'AIMÉ   Philippe Rustan
22 Avenue de Bédarieux, 34770 Poussan
Tel   04 67 78 98 32
domaine@iletaitunesoif.fr

MAP 8
Appointment strongly recommended.

Philippe's family goes back several generations, all *vignerons* at Poussan. Philippe travelled widely in his younger days, watching the vines all around his family *domaine* being torn up. He decided not only to save his own, but to explore and interpret the character of the many old grapes his great grandfather had planted on seven hectares dotted around the village. The *domaine* is named after him. Thus, you will find no syrah or mourvèdre here. His only white is a pure viognier called 'Adelaide' (D), from grapes he planted himself in 2000, and the wine is fermented and aged in barrel. The other wines are all (C): 'Les Raisins Oubliés' is pure grenache aged in wood, as is 'Il était une soif'. 'La Vieille Bataille' is a remarkable pure carignan, one of the best in Languedoc, from grapes planted in 1918. 'La Doyenne' is a blend of very old aramon (40%), carignan and grenache. 'Valaury' (if you can find old vintages) is pure alicante, vinified and aged in barrel, producing a wine of dense fruit and black colour. 'Sainte Catherine' is another pure grenache, this time from seventy-year-old vines. Unusually for this *domaine*, the alicante was trained *double guyot* rather than *en gobelet*, which is otherwise the rule here. The vines were however rented, and Philippe has had to give them back. The style and philosophy here is quite out of the mainstream, and Philippe has attracted huge attention since his first vintage in 1998. None of the wines here are racked or filtered.

B *** DOMAINE TERRE MÉGÈRE
Pierre Moreau
10 rue du Jeu de Tambourin, 34660 Cournonsec
Tel   04 67 85 42 85
terremegere@wanadoo.fr   www.terremegere.fr

MAP 9
Cellars open Monday to Friday, 11.30-12.30 and 17.00-19.00 Saturdays, 9.00-12.30. Otherwise by appointment.

Pierre Moreau comes from near Grenoble, where they have a grape called galopine, which is the same as, or a near relative of, viognier, so he has adopted the viognier grape and was one of its pioneers in the Languedoc. Today he and his son have a mere 11 hectares, of which seven are in the middle of the garrigue. His main viognier wine is still called 'Galopine' (B), in which he adds some marsanne, clairette and grenache blanc, all vinified together in barrel and kept there for six months. The result is top class. There is another viognier (A/B), this time 100%, raised in tank, but left two months on its lees. Their rosé (A) is largely cinsault with some syrah and grenache, and there is a range of reds: 'Clapas' (B) is largely mourvèdre (their other speciality grape) and partly aged in a mix of new and old barrels; 'Les Dolomies' (B) is mostly from tank-aged syrah only partly destalked, and from grenache crushed before vinification. Another tank-raised blend called 'Airelle' (A) is two-thirds Grenache and one-third mourvèdre, made for its fruit and with soft tannins. Finally, there is a pure cabernet sauvignon (A) and a mourvèdre -grenache blend called 'Garric' (B), partly raised in barrel.

***CLOS DE L'AMANDAIE
Philippe and Stéphanie Peytavy
Mas Arnaud, 34230 Aumelas
Tel   09 53 67 23 57
Mobile   06 86 68 08 62
GPS   43.361081   3.355511
closdelamandaie@free.fr   www.closdelamandaie.com

MAP 10
Cellars open Monday to Friday, 17.30-20.00 and on Saturday from 14.00-19.00.

Apart from mourvèdre, you will find all the usual Languedoc grapes on parade here at this 15-hectare *domaine* created as recently as 2002. Pursuing a policy of making something to please as many as possible, 'Chat Pitre' (A) opens the range with a trio of all three colours, quick and easy in style, and including an attractive rosé saignée from syrah, grenache and cinsault. Then go to 'L'Amandaie' (B), their traditional red and white, before ascending to another pair called 'Huit Clos' (C), where the red is half syrah, half grenache and aged in a mix of old and new wood. 'Les Menades' (D) is a late-harvested petit manseng aged in new wood. The new reception facilities here, as well as the quality of the wines, suggest an ambition to rise high in the ranks of Languedoc growers.

***CHÂTEAU DE L'ENGARRAN
Diane Losfelt and Constance Rerolle
(contact Isabelle Baertschi)
34880 Saint-Georges d'Orques
Tel   04 67 47 00 02
lengarran@wanadoo.fr   www.chateau-engarran.com

MAP 13
Visits during business hours seven days a week.

It is always a pleasure to visit this pretty *folie* of a *château* with its lovely iron gateway (actually imported from somewhere quite different). The welcome too is warm, like the wines, which are very successful and widely known. 40 hectares around the *château* and another 20 in a neighbouring village together constitute a sizeable vineyard, and thus there is a good range of wines, starting with 'Primeur' (A) from syrah for drinking at the end of the year of the vintage, with IGPs in all three colours. Notably, there is a delicious sauvignon, 'Cuvée Adelys' (A), rich in citrus flavours, hay and cut flowers, and a more-ish rosé (A) from cinsault and grenache. Then there are two reds (both A), one from young merlot and cabernet franc, supported by old carignan and raised in tank, the other, given 12 months in barrel and rather more serious. On to the AOPs, led by a rosé from grenache and cinsault (A/B) like its IGP cousin, which keeps longer than most, and three reds. 'Tradition' (A/B) is their best-seller, conventionally blended from syrah, grenache and carignan but given time in *foudres* and barrel, unlike 'Cuvée Sainte Cécile' (A/B), likened by the growers to a Loire for its elegance and gluggability. Don't miss the flagship 'Cuvée Quetton Saint Georges' (C/D), 70% syrah, raised half in wood and half in tank, the fruit surviving the toasty vanilla flavours from the wood, thanks perhaps to the smooth tannins. You can round off with a surprising *Vendanges Tardives*-style wine (C) from sauvignon, throbbing with flavours of preserved fruit, quince, honey and acacia flowers.

Robin Williamson, Domaine de Saumarez

***DOMAINE HENRY
François and Laurence Henry
2 Avenue d'Occitanie, 34680 Saint-Georges d'Orques
Tel   04 67 45 57 74
domainehenry@wanadoo.fr   www.domainehenry.fr

MAP 14
Cellars open Monday to Saturday, 9.00-12.00 and 16.00-19.30.

Through the capriciousness of French inheritance laws, M. Henry has 15 hectares of prime-sited vines at St Georges, but his fine winery is at some distance opposite the football ground. His family have been winemakers in the region for over 10 generations, so M. Henry knows a thing or two about his *terroir* and its potential. He makes only one white (B), a blend of chardonnay and terret blanc which he raises in tank. Of two rosés, he says of one that it is simple but authentic, comprising grenache and syrah (A), the other, made under the Saint Georges name is a food wine, full and fruity (B). Of the several reds, 'Le Coteau Rouge' (A) is an easy grenache/cinsault/syrah affair. 'Villefranchien' (B), as its name suggests, is from grapes grown on stony eponymous soil with a lot of *galets roulés*. 'Les Paradines' (B), from younger vines, is the 'second' wine of the domaine, 'second' that is to 'Le Saint Georges d'Orques' (C), typical

of its *terroir* with dark fruit flavours. 'Les Chailles' (C) has the biggest structure of all the wines here, its syrah, grenache and mourvèdre aged for two years in barrel. There are two curiosities: 'Le Mailhol' (D) is a reconstruction of what the wine hereabouts might have been like before the phylloxera, being made from forgotten old grape varieties and relatively light in alcohol; and an extraordinary sweet Grenache (C), late-picked and made like a sauternes, almost black in colour and very syrupy.

BD ***DOMAINE DE LA MARFÉE
Françoise and Thierry Hasard
Chemin de Cathala, 34570 Murviel-les-Montpellier
Tel   07 78 67 05 49
domainedelamarfee@gmail.com   www.la-marfee.com

MAP 15
Phone ahead.

Part of the *cru* called St Georges d'Orques, whose wines go back centuries and were the choice of, among others, Thomas Jefferson. This estate consists of several small parcels, which M. Hasard acquired and assembled in 1997. An individualist as well as being a biodynamic fanatic, he claims that wine critics are not interested in wines like his, preferring, he says, to confine themselves to "*domaines* of incontrovertible fame." Hasard has acquired such a reputation that he can already be listed as one of them. His winemaking is notable for the fact that he does not make any *assemblages* until after his wines have spent two years in barrel. Thus, the names and the blends may change from year to year. A snapshot in time reveals a white 'Frisson d'Ombelles' (C) from roussanne and chardonnay with a touch of petit manseng, and a late-picked sweetie called 'Sugar Baby Love' (C). Hasard has a penchant for mourvèdre – it makes up 50% of 'Les Gamines' (B/C) and 80% of 'Della Francesca' (C/D), a wine which he gives the St Georges label. 'Les Champs Murmurés' (D) is a blend of syrah/mourvèdre, while there is a pure carignan from one parcel of old vines which Hasard calls 'Les Vignes qu'on abat' (D). The French word '*précision*' is hard to translate into English wine-speak, but whatever it may mean, Hasard regards freshness and cleanliness as the key to achieving it. Outstanding but not cheap.

B **DOMAINE DE SAUMAREZ
Liz and Robin Williamson
Métairie de Bouisson, 34570 Murviel-les-Montpellier (on the road to St Georges d'Orques)
Tel 06 24 41 56 20
desaumarez@yahoo.fr   www.domainedesaumarez.com

MAP 16
Open Saturdays from 14.00-19.00, otherwise by appointment including Sundays.

Liz, who lends her name to the charming rosé, 'Fleur de Liz' (B), comes from New Zealand, Robin from London. They arrived in Languedoc in 2003, and have 12 hectares or so dotted around the village of Murviel, devoted largely to syrah and grenache. As time goes by they may develop a little more of their own personality into their finely made wines, and already they have managed to restrain their use of oak. In the meantime, the wines are really good: the white Cuve 'S' (B) and its red partner (mostly grenache). The latter very ripe and rich, and impressively deep in colour. 'Trinitas' (B) leads to their top wine 'Aalenien' (C), a nearly pure syrah, named after its particularly rocky *terroir* of limestone and quartz. A very exciting venture to be supported.

***DOMAINE BELLES PIERRES
Damien Coste
24 rue des Clauzes, 34570 Murviel-les-Montpellier
Tel 04 67 47 30 43
Mobile 06 08 88 61 27
www.domainebellespierres.com

MAP 17
Rendezvous sensible.

Damien took over 15 hectares scattered around the village

of Murviel from his father, Jo, in 1999 and immediately made a splash with his finely crafted wines. The property used to be called Les Clauzes, hence the name of his best-selling white and red wines, 'Les Clauzes de Jo' (B). The white is largely from roussanne and given nine months in wood, while the red is half syrah in tank, the rest grenache and mourvèdre in barrel. But first there is an easy-drinking white called 'Mosaïque' (A) to prepare the way for 'Ineptie' (C), a blend of roussanne, vermentino, viognier and muscat, vinified in barrel and aged for a year in the wood. Then follow some eccentric products of near genius: 'Monica' (C), a mix of syrah and grenache allowed to shrivel on trays before vinification; 'Passidore' (D), an unusual blend of gros and petit manseng; *passerillée* (C/D) in the same way; and finally 'Exception' (D+), a similar blend but in the *vendanges tardives* style and aged for three years in barrel. This *domaine* is for those seeking artisanal wines of a highly personal nature, far from the mainstream.

B ***DOMAINE DE LA PROSE
Bertrand de Mortillet
Route de St Georges d'Orques, BP 25, 34570 Pignan
Tel 04 67 03 08 30
domaine-de-la-prose@wanadoo.fr
www.domaine-de-la-prose.fr

MAP 18
Phone ahead

The signpost is small and has been much used in its time for target practice by the *chasseurs*. It points to an elegant *chais*, designed by Bertrand's father who was a surveyor. Bertrand himself is highly qualified as a winemaker, having worked (inter alia) at Château Montrose in Bordeaux. He is in charge of 28 hectares of vines which breathe in the fine sea air. This, in turn, gives the wines a certain freshness and elegance. For example 'Les Cadières Blanc' (B), half vermentino, the rest roussanne and grenache blanc, is lively and fruity, with hints of resin after its vinification and *élevage* in wood. There is also a lively and mineral rosé (B). The reds are headed by 'Les Cadières Rouge' (B), a blend of all five usual grapes, benchmark Languedoc, spicy and packed with red fruits, followed by 'Les Embruns' (B), an unusual blend of syrah and cinsault (40%), gamey and peppery, and 'La Grande Cuvée' (C), all oak-aged syrah and destined for a long life.

B **MAS DE LA RIME   Philippe and Brita Sala
Chemin des Proses, Route de Saint Georges d'Orques, 34570 Pignan
Mobile 06 86 18 11 84 or 06 08 18 32 73
philippesala@wanadoo.fr   www.masdelarime.com

MAP 19
Telephone for rendezvous.

Labelling at Clos de L'Amandaie

Philippe Sala worked for 40 years with telephones and electronics before he bought three and a half hectares of vines from Bernard de Mortillet (Domaine de la Prose, see above) in 2009. He has sensibly confided the care of the operation to Bernard, who is making a big name for this boutique enterprise. The first wines were made in 2010. The style is lean and meaty, allowing the fruit to speak for itself. For the moment, there are just two wines (both C), one white from roussanne and grenache, powerfully aromatic, partly aged in barrel, the other red from syrah and mourvèdre, wholly aged in wood. The acidity which comes from the *terroir* gives the aftertaste a fine bite. An exciting venture.

OTHER GOOD GRÈS DE MONT-PELLIER GROWERS

**MAS DU NOVI
(also Domaine de St. Jean du Noviciat)   Thierry Thomas
Route de Villevayrac, 34530 Montagnac
Tel   04 67 24 07 32
contact@masdunovi.com   www.masdunovi.com
MAP 1
Cellars open seven days a week from 10.00-19.00. A vineyard of 50 hectares, formerly part of the estate of the Abbaye de Vamagne.

**DOMAINES PAUL MAS   Jean-Claude Mas
Route de Villevayrac, 34530 Montagnac
Tel   04 67 90 16 10
info@paulmas.com   www.paulmas.com
MAP 2
Open at Côté Mas in Montagnac, Monday to Friday, 8.30-17.30. A string of properties, with a large range of wines ranging from the frankly commercial to the fairly ambitious.

B ** ABBAYE DE VALMAGNE
M. Le Baron d'Allaines
34560 Villevayrac
Tel 04 67 78 06 09
Mobile   06 03 03 04 85
info@valmagne.com   www.valmagne.com
MAP 5
Boutique open Monday to Saturday during usual hours. There is a charge to visit the interior of the buildings.
It would be too much to expect the wines here to match the splendour of the architecture, which make this one of the most visited historic monuments of the Languedoc. There is a ferme-auberge on site, and there are concerts and other events in the evenings.

** MAS DE BAYLE   Céline Michelon
34560 Villevayrac
Tel 04 67 78 06 11
contact@masdebayle.com   www.masdebayle.com
MAP 6
Cellars open Monday to Friday, 9.00-12.30 and 13.30-17.00.

B ** DOMAINE DE ROQUEMALE
Valérie Tabaries and Dominique Ibanez
25 Route de Clermont, 34560 Villevayrac
Tel 04 67 78 24 10
Mobiles 06 85 93 51 64 and 06 10 89 59 11
GPS 43 5032428 36012338.
contact@roquemale.com   www.roquemale.com
MAP 7
Appointment recommended, though cellars are in theory open 10.00-12.00 and 16.00-19.30 every day except Sunday and Monday mornings. The *servant* grape appears in a dessert wine, surprisingly spicy (B/C). Valérie is one of the Vinifilles (q.v.).

B ** CHÂTEAU BAS D'AUMELAS
Geoffroy and Jean-Philippe d'Albenas
34230 Aumelas
Tel 04 30 40 60 29
contact@chateaubasaumelas.fr www.chateaubasaumelas.fr
MAP 11
Appointment suggested.
Although this property has been in the Albenas family for three centuries, it was only in 2001 that the present scions took over the vineyards seriously, replanting 12 hectares organically.

** CHÂTEAU DE FOURQUES   Lise Fons-Vincent
Route de Lavérune, 34990 Juvignac
Tel 04 67 47 90 87
fourques@netcourrier.com   www.chateaudefourques.com
MAP 12
Guided tours of vineyard, cellar and tasting (about two hours, min. two people) 15€ per person bookable 48 hours in advance. Otherwise the cellars are open Monday to Saturday during usual hours.

** CLOS DES NINES
Isabelle Mangeart and Christian Marble
329 Chemin de Pountiou, 34690 Fabrègues
Tel   04 67 68 95 36
GPS 43 32 4873 3 46 1070
isabelle@closdesnines.com   www.closdesnines.com
MAP 20
Visits by appointment.
'Nines' is Languedoc for 'daughters', of whom these owners have three. They also have 10 hectares of vines all in one piece.

MORE GRÈS DE MONTPELLIER PROPERTIES ARE LISTED UNDER THE SECTION 'NORTH AND EAST OF MONTPELLIER'

The Road to Pic Saint Loup

The legend is that Saint Loup, returning from the Crusades, discovered that his beloved had married someone else in his absence – neither the first nor the last time that such a thing has happened. Unlike most others, he took his vows and lived a hermit on this mountain for the rest of his life.

From the west, this famous landmark. some 20 kilometres out of Montpellier to the north-west, looks like a quite large ordinary hill, but once you have travelled the valley which separates the Pic from the mountain of Hortus, the true face of the Pic is disclosed in dramatic fashion: a sharp tooth jutting out defiantly into the skyline. It has become the symbol of one of the most energetic and fashionable vineyards of the Languedoc. Although the media's searchlights have discovered the Terrasses du Larzac, the Pic remains the source of some of the finest wines of the region .

Pic Saint Loup has now received its own AOP status, the rules confirming previous practice ; the grape varieties must consist as to 90% of syrah, grenache and mourvèdre and the vines must be at least six years old before their juice qualifies for AOP. As elsewhere in the Languedoc, many new and often quite young growers have launched themselves, sometimes because they have decided to leave one or other of the *coopératives*, sometimes because, with a sound professional training behind them, they have persuaded their forebears to let them have a go and see what they can do with the family inheritance.

The excellence of the wines is due to a number of factors: especially a more temperate hill-country climate, with less extreme heat and a little more rainfall than on the plains to the south;

Near Domaine de l'Hortus

while the winds from the mountains to the north cool the vineyards at night and protect the grapes against rot and disease. These conditions are particularly suited to the syrah grape which in some other locations can suffer from drought.

The journey through these vineyards is described from south to north.

It should be remembered that in 2016 the northern half the district was severly damaged by hail and it remains to be seen how the vines recover. Notably Clos Marie and Château de Lancyre were very badly hit.

B *** DOMAINE CLAVEL Pierre Clavel
Mas de Périé
532 Avenue de Sainte-Croix de Quintillargues, 34820 Assas
Tel   04 99 62 06 13
Mobile   06 13 19 74 85
info@vins-clavel.fr   www.vins-clavel.fr

MAP 2
Appointment advisable, but in principle he's open Monday to Saturday in the afternoons.

Clavel's training is hardly usual for an innovative winemaker, even if his father was one of the founding fathers of the Syndicat of Languedoc producers and famous as an eminent wine-historian. Pierre left school at sixteen and took himself off into the mountains of the Cévennes, where he grew his hair long and became a goatherd. There he met George Dardé, then manager of the Cave Coopérative at Roquebrun, who kindled in Pierre the passion for wine which his father had somehow failed to ignite. After spells as a food salesman and a fisherman, Pierre decided to devote himself to wine and took a lease of a few hectares of vines in the suburbs of Montpellier, from where he still carries out part of his operations. His base is however today at Assas, where he has 12 hectares of syrah, grenache and mourvèdre from which he is making the same range of wines as he started out with though the labels are today a shade more chic: an exotic white called 'Cascailles'(B) from vermentino, roussanne and grenache blanc, a tip-top rosé in the provence style called 'Mescladis'(A), a much deeper and food-style 'Rosé à rougir'(B) from grenache, and a range of reds including among others the easy 'Le Mas'(A) , the medium-weight 'Les Garrigues'(B) and the top 'Copa Santa' (C), aged for a year in old barrels and bottled without filtration. The bulk of his production is exported. Excellent value.

B ✳✳✳ MAS DE MORTIÈS

Sylvie Guiraudon and Pascale Moustiès
34270 Saint-Jean-de-Cuculles
Tel   04 67 55 11 12
GPS 43.769885, 3.822856
contact@morties.com   www.morties.com

MAP 6
Cellar open Monday to Friday 15.00-19.00, Saturday 10.00-19.00 or by appointment.

One partnership succeeds another as the present owners of this pretty *mas*, who took over in 2008, carry on the good work started by Jorcin and Duchemin on their 25 hectares in 1993. There are two constants: the *régisseur* Olivier who is keeping very much to the style of the former gowers, and the carignan grape which was always favoured here and continues in the shape of 'La Mauvaise Herbe'(C), aged in tank to preserve its character. There is just the one dry AOP white, big, powerful and with hints of fennel(B/C) and one rosé 'Pénélope'(B) based on syrah. Apart from a sweet dessert wine from viognier, aged in oak (C), the rest of the wines are all red: a vin de soif (A), two syrah-based wines, one made by *macération carbonique*. the Pic wine(C) which is spicy and with notes of liquorice. You may be lucky to hit on 'Jamais Content'(C/D), a barrel-aged wine not made every year, but of which several old vintages going back to the former régime seem to be around still.

BD ✳✳✳ CLOS DES AUGUSTINS

Frédéric and Roger Mézy
111 Chemin de la Vieille, 34270 Saint Mathieu de Tréviers
Tel   04 67 54 52 77 and 04 67 54 73 45
mezyroger@me.com   www.closdesaugustins.com

MAP 7
Visits during normal business hours.

This 24 hectare vineyard is named after two great grand-fathers, both coincidentally called Augustin. Three generations of the Mézy family have had time to acquire a house-style, which has developed remarkably since they adopted biodynamic principles ten years ago. Yields are low (15/30 hl/ha), harvesting is done by *tris* and the wines are bottled according to the lunar calendar. The large cellar-space is

home to a striking painting of a woman in a red hat, whose composition is reflected in the labels of the wines from this *domaine*. The wines include the whites 'Les Bambins'(B) with 60% vermentino, fermented and aged in barrel; 'Joseph'(C) from low yielding chardonnay and roussanne; 'La Lueur du Jour' with marsanne added(D); and 'Les Secrets de Monique'(D), the *encépagement* of which is a guarded secret of the *domaine* (why? one wonders). Two rosés(A/B), one cinsault-based and deceptively pale, the other syrah/grenache, lead to the range of reds: 'Les Bambins'(B) from 60% syrah with mourvèdre and grenache, the ageing switching between cuve and wood; the popular 'Le Gamin' (B) from syrah and grenache, raised in a similar way; and 'Sourire d'Odile' with a longer *élevage*. The bigger reds have deep tannins, require ageing and are of top quality; Les Deux Rogers(D), with longer extraction and 15 months *élevage*; and finally 'L'Aîné'(D), from syrah and grenache yielding only 15 hl/ha, fermented in wood with gentle extraction and aged in new barrels for 18 months. Very good indeed.

BD ✳✳✳ ERMITAGE DU PIC SAINT LOUP

Jean-Marc, Pierre and Xavier Ravaille
Rue Carri lou Castellas, 34270 St. Mathieu de Traviers
Tel   04 67 54 24 68
GPS N430 45'99 55" E 3 JO' 79 45
ermitagepic@free.com www.ermitagepic.fr

MAP 8
Cellars open Monday to Saturday 9.00-12.00 and 14.00-18.00. Closed Sundays and holidays.

The grandfather of these three brothers sent all his grapes to the local *coopérative* which he was instrumental in founding in 1951. His son-in-law started planting syrah vines, and the new generation in 1992 decided to make their own wines, building a fine *cave* at the foot of the Pic itself and on the site of the former Château de Montferrand and the home of the bishops of Maguelone. The vines are surrounded by the trees, plants and flowers of the garrigue, whose influence, perfumes and flavours lend particular character to the wines here. The flowery white (B/C) is half roussanne, 30% clairette and the rest marsanne and grenache blanc (vinified and aged in barrel). The rosé(B) has a touch of cinsault otherwise is conventionally syrah, grenache and mourvèdre. The three reds start with 'Tour de Pierres'(B), a medium-weight typical Pic, raised partly in *foudre* and partly in barrel. 'Cuvée St Agnès'(B/C) is at its best between 5 and 10 years from the vintage, which gives an idea of its substantial but not overweening character. The top red is 'Cuvée Guilhem Caucelm'(D), a blend of syrah and 85-year-old grenache, grown *en gobelet* and aged in barrel for two to three years. The wine is named after the first person listed in the local archives as making wine in this region. The range of wines, though small, offers something for all tastes.

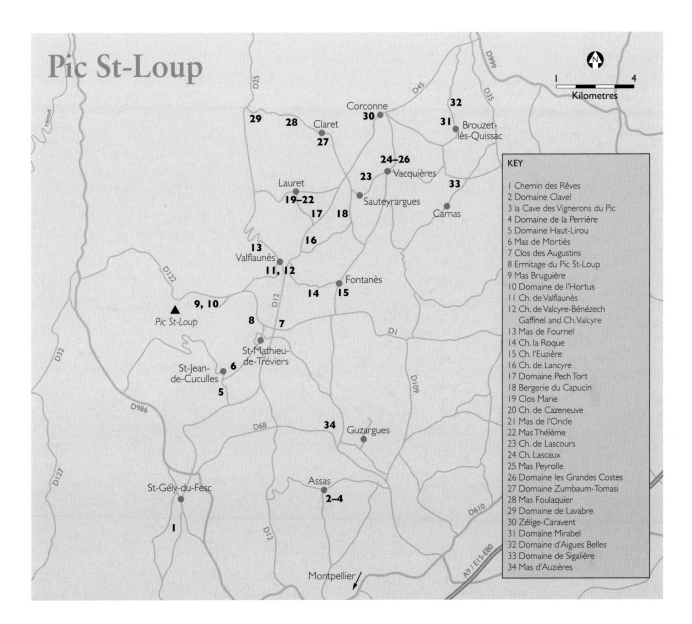

Pic St-Loup

KEY

1 Chemin des Rêves
2 Domaine Clavel
3 la Cave des Vignerons du Pic
4 Domaine de la Perrière
5 Domaine Haut-Lirou
6 Mas de Mortiès
7 Clos des Augustins
8 Ermitage du Pic St-Loup
9 Mas Bruguière
10 Domaine de l'Hortus
11 Ch. de Valflaunès
12 Ch. de Valcyre-Bénézech
   Gaffinel and Ch. Valcyre
13 Mas de Fournel
14 Ch. la Roque
15 Ch. l'Euzière
16 Ch. de Lancyre
17 Domaine Pech Tort
18 Bergerie du Capucin
19 Clos Marie
20 Ch. de Cazeneuve
21 Mas de l'Oncle
22 Mas Thélème
23 Ch. de Lascours
24 Ch. Lascaux
25 Mas Peyrolle
26 Domaine les Grandes Costes
27 Domaine Zumbaum-Tomasi
28 Mas Foulaquier
29 Domaine de Lavabre
30 Zélige-Caravent
31 Domaine Mirabel
32 Domaine d'Aigues Belles
33 Domaine de Sigalière
34 Mas d'Auzières

B * MAS BRUGUIERE**   Xavier Bruguière
La Plaine, 34270 Valflaunès
Tel   04 67 55 20 97
GPS   43 47" 18.8" 3 50" 33.10"
xavier.bruguiere@wanadoo.fr   www.mas-bruguiere.com

MAP 9
Cellars open from September to June; closed Wednesday, Sunday and holidays otherwise 10.00-12.00 and 14.00-18.00. July and August; open Monday to Saturday 10.00-12.00 and 15.00-19.00.

Although the vines here have been in the family for seven generations, it was Xavier's grandfather who, following the disastrous frosts of 1956, started the replanting of the vineyard with table grapes. His son Guilhem went a stage further and developed a wine-vineyard, leaving the *coopérative* and making his first vintage in 1986. But it's Guilhem's son Xavier who has taken the ultimate step of conversion to organic farming and expanding the vines to a total area of 20 hectares. The *mas* shares with Hortus the valley leading to the *col* which separates the latter from the Pic itself, and it is noticeable that the northern slopes of the valley are given over to mourvèdre, a grape which loves the sun and faces the sea, while the syrah is planted on the shadier side of the valley so as to limit the effect of heat and drought. There are also younger vines some 5 kilometres away, where vermentino has been added to the syrah, roussanne and marsanne. The hallmark of the domaine is 'fruit, freshness and finesse', showing in the white 'Les Mûriers'(B) from roussanne and marsanne, only 20% of which is aged in large *muids*. The pink 'L'Arbousé'(B) is mostly pressed directly from syrah and mourvèdre with a little grenache. A red of the same name(B) is made for immediate pleasure, and only half of it is shown wood, old 50-hl *foudres* at that. The there will be a tank-raised charmer called 'Caladiz'(A/B) from syrah and grenache; 'La Grenardière'(C), mostly syrah and aged for 18 months partly in *demi-muids* and partly in wooden

The Pic

cuves tronçonniques; and finally 'Le Septième'(D), almost all mourvèdre aged for 24 months in *demi-muids*.

***DOMAINE DE L'HORTUS

la Famille Orliac
34270 Valflaunès
Tel 04 67 55 31 20
GPS 43 47' 11.7456" 3 50' 12.9294"
contact@domaine-hortus.fr orliac.hortus@wanadoo.fr
www.domaine-hortus.fr www.vignobles-orliac.com

MAP 10
Cellars open Monday to Friday 8.00-12.00 and 13.00-18.00, Saturdays 10.00-12.00 and 15.00-19.00.

Jean Orliac, with next to no money but an unquenchable appetite for adventure, discovered some abandoned parcels of vines between the cliffs of Hortus and the Pic in the 1970's. Trained in agronomy at Montpellier he was equipped to recognise instantly the potential of the site for wine-making. To start with, only 4 hectares were planted, and hesitant steps towards a first vintage were firmed up by 1990, by which time the present extraordinary timber house and *cave* had been built. His four children were his invaluable back-up, each today bringing different talents to the establishment: François in the vines, Marie in the office, Yves on sales and Martin in the cellar. The 55 hectares of vine include today a vineyard some way to the west called 'Clos du Prieur' at the foot of the Larzac plateau, where the wines(C) are of a rather different style but equally good. There are basically two ranges of wine at the home-domaine: 'Bergerie de l'Hortus' in all three colours(B) (the red mostly from syrah), and the 'Domaine Grande cuvée'(B) in white and red. The former come from vines on the lower ground of the slopes, the white from the lowest of all. The vines here are more sensitive to heat and drought and the accent is on finesse, with shorter macerations and *élevage*. The 'Grands Vins'(C) on the other hand, whose grapes have the best exposure, drainage and depth of soil, are wines which are given longer vinification and life in barrel. The red is 45% each of grenache and mourvèdre with just 10% syrah, matured in barrels (2/3rds new) for 16 months. The whites are unjustly overshadowed by the reds which is a pity because they are every bit as good, though the production is smaller.

*** CHÂTEAU DE VALFLAUNÈS

Fabien Reboul
Rue de l'Ancien Lavoir, 34270 Valflaunès
Tel 04 67 55 76 30
Mobile 06 83 48 37 85
chateaudevalflaunes@gmail.com www.chateauvalflaunes.fr

MAP 11
Cellars open daily except Monday, and, October-April, Sunday.

Fabien has a varied experience in wine-making having studied and worked in the Rhône, Burgundy (Corton Charlemagne), Oregon and New Zealand, and while his travels have opened his mind, he has become a faithful devotee to the styles and terroir of Pic Saint Loup. He works organically, though not officially so. He makes his blends while the vinification is still in progress. The altitude of his 13-hectare vineyard here ensures that his first white(B) 'Pourquoi Pas' from a blend of marsanne and roussanne is minerally, crisp generous and both dry and full-bodied; 20% is raised in wood. The second white 'Encore une fois'(C), is from vermentino and marsanne. Fabien likes new wood. He says it is cleaner and doesn't carry extra aromas 'such as floor polish'. His rosé(A) AOP Pic-Saint Loup is largely from mourvèdre with some syrah and grenache, a pale salmon pink in colour, with red fruits and exotic ones too on the bouquet. It sells out fast. Fabien regularly makes two reds for the market: the first called 'Espérance'(B) (which has a touch of carignan in the blend) is complex, well-balanced between its acidity, its fruit and its tannins. This is his best-seller. Of it he has said "Hope is the flame which kindles the fire of all your plans". The top red(C) is called 'T'em T'em' and is noted for its concentration and structure. Unmistakeably *languedocien*, there is nevertheless a suspicion of Burgundian finesse in all Fabien's wnes, even this one, his biggest. Sometimes you will find one or both of two other reds: 'Encore Une Fois' a 100% mourvèdre(C), a fantastically experimental wine which he makes only in the years when conditions are suitable. You may also be able to taste and perhaps buy his pure carignan called 'Renverse-moi'(A) i.e. 'Pour some', and that speaks for itself. He made this first in 2010 and it has become all the rage. It is vinified for a mere three days in tank.

***CHÂTEAU L'EUZIERE

Michel and Marcelle Causse
9 Ancien Chemin d'Anduze, 34270 Fontanès
Tel 04 67 55 21 41
Mobile 06 27 17 90 77
leuziere@chateauleuziere.fr www.chateauleuziere.fr

MAP 15
Cellars open every day except Sundays and public holidays.

The Causse family can boast four generations at this excellent property, whose name derives from *yeuse*, the local word for the evergreen oaks which make up so much of the vegetation on the *garrigue*. The *chais* is in the middle of Fontanès, easy to find, which is more than be said of many local growers who seem intent on hiding themselves from public view. Most of the 25 hectares are devoted to syrah, with mourvèdre and grenache as backers-up. The small production of white wine is from vermentino, grenache blanc and roussanne. The first is called 'Grains de Lune'(B), round and full-bodied but fresh too. Another white is called 'L'Or des Fous', intense and oaky with pineapple, brioche and almond flavours(C). 'Tourmaline' is the first of the reds, an everyday quaffable and supple wine(A/B), then 'L'Almandin'(B), from low-yielding syrah which have smaller fruit than usual, and finally 'Les Escarboucles'(C), marketed in burgundy-style bottles. The cherries and flowers evident in the wine are never smothered by the discreet oaking. The house-style can best

Fabien Reboul, Château de Valflaunès

be summed up as preferring elegance to power, though the wines seem to manage surprisingly high degrees of alcohol never apparent on the palate.

***CHÂTEAU DE LANCYRE   Régis Valentin

Lancyre, 34270 Valflaunès,
Tel   04 67 55 32 74
contact@chateaudelancyre.com
www.chateaudelancyr.com

MAP 16
Visits every day except Sundays 10.00 to 12.30 and 14.30 to 18.30.

This domaine has grown from the 15 hectares or so when it was bought by the Durand and Valentin families in 1970, to 75 today. The long chain of family ownership and work keeps the domaine in the vanguard of modern Pic wines, the youth of some stakeholders blending with the experience of others. For example Bernard Durand tells how his grand-father kept sheep here and how charcoal-burners lived and made their product in the woods above the property. To the original carignan and cinsault have been added syrah (first planted in 1972), grenache and mourvèdre. The wines, near to the top of the tree in the area, are exceptionally good value, selling for half (or even less) of the price you might pay for their peers. The range includes the white 'Rouvière' (B), a roussanne/marsanne/viognier blend given some oak ageing; an excellent rosé(A) which enjoys a tremendous reputation for its exotic fruits; and a sequence of reds: 'Coste

d'Aleyrac'(A), an easy-going quaffer; 'Clos des Combes'(B), fruity and with a good finish; two Pic wines, 'Vieilles vignes'(B) from syrah and grenache; the 'Grande cuvee'C), huge, almost black, more obviously showing wood-ageing and needing time to show its best; finally 'Madame'(D). matured in tank and rather like a dry Banyuls without being fortified.

BD ****CLOS MARIE

Françoise Julien and Christophe Peyrus
Route de Cazeneuve, 34270 Lauret
Tel   04 67 59 06 96
clos.marie@orange.fr

MAP 19
Appointment essential.

Both Françoise's and Christophe's parents had been members of the local *coopérative*, but Christophe, a native of Cahors and once a marine, decided in 1990 that they should make and bottle their own wine from Françoise's family vineyard. They have since established this domaine (converted to bio-dynamic production in 2000) as just about the top reference for this *appellation*. Yields are low at this property and any replanting of vines is done at high density. Plants are not cloned but produced at the domaine by *selection massale*. *Cuvaisons* here are long and cool, avoiding the necessity for either filtration or fining. Note that the wines are hardly cheap. The domaine, which you may need help to find, is named after Françoise's grandmother. It consists today of about 20 hectares of grenache and syrah, with a little mourvèdre for the reds, and a variety of *cépages* for their *foudre*-aged white, called 'Cuvée Manon'(C) after their daughter. The all-grenache rosé(B) is one of the crispest and deepest in the area, very high class. 'L'Olivette'(B/C) is the first of the reds, a very superior entry-level wine, 'Cuvée Simon'(C/D), named after the son of the house, is aged in wood until it is bottled during the summer two years after the vintage. 'Métairies du Clos' in its white version is a classically vinified and oak-aged example(D), while the red(D) is mostly from old carignan and is aged in old barrels and *foudres*. The top red 'Les Glorieuses'(D) comes from their best parcels and spends two years in oak. Very fine wines indeed.

B ***CHÂTEAU DE CAZENEUVE

Anne et André Leenhardt
9 Route de Cazeneuve, 34270 Lauret
Tel   04 67 59 07 49
Mobile   06 63 10 16 61
chateaucazeneuve@orange.fr   www.cazeneuve.net

MAP 20
Appointment recommended.

Audrey Bonmarchand, Mas de l'Oncle

In 1988, André Leenhardt discovered that vines grew better at Pic St Loup than thyme or arnica, which had been his speciality in his days as a consultant on aromatic plants. So he bought this domaine complete with a range of outbuildings. One of these has since been converted into a week-enders' pilgrimage-restaurant, where the wine list contains over 100 Languedoc references. The vineyard today extends to 35 hectares. The 17th century winery has a rustic feel apart from the gleaming stainless steel tanks which line the walls. The estate was formerly given over to table-grapes, so André has replanted with the usual Languedoc varieties for his reds, and for his white wine roussanne, grenache blanc, vermentino, muscat and viognier. These make up his Coteaux du Languedoc(C), which he ages in barrel. 80 % of the vineyard is however given over to making reds, not forgetting an elegant rosé called 'Cynarah'(A/B), made and aged in wood. There are three reds: 'Les Calcaires'(B/C) partly raised in one-year old barrels for twelve months, the rest in tank, 'Le Roc des Mates'(C) given 18 months wholly in barrels 20% of which are new. This wine comes from the oldest syrah vines in the vineyard, low-yielding and harvested parcel by parcel. The top wine is 'Le Sang du Calvaire' (D), which is virtually all mourvèdre and aged for 2 years in new wood .

B *** MAS DE L'ONCLE

Audrey and Fabrice Bonmarchand
Place Miolane, 34270 Lauret
Tel 04 67 67 26 16
Mobil 06 47 71 72 06
contact@masdeloncle.com   www.masdeloncle.com

MAP 21
Caveau open May-September 10.00-13.00 and 14.00-18.00. October-April same hours but Wednesday, Friday and Saturday only.

Fabrice was once a building engineer, but returned to his native roots in the Pic to take over the vineyards once farmed by the previous owner's uncle. Hence the name of the *domaine*. Starting with 10 hectares in 2001 (a further five are being planted) the *domaine* is now wholly organic, with hand-harvesting and, in the cellar, no pumping over, and gravity feeding wherever possible. A feature of the domaine is the use of chenanson, a cross of grenache and jurançon noir, from which a varietal called 'Denis'(B) is made by *macération carbonique* and aged in barrel for 12-18 months. 2 hectares of grapes, mostly sauvignon and marsanne with just a little muscat, go to make a white 'Plaisir Blanc'(B), while a rosé 'Émy'(B) is mostly grenache with a little cinsault.

Merlot appears in a 'Plaisir Rouge'(A), while syrah-based blends include 'Cuvée Élégance' with grenache(B); the more ambitious 'Cuvée Jules' with carignan and cinsault as well; and 'Cuvée François'(D) with mourvèdre and raised in tank, not wood. This is an exciting and go-ahead estate.

B ***CHÂTEAU LASCAUX
Jean-Benoit Cavalier
Route de Brestalou, 34270 Vacquières
Tel   04 67 59 00 08
Mobile   06 15 10 51 34
info@chateau-lascaux.com   jb.cavalier@chateau-lascaux.com
www.chateau-lascaux.com

MAP 24
Phone ahead.

After a history of 13 generations, Jean-Benoit took direction of and re-created this *domaine* in 1984, consolidating the vineyards and restructuring the old *caves*. However you count up the hectares, this is a large *domaine* for the region, and justly one of the most respected. Unusually the white wines are as interesting as the red. There are two, a 'Classique' (B), dominated by vermentino, and a more ambitious 'Pierres d'Argent'(C) where marsanne and roussanne are the main stars, fermented and aged in a mix of old and new wood for 9 months and finished in tank. The rosés follow a similar pattern, a 'Classique'(B) and 'Carra Rosé'(B). A traditional red blend is sold as Languedoc AOP(B), and it can be drunk young or kept a few years. Jean-Benoit does not have much mourvèdre: it sometimes doesn't ripen up in this climate, so the reds follow a syrah/grenache pattern; 'Carra rouge'(B)is tank-raised while 'Les Nobles Pierres'(C) is aged in small part in new barrels, otherwise the wood is old. This wine manages to combine elegance and concentration. 'Les Secrets'(D) is from the best parcels and the syrah and grenache are blended together at the point of fermentation. Do not spurn the range of IGPs sold as Domaine Cavalier (A/B) which see merlot and cabernet added to the range of black grapes, and sauvignon to the whites.

B ***DOMAINE ZUMBAUM-TOMASI
Jorg Zumbaum
Rue de Cagarel, 34270 Claret
Tel   04 67 55 78 77

domainezumbaumtomasi@wanadoo.fr
www.domaine-zumbaum-tomasi.com

MAP 27
Phone for apppointment.

Zumbaum is a Berlin lawyer, Signora Tomasi his Italian wife. The winemaker is Moroccan so this is a cosmopolitan vineyard as well as being a very highly-regarded one. The principal wine year on year is called 'Clos Maginiai'(B/C), a blend of 80% syrah and 20% grenache. The élevage

nowadays is rather more subtle and gentle than it once was; about 20% of the wine is raised in barrel. Typically the wine offers up a bouquet of wild flowers and tobacco: big on the palate, soft velvety and very flavoursome. Much admired.

BD ***MAS FOULAQUIER
Pierre Jéquier and Blandine Chauchat
Route des Embruscalles, 34270 Claret
Tel   04 67 59 96 94
Mobile   06 09 52 77 53
contact@masfoulaquier.com   www.masfoulaquier.com

MAP 28
Cellars open June-September 10.00-12.00 and 15.00-18.00.
Otherwise by appointment.

Pierre Jéquier is a native of Switzerland and was once an architect before discovering Foulaquier in 1998. It is a more or less self-contained family village and the tastings are held on the threshold of the old bread oven. Blandine, a civil servant from Paris turned *oenologue*, arrived in 2003, bringing with her three hectares of vine to add to Pierre's 8 and they have since acquired some more vines bringing the total to about 15. Their single white 'La Chouette Blanche'(D) mostly from grenache blanc, redolent of pears but with fresh minerality, is a prelude to a list of six reds: 'Les Tonillières'(C), a syrah/carignan blend with the carignan very much to the fore; 'L'Orphée'(C) from syrah and grenache, with its complex fruity/gamey nose and hints of ratatouille on the palate; and 'Le Rollier'(C) from the same grapes, spicy and with good grip. There follow 'Les Calades'(C?D), with rather more syrah than Grenache; 'Le Petit Duc'(D), almost all grenache which Pierre thinks is the ideal grape for his terroir; and finally 'GranT'(D), a huge oaky and tannic wine which needs long keeping.

***DOMAINE DE LAVABRE
Émilie and Étienne Bridel
Route de Pompignan, 34270 Claret
Te   09 66 90 40 90 and   04 67 55 02 25
Mobiles Étienne 06 28 58 60 20   Émilie 06 14 58 16 82
emiliebridel@orange.fr

MAP 29
Cellars open Monday to Saturday 16.00-19.00 (Saturday 9.00-15.00) but rendez-vous still recommended.

Olivier Bridel has in his time been a maverick but sympathetic winemaker, hailing from Normandy where he used to run a successful electrical engineering business. He bought this domaine with just over 30 hectares in 1990, with its syrah going back to 1961 long before the grape became fashionable in Languedoc. It has now been passed to his children, Émilie and Etienne. Organic by nature but not by certification, the Bridels believe in hard pruning and high density planting, resulting in low yields, especially from the newer syrah. Much has been spent on both the vineyards and the cellar, the latter being on a slope and thus allowing much of the activity to be done by gravity rather than pumping. There are three reds produced from these 30 hectares: the *entrée-de-gamme* Pic Saint Loup(A/B), a traditional syrah/grenache/mourvèdre blend, light, fruity and irresistibly more-ish; 'Les Demoiselles'(B), mostly syrah and grenache with a touch of carignan, well-made and with fine balance, aged in old barrels, and 'Château Lavabre'(C), a much bigger proposition, but nowadays with the oak less prominent than at one time, and the wine altogether of a more classic and less New World character.

BD ***ZÉLIGE-CARAVENT

Luc and Marie Michel
Chemin de la Gravette, 30260 Corconne
Tel   04 66 77 10 98
Mobile   06 87 32 35 02
contact@zelige-caravent.fr www.zelige-caravent.fr

MAP 30
Appointment recommended.

'Zélige' refers apparently to a type of Moroccan tile, of which the landscape here reminds these owners; while 'Caravent' refers to caravanserai, a roadside inn along the old spice routes. Luc, reconnecting with his grandfather's roots as a vine-grower, and with help from Marie who still works as a painter and mother, took over just 3 hectares in Corconne in 1999. Today they have 15, divided among 25 different plots. The stony gravel and pebbly soil at Corconne can be up to 5 metres deep, allowing the vines to plunge without obstruction, and thus ensuring a good access to water. The Michels have also restored old plantations of olives, which had been largely destroyed in the frosts of 1956. Apart from the usual Languedoc black grapes, including an abundance of carignan, the vineyard also has some alicante and , for the whites some chasan as well as more recently planted roussanne. The chasan is a cross between chardonnay and listan and is at the base of the white(B) 'Un Poco Agitato' given three days of skin contact. There are a varying number of reds including 'Velvet'(C) from old family syrah vines blended with cinsault; 'Manouches'(B) a blend of alicante and cinsault which has to be labelled Vin de France;'Ellipse'(B), mostly carignan , a wine which needs keeping, 'Fleuve Amour'(D) is mostly from some of the oldest grenache and aged 20 months in barrel, while the pure alicante, 'Nuit d'Encre'(C) is named after the deep colour of this *teinturier* grape. Most recently there is 'Ikebouna(C)' largely from cinsault and carignan, with some grenache and syrah. None of the wines here are vinified or aged in barrel and they quickly sell out to an enthusiastic band of specialist *habitués*. Note that the blends but not the names are liable to change from year to year. The labels, designed by Marie of course, are as original as the wines. She says she hand-paints 4000 labels every year.

Marie Michel, Zélige-Caravent

BD *** DOMAINE MIRABEL

Samuel and Vincent Feuillade
30260 Brouzet-les-Quissac
Tel   04 66 77 48 88
Mobile   06 22 78 17 47 and 06 16 69 53 73
domainemirabel@neuf.fr

MAP 31
Appointment recommended.

The brothers Feuillade withdrew some of their grapes from the local *coopérative* in 2001 when they saw promise ruined by mass-production. Today the 12 hectares which they have retained for themselves are at the northern limits of the Pic *appellation*, with swings in temperature from day to night which ensure good acidity, elegance and finesse. Now fully biodynamic, their use of sulphur is limited to tiny quantities at the bottling stage. Yields are low at 20/25 hl/ha. Second fermentation is blocked for the white and the rosé. The white 'Le Loriot'(B) is 2/3rds viognier and 1/3rd roussanne, vinified in barrel. then transferred to vat before bottling. The apricot flavours associated with viognier are moderated here. A rosé(A) mostly from equal quantities of cinsault and grenache with a just a dash of syrah is just as attractive. Wait to see what is the result of his planting some petit manseng. There are three reds, vinified and aged in 20% new 400-litre barrels: 'Les Bancels' (60% syrah, 20% each mourvèdre and carignan, sometimes with some cinsault) is from vines grown on the higher ground, beautifully balanced and the wood is well integrated(B); 'Le Chant du Sorbier'(B) has 55% grenache, 35% mourvèdre and only 10% syrah, with richer fruit than the Bancels, and just as fine. The top red is 'Les Eclats'(C) half syrah, the rest equally grenache and mourvèdre; the fruit is soft and round , as are the silky tannins, but there is still lovely acidity to balance.

MAS D'AUZIÉRES   Philippe and Irène Tolleret
Route de Saint-Mathieu, 34820 Guzargues
Tel   06 25 45 16 60
philippe@auzieres.com   auzieres@gmail.com

MAP 34
Off the beaten track so appointment recommended.

Irène Tolleret and her husband set up this domaine in 2003. She had previously been a marketing executive for Val d'Orbieu before they bought this estate from Geneviève and Laurent Vidal, who afterwards moved to Mas Conscience on the Terrasses du Larzac (q.v.), The Tollerets had the good fortune to take over a well-managed vineyard, mostly syrah, but with some grenache and carignan too. They are just outside the official Pic Saint Loup area, and are still fighting to get inside it. So their entry wine is simply Languedoc AOP, a nice fruity jammy, straightforward effort(A). More exciting is 'Les Éclats', mostly syrah, sometimes smokey and meaty but well balanced and quite classy(B/C). 'Sympathie pour les Stones' is denser and altogether bigger(C), though it feels quite soft and the tannins are smooth. They don't do much oak, though they have one red which is given some barrel-ageing called 'Les bois de Périe'(B/C). Much recommended , this vineyard has a good following. ·

OTHER GOOD GROWERS AT PIC SAINT LOUP

CHEMIN DES RÊVES   Benoît Viot
218 Rue de la Syrah, 34280 St.Gély du Fosc.
Tel   04 99 62 74 25
Mobile   06 85 73 29 33
contact@chemin-des-reves.com   www.chemin-des-reves.com
MAP 1
Visits Monday to Saturday 16.00-19.00.

*LA CAVE DES VIGNERONS DU PIC
285 Avenue de Sainte-Croix, 34820 Assas
Tel   04 67 65 93 55
www.vigneronsdupic.net
MAP 3
Cellars open Tuesdays to Saturdays (also Monday during summer) from 9.00-12.00 and 14.00-18.00. There is another branch at Saint-Gély-du-Fesc a few kilometres to the west.

**DOMAINE DE LA PERRIÈRE
Véronique and Thierry Sauvaire
Route de Saint-Vincent de Barbeyrargues, 34820 Assas
Tel   04 67 59 61 75
thierry.sauvaire@free.fr   www.domaine.perriere.free.fr
MAP 4
Cellars open Monday to Friday 17.00-19.00, Saturdays 9.00-19.00 otherwise by appointment.

**DOMAINE HAUT-LIROU
Jean-Pierre Rambier fille et fils
34270 Saint Jean de Cuculles,
Tel   04 67 55 38 50
GPS 43. 45'45.92"N 03. 50'39.36"E
info@hautlirou.com   www.hautlirou.com
MAP 5
Cellars open Monday to Saturday 9.00-12.30 and 14.30-18.30 and (summertime only) on Sunday 10.00-12.30 and 14.30-19.00.

**CHÂTEAU DE VALCYRE-BÉNÉZECH GAFFINEL
Alexandre Bénezech Gaffinel and Jacques Gaffinel
Château de Valcyre, 34270 Valflaunès
Tel   04 67 55 28 99
Mobile   06 11 21 56 71
This property is twinned with Château Valcyre (or at least they share some facilities), and between them they produce a range of good value wines.

**CHATEAU DE VALCYRE
Tel   04 67 55 22 03
Mobile   06 03 46 45 11
contact@chateau-valcyre.fr   or valcyre-gaffinel@orange.fr
www.chateau-valcyre.fr
MAP 12
Cellars open Wednesday Thursday and Friday 17.00-19.00 and Saturday 14.00-19.00.

MAS DE FOURNEL   M. Gérard Jeanjean
34270 Valflaunès
Tel   04 67 55 22 12
masdefournel@free.fr   www.masdefournel.com
MAP 13
Rendez-vous recommended.
Can this M. Jeanjean be immortal ? Well into his eighties, and a man who started a new career in winemaking at the age of 70, now presides over a small and less well-known estate towards the northern end of the Pic district, making classy wines which need keeping.

BD **CHATEAU LA ROQUE**   Jacques Figuette
La Roque, 2 chemin de St Matthieu, 34270 Fontanès
Tel   04 67 55 34 47
contact@chateau-laroque.fr   www.chateau-laroque.fr
MAP 14
Cellars open Monday to Friday from 13.00-17.00 and Saturdays by appointment.
M. Figuette took over this property in 2008 and immediately set about converting its 32 h to organic production.

Délestage in progress

**DOMAINE PECH TORT

Nadège and François Jeanjean
419 route de Pompignan, 34270 Valflaunès
Tel   04 67 55 27 53
Mobile   06 18 92 65 08
nadegejeanjean@domaine-pech-tort.com
www.domaine-pech-tort.com
MAP 17
Cellars open ; Tuesday to Friday 17.00-19.00, Saturday and Sunday
10.00-12.00 and 16.00-20.00 .
Another family of ex-*coopérateurs*, who left to make their own first
vintage in their new *cave* in 2008.

**BERGERIE DU CAPUCIN

Guilhem et Christelle Viau
Mas de Boisset, 34270 Valflaunès.
Tel   04 67 59 01 00
Mobile   06 87 83 11 84
contact@bergerieducapucin.fr   www.bergerieducapucin.fr
MAP 18
Visits to new cellar every Friday and Saturday 10.30-12.30 and
16.00-19.00, otherwise by appointment (by mobile).
This is a 12-hectare vineyard., with organic tendencies, where Guil-
hem intends to re-roof with solar panels, to produce his own bio
fuels and to recycle water.

**MAS THÉLÈME   Fabienne and Alain Bruguière

Route de Cazeneuve, 34270 Lauret
Tel   04 67 59 53 97
mas.theleme@orange.fr   www.mas-theleme.com
MAP 22
Appointment required on weekdays. Open Saturdays 10.00-12.00
and 17.00-19.00 and Sundays (except Sundays in January) 10.00-
12.00.

**CHATEAU DE LASCOURS

Claude, Elyette and Lise Arles
Hameau de Lascours, 34270 Sauteyragues
Tel   04 67 59 00 58
domaine.de.lascours@wanadoo.fr   www.chateau-lascours.com
MAP 23
Cellars open every day 10.00-12.00 and 14.00-18.00.

B **MAS PEYROLLE Jean-Baptiste Peyrolle

Route du Brestalou, 34270 Vacquières
Tel   04 67 55 99 50
Mobile   06 12 29 53 91
GPS 43 50 44.008N 3 56 48.419 E
jbpeyrolle@yahoo.fr   www.maspeyrolle.com
MAP 25
Appointment necessary.

***DOMAINE LES GRANDES COSTES

Jean-Christophe Granier
2 Route du Moulin à Vent, 34270 Vacquières
Tel   04 67 59 27 42
Mobile   06 89 10 10 68
contact@grandes-costes.com   www.grandes-costes.com
MAP 26
Visits Monday to Saturday by appointment.
Jean-Christophe was director of publicité at La Revue du Vin de
France at a time when his grandfather, at the end of a long line of
vignerons, retired at the age of 88.

**DOMAINE D'AIGUES BELLES

Gilles Palatan, Patrice et Thierry Lombard
30260 Brouzet-les-Quissac
Tel   06 07 48 74 65
www.aigues-belles.com
MAP 32
This is an all-IGP domaine. Very good value here, all (B) and any
oak is usually well-handled.

*DOMAINE DE SIGALIÈRE André Moulière

Ancien Chemin de Carnas, 30260 Carnas
Tel   04 66 35 50 64
Mobile   06 63 01 39 90 and   06 81 03 11 92
marie.vins.sigaliere@gmail.com   www.vins-sigaliere.com
MAP 33
Phone in advance.
These vineyards were formerly part of a much larger estate, the domaine
de Monteil, a one-time important abbey. The wines are good
and are reasonably priced.

North and East of Montpellier

This section covers those parts of the Grès de Montpellier to the north and east of Montpellier, including those crus of Vérargues, Saint Christol, Saint Drézéry and La Méjanelle, which are entitled to add those names on their labels. In general, the rules for the *appellations* are the same as for the rest of the Grès on the other side of Montpellier, with a preponderance of grenache, syrah and mourvèdre in the wines. So as to qualify, each *assemblage* must have at least 70% of these grapes, of which there must be at least two in the make-up.

As elsewhere, the rigidity of the rules has persuaded many growers to make wines outside the appellations, for example, to make good use of their carignan and cinsault which can appear as only minority grapes in the AOP wines. As ever, the identity of the grower is more important than the régimes under which he/she makes his/her wines.

A general feature of these wines is their spicy, aromatic character.

** DOMAINE ELLUL FERRIERES
Sylvie et Gilles Ellul
D 610 Fontmagne, 34160 Castries
Mobile   06 15 38 45 01
contact@chateau-ellul.com   www.domaine-ellul.com

MAP 1
Cellars open Monday to Saturday from 17.00-19.00.

Sylvie is a trained oenologist, formerly president of the Syndicat des Producteurs de Vins de Pays d'Oc. Gilles was formerly a property man, for whom the transition to *vigneron* has been his road to Damascus. Starting in 1997 with just three hectares of grenache, grown *en gobelet* and embedded in a thick layer of *galets roulés*, today the *domaine* still does not extend beyond five, which include some syrah. Their rosé, 'Demoiselle Laure' (B) is a blend of the two, raised in new barrels for a period of four months. The *élevage* is limited so that the wine is ready for bottling the following spring. 'Libre Ellul' (A) is their first unoaked red, and 'Les Romarins' (B) their second (it has a little mourvèdre too). Both are easy-drinking wines in a traditional style. 'Grande Cuvée' (C) is more ambitious, aged in barrel for a year and then another year in tank before bottling. Finally, there is a sweet red grenache (C) from super-ripe grapes which have been allowed to shrivel on the vine. With 16% alcohol, the wine has 60 grams of residual sugar on average. A small but exciting *domaine*.

Rémy Pédréno, Roc d'Anglade, p.264

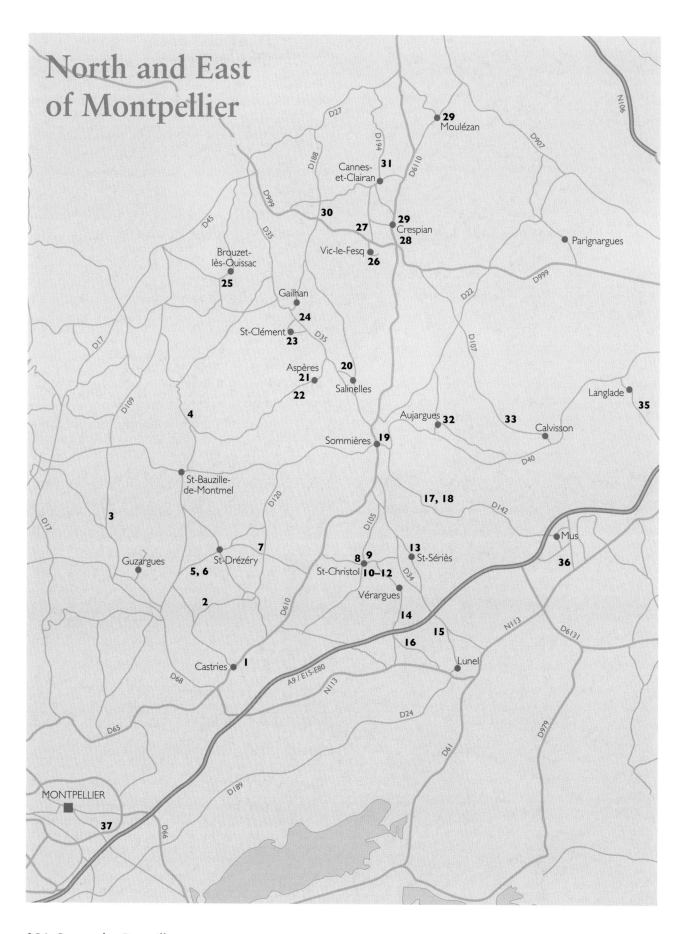

North and East of Montpellier

29 Moulézan

31 Cannes-et-Clairan

30

27 **29** Crespian

28

Vic-le-Fesq

26

Parignargues

Brouzet-lès-Ouissac

25

Gailhan

24

St-Clément

23

Aspères

21 **20**

22 Salinelles

Langlade

35

4

Aujargues **32**

33

Calvisson

Sommières **19**

St-Bauzille-de-Montmel

17, 18

3

Mus

7

13

36

Guzargues

St-Drézéry

8 **9** St-Sériès

5, 6

St-Christol **10–12**

2

Vérargues

14

15

16

Castries **1**

Lunel

MONTPELLIER

37

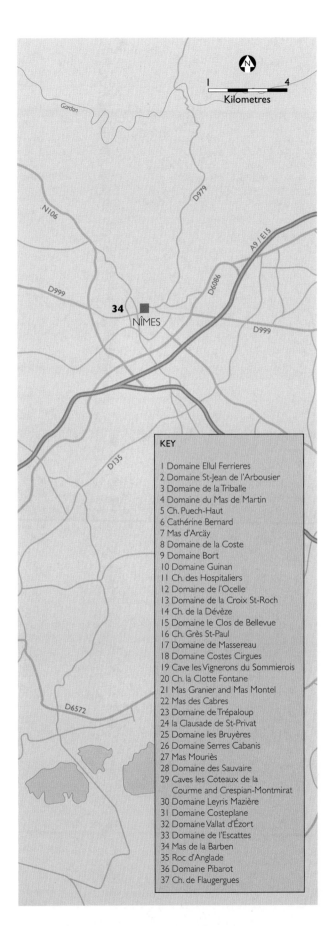

KEY

1 Domaine Ellul Ferrieres
2 Domaine St-Jean de l'Arbousier
3 Domaine de la Triballe
4 Domaine du Mas de Martin
5 Ch. Puech-Haut
6 Cathérine Bernard
7 Mas d'Arcäy
8 Domaine de la Coste
9 Domaine Bort
10 Domaine Guinan
11 Ch. des Hospitaliers
12 Domaine de l'Ocelle
13 Domaine de la Croix St-Roch
14 Ch. de la Dévèze
15 Domaine le Clos de Bellevue
16 Ch. Grès St-Paul
17 Domaine de Massereau
18 Domaine Costes Cirgues
19 Cave les Vignerons du Sommierois
20 Ch. la Clotte Fontane
21 Mas Granier and Mas Montel
22 Mas des Cabres
23 Domaine de Trépaloup
24 la Clausade de St-Privat
25 Domaine les Bruyères
26 Domaine Serres Cabanis
27 Mas Mouriès
28 Domaine des Sauvaire
29 Caves les Coteaux de la
   Courme and Crespian-Montmirat
30 Domaine Leyris Mazière
31 Domaine Costeplane
32 Domaine Vallat d'Ézort
33 Domaine de l'Escattes
34 Mas de la Barben
35 Roc d'Anglade
36 Domaine Pibarot
37 Ch. de Flaugergues

**DOMAINE SAINT-JEAN DE L'ARBOUSIER Jean-Luc, Nicolas and Catherine Viguier
34160 Castries
Tel 04 67 87 04 13
Mobile 06 15 74 17 56
GPS 43 . 71'2712" 3.96' 83 0557
contact@domainearbousier.fr www.domainearbousier.fr

MAP 2
Cellars open out of season, Saturdays from 9.00-12.00 and 14.00-19.00 or by appointment; in the summer, Monday to Saturday from 9.00-12.00 and 14.00-19.00.

The Viguier family have been at their lovely estate for a long time with more than a hundred hectares, forty of which are under vine, surrounded by umbrella pines and *arbousiers*, trees which bear a strawberry-like fruit in autumn. The pretty buildings form three sides of a square and the Viguiers are much into oeno-tourism, including the provision of '*cabanes*' in the trees as well as on the ground for people wanting to stay. There are also arts and crafts days, walks through the vineyards, and at Christmas and the New Year, a Provençal-style crèche and open-air farm. The good news is that the wines do not take second place to all this. A range of very satisfactory good-value bottles (all A/B) start with a white blend including some viognier and vermentino, giving a fairly explosive aromatic wine. The red AOP Languedoc from syrah and grenache usually offers cassis, spices, good depth and structure. The IGPs from cabernet, merlot and some syrah in the blend are less noteworthy but very drinkable all the same. A fun visit.

B ***DOMAINE DU MAS DE MARTIN
Christian Mocci, Oenologist Jean-Philippe Bourlès
Route de Carnas, 34160 St Beauzille-de-Montmel
Tel 04 67 86 98 82
Mobile 06 09 88 22 95
GPS 43 47'26" 3 57'41"
masdemartin@gmail.com www.masdemartin.fr
boutique@masdemartin.fr

MAP 4
Cellars open every day 9.00-12.00 and 13.30-18.00.
Rendezvous to visit the vineyards.

Mocci was once a history professor, and his sense of the importance of the past does not impede his recognition that the production of wine also advances from day to day. He established himself at this Mas with its 19 hectares some 20 years back, and has since planted what he considers the important grapes for him, as well as modernising the *chais* and cellars. Organic certification has been in place since 2012. Bourlès is in permanent residence with a complement of three personnel. The grapes are hand-picked and sorted twice to ensure elimination of poor fruit. The wines are aged in barrel for periods varying from nine to 18 months, neither filtered nor fined and accorded only the minimum of sulphur. The wines are far from conventional. Try the sweet rosé (A/B), made from muscat d'Hambourg, normally a table grape; 'Amour et Psyché' (A), a sweetish white muscat in 50-cl. Bottles; and the range of eight reds which span

Working *cave*

all styles and price ranges. There is 'Casanova' (B), round and long on the palate; 'Venus' (B), appropriately soft and warm; 'Terra du Languedoc' (C) dark and fruity; 'Plein Sud' (C), dark and balsamic; 'Cinarca' (C), mostly grenache, chocolatey and spicy, with blackberries and cherries, elegant and powerful at the same time; 'Utreia' (D), with the accent on sweet syrah; and 'Ecce Vino' (D), half mourvèdre and given two years in new wood.

✶✶✶CHÂTEAU PUECH-HAUT Gérard Bru
2250 route de Teyran, 34160 Saint-Drèzéry
Tel   04 99 62 27 27
contact@pech-haut.com   www.puech-haut.com

MAP 5
Cellars open Monday to Saturday usual hours, also Sundays from April through October.

Gérard Bru, a native of the Minervois where his father had had some vines, was already a successful businessman who had made for himself a substantial personal fortune by the age of 25. Lucky to be able to take such early retirement, he discovered this remote *domaine*, where he planted 100 hectares of vines (today there are 115), built a semi-underground *chais*, transported to site a substantial 19th century house, and within 10 years established himself as one of the most successful producers of the region. Nothing unusual about the grapes he chose: the usual Languedoc quintet for the reds and rosés, and roussanne, marsanne and grenache blanc for the whites. But his barrels are highly original, painted and decorated by over 100 painters and sculptors. All his wines (with one exception) are aged in them, the whites fermented in them too. The wood is renewed on a three-year cycle and the house style can be described as mainstream-modern. He has attracted the attention of Parker and Rolland. 'Le Benjamin' (A), unoaked, is the nearest you get here to a *vin des copains*, while 'Prestige' (B) and 'Tête de Cuvée' (C) describe both the two whites and two reds. The rosé 'Prestige' (B) has gained a phenomenal success as one of the best in France. A second range of wines is marketed under the title 'Complices de Puech-Haut' (A) and Bru is not ashamed to route much of his production through the *grandes surfaces*. His business instincts have no doubt prompted him to realise that the marketing of 100 hectares of grand cru wine is hard indeed in these days. Mention should also be made of a wine he makes from vines in the Pic Saint Loup, called 'Le Loup du Pic' (B/C).

B ✶✶CATHÉRINE BERNARD
34160 Saint-Drézery
Tel   04 67 79 02 01

MAP 6
Appointment essential.

Cathérine was (and still is when she has time) a journalist, and nowadays the proud possessor of three and a half hectares of vines as a near neighbour of Gérard Bru (see above). She has only black grapes: grenache, mourvèdre, marselan and smattering of cinsault. She would like to make white wine too one day, but meanwhile contents herself and her many customers with a

Serge Martin-Pierrat, Château des Hospitaliers

charming rosé, an all carignan *Vin de France*, as well as an IGP red blended from all her grapes. She does not leave them long on the skins and the wines are elegant and fresh with lovely light fruit and soft tannins. They are even better tasted the day after opening. They are much sought after and well worth following. All Price (B).

✶✶✶DOMAINE DE LA COSTE
Luc and Elisabeth Moynier
Chemin du Mas de la Coste, 34400 Saint-Christol
Tel   04 67 86 02 10 and 04 67 86 65 27
Mobile 06 88 90 65 20
luc.moynier@wanadoo.fr   www.domaine-coste-moynier.fr

MAP 8
Cellars open Monday to Saturday 9.00-12.30 and 13.30-19.30 Sundays from 9.00 by appointment.

For wines of this quality, the prices are still very reasonable, especially in view of the many medals these growers have won. Luc, a mustachioed giant with a gentle charm of manner, settled here in the 1970s, and for the first few years the couple sold their wine *en négoce*. Their first vintage on their own was 1981, with just 500 hectolitres of wine. In 2005 they made their first white (B) from roussanne and viognier which they had planted in 2001. Their 30 hectares of AOP vines are all on typically pebbly soil, which commentators invariably liken to that of Châteauneuf-du-Pape. There is also a deal of rather scruffy sandstone. Together, this *terroir* gives the wines a depth and power, even a rusticity rather than elegance. It also suits mourvèdre, their favourite red grape, which, being not far from the sea, thrives. The property is noted for its delightful rosé (A), a basket of ripe red fruits. Their reds range from IGPs from non-conforming grapes (B) to AOPs such as their 'Tradition' (A) from the quintet of the usual Languedoc varieties. There is also 'Cuvée Prestige' (A), mostly mourvèdre, then 'Cuvée Merlette' (B), with even more mourvèdre, and finally their 'Sélection Fûts' (B), their only oaked wine which they make from 80% syrah and 20% grenache.

B **DOMAINE BORT Frédéric Bort
154 Avenue de Platanes, 34400 Saint-Christol
Tel 04 67 86 06 03   Mobile 06 40 20 68 33
sceadomainebort@orange.fr www.domainebort.fr

MAP 9
Cellars open Monday-Friday, 9.00-12.00 and 14.00-18.00. Weekends and holidays by appointment. Groups on Saturdays.

At this newly created *domaine* (there is no *château* but the cellars are ultra-modern) they don't believe in the hierarchisation of wines, and they work to free themselves from the history of the region and the bad habit of rating the wines of Languedoc as being second class. With a relatively large area of 60 hectares, there is as yet only one white wine – a pure roussanne, part of a range called 'NO.1' (B). A rosé from syrah and grenache is called 'Bleu de Ciel' (B), 'Infiniment Rouge' (C) is from old-vine carignan and grenache which yield only 15 hl/ha, 'Secret de Famille' is the name given to another rosé and a red, both (A), from merlot, and another red from Languedoc grapes, 'Cuvée Prestige' (C) is as yet their top wine. A grower to watch.

**CHÂTEAU DES HOSPITALIERS
Serge Martin-Pierrat   Manager Sylviane Lepâtre
923 Avenue Boutonnet, 34400 Saint-Christol
Tel 04 67 86 03 50
GPS 43 / 44'07" N 4/05'28" E
martin-pierrat@wanadoo.fr www.chateaudeshospitaliers.fr

MAP 11
Cellars open every day from 9.00-19.00

Serge's parents were teachers, and when they found a house in the village of Saint Christol they found they had also to nurture four and a half hectares of vines. Serge, bitten by the bug of perhaps becoming a *vigneron*, looked around for more (he now has 32), but met a lot of opposition from the local *chasseurs*, who of course would be shut out of any land planted with grapes. Mistrustful of the aggressive non-interventionism of organic producers, he maintains on the other hand that copper, which they authorise, is deadly for a vineyard and will render the soil sterile

after 40 years of use. He also believes in hand-harvesting, the maximum use of gravity to avoid over-working, and the minimum use of sulphur. The cru Saint-Christol accounts for only a third or so of his output. The partly subterranean cellar was built by Serge himself in time for the 2004 harvest, and it has an open-air garden with a cooling pond in the middle. His whites (A/B) include a pure chardonnay from 80-year-old vines, and another which blends a lot of ugni blanc with it. His rosé (A) from syrah and grenache is partly vinified in barrel but aged in tank. His 'Rouge Sélection' (B), largely from mourvèdre blended with some syrah and grenache is aged in a mix of old and new barrels for two years, and then spends more time in tank before bottling. These are but few of the large range of wines here (all A and B), for which the repertoire of grapes includes gewurztraminer and sangiovese which make the pinot noir and ugni blanc relatively normal. The sangiovese is blended with 25% syrah to produce a wine raised in barrels for a year. An attractive and adventurous *domaine*, and good value, too.

SOMMIÈRES

This separate cru of Languedoc extends over an area 20 kilometres or so to the west of Nîmes, and enjoys (if that is the right word) the influence of the mistral. The vines are mixed in with olive trees, truffle oaks and the *garrigue*. Syrah and grenache are the order of the day here, but many growers, not wishing to be bound by the rules of any *appellation*, are making some of their wines (including the best ones) as IGPs. The wines of Langlade are said to have been favourites of the Avignon Popes and the nobility of the Midi, and are among the best Sommières wines today.

The vineyards are listed starting in the far north, continuing towards Nîmes before tracking backwards towards Montpellier via Lunel. If regarded as an itinerary, it could well be tacked on to the end of the Pic St. Loup growers.

BD **DOMAINE COSTES CIRGUES

Béatrice Althoff
1531 route d'Aubais, 30250 Sommières
Tel 04 66 71 83 85
Mobile   06 77 14 09 69
costescirgues@gmail.com   www.costes-cirgues.net

MAP 18
Cellars open Monday, Tuesday, Thursday and Friday
9.00-12.00 and 14.00-18.00.

Mme Althoff and her husband, a Swiss partnership, bought this beautiful property in 2003, when there were just 10 hectares of vines surrounded by olive trees and plenty of garrigue. Today there are 18 hectares and a brand new *chais*, built in 2007, where the winemaking is made by gravity and without pumps. Their son David, a qualified oenologist is in charge. The style here is for natural winemaking, and though many biodynamic principles are observed, cultured yeasts are used to enhance the natural ones. On the other hand, the wines are all sulphur-free. David has been making the wines during the last few years, and they are getting better all the time. The blends and the titles may vary, but currently there is a white from grenache blanc, viognier, vermentino and muscat (A/B), a rosé from syrah and carignan, picked early, so not *saigné* from the later reds (A/B). These include a carignan-led 'Montplaisir' (A/B) with dark cherries and spice, a very Languedoc 'St Cyr' (B) from grenache, and 'Bois du Roi' (B/C), for which the *élevage* may vary from being almost barrel-free to the use of wood for the syrah and grenache. 'Cuvée Syrah' (C) is their last red, 80% from that grape with 20% grenache. The wine is aged in oak, the barrels being renewed on a three-year cycle.

***MAS GRANIER and MAS MONTEL

Dominique and Jean-Philippe Granier
Cellier du Mas Montel, Cedex 1110, 30250 Aspères
Tel   04 66 80 01 21
GPS 43 ; 48' 41.4N   4 2'25.9"E
dgranier@masmontel.fr   www.masgranier.fr

MAP 21
Cellars open Monday to Saturday and by appointment on Sundays and holidays.

The *cave* here used to be an olive mill, then, once converted to a winery, it was lined with huge old *foudres* which are still there today – for decoration. The Granier brothers (Jean-Philippe, a consultant oenologist and Dominique, an economist) today make both AOP wines (Mas Granier) and IGPs (Mas Montel). The young Jean-Baptiste is currently doing his own thing with Olivier Jullien up on the Terrasses du Larzac, but maybe he will one day come home to the family *domaine*. The Montel vines are on the lower ground close to the Mas where the soil is *argilo-calcaire*, while the Granier vines are further up in the hills on wild stony ground. The best sellers here are 'La Petite Syrah' (A/B), a charmer with both good fruit and spice, a versatile more-ish style of wine, and 'Cuvée Psalmodi' (A), with a

high merlot content, given a short and sharp vinification for 12 days or so. But there is also 'Cuvée Jéricho' (B), a syrah/grenache blend, an AOP which shows its garrigue origins well. There are two whites: 'Bouquet de Blancs' (A) and 'Les Marnes' (B) from roussanne, grenache blanc and viognier, aged for nine months in wood. The rosés too are charmers (A). Fantastic value here – one of the best bets of the region.

B **DOMAINE DE TRÉPALOUP

Rémi and Laurent Vandôme
Rue du Moulin à L'Huile, 30260 Saint-Clément
Tel   04 66 77 48 39
Mobile   06 71 65 73 30
trepaloup@gmail.com   www.domainetrepaloup.com

MAP 23
Cellars open Wednesday and Friday 17.00-19.30 and Saturday 15.00-19.30. Otherwise by appointment.

The 20 hectares here are on chalky clay supported by pebbly hard chalk which drains well. They are surrounded by flavour-giving garrigue. There is no cinsault in the traditional mix of grapes, but there are some cabernet and merlot. Varietal IGPs (B) are made from sauvignon and viognier, carignan, mourvèdre, grenache, syrah, merlot and cabernet. Of the blends, 'La Raiole' is the easiest and fruitiest, 'Les Costes' a traditional tank-raised AOP (both B), while 'Clos des Oliviers' (C) is a syrah/mourvèdre blend given a year in barrel. Merlot is added for the 'Cuvée Réserve' IGP (C). There is a white grenache blanc/roussanne AOP (C), vinified and aged in barrel, and to round off try the VDN 'L'Or du Temps' (C) from sauvignon and roussanne, over-ripened on racks rather like prunes for a month before being pressed.

**DOMAINE DES SAUVAIRE

Sylvie and Hervé Sauvaire
Mas de Reilhe, 30260 Crespian
Tel   04 66 77 89 71
Mobile   06 85 80 94 52
sylvie@domaine-sauvaire.com   hervé@domaine-sauvaire.com
www.domaine-sauvaire.com

MAP 28
Cellars open 1st May-30th September, Monday-Saturday 9.30-12.00 and 15.00-19.00.
1st October-30April, Saturdays only 10.00-19.00. Otherwise by appointment.

The vineyard and the wines are named after the growers, but the name of the property is Mas de Reilhe, part of which goes back to the 16th century, subsequently enlarged to include twin gateways leading to a place where horses could be changed. 28 hectares of vines include some which are destined for IGPs. Otherwise the AOP grapes (the usual Languedoc varieties) are grown on a soil which is mostly sandstone. There are three ranges of wines under the name 'Mas Sauvaire', all IGPS (A). The white is almost all from vermentino with just a touch of grenache, the rosé from syrah, grenache (*saigné*) and cinsault (directly pressed), while the red has a spot of cabernet to add to a wine otherwise mostly grenache. 'Domaine de Sauvaire' (A/B) is an AOP group of wines in all three colours, as is 'Domaine de Reilhe' (B), where syrah (aged two years in tank) dominates the red and pink, and vermentino, showing nice acidity and roundness, again represents the white. No barrels here, at least not yet. Good value.

B ***DOMAINE LEYRIS MAZIÈRE
Odile and Gilles Leyris
Chemin des Pouges, 30260 Cannes et Clairan
Tel 04 66 93 05 98
Mobile 06 11 35 74 21
GPS 43 90'025" 4.08'019"
gilles.leyris@wanadoo.fr anaellegallou@gmail.com
www.domaineleyrismaziere.e-monsite.com

MAP 30
Visits by appointment.

A 15-year-old *domaine* which has been certified bio since 2004. The Leyris grow on their 11 hectares a deal of alicante, which makes up with 20% carignan their *haut de gamme* wine from that grape. Yields from it are exceptionally low, a mere 10 hl/ha, which explains the price (D). Their production is half inside and half outside the Languedoc *appellation*, so there is a grenache/merlot blend (A), as well as an unoaked AOP called 'L'Aiguier' (A), which is half grenache, the balance coming from carignan and syrah. The oaked red is called 'Les Pouges' (C) and is mostly syrah. 'L'Aiguier' (A) is also the name given to a modest pink and a white, both unoaked.

BD **DOMAINE COSTEPLANE
Françoise and Vincent Coste
30260 Cannes et Clairan
Tel 04 66 77 85 02
Mobile 06 46 46 79 49
GPS N43.55.071 E.4.05 390
domaine.costeplane@gmail.com www.costeplane.com

MAP 31
Visits by appointment.

These growers reopened the cellar of the *domaine* in 1982, after it had been shut up by Vincent's grandfather for seven years. They ripped out their aramon and gradually reduced the area of carignan to five hectares, replanting what they call "more interesting varieties such as chardonnay, cabernet sauvignon, merlot, grenache, syrah and even vermentino." They have a total of 30 hectares and the *domaine* is isolated, deep in the countryside. Biodynamic since 2010 (certified Demeter), they produce three ranges of wine: some *Vins de France* for easy drinking (A), IGPs from single varieties, e.g. vermentino and chardonnay (B), and AOP Languedoc wines, 'L'Arboussade rouge' (A/B), 'Le Pioche

de l'Oule' (B), which is quite spicy and more concentrated, and 'Les Cistes' (B/C) for which their syrah is raised in new wood, the grenache in *cuve*.

*DOMAINE VALLAT D'ÉZORT Frédéric Martin
30250 Aujargues
Mobile 06 28 33 06 38
vallat.dezort@sfr.fr

MAP 32
Telephone ahead.

An excellent good-value *domaine* which produces some interesting out-of-the way wines. Frédéric trained with François Caumette at L'Ancienne Mercerie in Faugères, so he is well qualified in Languedoc terms. But the wines (A/B) are not always typical: for example, the pure cinsault called 'Alégria' is light, fine and elegant with good acidity and no sign of that overweight muscle sometimes shown by lesser producers. The AOP red, 'Fantastica', has the same qualities, though the wine is bigger (a syrah/carignan/grenache blend). Don't forget either the rosé, which is a carignan/cinsault blend, very unusual and which shows a surprising gentleness.

ANGLADE

This commune is the most easterly of the Sommières region. It has at least three claims to fame: it was the home of Lawrence Durrell for many years; its wines were in the nineteenth century thought to be as good as those of Burgundy; and today it is home to a small bunch of fine winemakers. There are but six of them with a total of 90 hectares, a mere fraction however of the acreage under vine before the phylloxera.

*MAS DE LA BARBEN
Véronique and Marcel Hermann
vines at D 999, 30870 Parignargues, otherwise route de Sauve, 30900 Nîmes
Tel 04 66 81 15 88
GPS 43.85'6872" 4.24'1506"
masdelabarben@wanadoo.fr www.masdelabarben.com

MAP 34
Cellars open Monday to Friday 10.00-12.00 and 15.00-19.00
Saturday 10.00-12.30 and 15.30-19.30.

A family affair, this vineyard started in 1964 and there are now 45 hectares planted with the usual Languedoc varieties. The Mas itself is just outside Nîmes, and therefore convenient for visitors to that city. An easy-going entry range of wines, available also in bag-in-box format, is called 'Improviste'. The white is roussanne /vermentino, the pink grenache/cinsault and the red grenache/ syrah (all A). So far nothing remarkable, but there is consistent praise for other reds: 'Lauzières' (B), raised in *cuve*, where the grenache dominates, and 'Les Sabines' (C), where syrah is the major contributor, raised in *barriques* for up to two years. There is a top wine called 'Calice' (D), which is nearly all grenache and which was once viewed with favour by Robert Parker. A curiosity is the sweet blend of grenache and clairette called 'Omission' (C).

****ROC D'ANGLADE Rémy Pédréno
700 Chemin de Vignecroze, 30980 Langlade
Tel   04 66 81 45 83
contact@rocdanglade.fr   www.rocdanglade.fr

MAP 35
Telephone well ahead to make an appointment.

A rock indeed! Rémy came to wine rather later in life than most. Until his early 20s he never drank the stuff. Working on an IT project for the Tavel wine growers, he suddenly discovered the joys. He acquired a few vines near St. Gilles close to the Camargue, where he dipped his toe gently into one solitary barrel of carignan. The following year his production quadrupled (from less than an acre at nearby Clos de la Belle) and he made his wine in his parents' garage in Langlade. From there it was a short step to acquiring vines nearer home (today he has 10 hectares), but not before he had entered into a four-year partnership with the famous grower René Rostaing from the northern Rhone to supply Rostaing with wine for the latter's *vins de pays*. Independence as a fully grown winemaker came in 2002, with his first vintage on his own. He was an instant hit, making a play for the primacy of elegance and finesse over the brute force of many producers in the Midi. Since then he has become more and more enamoured of the carignan grape, which forms an increasing percentage of his one sole red (D). His style seems to lend itself to 'off' vintages like 2002 and 2008, and he does not aspire to high alcohol levels. He uses *demi-muids* for *élevage*, and even so only one-fifth of them are new, so the oak influence is very discreet. Rémy also makes a dry white chenin (D) from vines which he acquired from nearby Domaine Arnal before that estate closed. He ferments this in his *demi-muids* and he ages it there for the best part of two years. There is a rosé too (C), with a pronounced carignan character, so, although fairly powerful, the typical Pédréno elegance is still very present. Rémy does not bother with *appellations* or with organic certification, although he has been working biologically for many years. He is an absolutely outstanding if atypical winemaker, whose production is worth every euro of its high price.

LUNEL

There is a separate *appellation* for the Muscat wines made in the area around this town, half way between Montpellier and Nîmes. Some of the wines are conventional dry table wines, others are sweet and some are fortified. Because the total area of muscat is but 300 hectares and the *coopérative* at Vérargues has the lion's share, the growers also make wine (mostly red) under the usual Languedoc *appellations* and *crus*.

***DOMAINE DE LA CROIX SAINT-ROCH
Anne and Jean-Pierre Boissier
34400 Saint-Sériès
Tel   04 67 86 08 65
Mobile   06 84 24 28 58
info@lacroixsaintroch.com   www.lacroixsaintroch.com

MAP 13
Cellars open Monday to Saturday 10.00-12.00 and 16.00-18.00.

The *domaine* takes its name from the Mission cross which stands at the entrance to the vineyards. Jean-Pierre is passionate about his muscat grapes, from which he makes a diverse range of very different wines. His 'Piochs Blanc Sec' (A/B) is traditional, but Jean-Pierre believes that its character is influenced by the *garrigue* which surrounds the parcel from which this wine comes. Then there are two sweet wines from the same grape, but without the benefit of added alcohol. The more noteworthy of these comes from a parcel where the yields are only 10 hl/ha and the resulting wine (B/C) is said to be capable of lasting 50 years. The oddity from this *domaine* is called 'Le Must d'Ambrussum' (B) and is Jean-Pierre's idea of what the Romans might have drunk when they were camped in the nearby settlement of the same name. The wine is three-parts sweet and reaches only 12 degrees of alcohol. It is made from late-picked grapes, but fermentation is stopped before the wine can become fully sweet. A salmon-coloured rosé (A) derives from cinsault and syrah, from which the juice is *saigné*. Sometimes it suggests fennel as well as wild fruit, and is full-bodied. The first of two reds is, like the dry white, called 'Les Piochs' (A/B), and is a traditional syrah/ grenache/mourvèdre blend. The second, 'Via Villa' (B/C), has carignan added and enjoys 12 months in barrel. Eccentricity continues with a sweet carignan wine, 'Les Thermes d'Ambrussum' (B), a kind of red brother of the 'Must'. Finally, there is a range of old sweet wines, for which you will need a well-furnished credit card, but the newer wines are extremely good value.

**CHÂTEAU GRÈS SAINT PAUL

Jean-Philippe Servière
1909 Route de Restinclières, 34400 Lunel
Tel 04 67 71 27 90
Mobiles   06 08 89 09 54 and 06 08 31 83 02
contact@gres-saint-paul.com   www.gres-saint-paul.com

MAP 16
Cellars open Monday to Saturday 9.30-12.30 and 14.30-19.00.

The present *château*, built at the beginning of the last century, is on the site of a former church, built alongside the old Roman *Via Domitia* linking Provence with Spain. It is a suitable reminder of the opulence of Languedoc at the time before the eclipse of the wines of the Midi a hundred years ago. Servière, whose family goes back six generations to the 1830s, today has 24 hectares mostly given over to the muscat grape, which provides four styles of wine: a *Pétillant* (B) which is *moëlleux* in character; a dry white (A); a still *Moëlleux* (B); and a fortified sweet white (C) with 120 grams per litre of residual sugar. There are Languedoc reds too, all quite southern in style but raised in concrete tanks. The syrah, grenache and mourvèdre which go into these represent about 2/3rds of the total vineyard area. The grapes are grown on banks which follow the course of a long-since dried up river with lots of pebbles and smaller stones. 'Grange Philippe' (A) is the name given to a range of varietals from mourvèdre, syrah, merlot, chardonnay, sauvignon and viognier, as well as a pair of rosés, one from syrah, the other grenache. The reds are AOP Languedoc Grès de Montpellier, so a little mourvèdre is blended into 'Syrhus' (D), with some grenache too in 'Antonin' (B), and even more in 'Romanis' (B). 'Côté Sud' (C) is an all-merlot IGP. Good value for money here, especially in the middle ranges.

LA MÉJANELLE

The city of Montpellier has expanded in the same way as Bordeaux to incorporate within its urban area a number of vineyards. Those in the district called La Méjanelle have been absorbed into the Grès de Montpellier regional *cru*, but are still entitled to put the local name on their bottles. The fine wines made by Pierre Clavel are noted in the Pic Saint Loup section, and he retains vines in La Méjanelle as well as having planted new vines in his vineyard at Assas. La Méjanelle also includes:

***CHÂTEAU DE FLAUGERGUES

le Comte Henri de Colbert
1744 Avenue Albert Einstein, 34000 Montpellier
Tel 04 99 52 66 37
caveau@flaugergues.com   visiter@flaugergues.com
www.flaugergues.com

MAP 37
Cellars open Monday to Saturday all year from 9.00-12.30 and 14.30-19.00.
Also in the afternoons on Sundays and public holidays in July and August.

Montpellier is surrounded by *folies*, many built by tax farmers and other dignitaries before the Revolution. They were the new aristocracy. Etienne de Flaugergues had taste, and this very Tuscan mansion with its many cypress trees remains unchanged architecturally since 1740. The architect is unknown, but the building is remarkable for its internal iron staircase, which at first sight appears to have no visible means of support. Visitors cannot fail to be impressed by the magnificent furniture and furnishings, particularly the tapestries that adorn the staircase. The park and gardens are no less remarkable. A complete two-hour tour (well worth the modest charge) is a long one, especially for those who thought they were visiting a vineyard, but Monsieur le Comte is as charming as he is erudite, and the thirsty should be patient. He is careful to keep a just balance between his heritage and the wine business which helps to support it. If visitors don't want the full treatment they can just visit the *caveau* for free. The 30 hectares of vineyards, which go back to Roman times, were replanted from 1976 onwards. The good-value wines are exceptional in that the bottles are generally screw-capped, but that is no reflection on their quality. Two white blends, (A) and (B) respectively, and a pink 'Cuvée Rosée' (B) are perhaps less remarkable than the range of reds. A charming IGP merlot/cabernet blend called 'Cuvé de l'Oncle Charles' (A) is a prelude to three AOPs: 'Cuvée les Comtes' (B), a traditional blend raised in tank; the grenache-led 'Cuvée Sommelière' (B), the free-run wine being aged 18 months before bottling; and 'Cuvée Colbert' (C), the only barrel-aged wine here, two parts syrah, one part grenache with just a touch of mourvèdre.

OTHER GOOD GROWERS NORTH AND EAST OF MONTPELLIER

B *DOMAINE DE LA TRIBALLE

Olivier and Sabine Durand
34820 Guzargues
Tel 04 67 59 66 32 and 04 67 59 70 33
la_triballe@club-internet.fr   www.la-triballe.com
MAP 3
Visits Monday to Friday 17.30-19.00; Saturdays 10.00-12.30 and 16.30-19.30.

**MAS D'ARCÄY   Jean Lacauste
1080 route de Beaulieu, 34160 Saint-Drézéry
Tel   04 67 29 75 93
Mobile   06 76 04 21 11
lacaustej@yahoo.fr   www.arcay.fr
MAP 7
Cellars open Monday to Friday 17.00-19.00 and Saturday mornings 9.00-12.00. Otherwise by appointment.
Lacauste has been making and bottling his own wine only since 2011 from five of the 20 hectares he owns. They have attracted quite a bit of notice.

**DOMAINE GUINAND   Alain, Claude, Serge and Pierre Guinand
36 rue de l'Epargne, 34400 Saint Christol
Tel   04 67 86 85 55
contact@domaineguinand.com   www.domaineguinand.com
MAP 10
Cellars open Monday to Friday 10.00-12.00 and 15.00-18.00.
Saturday 9.00-12.00 and 14.00-18.00 (19.00 from May to October).

*DOMAINE DE L'OCELLE
Arnaud Warnery and Filipe da Silva
28 Avenue des Platanes, 34400 Saint-Christol
Tel   04 67 86 04 26
domainedelocelle@saint-christol.com   www.domainedelocelle.com
MAP 12
Appointment recommended.

*CHÂTEAU DE LA DÉVÈZE   Claudine Navarro
Route de Lunel, 34400 Vérargues
Tel   04 47 86 00 47
www.chateaudeladeveze.fr
MAP 14
Cellars open Monday to Saturday 9.00-12.00 and 14.00-18.00.
This property is not to be confused with the Domaine de Dévèze at Montoulieu near Ganges (q.v. under Terrasses du Larzac).

*DOMAINE LE CLOS DE BELLEVUE
Nicolas Charrière
Route de Sommières, 34400 Lunel
Tel   04 67 83 24 83
Mobile   06 83 24 11 85
GPS   43 41' 56.50 N   4 07'10.00 E
leclosdebellevue@gmail.com
www.domaine-le-clos-de-bellevue.com
MAP 15
Cellars open Monday to Saturday 09.00-12.30 and 15.00-19.00.

*DOMAINE DE MASSEREAU   Arnaud Freychet
30250 Sommières
Tel   04 66 53 11 20
vin@massereau.com   www.masserau.com
MAP 17
Guided visits Tuesday and Thursday at 17.00. Otherwise telephone ahead.
As well as 50 hectares of vines, this most attractive *mas* also plays host to a five-star camping, as well as offering a variety of facilities for weddings, seminars etc.

*CAVE LES VIGNERONS DU SOMMIÈROIS
contact Mary Daire or Charlotte Duverdier
2 rue de l'Amède, 30250 Sommières
Tel   04 66 80 03 31
Mobile   06 76 63 84 94
contact@les-vignerons-du-sommierois.com
www.les-vignerons-du-sommierois.com
MAP 19
Cellars open Monday to Saturday 09.00-12.30 and 15.00-19.00.
Sunday mornings during summer.
This is one of the better local *coopératives*, in fact a merger of three.

*CHÂTEAU LA CLOTTE FONTANE
Maryline et Philippe Pagès
30250 Salinelles
Tel   04 66 80 06 09
clotte@club-internet.fr   www.clotte.free.fr
MAP 20
Make an appointment to be on the safe side.

*MAS DES CABRES   Florent Boutin
12 le Plan, 30250 Aspères Cedex 1160
Mobile   06 23 68 14 24
GPS   43 80'779"N   4 03'852"E
masdescabres@hotmail.fr   www.masdescabres.com
MAP 22
Cellars open in April through September, Monday to Saturday 11.00-13.00 and 17.00-20.00; October through March, Monday to Saturday 17.00-19.00. Or by appointment.
In the 18th century, the owners used to farm goats here, hence the name. The wines are meaty in all senses of the word.

*LA CLAUSADE DE SAINT PRIVAT
Mathilde and Christophe Trémoulet
Chemin de la Tuilerie, 30260 Gailhan
Mobile   06 15 33 65 12
domaineclausadesaintprivat@orange.fr   www.clausade-saintprivat.fr
MAP 24
Cellars open Saturday morning 9.30-14.00, otherwise appointment recommended.

**DOMAINE LES BRUYÈRES
Christophe Combaluzier,30260 Brouzet-les-Quissac
Mobile ; 06 07 11 51 19
www.domaine-les-bruyeres.fr
MAP 25
Appointment essential.

*DOMAINE SERRES CABANIS   André Baniol
30260 Vic-le-Fesq,
Tel   04 66 77 93 15
Mobile   06 11 50 97 39
contact@serrescabanis.com
www.serres.cabanis.pagesperso-orange.fr/portail.htm
MAP 26
Appointment recommended.

B **MAS MOURIÈS   Eric and Solange Bouet
30260 Vic-le-Fesq
Tel   04 66 77 87 13
bouet.eric@wanadoo.fr   www.mas-mouries.com
MAP 27
Cellars open Monday to Saturday from 9.00-19.00. Sundays by appointment.
The 20 hectares of this family property rise from the river valley in terraces facing south and thus protected from the Mistral. A domaine well worth searching out.

*CAVES LES COTEAUX DE LA COURME and CRESPIAN-MONTMIRAT
30350 Moulèzan and 30260 Crespian
Tel   04 66 77 81 02
lescoteauxdelacourme@wanadoo.fr
www.lescoteauxdelacourme.com
MAP 29
Cellars open Monday to Saturday 9.00-12.00 and 15.00-18.00
This is a 70-member *coopérative* in the far north of the Sommières region, more a part of the Cévennes than Languedoc proper, but still making a range of wines from the local varieties.

B *DOMAINE DE L'ESCATTES
Dominique, Michelle and François Robelin
30240 Calvisson
Tel   04 66 01 40 58
snc.robelin@wanadoo.fr
MAP 33
Cellars open Tuesday, Thursday and Friday from 14.30-18.30 and Wednesday and Saturday from 8.30-12.30. Otherwise by appointment.
The *domaine* sits in a hollow surrounded by *garrigue* just north-east from Sommières. The Robelin family produce good-value no frills wines which show regular quality above the mainstream in the region.

B **DOMAINE PIBAROT   Philippe Pibarot
429 rue du Pont Neuf, 30121 Mus
Tel   04 66 53 36 35
Mobile   06 23 91 29 32
contact@domaine-pibarot.com
www.domaine-pibarot.pagesperso-orange.fr
MAP 36
Cellars open daily (10.00-12.00 and 17.00-20.00), except Wednesdays.

Costières de Nîmes

The Costières (meaning *'coteaux'*) form the cultural border between the Rhône Valley and Languedoc. Geographically they mark the point at which the garrigue and the Cévennes behind swing westwards away from the Rhône basin and start to run parallel with the Mediterranean coast. Reflecting its border status, the Costières can be said to be part either of Languedoc or of the Rhône Valley wine system. A limited selection of its best growers is included in this book because of tradition, because so many of its grape varieties belong in the Languedoc repertory rather than the Rhône, but so much of its *terroir* is more typically Rhône Valley.

The area of the Costières is lozenge-shaped, running parallel on one side with the canal linking the Rhône to the port of Sète, and on the other with the A9 motorway. At its southern tip is the ancient town of Saint-Gilles, an embarkation point for the crusaders in the Middle Ages when it was an important port near the mediaeval fortress of Aigues-Mortes. Beyond are the marshlands of the Camargue, and then the sea, next to which IGPs are made from grapes literally grown on the sand and called 'vins de sable'.

The Costières constitute a low-lying terrace between the prehistoric course of the river Rhône – which at one time ran just close to Nîmes and Montpellier – and the present-day estuary to the south. It rises from sea level to a height of not much more than 100 metres. Nîmes was the first city to be built by the Romans when they expanded their empire by crossing the Rhône. Its buildings are famous: there is the Maison Carrée, the vast arena in the centre of the city, and above all the world-famous Pont du Gard, which used to carry the water supply to the city from the hills beyond.

The countryside around Nîmes is statistically one of the hottest regions in France, but the Mediter-

Château Beaubois

ranean climate is somewhat modified by the wind. The Mistral can blow hard here, but it quickly clears the sky and dries the vines after summer storms. Further geographical advantage is provided by the thick protective layers of pebbles which prevent the subsoils from drying out completely during the summer, enabling the roots of the vines to plunge deep into the ground. These are the famous *galets roulés*, washed down the Rhône when the Alps burst forth from the earth in prehistoric times. These stones are like the ones to be found at Châteauneuf-du-Pape and in various vineyards to the north of Nîmes. Being large they have the capacity to retain the heat of the midday sun and reflect it back on to the underside of the grapes during the night, thereby hastening the ripening of the fruit. They characterise the *terroir* of the region, especially at its eastern and western ends, which sandwich an area of more clay in the middle. Rain, though it comes seldom, buckets down on the few wet days there are. It quickly sinks through the *galets* and forms an underground reservoir of damp which prevents the plants burning in the sun.

The wines of Nîmes are among France's oldest. They quenched the thirst of Popes throughout their residence in Avignon during the 13th century. They were exported widely from the 16th century onwards, and were much admired by writers who likened them to the best of Rhône wines. After the phylloxera plague they suffered a decline, as did so many other vineyards, and it was not until the middle of the last century that a renaissance occurred.

Today it is all change. As well as mirroring the improvements elsewhere in the south, a study in depth of the geology and the hydrology of the region has made planning for the future easier. AOC (now AOP) status was granted in 1986. Until then, the area was known as Costières du Gard, but at about the same time its name was changed to Costières de Nîmes to distinguish the *appellation* wines from the *vins de pays* which then carried (and still do as IGPs) the name of Gard.

Today there are just over 100 independent producers, many of whom are making wines worthy of the best the Midi can offer. There are seven *coopératives* too, some the result of recent mergers which have been made to reflect the switch from cooperative to independent production, as well as the fact that so many minor producers have ripped up their vines altogether. Only about a third of the total area under vine qualifies for AOP status. Carignan is no longer king here, many growers saying it is not suited by the *terroir*. Mourvèdre, as might be expected, is in its element, though it is not easy to grow at the best of times. It much appreciates the influence of the moisture coming in from the sea. Rosé wines form about a quarter of the total production, but white wines are to be found much less often, even if growers are still faithful to the old varieties, clairette and maccabeu. There is a small part of the area, Clairette de Bellegarde, which is entitled to its own *appellation*, and where the wine is exclusively from that grape.

In general, the wines coming from nearer the sea and the *étangs* are lighter and more elegant than those grown further inland, and can be drunk young. The best will of course keep. The whites are floral and fruity, excellent with goats' cheeses, such as the local *pélardons*.

The list below can either be followed starting in Montpellier or Nîmes; in either case, you will end up back in the suburbs of the latter.

B ＊＊CHÂTEAU DE NAGES / MAS MOLINES

Michel Gassier
Chemin des Canaux, 30132 Caissargues
Tél 04 66 38 44 30
info@michelgassier.com www.michelgassier.com

MAP 1
Cellars open Monday to Saturday usual hours.

Nages is a 70-hectare vineyard planted largely with syrah, some grenache and a little mourvèdre, with rousanne and blanc for the white wines. Molines is more experimental and given over to a wider variety of *cépages*. The Nages wines come in three ranges: 'Réserve' (A) in all three colours, the pink surprisingly tannic sometimes, the white fresh and aromatic after ageing on its lees, and the red with vivid fruit and spices and intended for early drinking. The red 'Vieilles Vignes' (B) is tank-vinified, the white with the roussanne and a little viognier is barrel-fermented, peachy and floral but with some minerality. 'Cuvée JT' (B/C) is almost all roussanne in its white version and fermented in new barrels – a fat wine with a lush finish, it is twinned with a syrah-based red, aged in barrels which are renewed on a three-year cycle. It is a powerful Par-ker-style wine.

The Molines wines start with a pair of varietals from cabernet sauvignon and viognier for enjoying on their light fruit (A). The 'Piliers' range (B) are again varietals from cabernet, syrah and viognier, all barrel-aged. Density and weight return with 'Nostre Pais' (B/C), a pair of substantial modern-style wines in the New World manner.

＊＊CHÂTEAU DE LA TUILERIE

Chantal and Pierre-Yves Comte
Route de Saint- Gilles, 31000 Nîmes
Tel   04 66 70 07 52
contact@chateautuilerie.com www.chateatuilerie.com

MAP 2
Visits Monday to Friday 9.00-18.00.

Since 1955, this important 60-hectare estate has been a leading light in the Costières. On the crest of a small hill it gets the full force of the mistral, which dries the grapes after rain, hence the top *cuvées* both white and red being called 'Éole' (D). These are modern oak-aged wines in international style, with plenty

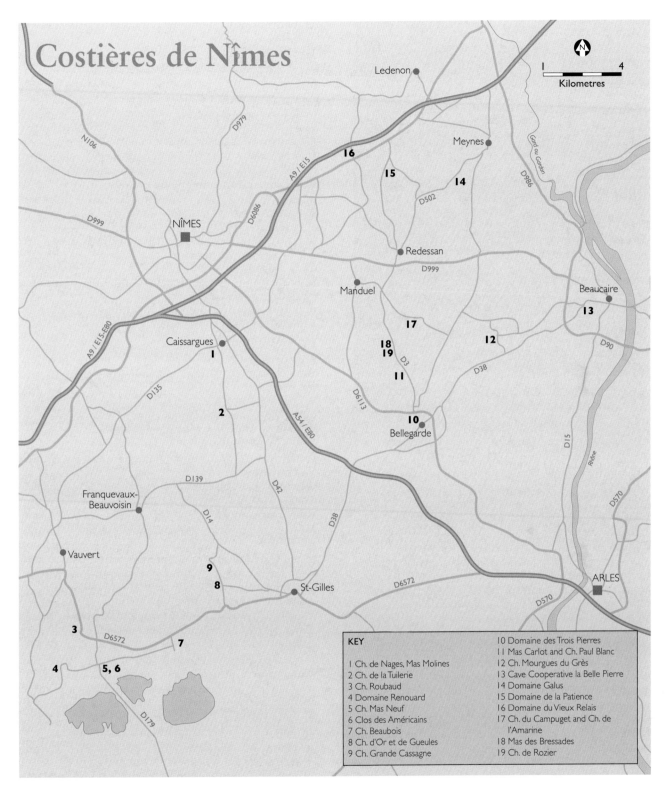

Costières de Nîmes

KEY

1 Ch. de Nages, Mas Molines
2 Ch. de la Tuilerie
3 Ch. Roubaud
4 Domaine Renouard
5 Ch. Mas Neuf
6 Clos des Américains
7 Ch. Beaubois
8 Ch. d'Or et de Gueules
9 Ch. Grande Cassagne
10 Domaine des Trois Pierres
11 Mas Carlot and Ch. Paul Blanc
12 Ch. Mourgues du Grès
13 Cave Cooperative la Belle Pierre
14 Domaine Galus
15 Domaine de la Patience
16 Domaine du Vieux Relais
17 Ch. du Campuget and Ch. de l'Amarine
18 Mas des Bressades
19 Ch. de Rozier

of vanilla and spices, though there is still elegance to tame the power. More modest and affordable are the other ranges: the easy-drinking 'Dinette et Croustilles' (A) in all three colours, and 'Diner de chasse' (A). The 'Château de la Tuilerie' (B) red and white are a little more ambitious. The family also has interests in Martinique, from which it brings in its own range of rums.

**CHÂTEAU ROUBAUD
Françoise and Guilhem Molinier
Gallician, 30600 Vauvert
Tel 04 66 73 30 64
chateau-roubaud@wanadoo.fr   www.chateau-roubaud.fr

Fanny Molinie-Boyer, Château Beaubois

MAP 3
Visits Monday to Friday usual hours, Saturday mornings by appointment.

This is a long-established *domaine* in the Costières, going back a century and more, and one of the first to bottle its wines under *appellation* as Côtes du Rhone in 1927. It is a reliable *'valeur sur'*, (a safe bet), the wines from its 70 hectares combining good quality and reasonable prices. There are two ranges of wine. 'Cuvée Passion' comes in all three colours, a small production of white from a roussanne/grenache blanc blend with a floral, honey character and making an excellent aperitif. The rosé, notable for its cherry and redcurrant flavours, is from equal quantities of syrah with just a touch of grenache blanc, and the spicy, well-built red is from the older vines of syrah and mourvèdre, again with a touch of grenache blanc. There is no white in the second range, called 'Cuvée Plaisir', the rosé having a little cinsault to give a clean flowery style, the red as before with good spice to taste up the fruit. All wines are (A/B).

**CHÂTEAU MAS NEUF Luc Baudet
Gallician, 30600 Vauvert
Tel   04 66 73 33 23
GPS   43.65574 N 4.30216E
info@chateaumasneuf.com   www.chateaumasneuf.com

MAP 5
Cellars open Monday to Friday usual hours. Weekends by appointment.

A large estate (65 hectares under vine), where all the main Languedoc grapes are grown. Inexpensive IGPs (A) begin the range here under the name 'Conviviales'. The entry-level AOP wines, 'Paradoxe' (B), white, pink and red, are raised in tank. The white is made at low temperature without a second fermentation, the pink is partly directly pressed and partly *saigné* from the red juice. The red is kept in *foudre* for a few months after the fermentation is finished. There are superior white and red wines under the labels 'Compostelle', 'Parcellaires' and 'Armonia' (all C/D) in ascending order of weight and price. All are of good quality, and aim for high standards in their production Multi-medal winners and praised in the main French guides.

B **CHÂTEAU BEAUBOIS
Fanny Molinie-Boyer and François Boyer
Route de Franquevaux, 30640 Franquevaux-Beauvoisin
Tel   04 66 73 30 59
Mobile   06 19 81 47 36
GPS   Long 04 25'12"E Lat 43 40'31"N
chateau-beaubois@wanadoo.fr   www.chateau-beaubois.com

MAP 7
Cellars open Monday to Saturday until 18.00.

Four generations of the Boyer family have been farming this 50-hectare-plus *domaine*, which is close to the étangs of the Camargue. Fanny maintains that their vines are cooled by the proximity of the water and are thus lighter and less Rhoneish than those further inland. The property was once a farm, an annexe to the Abbey at Franquevaux. There is still an old well which fed not only the farm and the Abbey, but the whole village. The tomb of a former monk now serves as a raised flower bed. As long ago as the 13th century, Franquevaux had been identified as a fine *terroir* for wine production. Today, this brother and sister enterprise (Fanny is one of the Vinifilles, q.v.) are proud of the elegance and harmony which they bring to their wines. There are four ranges. In ascending order of quality and ambition, start with 'Expression' (A), represented in all three colours, as is 'Élegance' (B), where the white is aged on its lees. The 'Confidence' range (B) does not offer a rosé, while 'Harmonie' (D) is only offered as red, mostly from syrah and grenache. These are the grapes widely used for their reds, with a touch of cinsault for their rosé, 'Élégance'. There is a flamboyant red *tête de cuvee*, 'L'Idole' (D), from all the usual grapes bar carignan (which they don't grow), and which is aged in *demi-muids*. Viognier, roussanne and grenache blanc make up the whites. A red IGP is made from a 50/50 blend of marselan and mourvèdre. The wines here, while they may be drunk young, will age well, particularly in the upper ranges.

State-of-the-art *cave*

✳✳✳CHÂTEAU D'OR ET DE GUEULES
Diane de Puymorin and Mathieu Chatain
Chemin des Cassagnes, Route de Générac, 30800 St. Gilles
Tel   04 66 87 32 86
Mobile   06 46 31 00 20
chateaudoretdegueules@wanadoo.fr

MAP 8
Cellars open Monday-Saturday 10.00-19.00; autumn and winter 10.00-18.00

The property is old and extensive, named today after the colours on Diane's family shield. She bought it in 1999. Today there are 50 hectares of vines grown on south-facing slopes, rising above the plains by the sea on a *terroir* covered with *galets roulés*. The house style is for sweet, floral and well-structured wines, with plenty of *matière*, but which are not exaggerated, despite the flattering attentions of Robert Parker. Of the entry range ('Cimels') note especially the unoaked syrah called 'La Charlotte' (B). The top range of blends is called 'Trassegum' (A/B), all given more or less oak, while three near-varietals include an 80% carignan 'Qu'es Aquo' (C), meaning *'Qu'est-ce-que-c'est'*, a mourvèdre called 'Bolida' (D) and a grenache, 'Castel Noir' (B). Finally, there is an ambitious, generously oaked syrah/grenache/mourvèdre blend (D+). The property is undergoing conversion to organic production and may thereafter go the whole hog to biodynamic

certification. It combines a certain seriousness with commercial flair.

✳✳✳MAS CARLOT / CHÂTEAU PAUL BLANC
Nathalie Blanc-Marès
30127 Bellegarde
Tel   04 66 01 11 83
mascarlot@aol.com   www.mascarlot.com

MAP 11
Visits 8.00-12.00 and 13.00-17.00 Monday to Thursday and until 16.00 Friday. Or by appointment. Closed one week mid-August.

Nathalie, a trained oenologist, took over the 70 hectares of this estate in 1998 from her father Paul Blanc, who once owned the famous Au Pied de Cochon restaurant at Les Halles in Paris. She is also the wife of Cyril Marès (Mas des Bressades, q.v.) and they have four children, so together the parents have their work cut out. Nathalie is one of the few growers still producing 'Clairette de Bellegarde', an orangey-apricot-peachy wine from 60-year-old clairette vines, of which she ferments and ages 20% in barrel. More conventionally, her 'Tradition' range of AOP Costières (all A) is for early drinking on their fruit, starting with a roussanne/

Intruders from the Carmargue

particularly a fine rosé). One step up are the red and white 'Terre d'Argence' (B), while the top range is called 'Les Capitelles' (B) and, unlike the other ranges, it is partly aged in wood, even the rosé (A), which is unusual. An interesting red called 'Terre de Feu' (B) is almost all grenache with just a touch of syrah, and is made only in years when the grape is particularly successful.

**DOMAINE DU VIEUX RELAIS

Christiane Bardin
30129 Redessan
Tel   04 66 20 07 69
c-bardin@wanadoo.fr

MAP 16
Visits by appointment.
A legendary *domaine* whose wines from earlier vintages (they keep well) may still be found on restaurant lists and some serious wine shops. Pierre Bardin (who died recently) made just two reds, the first mainly from syrah with just a little carignan, and a second based on mourvèdre and notable for its wonderful depth and complexity. He presided over a tasting bar, reminiscent of a village post office. His daughter Christiane is following in his footsteps and the wines (A/B) should not be missed.

***MAS DES BRESSADES   Cyril Marès

Le Grand Plagnol, 30129 Manduel
Tel   04 66 01 66 00
masdesbressades@aol.com   www.masdesbressades.com

MAP 18
Open Monday to Friday usual hours, but mornings in summer only. Not first two weeks of August. Appointment recommended.

Cyril is as contemporary, dapper and *soigné* as the underground cellar which he built himself to store his precious oak barrels. He is a great lover of new wood, and the wines here feel like a personal credo of the maker. With a faultless training pedigree (Cos d'Estournel and Château Margaux in Bordeaux), Cyril sets himself the highest standards, and is a top contender for best Costières grower. His 'Tradition' range comprises a 50/50 syrah/grenache red, which has good fruit, some power but also elegance; a white without a malolactic fermentation with prominent peaches and citrus fruits; and a peppery rosé containing some cinsault (all A). There are two 'Cuvées d'Excellence' (B): one white mostly from roussanne fermented in new barrels and raised with frequent *bâtonnage*; and the other red virtually all syrah and raised in a mix of new and old wood. The family's Bordeaux background shows in a cabernet/syrah blend called 'Vignes de Mon Père' (C), which is given 12 months in new wood. To finish, there is a *vendanges tardives*-style wine from viognier called 'Les Vignes Oubliées' (C), not too sweet (60 grams of residual sugar). Cyril is married to Nathalie Blanc from Mas Carlot (q.v.).

marsanne blend (with a touch of viognier) which has something of the same rich fruit as the clairette. The pink wine is mostly saigné from syrah, medium-weight and quite long, and the red has a little mourvèdre added. Still under the Mas Carlot banner, 'Les Enfants Terribles' (A/B) is half mourvèdre, half syrah, partly aged in barrel and can be kept for four to 10 years. In honour of her father, Nathalie makes under his name a white (B), mostly roussanne, wholly made and aged in barrel, but without a second fermentation, and a red (B), mostly syrah and also raised in barrel.

***CHÂTEAU MOURGUES DU GRÈS

Anne et François Collard
Route de Saint Gilles, 30300 Beaucaire
Tel   04 66 59 46 10
chateau@mourguesdugres.com   www.mourguesdugres.com

MAP 12
Visits at usual hours Monday to Friday and Saturday morning. Saturday afternoon by appointment.

The sundial proclaims "Nothing without sunshine," and this is reflected in these Rhone-style wines. It is not surprising, because this is probably the Nîmes vineyard closest to the river, and the wines bear all the hall-marks of the Rhone style. Carignan augments the red palette and vermentino the white. Otherwise the grape varieties are as you would expect. The wines are thought by some to be the best in this *appellation*. The 'Galets' range (A) provides good-value refreshment in all three colours (note

Diane de Puymorin, Château d'Or et de Gueules, p.273

OTHER GOOD GROWERS ON THE COSTIÈRES DE NÎMES

B **DOMAINE RENOUARD
Franck and Nadine Renouard
Chemin des Coquillons, 30600 Vauvert
Postal address 7 rue Gambetta, 92320 Chatillon

Mobile   06 15 38 63 07
scamandredvr@gmail.com   www.scamandre.com
MAP 4
Phone ahead for appointment. Only old barrels are used here and they come from Vega Sicilia.

Syrah in the spring with poppies

**CLOS DES AMÉRICAINS
Annette and Bruno François and Pierre Villebrun
Chemin des Salines, Gallician, 30600 Vauvert
Tel   04 66 88 85 61
Mobile   06 19 27 85 48
GPS   43.6693641 4.2982657
contact@closdesamericains.com   www.clos-des-americains.com
MAP 6
Cellars open daily 9.00-19.00
This property owes its curious name to the fact that it was one of the
first vineyards in the area to replant with immune American stock after
the phylloxera.

B *CHÂTEAU GRANDE CASSAGNE
Laurent and Benoit Dardé
2057 Chemin Generac Aux Palus, 30800 Saint Gilles.
Tel   04 66 87 32 90
chateaugrandecassagne@wanadoo.fr
MAP 9
Visit by appointment.

**DOMAINE DES TROIS PIERRES
c/o Vignerons Créateurs
31 bis Ancienne Route d'Arles, 30127 Bellegarde
Tel   04 66 35 72 26
 f.languillat@vigneronscreateurs.com
www.vigneronscreateurs.ncom

MAP 10
Open Monday to Saturday usual hours.
Vignerons Créateurs are a merger of four *coopératives*. This is one of a
handful of single *domaines* which they make.

*CAVE COOPÉRATIVE LA BELLE PIERRE
(Caveau de la Croix Couverte)
590 Route de Fourques, 30300 Beaucaire
Tel   04 66 59 82 75
contact@la-belle-pierre.com
MAP 13
Open usual business hours (not Saturday afternoon or Sundays).

B **DOMAINE GALUS
Fanettte and Jean-Baptiste Paquet
Route de Redessan (D 502), Pazac, 30840 Meynes
Tel   04 66 22 88 37
Mobile   (Fanette) 06 21 15 85 83   (Jean-Baptiste) 06 14 47 79 60
fanette@domainegalus.fr   jeanbaptiste@domainegalus.fr
www.domainegalus.fr
MAP 14
Cellars open all year, but appointment advisable.

B *DOMAINE DE LA PATIENCE
Christophe Aguilar
Chemin de Serre Plouma
30210 Ledenon
Tel   04 66 75 95 94
domainedelapatience@orange.fr   www.domaine-patience.com
MAP 15
Visits Monday to Saturday usual hours but not after 18.00 in winter.
Christophe also has a shop where he sells his olives and their oil as well
as a range of 'oc' produce. An enterprising and good value-for-money
estate.

*CHÂTEAU DU CAMPUGET /
CHÂTEAU DE L'AMARINE   Jean-Lin Dalle
30129 Manduel
Tel   04 66 20 20 15
campuget@campuget.com   www.campuget.com
MAP 17
Cellars open Monday to Saturday usual business hours.
This large and commercially competent *domaine* is essentially devoted
to syrah and grenache for the reds and rosés, and to grenache blanc and
roussanne for the whites.

*CHÂTEAU DE ROZIER   David Guillon and Julien Paille
30129 Manduel
Tel   04 66 01 14 11
MAP 19
Visits by appointment. An all-red wine property.

Vineyards by the Sea

FROM MONTPELLIER TO SÈTE: MUSCAT COUNTRY

The coastal area between Montpellier and Sète is home to some of the oldest and best-known sweet fortified muscat wines, those from Frontignan and Mireval being the most familiar, particularly to French drinkers. They are similar in style, but some say those from Mireval are bigger and richer. It is sad that the fashion for these sweet wines is in decline, which explains why many growers have switched either wholly or in part to the production of red table wines under the Grès de Montpellier banner, or simply as IGPs.

The cathedral serving Montpellier was once situated right on the sea at a place called Maguelone. The see was transferred to Montpellier in 1553, but the original Maguelone church still stands (more or less) and is looked after by a dedicated preservation society. Being a once-fortified Romanesque building, it is well worth a visit.

Across the *étang* to the north is the village of Villeneuve-lès-Maguelone, today almost an extension of the city of Montpellier itself. But it is home to an excellent wine-*domaine*.

** CHÂTEAU D'EXINDRE LA MAGDELAINE Catherine Sicard Géroudet
3450 Villeneuve-lès-Maguelone
Tel 04 67 69 49 77
 GPS 43.5304 N 3.8336 E
catherinegeroudet@yahoo.fr www.exindre.fr

MAP 1
Cellars open Monday, Tuesday, Thursday and Friday all the year from 15.00-19.00. Saturday from 9.00-12.00.

The Sicard family have been proprietors here for seven generations, having acquired the estate in 1799 after the shake-out caused by the Revolution. Winemaking is a more recent development, rather a resumption of a long history of vine-growing. The present range of wines includes an IGP choice (A) in three colours, a varietal white Chardonnay (A/B) for drinking as an aperitif or with shellfish, an all-purpose cinsault-dominated rosé, and a red blend of merlot, cabernet and grenache. The AOP reds include 'Magdalia' (B), half old carignan and raised in tank, sometimes redolent of chocolate and prunes, and 'Amelius' (B), mostly syrah and aged a year in barrel. Of the two muscats, the first is fairly traditional and sold under the Mireval banner as 'Vent des Anges' (B). It is from grapes picked fairly late. The second is altogether atypical, called Garhilofilatum' (D), it is a marriage between grapes and certain rare plants and spices, and is said to have been a favourite of King Henry III of England. The recipe is a secret, and this *domaine* claims an exclusivity.

***DOMAINE DE LA CAPELLE

Alexandre Maraval
5 Avenue Gambetta, 34110 Mireval
Tel 04 67 78 15 14

MAP 2
Cellars open every day 9.30-12.00 and 14.00-19.00 (except Sundays and the last week in November and the first in December).

The cellars are in the centre of town, but the vineyards are away to the north, up in the heart of the garrigue, where the drainage is good and the grapes can enjoy the benefit of the sea moisture. The family have been here a long time, and their customers have included the Ritz in Paris, the Troisgros restaurant in Roanne, and even the Élysée itself. To combat the decline in the market for sweet muscats, Alexandre has been quick to produce a dry version (B), lively and with good acidity and a good accompaniment to asparagus. But it is the fortified wines which have made the fame for this domaine, notably 'Parcelle 8' (D), whose glistening appearance belies a big and viscous structure. This is a wine which manages to combine elegance and minerality with a sumptuous richness that does not cloy on the palate. Prices are not cheap here, because yields are low and the vineyards are gone over several times to ensure that only the perfect grapes are picked, and at just the right moment of ripeness.

**DOMAINE DE LA RENCONTRE

Pierre and Julie Viudes
50 chemin de la Condamine, 34110 Vic-la-Gardiole
Tel 07 85 84 37 72
Mobile 06 24 05 39 46
julie@domainedelarencontre.com www.domainedelarencontre.com

MAP 3
Telephone ahead.

As if to buck the trend against the decreasing popularity of sweet muscats from this part of the world, Pierre and Julie (whose personal 'rencontre' was in Central America) set up this *domaine* as recently as 2010, having bought their first eight hectares two years previously. The grapes had, until 2014, been contracted to the *cooperative*, so they have rented another five hectares from which to make their own wine. This was also the 'rencontre' of the painter Gustave Courbet, in whose honour there is a statue to memorialise his painting of that name. It is still early days for these growers, but for the moment they concentrate on a wholly dry wine called 'Rencontre' (A), flowery and refreshing; another wine which they call 'Philosophe Entre Deux' (B), off-dry and containing sometimes some wine from an earlier vintage which has seen some wood; and two vins doux naturels, which share a distinctly lemony character while being sweet. 'Eclat' (B) is perhaps a bit richer than 'L'Hédoniste' (C). A very promising and interesting *domaine*.

**DOMAINE DU MAS ROUGE Julien Cheminal,
30 Chemin de la Poule d'Eau, 34110 Vic la Gardiole
Tel 04 67 51 66 85
alice@allforonewines.com www.domainedumasrouge.com

MAP 4
Visits to the *domaine*, *chais* etc. through the Office de Tourisme at Vic (Tel; 04 67 78 94 43) every Friday in June, July, August and September.
Tutored tastings during the same period through the Office de Tourisme at Sète (Tel; 04 99 04 71 71).

Cheminal acquired this estate in 1997 and entirely rebuilt the chais within its old picturesque shell in 2002. This is essentially a muscat house, though there may be some IGP reds and even a Rosé (A). The unfortified whites include two dry and two sweet muscats (A/B), and a pair of sweeter wines (B) from later-picked grapes, one of which, 'Hautes Fleurs', is aged in barrels and demi-muids for a year. Cheminal also makes sweet fortified mus-cats under both the Mireval and Frontignan *appellations* (all B). It is hard to distinguish the two – the Mireval perhaps the more flowery and the Frontignan the more exotic. All good examples of their styles.

B **CHÂTEAU DE STONY

Lydie and Frédéric Nodet
Route de Balaruc, La Peyrade, 34110 Frontignan
Tel 04 67 18 80 30
Mobile 06 49 95 86 89
GPS 43.4362024 N 3.72226238 E
chateaudestony@orange.fr www.chateaudestony.fr

MAP 5
Cellars open Monday to Friday, 9.00 (10.00 in summer) -12.30 and 14.00 (15.00 in summer) -18.30.

In the old days, this part of France was home to the making of vermouth, and this flamboyant property was founded by one of those who had made a fortune from this trade: Hippolyte

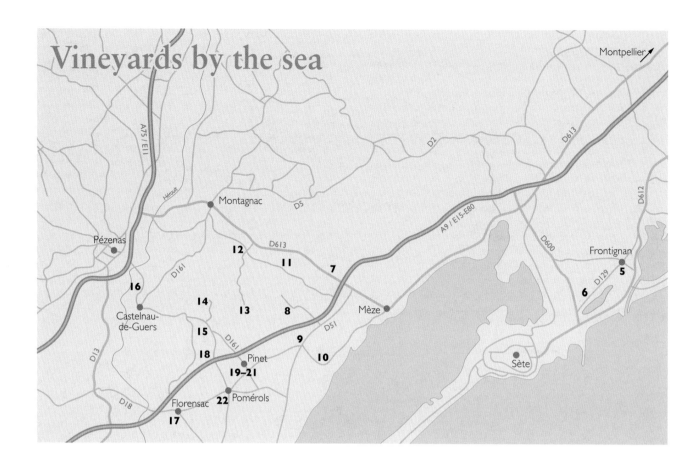

Chavasse, who came from Savoie. But muscat grapes were not made into table wine here until 1983. At first, Frédéric Nodet experimented with just two hectares, but the domaine has grown little by little and has in the process become organic. Their muscat production ranges from the dry 'Amétlier' (A), through a moëlleux 'Fleur de Muscat' (A/B), two muscat vins doux naturels (B), and a dessert unfortified muscat (B). A range of more conventional table wines starts with a rosé called 'Pétale de Ciste' (A), a fruity red called 'Lentisque' (A), a heftier 'Garance' (A/B), and ends with a powerful 'Kermes' (C). There is even an eau-de-vie from muscat and some pure muscat juice.

**CHÂTEAU DE LA PEYRADE

Yves, Bruno and Rémi Pastourel,
Rond-Point Salvador Allende, 34110 Frontignan
Tel   04 67 48 61 19
info@chateaulapeyrade.com   www.chateaulapeyrade.com

MAP   6   Cellars open Monday to Saturday 9.00-12.00 and 14.00-18.30 (19.00 in July and August).

The Pastourel family have a really pretty waterside château, but the *chais* where the wines are made is separated from it by some of the 26 hectares of vines which make up this *domaine*. They are entirely devoted to the muscat grape, so it is surprising that the estate manages to ring the changes and produce such a range of AOP muscats de Frontignan and a range of IGPs all from the same grape. The owners believe that modern taste is for a less cloying style of sweet wines, and therefore the house style is somewhat light and more in keeping with the taste of the market. Since the *appellation* for Frontignan is uniquely for fortified wines, the unfortified all appear under the IGP banner (A). There is the sugarless but very muscaty 'Les Lilas', 'Patrodou', more *moëlleux* in style, and 'Vendange d'Automne', a fully sweet wine from late-picked grapes with 80 gr/litre residual sugar. There is also a sparkling off-dry 'Bulles de Lilas' (B), discreetly muscaty and made by the champagne method. The AOP range of fortified wines includes the 'Tradition' (B) wine from the château; a 'Prestige' version (B), perhaps with more finesse and subtlety; the lighter but exotic 'Sol Invictus' (B); and a barrel-aged version of the 'Tradition', called simply 'Barriques Oubliées' (B), in 50-cl. bottles. You can also buy a big range of wines from other Midi producers at this cellar, which makes a visit a very attractive proposition.

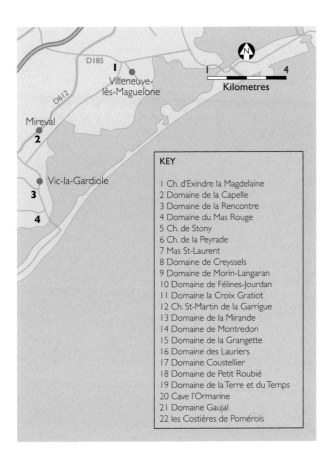

KEY

1 Ch. d'Exindre la Magdelaine
2 Domaine de la Capelle
3 Domaine de la Rencontre
4 Domaine du Mas Rouge
5 Ch. de Stony
6 Ch. de la Peyrade
7 Mas St-Laurent
8 Domaine de Creyssels
9 Domaine de Morin-Langaran
10 Domaine de Félines-Jourdan
11 Domaine la Croix Gratiot
12 Ch. St-Martin de la Garrigue
13 Domaine de la Mirande
14 Domaine de Montredon
15 Domaine de la Grangette
16 Domaine des Lauriers
17 Domaine Coustellier
18 Domaine de Petit Roubié
19 Domaine de la Terre et du Temps
20 Cave l'Ormarine
21 Domaine Gaujal
22 les Costières de Pomérols

PIQUEPOUL (PICPOUL) COUNTRY PICPOUL DE PINET

It would be hard to imagine a more pleasant experience than taking a seat at one of the seaside tables at Bouzigues on a warm sunny day and ordering a plate of oysters or mussels to enjoy with a bottle of the local Picpoul de Pinet. This is the name given to the white wines from a quite self-contained AOP area, limited to the six communes of Castelnau-de-Guers, Florensac, Mèze, Montagnac, Pinet and Pomérols, all lying between Pézenas and the Bassin de Thau. The Bassin is a salt water lagoon devoted to the cultivation of oysters and mussels, with which this wine forms a perfect partnership.

Picpoul's particularity derives from the grape, here confusingly spelt Piquepoul. In any event, it is nothing to do with the grape bearing the same name grown in the Gers as a basis for armagnac.

It is undoubtedly traditional in the Languedoc, in three guises: black, gris and white. Here we are concerned only with the white grape, which has a history in the south going back at least to the sixteenth century.

Picpoul de Pinet may contain no other juice than that of the piquepoul blanc, which thrives on the sandy soil mixed with pebbles, sometimes with gravelly stone, to be found in this maritime location. Typically the wine will have good acidity, but with some suavity and just a touch of bitterness on the finish. Citrus and grapefruit flavours have been detected by many, as well as a floral character. Others describe the wine as being 'in the Italian style.' Parallels with muscadet are misleading, because the style of picpoul is much more southern; it is, on the whole, less variable in quality. The *appellation*, which covers 1,400 hectares, extends a few kilometres inland, and the best wines are made from grapes grown on the slightly rising ground away from the shore. The grant of AOP status has acted as a great spur to increase quality at the expense of yield, and to upgrade the standards of vinification. 'Rather flabby' may have been an apt description of these wines 20 years ago, but it will not do today for most of them. On the other hand, attempts by some growers to age the wine in wood tend to deny the terroir and the partnership with shellfish. The permitted maximum yield for the grapes is 50 hectolitres per hectare, and the annual production runs at about 70,000 hectolitres (very nearly a million bottles). Four *coopératives* dominate the production in a ratio of four to one, and the standard there is high.

This list of good growers begins at Mèze and goes in a circular fashion through Montagnac, Castelnau-de-Guers, Florensac, Pomerols and Pinet itself. If more convenient, you can start at the end and go back to the beginning.

Unusually, and unlike in other sections of this book, stars denote the quality of the picpoul, rather than the total output of the vineyard. This is because it is sometimes only the picpoul which is of real interest. All the picpouls mentioned here are (A), sometimes (A/B), except where otherwise and rarely noted. Picpoul does not aspire to greatness, but for a delicious white at amazingly good prices, it is hard to beat and is enjoying a considerable vogue.

* * * MAS SAINT LAURENT   Roland Tarroux
Montmèze, 34140 Mèze
Tel   04 67 43 92 30
GPS Lon : 3.550762   Lat : 43.452577
massaintlaurent@wanadoo.fr

MAP 7
In theory, open Monday to Saturday all year round, but a phone call ahead is a good idea.

Although the Tarroux family has been making wine here for a mere four generations, the *domaine*, on the road from Mèze to Montagnac, can trace back millions of years to the time when there was a dinosaur colony living here – and there are authenticated remains of fossilised eggshells to prove it. Whether this affects the *terroir* (mostly on argilo-calcaire) is hard to say, but Tarroux is making some of the most distinctive picpoul from his 32 hectares of vines. Some of these are also devoted to making IGPs, for example his syrah/cabernet/grenache blend (A) or his rosé based on cinsault, carignan and grenache, both very drinkable. His picpoul (A) is drier, has more acidity, and speaks 'shellfish' more loudly than some of the wines made nearer the shore, and certainly ranks among the best. Excellent value here, too. If you and he have had a good time, he may even give you a few bits of dinosaur eggshell to take home for the kids.

* * * DOMAINE DE MORIN-LANGARAN
Albert Morin
Route de Marseillan, 34140 Meze
Tel   04 67 43 71 76
domainemorin-langaran@wanadoo.fr

MAP 9
Visits all year round during usual hours, but closed on Sundays in January and February, and public holidays.

This is an estate with a venerable tradition: Pasteur stopped here to take away some samples, and the Empress Eugénie contemplated buying it as a second home. The Morins arrived in 1966, when there were already 16 hectares of piquepoul planted. Today, M. Morin makes a very fine example, and he is a good all-rounder. He has to join his name to the Langaran name to avoid confusion with another estate with a similar name, over which there was a long and unnecessary lawsuit many years ago. Morin also makes some nice IGPs (A), which may include varietals from chardonnay and sauvignon. Or you might find a lightly oaked roussanne. There may be reds, too: syrah/cabernet/

merlot blends. It is to be hoped that Morin will continue with his sweet Muscat (B), a meticulously clean version which gets special attention at the bottling stage.

* * * DOMAINE DE FÉLINES-JOURDAN
Claude Jordan
34140 Mèze
Tel   04 67 43 69 29
claude@felines-jourdan.com   www.felines-jourdan.com

MAP 10
Cellars open by appointment Monday to Friday, 8.00-12.00 and 13.00-16.00.

Claude Jourdan's *domaine* is close to the sea, a few kilometres out of Mèze, where she has a considerable plantation of vines which go to make up her range of IGPs. Her piquepoul grapes (which represent only one third of her total production, but still make her the biggest independent producer) are however grown inland on the higher ground away from the sea, and further west at Pomerols. Claude explains that piquepoul ripens over a longer period than most grapes in Languedoc, because it matures after the fiercest heat has gone. This means that it can give a variety of different styles. Hers – and she makes just the one *cuvée* (A/B) – tends, after she has blended the early and the late, to be fruitier and more generous than most, with some *gras* and hints of butter and pears, though she insists that it remains fresh and lively. Her reputation as one of picpoul's best advocates should not blind you to the merits of her other wines, which are fruity and very drinkable, such as her syrah/grenache AOP blend, which you may or may not prefer to her grenache varietal (both A). There is too a mostly roussanne AOP (A), quite fruity and elegant, and a range of IGPs (all A) designed to quench your thirst. Even so, it is the picpoul which distinguishes this domaine as one of the best producers of this wine.

* * * DOMAINE LA CROIX GRATIOT
Anaïs and Yves Ricome
34530 Montagnac
Mobile   06 13 42 10 68
croixgratiot@gmail.com   www.croix-gratiot.com

MAP 11
Open Monday to Friday, usual hours.

Anaïs and her father Yves run this estate of 27 hectares together. They bought it in 1981 and sent their grapes to one of the *coopératives*, but in 2004 they decided to make and bottle their own wines and built the rather fine *cave*. Travels way beyond the boundaries of Languedoc instilled in Anaïs a love of the pinot noir grape, from which she makes a rather *sudiste* wine (B), with the help of a little oak. But as usual it is the picpoul wines which command attention, and Anaïs makes two, neither of them oaked. The first (A) is very dry and typical of the style, the second, called 'Bréchallune' (B), is matured on its lees and thus somewhat richer with some *gras*. In the range she calls 'Coeur de Gamme' (all A), there is a blended white from viognier, chardonnay, roussanne and muscat called 'Désir Blanc', a rosé called 'Roséphine' from syrah and cabernet sauvignon, and a red 'Rouge Cérise', a

Anaïs Ricome, Domaine la Croix Gratiot

The harbour at Bouzigues

pure syrah.

***DOMAINE DE LA MIRANDE
Joseph Albajan
34120 Castelnau-de Guers
Tel 04 67 98 21 52
vinmirande@hotmail.com   www.domainedelamirande.com

MAP 13
Open every day from 8.00-12.00 and 15.00-19.00

Joseph Albajan had been long associated with this *domaine* before he bought it in 1988 from its former Bordelais owners. Today he has 30 hectares of vines, from which he and his daughter make a range of five wines, headed naturally by his picpoul de pinet (A), rather grapefruity on the nose but with a good balance of *gras* and acidity. You should see whether you like his oaked version called 'Cuvée Marie Laure' (A/B), the oaking of picpoul being controversial. This comes from very old vines and lives in barrel for six months. 'Cuvée Perle Marine' (A) is an AOP blend from roussanne and grenache blanc, with 20% vermentino, and exempt from barrel. 'Cuvée Jérôme' (A/B) is a vanillin cabernet/merlot blend, given a long vinification and some oak-ageing. There is also an easy quaffing pink wine called 'Rose du Moulin' (A), mainly cinsault and carignan.

***DOMAINE DE LA GRANGETTE
la famille Moret
La Grangette-Sainte Rose, Route de Pomerols,
34120 Castelnau-de-Guers
Tel 04 67 98 13 56
info@domainelagrangette.com   www.domainelagrangette.com

MAP 15
Open 9.00-12.00 and 16.00-20.00, Monday to Saturday. Closed Sunday. The cave is four kilometres down the road from Pomerols.
Their white picpoul de pinet, 'L'Enfant Terrible' (A/B), is all the

rage here, which is hardly surprising since it is one of the best to be had. It's a pity it is overshadowed in volume by the other wines of the property, because it represents only about 10% of the vines planted, which cover 30 hectares in total. There is an oaked version of the white picpoul called 'La Part des Anges' (B) (why do they do this?), but also an interesting rosé and red from the rare piquepoul noir (A/B). White IGPs include a pure dry muscat and a sauvignon/muscat blend, as well as a sweet sauvignon from late-harvested grapes given 12 months in barrel. As well as a red 'Tradition', there is a fancier oak-raised syrah/grenache blend called 'Rouge Franc' (C), and a sweet red grenache called 'Mi Ange mi Démon' (C).

B ***DOMAINE DE PETIT ROUBIÉ
Olivier and Floriane Azan
BP4, 34850 Pinet
Tel 04 67 77 09 28
petitroubie@gmail.com   www.petit-roubie.com

MAP 18
Cellars open Monday to Friday 9.00-12.00 and 13.30-18.00 (17.00 Friday).

The picpoul is so good here that one wonders why they bother to make an oaked version, 'L'Arbre Blanc' (B). The basic version is very lively and sprightly on the palate, with notes of exotic fruits and flowers. Of the range of varietals (all A), note the powerful tannat, given a long *cuvaison*, as well as the more usual merlot, marsanne and viognier. Two inexpensive ranges (both A) are called respectively 'Spirit of Nature' (including a white blend of terret, piquepoul and viognier) and 'Le P'tit Roubié', which includes a rosé and a red, both 100% cabernet. The top red, 'L'Arbre Blanc' (B), is a mix of merlot, syrah and cabernet, aged in barrel for 12 months. This is one of the two fully certified organic estates in Picpoul.

***DOMAINE DE LA TERRE ET DU TEMPS (MAS AUTANEL) Jean-Claude Zabalia
34850 Pinet
Business address Route des Crozes,
Le Mas Rouch, 34800 Cabrières
Tel 06 85 42 92 35
contact@laterreletemps.com   www.laterreletemps.com

MAP 19
Shop open every day from April to September.

Zabalia was until recently in charge of Ch. St Martin de la Garrigue, so is not lacking experience in making good picpoul. Since that property was sold abroad, Zabalia has rented a couple of hectares at Pinet, where he is making quite a rich version from late-picked grapes. The wine (B) is matured on its lees to give extra weight. No oak though. An excellent start.

***CAVE L'ORMARINE

13 Avenue du Picpoul, 34850 Pinet
Tel 04 67 77 03 10
contact@caveormarine.com   www.cave-ormarine.com

MAP 20
Open seven days a week during usual hours.

This is the largest and one of the two best *coopératives* making picpoul. It has over 500 members, and between them they cover over a third of the total AOP area. In 2003 they formed a partnership with the big *négociant* Jeanjean and created the brand name Ormarine, particularly for the marketing of picpoul. The *cave* has also absorbed over the years growers from well-known estates such as Roquemolière. Apart from the range of picpoul (note especially 'Cuvée du Cheval des Mers'), the rest of the production is divided between varietals from just about every grape in just about every blend you can think of, including terret, carignan and the white grenache. All the wines here are inexpensive and good value.

**DOMAINE GAUJAL Ludovic Gaujal

1 rue Ludovic Gaujal, BP 1, 34850 Pinet
Tel 04 67 77 02 12
lg@gaujal.fr   www.gaujal.fr

MAP 21
Cellars open Monday to Friday, 10.00-12.00 and 14.00-18.00 (19.00 July and August).

Ludovic's grandfather, so the story goes, once turned down an offer from the owners of Château d'Yquem to swap properties. Such was the family confidence in the virtues of picpoul that Gaujal declined. Readers can decide whether this was the right decision. Certainly, the AOC picpoul here is benchmark. Ludovic has 30 hectares of vines and distinguishes himself from what he calls 'les grandes structures': *"nous ne jouons pas dans la même cour"*. Ludovic also makes a merlot varietal called 'Domaine de la Rouquette' and a pure chardonnay called 'Fontaine'. The range is rounded off by a *vendanges tardives* style pure merlot (C), the grapes picked a full month after the piquepoul. Apart from this, all wines here are (A).

**LES COSTIÈRES DE POMÉROLS

Avenue de Florensac
34810 Pomérols
Tel 04 67 77 01 59
info@cave-pomerols.com   www.cave-pomerols.com

MAP 22
Open Tuesdays to Saturdays 7.00-12.00 and 15.00-20.00

A merger with the caves at Mèze and Castelnau-de-Guers has made the combined unit an important player in this region. The picpoul de pinet in particular is a bestseller, though it represents less than 10 percent of the total output, which includes varietals from about one third of the vines grown by its members. These are rather less interesting than the picpoul, which presents aromas of citrus fruits and apples. It tends to be lighter than the average picpoul, but is full of character.

OTHER GOOD PICPOUL GROWERS

B **DOMAINE DE CREYSSELS Julie Benau

Route de Marseillan, 34140 Meze
Tel 04 67 43 80 82
contact@creyssels.fr
MAP 8
Open all year round from 10.00-12.30 and 15.00-18.30. There are flats adjoining the château and a restaurant is open at week-ends.

**CHÂT. ST MARTIN DE LA GARRIGUE

Groupe Vaskoveyskoe   Manager Jean-Luc Parret
34530 Montagnac
Tel 04 67 24 00 40
contact@stmartingarrigue.com   www.stmartingarrigue.com
MAP 12
Open every day in July-August, otherwise Monday to Friday only. Usual hours, but not before 10.30 at weekends in summer.
A large estate, now in absentee Russian ownership. The Picpoul is lively and typical of the style, for which the grapes are usually picked later (because of the altitude of the vineyard) and are from low-yielding vines.

**DOMAINE DE MONTREDON

Bruno and Christine Cantié
34120 Castelnau-de-Guers
Tel 04 67 98 95 69
sceadomainedemontredon@nordnet.fr
MAP 14
Open Tuesdays and Thursdays usual hours, Wednesday and Friday afternoons only. Closed weekends and Mondays.

*DOMAINE DES LAURIERS Marc Cabrol

15 Avenue de Pezenas, 34120 Castelnau-de-Guers
Tel 04 67 98 18 20
Mobile 06 07 59 32 14
GPS 43.4381 3.4387
contact@domaine-des-lauriers.com
www.domaine-des-lauriers.com
MAP 16
Wine tasting and sales facility open Monday to Friday, 8.30-12.00 and 14.00-17.30. Otherwise by appointment.

**DOMAINE COUSTELLIER La Famille Coustellier

5 Boulevard Magenta and 10 rue du Général Montbrun, 34510 Florensac
Tel 04 67 62 38 80
Mobile 06 75 23 36 16
louiscoustellier@wanadoo.fr
MAP 17
Not such a high-profile *domaine*, but one rather well respected particularly in restaurant and sommelier circles.

Vinifilles

In many vineyards, women play a major and often principal role in the *domaine*: sometimes as wife or partner, sometimes as daughter, sometimes as sole proprietor. Others are growers, or winemakers in the chais. Some are born and bred in Languedoc, others have come to winemaking from beyond the region; some have never before had any experience of winemaking, others have it in their blood. They all have in common an interest in asserting their competence and influence, and showing that in the world of wine, women are just as important as their male counterparts. So many have come together to form their own 'trade union' called 'Vinifilles.'

'Dictionary Definition' (their own);

n.f.pl. Females of the species, practising the art of winemaking in Languedoc-Roussillon, formed into a group in 2009, driven by the joy and richness of their profession, individually and collectively beautiful, rebellious, active, fun, sociable, vivacious and dynamic.

The Members

Séverine Bourrier, Château de l'Ou, 66200 Montescot, see p.58
Laetitia Piétri-Clara, Domaine Piétri-Géraud, 66190 Collioure, see p.68
Sophie Guiraudon, Clos de l'Anhel, 11220 Montlaur, see p.90
Caryl Panman, Domaine Rives Blanques, 11300 Cépie, see p. 106
Françoise Antech-Gazeau, Antech Limoux, 11300 Limoux, see p.107
Françoise le Calvez Frissant, Château Coupe-Roses, 34210 La Caunette, see p.138

Françoise Ollier, Domaine Ollier-Taillefer

Véronique Étienne, Château la Dournie, 34360 Saint-Chinian, see p.154
Isabelle Champart, Mas Champart, 34360 Saint-Chinian, see p.155
Françoise Ollier, Domaine Ollier-Taillefer, 34320 Fos, see p.170
Hildegarde Hort, La Grange de Quatre Sous, 34360 Assignan, see p.159
Liedewij Van Wilgen, Mas des Dames, 34490 Murviel-les-Béziers, see p.183
Bernadette Roquette, Domaine des Trémières, 34800 Nébian, see p.192
Marie Chauffray, La Reserve d'O, 34150 Arboras, see p.205
Pascale Rivière, La Jasse Castel, 34150 St. Jean de Fos, see p.208
Valérie Tabaries-Ibanez, Domaine de Roquemale, 34560 Villevayrac, see p.238
Isabelle Mangeart, Clos des Nines, 34690 Fabrègues, see p.238
Fabienne Bruguière, Mas Thélème, 34270 Lauret, see p.252
Fanny Molinié Boyer, Château Beaubois, 30640 Franquevaux, see p.272
Cathy Sisquelle, Château de Rey, 66140 Canet-en-Roussillon

and just beyond the scope of this book:
Emmanuelle Schoch, Mas Seren, 30140 Anduze

Glossary

Agrumes citrus fruits whose character is sometimes found on the aroma of white wines

Ambré amber, the colour acquired by old *vins doux naturels*; also the style of such wines

Appellation d'origine contrôlée/protégée
> (AOC/AOP) a statutory legally controlled area of production

Argileux composed of clay

Argilo-calcaire clay mixed with chalk or limestone

Assemblage the creative blending of wine from different *cuvées* from the same winemaker

Barrique barrel or cask, usually of a size containing 225 litres

Bâtonnage breaking up with a stick (or similar) solid matter developing in a cask during fermentation

Bidon a plastic container for holding liquid, from five litres upwards

Bonbonne a demi-john, a glass measure of five litres or more

Botrytis a fungoid disease which rots the skins of grapes, rare in the Midi

Bouquet the aromas produced by wine when it is poured, other than the basic smell of wine;
> also called 'nose'

Brut bone-dry (of sparkling wine)

Cagette a small container for carrying grapes from the vineyard to the *chais*

Calcaire chalk or limestone

Capitelle a small stone building in vineyards for housing implements and giving shelter to vineyard
> workers in bad weather; in Catalan called **Casot**

Cart(h)agène an aperitif made from unfermented grape juice and fortified with spirits

Cassis blackcurrants

Cave wine cellar

Caveau a showroom or shop having the character of a *cave*

Caviste a specialist wine retailer

Cépage grape variety

Cépage améliorateur a grape variety, usually syrah or mourvèdre, encouraged by the authorities to
> replace older, less-esteemed varieties

Chai(s) winery for making and/or storing wine

Champenoise as in Champagne

Chapeau the cake-like solid mass of matter, (grape, skins etc.) thrown to the surface of a vat
> during fermentation

Chef de culture vineyard manager (c.f. maître de chais)

Chêne oak

Clairet a red wine, pale in style but deeper than a rosé

Climat a subdivision of a vineyard

Clos a vineyard, strictly speaking enclosed by a wall

Collage the process of forcing to the bottom of a container the solid particles contained in a wine; also called 'fining'

Coulure a disease of vines inhibiting young grapes from developing, ultimately causing them to rot and drop off the plant

Crachoir a spittoon

Cru a specially selected wine

Culture raisonnée the voluntary practice of neo-organic production but without obligation

Cuvaison the period, including the time following the end of the first fermentation, during which the wine remains in contact with the skins, stalks and pips of the grapes

Cuve a vat of whatever material

Cuvée the wine drawn off one or more vats

Dans un seul tenant one continuous vineyard

Débourbage the racking or settling of the must prior to fermentation

Délestage the draining of a vat during vinification and the re-homogenisation of the must, which is then returned to the vat. An alternative to *remontage (q.v.)*

Demi-Muid a barrel larger than a *barrique (q.v.)*, usually 300 or 400 litres

Eau-de-Vie the distilled juice of grapes/other fruits

Éffeuillage the removal of surplus leaves from a vine to ensure maximum exposure of the grapes to the sun

Égrappage the removal of stalks from bunches of grapes prior to vinification

Égrappoir a machine for doing this

Élevage the ageing or maturing of wine

En cordon royat a way of training the vine, usually on wire, so that it produces two principal stems, the maximum number of shoots on each being prescribed by local rules

En espalier grown as on a trellis

En gobelet grown in bush form, the shape reminiscent of a goblet

Encépagement the proportion of different grape varieties in a vineyard or in a wine

Feixe (catalan) the stone wall of a vine terrace

Fine *eau-de-vie* (q.v.)

Finesse the opposite of roughness, a quality of subtlety, elegance and softness

Floraison the flowering of the vine

Foudre a large old-fashioned barrel measuring a tun, usually with oval ends

Fouloir a machine for crushing grapes sometimes combined with an égrappoir

Fût a cask, often denoting new wood

Galet a large round pebbly stone, as found by riverbeds

Garrigue a heath-like terrain valued for its herbs, flowers and other wildlife

Gouleyant easy to drink, quaffable

Goût du terroir a taste deriving from a combination of soil, locality, grape variety and climate that is exclusive to a particular wine

Gras rich, buttery, fleshy, literally fat – a term applied to white wines

Graves (of the soil) gravelly, of tiny stones

Greffe a vine graft

Gris a vin rosé so pale that it is called 'grey' rather than pink

Guyot the training of vines along one main shoot

Hectare an area of 10,000 square metres, about 2.5 acres

Hectolitre 100 litres

INAO French National Institute for wines of controlled appellation

Liquoreux the sweetest grade of wines, not to be confused with liqueur

Macération the leaving of the grape skins, stalks, pulp and juice in contact with each other, before, during or after fermentation

Macération carbonique a winemaking technique where the grapes are not crushed but allowed to disintegrate by themselves under a protective layer of carbonic gas

Macération pelliculaire maceration at a cool temperature prior to fermentation

Madérization excessive oxidisation of wine, producing an effect not unlike the smell and taste of Madeira

Maillole (catalan) a young vine not yet capable of producing fruit

Maître du chais cellar-master

Malolactic (fermentation) a second fermentation of wine after the first alcoholic fermentation has finished, which converts the harsh malic acid in the wine into milder lactic acid. Sometimes called '**Malo**' for short

Mas a farm, sometimes a larger group of farm buildings

Méthode ancestrale the original method of making sparkling wines, as in Limoux

Méthode champenoise the way of making sparkling wines, as in champagne

Méthode traditionelle the name under which the *champenoise* method is obliged to go outside the champagne area

Microbullage the introduction of tiny quantities of oxygen into a maturing wine, so as to avoid the necessity of racking the wine and thereby disturbing the lees

Moëlleux mellow and full, usually denoting a measure of sweetness

Mono-cépage a wine made from only one grape variety, a so-called 'varietal' wine

Must the contents of a *cuve*, liquid and solid during fermentation

Mutage the 'silencing' or stopping of fermentation by the addition of alcohol

Négociant a dealer in bulk wines

Nerveux vigorous and lively (to describe a wine)

Oxidisation chemical effect of oxygen on wine

Pain grillé an element in bouquet, reminiscent of toasted bread

Palissage the training of vines over wire trellises rather than allowing the plants to grow in bush formation

Passerillage over-ripeness of grapes obtained by leaving them to shrivel and partly evaporate in the sun

Peus de gall (Catalan) a system of combined vertical and diagonal drainage in Banyuls and Collioure

Phylloxera a rapidly multiplying aphid feeding on and destroying wine roots. First appeared in the Midi in the 1870s

Pierre à fusil the smell or taste of gunflint

Pigéage the breaking up of the *chapeau* (q.v.) to give fermenting juices access to the solids

Porte-greffe rootstock

Racking transferring wine from one *cuve* to another to aerate it, and then returning it to its original cask. If performed during the ageing of the wine, this shortens the period of maturation

Rafle the wood and fibre, as opposed to the fruit, in a bunch of grapes
Rancio the character of an old oxidised *vin doux naturel*, Madeira-like
Récolte harvest, crop
Régisseur the overall manager of a vineyard
Réglisse liquorice
Remontage the circulation of wine in the vat by pumping it back into the top of the container
    to submerge the *chapeau* (q.v.)
Rendement the yield of a vineyard, quantitatively, usually expressed in the proportion of volume of
    juice to the hectare
Rimage see Vintage
Robe colour or appearance of a wine
Sable, vin de wine from grapes grown in a very sandy soil, especially close to the sea
Saignage drawing off ('bleeding') pink juice from fermenting red grapes to make a vin rosé
Selection massale the propagation of vines through direct cuttings from a plant, rather than cloning
Stage a programme of internship
Tête de cuvée the top wine of a producer
Tonneau a large cask, a hogshead
Tonnelier a barrel-maker or cooper
Torréfaction the smell of hot, dry roasting, as of the coffee bean
Tri(e) the selective picking of well-ripened grapes; also the hand-sorting of grapes prior to vinification
Tuilé the colour of old tiles, often a feature of old red *Vins Doux Naturels*.
    Also the name given to wines of that character
Typicité the individual character distinguishing one wine area from another
Vendange the grape harvest
Vendange tardive the late harvesting of overripe grapes, a term officially once limited to Alsace
    but frequently used elsewhere
Vendange verte the removal of some unripe bunches of grapes in July, to promote
    quality and concentration in the remaining bunches
Vigneron a grower of vines, a winemaker
Vin de cépage a wine made from a single grape variety, a varietal or *mono-cépage*.
Vin de France a wine made in France but not required to confirm to any specific rules
    (formerly called *Vin de Table*)
Vin de garage wine, usually from a small property, made in tiny quantities,
    to the highest specification and sold usually at high prices
Vin de garde a wine that requires ageing
Vin de Pays (IGP) a wine from a recognised locality but not within an area of AOP.
    Also a wine which may be made in that area but which may not comply with its rules
Vin de presse the wine that results from the pressing of the solid matter/grape skins etc. at the bottom
    of the *cuve*
Vin doux naturel a naturally sweet wine of any colour, fortified by the addition of pure alcohol
Vintage a style of vin doux naturel bottled young and allowed to mature like port (also called *rimage*)
Vrac in bulk; large containers other than bottles

INDEX of *domaines* and growers

Index

Index

Index

Index